Crouching Tiger, Hidden Dragon?

Crouching Tiger, Hidden Dragon?

Africa and China

Edited by

Kweku Ampiah and Sanusha Naidu

University of KwaZulu-Natal Press

Published in 2008 by University of KwaZulu-Natal Press
Private Bag X01
Scottsville 3209
South Africa
E-mail: books@ukzn.ac.za
Website: www.ukznpress.co.za

ISBN: 978-1-86914-150-9

Cover design: Kult Creative

Printed and bound by Interpak Books, Pietermaritzburg

Contents

Abbreviations

AAF	Angolan Armed Forces
ACOTA	African Contingency Operations Training Assistance
ACP	African, Caribbean and Pacific
ACRI	African Crisis Response Initiative
ADB	African Development Bank
AENF	Alliance of Eritrean National Forces
AFLEG	African Forest Law Enforcement and Governance Process
AFRICOM	(United States) Africa Command
AGOA	African Growth and Opportunity Act
AHSG	African Heads of State and Government
AMIS	African Union Mission in Sudan
ANC	African National Congress
ANIP	Angolan National Agency for Private Investment
APEC	Asia-Pacific Economic Cooperation
APRM	African Peer Review Mechanism
APT	ASEAN Plus Three
ARF	Asia Regional Forum
ASEAN	Association of Southeast Asian Nations
ASGISA	Accelerated Shared Growth Initiative for South Africa
AU	African Union
BEE	black economic empowerment
BNC	(China-South Africa) Bi-National Commission
CADF	China-Africa Development Fund

CAITEC	Chinese Academy of International Trade and Economic Cooperation
CCP	Chinese Communist Party
CFA	Communauté Française Africaine
CFELG	Central Foreign Affairs Leadership Small Group
CIA	Central Intelligence Agency
CIAT	International Committee in Support of the Transition
CICIR	China Institutes of Contemporary International Relations
CICMH	Huazhou Industrial and Commercial Mining Company
CIF	China International Fund
CIIS	China Institute of International Studies
CMC	Central Military Commission
CMEC	China National Machinery and Equipment Import-Export Corporation
CNMC	China Nonferrous Metal Mining
CNOOC	China National Offshore Oil Cooperation Ltd
CNPC	China National Petroleum Corporation
COMESA	Common Market of East and Southern Africa
COMIBEL	Compagnie Minière de Bélinga
COMILOG	Compagnie Minière de l'Ogooué
COVEC	China Overseas Engineering Company
CPA	Comprehensive Peace Agreement
CPLAC	Central Political and Legal Affairs Commission
CREC	China Railway Engineering Company
CU	Customs Union
CVRD	Companhia Vale do Rio Doce
DAC	Development Assistance Committee
DEG	diethylene glycol
DPA	Darfur Peace Agreement
DRC	Democratic Republic of Congo
EAC	East African Communtiy
EAMA	Etats Africains et Malgache Associés
EBA	'Everything but Arms'
EC	European Commission

ECOSOC	Economic and Social Council
ECOWAS	Economic Community of West African States
EDF	European Development Fund
EITI	Extractive Industries Transparency Initiative
EMU	European Monetary Union
EPA	Economic Partnership Agreement
EU	European Union
Exim	Export-Import (Bank)
FAFDAC	National Agency for Food and Drug Administration and Control
FAW	First Automotive Works
FDI	foreign direct investment
FNDP	Fifth National Development Plan
FOCAC	Forum on China-Africa Cooperation
FTA	foreign trade agreement
FTA	free trade agreement
G8	Group of Eight
G77	Group of 77
GATT	General Agreement on Tariffs and Trade
GDP	gross domestic product
GEDA	Gauteng Economic Development Agency
GNI	gross national income
GNPOC	Greater Nile Petroleum Operating Company
GRN	Gabinete de Reconstruçcão Nacional
HIPC	heavily indebted poor country
IBSA	India-Brazil-South Africa
ICBC	Industrial and Commercial Bank of China
ICC	International Criminal Court
ICG	International Crisis Group
IDRF	infrastructure development resources backed finance
IFCC	International Fellowship of Christian Churches
IFI	international financial institution

IGAD	Inter-Governmental Authority for Development
IMF	International Monetary Fund
JIPSA	Joint Initiative for Priority Skills Acquisition
LDC	least developing country
LLDC	least landlocked developing country
LNG	Liquified Natural Gas
LSG	leadership small group
MCA	Millennium Challenge Account
MCC	Metallurgical Corporation of China
MDC	Movement for Democratic Change
MDG	Millennium Development Goal
MFA	Ministry of Foreign Affairs
MFA	Multifibre Arrangements
MND	Ministry of National Defence
MOFCOM	Ministry of Foreign and Commercial Affairs
MONUC	Mission des Nations Unies en République Démocratique du Congo [United Nations Mission in the Democratic Republic of Congo]
MOU	memorandum of understanding
MPLA	Popular Movement for the Liberation of Angola
NAFDAC	National Agency for Food and Drug Administration and Control
NAM	Non-Aligned Movement
NATO	North Atlantic Treaty Organisation
NEPAD	New Partnership for Africa's Development
NFC-Africa	Non-Ferrous Africa Mining Plc
NGO	non-governmental organisation
NIF	National Islamic Front
NIIA	Nigerian Institute of International Affairs
NNPT	Nuclear Non-Proliferation Treaty
NOCs	National Oil Corporations
NORINCO	China North Industries Corporation
NPC	National People's Congress
NRZ	National Railways of Zimbabwe

OAU	Organisation of African Unity
ODA	Overseas Development Aid
OECD	Organisation for Economic Cooperation and Development
OEM	original equipment manufacturer
OPEC	Organisation of Petroleum Exporting Countries
PBMR	pebble-bed modular reactor
PDOC	Petrodar Operating Company
PEPFAR	President's Emergency Plan for Aids Relief
PIP	Programme of Public Investments
PLA	People's Liberation Army
PRC	People's Republic of China
PRSP	Poverty Reduction Strategy Paper
RASCOM	Regional Africa Satellite System
RDP	Reconstruction and Development Programme
REC	Regional Economic Community
RPF	Rwandan Patriotic Front
SAA	South African Airways
SABC	South African Born Chinese
SACU	Southern African Customs Union
SADC	Southern African Development Community
SARS	severe acute respiratory syndrome
SETA	Skills, Education and Training Authority
SEZ	special economic zone
Sinopec	China Petroleum and Chemical Corporation
SOE	state-owned enterprise
SOMIFER	Société des Mines de Fer de Mékambo
SPLA	Sudan People's Liberation Army
SSI	Sonangol-Sinopec International
TAC	Treaty of Amity of Cooperation
TAM	Turn Around Maintenance
TAZARA	Tanzania-Zambia Railway
TDCA	Trade, Development and Cooperation Agreement

TICAD	Tokyo International Conference on African Development
TNC	transnational corporation
TSCTI	Trans-Sahara Counter-Terrorism Initiative
UFWD	United Front Work Department
ULP	United Liberal Party
UNAMID	United Nations-African Union Mission in Darfur
UNCTAD	United Nations Conference on Trade and Development
UNICEF	United Nations Children's Fund
UNITA	National Union for the Total Independence of Angola
UNMIS	United Nations Mission in Sudan
UPND	United Party for National Development
USAID	United States Agency for International Development
WHO	World Health Organisation
WMD	weapons of mass destruction
WTO	World Trade Organisation
XOCECO	Xiamen Overseas Chinese Electronics Co. Ltd
YNCIG	Yunnan Copper Industry
ZANU-PF	Zimbabwe African National Union Patriotic Front
ZAPU	Zimbabwe African People's Union
ZESA	Zimbabwe Electricity Supply Authority
ZESCO	Zambia Electricity Supply Corporation
ZISCO	Zimbabwe Iron and Steel Corporation
ZTE	Zhongxing Communications

Acknowledgements

We are grateful to the Centre for Conflict Resolution (CCR) in Cape Town, South Africa, for commissioning and managing this project. We would also like to extend our appreciation to the participants at the policy seminar on China and Africa, organised by CCR in September 2007, whose comments helped to shape this publication.

We would like to express our gratitude to the funders of CCR's Africa Programme who supported the policy seminar and the publication of this book: the governments of Denmark, The Netherlands, Sweden, Norway and Finland; the United Kingdom's Department for International Development (DFID); and the Swiss Agency for Development and Co-operation (SDC).

We would like to convey particular thanks to Adekeye Adebajo, Executive Director of CCR, for his guidance, enthusiasm and perseverance, without which this publication would not have been possible. We would also like to mention Ken McGillivray for his thoroughness in the copy-editing and proof-reading process. We thank Elizabeth Myburgh, Selma Walters, Dawn Alley, and CCR's communications and finance departments for their organisational support.

We are grateful to all the contributors for their valuable input and their commitment to this project and we thank the team at the University of KwaZulu-Natal (UKZN) Press for their hard work. Finally, we would like to thank our families and friends for their encouragement and support.

Kweku Ampiah and Sanusha Naidu

PART 1

Context

1

Introduction

Africa and China in the Post-Cold-War Era

Kweku Ampiah and Sanusha Naidu

The evolving relationship between China and Africa could be one of the most important developments in the international relations of the post-Cold-War era. In the last two decades, there have been profound changes in Africa's relations with China, not least in the phenomenal growth in trade and investment between Beijing and several African countries. This transformation of the relationship between China and Africa has undoubtedly placed this engagement at the centre of the debate about Africa and its future prospects, thereby confirming Beijing as an important actor in the continent's development objectives.

The geo-political implications of these developments are profound, if only because China is now seemingly challenging the hegemonic positions long monopolised by the United States (US), Britain and France in Africa. There are anxieties in certain quarters about the spreading shadow of a non-traditional foreign power in the region, and questions about China's intentions with respect to Africa. Such concerns manifest themselves in a variety of ways, including concerns over how China is 'venturing into the traditional sphere of influence of the dominant powers'; and undermining certain 'noble' goals of the West such as 'isolating rogue governments for failing to promote democracy, comply with international law . . . or respect human rights'.[1] As such, China's interest in Africa has spawned a perplexing variety of commentary, which has led to the emergence of two polarising views concerning the Middle Kingdom's deepening engagements across the African continent.

The first view consists of those who are perturbed by the colonialist resonances of China's engagement with Africa.[2] Scholars argue that Beijing's emergence in Africa, considering the region's colonial history, evokes visions of a 'Second Scramble', resulting in yet another impending round of foreign plunder of Africa's natural resources.[3] There are others, still, within the scholarship that assess China's late arrival in Africa as an anachronism, synonymous with a bright yellow construction crane in the depths of the continent, destroying the region's rain forests and natural beauty.

Essentially this interpretation embodies a growing hysteria concerning China's emergence as a powerful nation in the post-Cold-War era and even more so in Africa. These authors often analyse Beijing's economic ascendancy within the context of a 'threat theory' or 'yellow peril', and typically view China's initiatives toward Africa as having an imperialist agenda. They also tend to see the relationship between China and African countries as potentially deleterious to achieving 'good governance' and democratic state-building.[4] In short, this view portends that China's engagement in Africa is purely exploitative, extractive and destructive, and will perpetuate Africa's underdevelopment. But there is an underlying dynamic to this argument that 'China's new engagement in Africa is part of a long-term strategy aimed at displacing the traditional Western orientation of the continent by forging partnerships with African elites under the rubric of South-South solidarity' geared towards some form of '. . . political control over African territories'.[5]

The second view offers a more nuanced assessment of the relationship that can be defined along the lines of 'benign engagement'. Proponents of this thinking approach the topic with less aggression[6] and tend to perceive Africa's engagements with the East Asian giant as a 'catalyst for development and, with that, a new level of improved livelihoods such as Africa had not known for decades'.[7] They also invoke a non-ideological cost-benefit analytical construct that allows for a more rigorous assessment of the evidence.

In this mix, the views of African policy-makers must also be considered. In their opinion, China's interest in the continent (along with the increase in economic assistance from Beijing to their countries) is refreshing and therefore laudable, compared to what many view as the often paternalistic, patronising and culturally prejudiced attitudes of the West and Japan towards Africa. Thus, according to the former Nigerian Finance Minister, Ngozi Okonjo-Iweala, 'China should be left alone to forge its unique partnership with African countries, and the West must simply learn to compete'.[8]

These contending views tend to compartmentalise the significance and implications of China in Africa along the lines of partner, competitor or coloniser.[9] While these impressions are accurate to some extent in their assumptions about China's behaviour, intentions and pending outcomes for African development, their arguments are shaped by a Manichean psychology.

Being mindful of these competing visions, this volume on China's growing footprint across Africa aims to make an informed contribution to the debate and discourse on the topic. Without disregarding concerns about China's engagement with corrupt regimes in Sudan, Angola and elsewhere, as well as the potential problems in China's expanding economic interests in Africa, the arguments set out in the proceeding chapters provide more of the African perspectives on the subject, which at times are either in short supply or merely subsumed within the existing scholarship as the African voice.

With this in mind, the editors and contributors of this volume seek to emphasise how the continent can build a relationship with China that can promote mutual economic benefits and development. What distinguishes this publication from others is its explicit emphasis on the active role of African governments and the experiences of ordinary Africans in the growing affinity between China and Africa, in contrast to the popular postulations that the continent is merely a passive agent in this relationship. This is achieved in three major ways: first, through a thorough understanding of the historical and foreign policy imperatives in this relationship; second, an emphasis on contemporary African perspectives and empirical assessments of nine bilateral case studies across four African sub-regions; and third, in focusing on the comparative approach of China and other external actors such as the US, France, Japan, India and the European Union (EU) to Africa in key areas of politics, trade and security. By comparing American geo-strategic interests in Africa to those of France, the EU, Japan, India and China, this book aims to provide a more nuanced assessment of the international concerns about the exploitative nature of China's engagement with Africa.

The volume therefore interrogates the campaign of suspicion by much of the Western media at China's 'new-found' power, which, at times, is labelled as Chinese exceptionalism. As a result, critics of the West, for example, see this myopic approach as pernicious and hypocritical, especially when viewed in relation to the effects of America's 'War on Terrorism' on democratic governance and civil liberties in Africa, as well as France's long history of neo-colonial military interventions and support for autocratic regimes on the continent.

In addition, *Crouching Tiger, Hidden Dragon?* aims to highlight the discourse on development and the issue of the relevance and viability of the Chinese economic model to Africa's economic situation, based on the assumption that certain aspects of China's experience and expertise in development issues may well be useful for the continent. Beijing – which often describes itself as a poor country of the 'global South' – is approaching development challenges that are frequently similar to Africa's problems with some remarkable results. As Ngozi Okonjo-Iweala notes, 'African countries are clear that when it comes to economic growth and transformation, China has much to offer that is relevant to present-day Africa.'[10]

AN EVOLVING ENGAGEMENT

Contemporary relations between China and Africa have their origins in the 1950s, when at the Bandung Conference of 1955, 29 Asian and African countries met in Indonesia to confront colonialism and the divisive nature of the Cold War. While China's participation in Bandung encouraged the forces of decolonisation, Beijing's presence caused consternation for the West, especially the US, which saw China's involvement in the conference as a calculated attempt on the part of the neutralist members of the Bandung group of states (India, in particular) to undermine American hegemony in Asia. Chinese premier, Zhou Enlai, cut an impressive figure in Bandung as he inspired the African representatives with his messages of solidarity and encouraged them to forge ahead with their struggle for the total decolonisation of the continent, as well as economic self-reliance. Following the historical events at Bandung, the relationship between China and Africa revolved, in the 1960s and 1970s, mainly around ideological solidarity, with several socialist African countries, such as Tanzania, Zambia and Zimbabwe generally supporting the liberation war against 'capitalism' and 'imperialism' and assisting in infrastructural development in a handful of countries, notably Tanzania and Zambia.

But China's engagement in Africa was also motivated by another protagonist's influence amongst liberation movements on the continent, i.e. the Soviet Union. For all of Chairman Mao Zedong's rhetoric of Third World solidarity and independence, the cross-currents of the Cold War brought together 'the different power protagonists – the Soviet Union, the US and China – that helped them to carve spheres of influence which resulted in the de facto (if not neo-colonial) balkanisation of Africa'.[11] Such foreign policy leanings are explored in Garth le Pere's Chapter 2 on the geo-strategic dimensions of China's engagement in Africa, which is noted to have been ideologically driven and determined by Cold-War rivalries based on the Sino-Soviet Split and Mao's Theory of the Intermediate Zone.[12]

In the current trajectory of relations, Beijing's Africa policy has undergone a transformation. Reasons for this shift are supplied by Suisheng Zhao's Chapter 3, where he argues that the rationality of the decision-making process in China's foreign policy is based on the pragmatism of subsequent Chinese leaders following Deng Xiaoping's leadership (from 1978 to 1992). Zhao claims that this is being shaped by a set of bureaucrats who have been educated abroad and are institutionalising and approximating Beijing's external engagements based on its global rise. He also makes note of the trend towards the corporate pluralisation of foreign policy decision-making and reflects on the decentralisation of power in the bureaucratic hierarchy, which suggests that the central government and provincial governments could pursue different aims and objectives in Africa.

This is evident in Le Pere's historiography of Sino-African relations, which in the present context signals an institutionalisation of engagements through the establishment of the Forum on China-Africa Cooperation (FOCAC) in 2000 and the launch of the White Paper on China's Africa Policy in January 2006. This also seems to be complimented by the push and pull factors that are aligned to China's insatiable domestic needs to feed its spectacular economic development.

THE POLITICAL-ECONOMIC NEXUS

Since the initiation of its 'open-door' policy in 1978, and following the astounding developments in its economy, some estimate that China will become the world's largest economy by 2025. In pursuit of this objective, China has sought key raw materials for its development from Africa and attempted to consolidate its relations with several African countries through trade and other economic initiatives. Beijing has based its Africa policy on the basis of the Five Principles of Peaceful Coexistence:[13] mutual respect for each other's territorial integrity and sovereignty; mutual non-aggression; mutual non-interference in each other's internal affairs; equality and mutual benefit; and peaceful coexistence. In 1996, Chinese President, Jiang Zhemin, further underlined these policies with his Five Points of Principle to seal the bonds between China and Africa: sincere friendship; equal treatment; true reciprocity; dynamic cooperation; and common goals for the future.[14]

The interaction between the political and the economic has become a significant feature of China's contemporary Africa policy. This is affirmed through the three successive FOCAC summits, where Chinese leaders have confirmed their country's desire to (1) strengthen consultation and expand cooperation with relevant African states; and (2) promote political dialogue and economic cooperation and trade with African countries 'with the view to seeking mutual reinforcement and common development', which was termed as 'a new strategic partnership' at the FOCAC summit in 2006.

This strengthening of economic ties is further amplified through the historical lens, which is demonstrated in each of the case study chapters where reflections of

China's continuity with the past, predicated on a South-South partnership, is noted. However, even in cases where any meaningful relationship between Beijing and the liberation movement of choice was minimal, there seems to be some form of selective amnesia in the current buoyancy of relations.

Nevertheless, while the historical-political dynamic provides a foundation to the contemporary nature of Sino-African engagements, the growing economic ties between China and Africa are the primary determinants of the bonds in this evolving relationship. This again dovetails with the outward expression of Beijing's institutional and policy documents. The White Paper on China's Africa Policy and the FOCAC processes have explicitly become platforms in promoting and concretising China's economic interests on the continent. Consider, for example, the following text from China's Africa Policy Paper:

> The Chinese government encourages and supports competent Chinese enterprises to co-operate with African nations in various ways on the basis of the principle of mutual benefit and common development, to develop and exploit rationally their resources, with a view to helping African countries to translate their advantages in resources to competitive strength, and realise sustainable development in their own countries and the continent as a whole.[15]

In 2006, China's trade with Africa reached US$55 billion, up from US$40 billion in the previous year. Oil alone represented 71 per cent of Africa's exports to Beijing.[16] In 2005, Nigeria, Angola, Equatorial Guinea, Gabon, Congo-Brazzaville, Sudan and Chad supplied 28 per cent of China's crude oil imports, compared to 9 per cent in 1995 from Nigeria, Angola and Gabon. This compares with the Middle East's 47 per cent and 45 per cent respectively in the same period; East Asia's 7 per cent and 41 per cent; and Russia's 10 per cent and 0 per cent. As a result of China's increased dependence on Africa for crude oil, the trade statistics between Beijing and Africa continue to rise. This is followed by metal-ferrous ore, which accounts for 13 per cent.

Chinese exports to Africa are more diversified: textiles (16 per cent); clothing and footwear (14 per cent); transport vehicles (8 per cent); electrical appliances (7 per cent); industrial equipment (5 per cent); and other (42 per cent).[17] Chinese foreign direct investment (FDI) into Africa is also growing steadily. Between 1979 and 2002, almost 10 per cent of Chinese FDI went to Africa; while by 2004, China provided Africa with over US$900 million of the total US$15 billion in FDI that the continent received. Chinese official sources have also noted that, in the first ten months of 2005, 'Chinese companies invested a total of $175 million in African countries, primarily on oil exploration projects and infrastructure'.[18]

At the 2006 FOCAC summit, Premier Wen Jiabao surmised that China's total trade with the continent will reach US$100 billion by 2010. At the conclusion of the Summit, more than a dozen investment agreements were signed between eleven Chinese companies and African governments and businesses. These totalled US$1.9 billion and ranged from primarily resource and infrastructure development to deals on manufacturing. FOCAC 2006 also saw China launch the US$5 billion China-Africa Development Fund (CADF) and US$5 billion in loans and credits, as well as the unveiling of the construction of three to five Special Economic Zones across the continent. The design for the first zone in Zambia's Copper Belt region has already been completed.

These commitments will certainly increase the footprint of Chinese corporations and commercial interests in the African market. Beijing has become a significant development partner to African countries. Since the inception of FOCAC, China has cancelled US$1.3 billion of the debt owed by African countries and aligned its development assistance more broadly to the objectives of the UN's Millennium Development Goals (MDGs) to halve poverty by 2015. At the 2006 FOCAC summit in Beijing, China pledged another US$1.25 billion in debt write-offs, promised to double aid to Africa by 2009, provide a pool of 100 agricultural experts, train 1 500 professionals, build 100 schools, 10 agricultural demonstration centres, 100 hospitals and 30 malaria clinics, grant zero tariffs for 440 African products to enter the Chinese market and increase the number of Chinese scholarships offered to Africans to study in China.[19] All of this signals a long-term focus on the continent.

Perhaps the most profound element of China's engagement with Africa is to be found in its behaviour as an alternative source of credit to the International Monetary Fund (IMF) and the World Bank. The generous aid packages and soft loans that African governments are receiving from Beijing are exemplified in Chapter 6 on Angola by Lucy Corkin (and the other case studies) where the Eduardo dos Santos government benefited from securing a US$2 billion loan from China.[20]

At the same time, and not surprisingly, there are enormous risks involved in the economic ties between China and Africa. For example, there are concerns that Beijing's economic largesse masks the realities that African economies are becoming dumping grounds for cheap consumer retail products, such as textiles, garments, leather goods and electronic products, which is undermining the efforts of local competitors. This invariably leads to local unemployment in these sectors, which begs the obvious questions: do African economies gain if China is dumping its low-priced products on African markets and, is China using its comparative advantage in the manufacturing industry to inhibit growth, investment and development in Africa? These are questions that are most relevant and reflected as a constant theme in the case study chapters, especially in countries like South Africa and Nigeria, which have growing manufacturing industries.

Apart from the trade impasse, Chinese investments have also come under the spotlight. The recent public opposition from key political actors in Zambia, as well as criticism from civil society actors noted in chapters on South Africa, Nigeria and Zimbabwe have raised questions about the development impact of China's trade and investment engagements in Africa.

THE DEVELOPMENT IMPASSE?

It has been suggested by Martyn Davies that 'considering the general low volume, relatively small economies of scale, and the poor levels of competitiveness of Africa's manufacturing capacity, the continent is in all probability best positioned to serve as a supply function to China'.[21] Another postulation by the South Africa-based Brenthurst Foundation is that since 'Asian countries will probably dominate industries like cheap clothing and footwear for [the foreseeable future], thereby inhibiting most African countries climbing the traditional first step of the industrialisation ladder, a combination of natural resource exploitation, agricultural self-sufficiency and high-value agro-exports, and the expansion of its unique range of service industries including tourism, would seem to be the most likely and rewarding growth path for many African states'.[22]

An added dimension to this development impetus is the view of proponents of China's Africa policy that Beijing's 'thirst for [Africa's] natural resources sets it apart from the 19th century scramble for Africa by the fact that now the economic engagement is accompanied by investment in and upgrading of infrastructure and transport facilities, which are central to Africa's development trajectory'.[23] This has led commentators like Davies to assert that China is transporting its development model to Africa.[24] But such an observation has produced a set of ambivalent responses.

On the one hand, Chinese policy mandarins, development practitioners and diplomats have cautioned that China's engagement in Africa should not be confused as a panacea for the continent's development deficiencies. Nor should China's home-grown development model be considered as a brand to be exported and replicated as an alternative to the Washington Consensus. Instead most Chinese commentators and high-ranking officials have argued that China's trade, investment and aid to the continent is primarily intended at enabling African governments to achieve self-sufficiency by finding their own development brand rather than creating what some have called a 'Beijing Consensus'.

On the other hand, others less convinced of the Chinese argument believe that there is very little substance to the way the engagement is structured, which raises questions about whether it will assist Africa in its sustainable development mandate. For these critics, such as Eisenman and Kurlantzick, Africa is essentially part of Beijing's global strategy of finding export markets for its cheap goods while simultaneously accessing energy resources and raw materials to fulfil its economic ambitions.[25]

These two juxtapositions are reflected upon in the case study chapters. Each of the authors explore to what extent China's engagement with particular countries creates opportunities for development or threatens its reversal. Indeed, what is keenly observed, especially amongst the small band of oil-producing and mineral-rich countries like Angola, Nigeria, Democratic Republic of Congo (DRC) and Sudan is the delicate nature of these economies slipping into a 'Dutch disease' (a phenomenon in which the revenues of natural resource extraction have an unintended corrosive effect on the political economy of the exporting country). Even in countries like South Africa, it is demonstrated that China's competitive advantage has created inherent pressures for the industrial base of these countries.

But while the country chapters raise significant issues regarding the comparative advantage of African economies vis-à-vis China's industrial prowess, they also point to a deeper issue: whether Africa has any strategies in its engagements with China and if so, whether they are appropriate. Clearly what is demonstrated in most of the case studies is that the economies of the African states are quickly becoming overly dependent on commodity exports to China, while at the same time ignoring the need to devise robust and coherent national industrial policies. The IMF reported in its 2006 World Economic Outlook Report that sub-Saharan Africa's growth rate could rise to 6.3 per cent from the current 5–5.5 per cent range as a result of the rise in oil prices and the commodity boom. But if Africa is to integrate itself more effectively into the global economy, it has to shift its current activities in the natural resource sector towards secondary and tertiary production.

This seems to be a recurrent theme in most of the case studies, which leads to another issue regarding debt sustainability. A contentious issue that is raised mainly within Western circles, the argument is that the new loans incurred by African governments through export credits and concessional finance will create new forms of debt vulnerability. A central concern is that China is undermining or 'free-riding' on the debt relief granted through bilateral (Paris Club) and multilateral initiatives (namely the Multilateral Debt Relief Initiative and the Highly Indebted Poor Countries programme).

Such fears are to be found in what is becoming a view that China is perceived to be increasing its concessional loans and decreasing its grant assistance to Africa. This is exemplified by the increased role of the Export-Import Bank of China (Exim)[26] and the authorisation by the Chinese government for the China Development Bank to administer the China-African Development Fund.[27]

Most of the case study chapters allude to the fluidity of the economic relations between China and the respective countries. But, in each case, a fundamental question is being raised: how do we interpret China, as a development partner or a scrambler?

STRUCTURE OF THE BOOK

Starting with this Introduction, Part 1 provides a contextual understanding of the political, economic and geo-strategic dimensions of the China-Africa engagement.

From a historical perspective to the more nuanced assessments of the current plateau of relations, in Chapter 2, Le Pere weaves a broad purview around the nature of relations in which he highlights that amongst Beijing's trajectory of interactions with the developing world, Africa has featured as and remains a prominent and strategic sphere of engagement. Against this background, he highlights the fact that China's Africa policy is a reflection of the 'dialectical interplay with China's definition of its self-image, national interest and world view'. In so doing, Le Pere provides a valuable framework of how this synergises with Africa's reintegration into the global system, based on Beijing's perceptions of a unipolar international order and the notion of peaceful rise and development, which he sees as an integral part of the three imperatives that drive China's global agenda: 'access to raw materials, market access and a greater role in international relations'. He concludes by offering valuable advice to Chinese and African policy-makers, academics and activists engaged in the China-Africa debate on how the engagement can be made more cogent. This can be done by each leveraging the relationship towards achieving global initiatives like the MDGs through better formulated policies and more transparency in the governance realm.

Zhai's Chapter 3 interfaces with Le Pere's considerations that underline China's global agenda. In this chapter on China's foreign policy, Zhao notes the pluralism and actors that underpin the reorientation of Beijing's external relations. It is evident how this aligns with Beijing's global agenda and what some see as China's becoming more conscious of its 'soft power' outreach.

Part 2 of the book focuses on the arguments from the previous section with a deeper analysis of how nine individual countries in four African sub-regions are managing their engagements with China. Each of the country chapters examine the push and pull factors and draws significant conclusions about what influences this will have on these countries' future relations with Beijing. As an indirect corollary, the case-study chapters reflect on Le Pere's advice and Zhao's foreign policy pluralism.

Chapter 4 by Sharath Srinivasan focuses on Sino-Sudanese relations in the context of Darfur and argues that Beijing's foreign policy towards Africa is being tested to its limit. It further intimates that the Darfur component to China's relations with Africa demonstrates an evolution from the proverbial People's Republic of China position of 'no interference' to a pragmatic acceptance of the need to apply its influence where necessary. This also suggests an acceptance on the part of Beijing of some measure of multilateral approach in its relations with African states, rather than the stubborn position of approaching African countries on a bilateral basis.

By examining the myriad factors influencing the political economy of the DRC, Chapter 5 by Devon Curtis starts with an evaluation of the relations between China and the Congo in the Cold-War era before engaging with the issues surrounding the contemporary relationship. It poses some critical questions about China's growing economic relations with the DRC and takes particular note of the US$8 billion draft agreement signed in September 2007 which, as the chapter suggests, would tie up some of Congo's mineral resources in exchange for infrastructure projects and loans. Such agreements between the two countries also undermine efforts by the IMF and the World Bank to inject some discipline and transparency into the national budget of the DRC. The chapter further warns that although 'China has extricated itself from the burden of a "civilising mission" there is no reason to believe that this has freed it from exploitative practices'.

This is contrasted with Chapter 6 by Lucy Corkin on Angola where she highlights international donors' concerns about China's role in Angola, with specific reference to the lack of transparency in the various bilateral economic negotiations between Beijing and Luanda. These negotiations have invariably led to agreements that have made it possible for the entry of state-owned Chinese enterprises into the Angolan economy. Of these, as the chapter informs us, the high-level oil deals have been the most outstanding, not to mention the positive contribution that Chinese companies have made to the development of the national infrastructure. Corkin suggests that within these dynamics of Sino-Angolan relations may lie the potential for Angola's economic self-determination.

Lloyd Sachikonye's perspective on Zimbabwe's relationship with China in Chapter 7 examines the dividends of Robert Mugabe's 'Look East Policy'. In his analysis, Sachikonye notes that in spite of the rhetoric that governs the relations between Harare and Beijing, there seems to be a cautious approach by China in strengthening ties with the Mugabe regime. He notes that the continuing political and economic crisis that bedevils Zimbabwe is one of the factors that shapes this approach. He concludes that 'while the strategic and economic value of a non-oil producing country such as Zimbabwe to China is much more limited, it would be interesting to see if China invests in a diplomatic initiative in Zimbabwe, as it has done in Sudan'.

Muna Ndulo's Chapter 8 concerns itself with China's growing economic interests in Zambia and the investments that are being generated as a result in the Zambian economy. The chapter affirms that the Chinese investments are in line with the ambitions of the Zambian Fifth National Development Plan, which seeks to promote investments in the mining sector. The real issue that this increasing collaboration between the two countries raises, as the author notes, is whether Zambia's need for investments and China's raw material requirements (in a form of mutual exchange) can bring about the requisite economic changes to alleviate poverty in both countries. The chapter indicates potential problems for Zambia in such an engagement but these are, on the whole, problems that may result from any kind of rapid economic development. On the whole, the chapter encourages China's economic initiatives in Zambia.

Chapter 9 by Mwesiga Baregu on Tanzania provides a well-documented overview of relations with Beijing that spans a 40-year period. While acknowledging the rich history of relations, Baregu notes that China's engagements with Tanzania should not be viewed as anything less than part of Beijing's overall Africa policy, which he sees as being motivated by national interests. But instead of surmising that this should be interpreted as a zero-sum game, Baregu opines that this can be a positive-sum game for Tanzania, in particular, and Africa, more generally. Of course he argues that this depends on what he terms as 'objective conditions of demand and supply', which can be mutually reinforcing. He concludes by noting that for these objective conditions of complementarity to be realised, Tanzania would need to work through a coherent multilateral Africa strategy instead of through bilateral engagements.

In Chapter 10 on South Africa, Sanusha Naidu explores the meaning of the strategic partnership between Pretoria and Beijing. While recognising that the engagement is governed by the Bi-National Commission signed between the two countries in 1998, she is of the view that for the partnership to be strategic Pretoria has to become more proactive in its engagements with Beijing and extend beyond the 'normative agenda of like-mindedness' in the areas of reforming the international order, Africa's development programme and South-South cooperation. She concludes that for the South African government to balance its relations with China more strategically, its engagement should be predicated more along the lines of the 'business of business is business' within the confines of realpolitik.

Alaba Ogunsanwo's Chapter 11 on Nigeria dovetails with Chapter 9 in terms of its historical record. While the author makes reference to the significance of the engagement with Beijing, he is less convinced that the 'win-win' rhetoric that accompanies Beijing's relationship with Abuja will be mutually reinforcing. For him, the relationship with China, which is predicated on Nigeria's oil industry, sees Beijing deriving greater benefits. What is explicitly reflected upon in Ogunsanwo's chapter is the issue of political will and internal politics of the Nigerian authorities to be transparent about their engagements with Beijing, especially in terms of how much oil is being extracted from its oil fields. Ogunsanwo concludes his chapter by raising a significant issue around the Dutch disease wherein he asks that since the West was not able to assist Nigeria in achieving an economic miracle, will China be able to do so?

Starting with useful background information on the rise of Omar Bongo in Gabon, the final case study in Chapter 12 by Douglas Yates explores the relations between France and Gabon and brings into perspective the role of the international mining companies in the Gabonese economy. It is in this context that the chapter introduces the sudden emergence of China as a prominent player in the economy of the Central African state, alerting us to the potential advantages and disadvantages about the role of China in the development of Gabon.

Following from the case study chapters, Part 3 of the book focuses on Africa's global geo-strategic position. In this section, the authors assess the interplay of relations between the dominant powers on the one hand and China on the other hand.

Since the beginning of the twenty-first century, Africa's geo-political and geo-economic strategic concerns regarding the continent's relationship to the global order have become significant. By the start of the 1990s, Africa's role within the global economy was marginal. Yet by the turn of the twenty-first century, Africa's global trajectory had shifted gears. Much of this was aligned to the demand for Africa's renewable and non-renewable resources, but also lent itself to the 'War on Terrorism' led by the US 'Coalition of the Willing'.

As these geo-strategic dimensions to Africa's global position became more profound, it became increasingly apparent that these considerations were shaping a renewed interest in Africa amongst the traditional foreign powers on the one hand and the emerging powers on the other hand. These issues underpinning Africa's relations with these powers are reflected upon in the chapters on the US and France at one level, the EU and Japan at another and India on the periphery. Of course, each of the chapters in this section provides a view of the push and pull factors and how they are being played out across the continent and the implications this will have for Africa's international relations.

Chapter 13 by Adekeye Adebajo examines the cross-currents of US, France and China's relations with Africa; it takes an historical approach and assesses aspects of the political, military and economic roles that all three countries have played and are currently playing on the continent. Borrowing from the anthology of Bushism, the chapter attempts to depict these actors as three cowboys in a spaghetti western of 'the Good, the Bad and the Ugly'. Essentially, the chapter seeks to shatter the 'Orientalist' myth that often describes China's role as that of a 'yellow peril' seeking to monopolise markets, coddle caudillos and condone human rights abuses on the continent; while Western powers such as the United States and France are portrayed by contrast almost as knights in shining armour, seeking to assist Africa's economic recovery, spread democracy and contribute to conflict management efforts.

Covering some of the same territory as Adebajo but in a more contemporary vein and broader canvas, Adam Habib's Chapter 14 delineates the triangular relationship between the US, the West, China and India in Africa. Habib places the US engagement more in terms of Washington's global hegemonic position and argues that China's behaviour in Africa is guided by this condition. He notes, too, that Delhi remains a peripheral actor in Africa. It is, however, tempting to suggest that although currently muted, India's interests in Africa should neither be underrated nor overlooked.[28] There are emerging signs that Delhi is becoming more aware of its interests in Africa vis-à-vis China, and the first India-Africa Forum Summit was held in New Delhi in April 2008.

Daniel Bach argues in Chapter 15 that the EU-Africa Partnership is not being governed by the China dimension, although there are intimations that in an indirect way Brussels is considering the merits of a cooperation partnership with China, which is seen as beneficial in strengthening Africa's development agenda.

Kweku Ampiah's Chapter 16 on Japan and China argues that Tokyo's engagement remains more of the same in terms of its historical perspective in spite of the Tokyo International Conference on African Development (TICAD) process. As he argues, Japan seems more committed to the discourses at the multilateral level about the 'Africa problem' and therefore has been unable to define Africa as a potential economic partner as China has. Tokyo is thus constrained by the big-power perception of Africa as an entity that needs to be 'aided along'.

The final substantive chapter in the book provides a comparative perspective, as well as the lessons that Africa can learn from China's relations with its Southeast Asian neighbours. By exploring the nature of these relationships, Chapter 17 by Amitav Acharya leaves us with resounding advice: Africa will lose if it deals with China – including its demand for its resources – exclusively through bilateral channels, as a house divided against itself, with individual African nations competing among themselves for Chinese economic aid or political backing. In other words, African states would be better off working as a coherent entity, rather than allowing China to divide and rule them. Consequently, Acharya makes 'a strong case for a multilateral dialogue between China and the African Union (AU) and China and Africa's myriad sub-regional groupings'. Finally, Chapter 18 concludes with an analysis of the possibilities of the developing partnership between China and the continent of Africa.

NOTES

1. D. Zweig and B. Jianhai, 'China's Global Hunt for Energy', *Foreign Affairs* 84(5), September/October 2005: 32.
2. See D. Tull, 'China's Engagement in Africa: Scope, Significance and Consequences', *Journal of Modern African Studies* 44(3), September 2006: 459–79.
3. See M.C. Lee, 'The 21st Century Scramble for Africa', *Journal of Contemporary African Studies* 24(3), September 2006: 303–30; I. Taylor, 'China's Oil Diplomacy in Africa', *International Affairs*, September 2006: 937–59; *The Economist*, 'Never Too Late to Scramble' (26 October 2006).
4. See I. Taylor, 'Beijing's Arms and Oil Interests in Africa', *China Brief* 5(21), 13 October 2005; H.W. French, 'Commentary: China and Africa', *African Affairs* 106(422), 2006; articles by *The Economist*, such as 'Africa and China: Wrong Model, Right Continent' and 'China in Africa: Never Too Late to Scramble' (28 October–3 November 2006).
5. C. Alden, *China in Africa* (London and New York: Zed Books, 2007), p. 6.
6. See G. le Pere and G. Shelton, *China, Africa and South Africa: South-South Co-operation in a Global Era* (Johannesburg: Institute for Global Dialogue, 2007); F. Manji and S. Marks (eds.), *African Perspectives on China in Africa* (Oxford: FAHAMU, 2006); G. le Pere (ed.), *China in Africa: Mercantilist Predator or*

Partner in Development? (Johannesburg: Institute for Global Dialogue and the South African Institute of International Affairs, 2007); G. le Pere (ed.), *China Through the Third Eye: South African Perspectives* (Midrand: Institute for Global Dialogue, 2004); P. Draper and G. le Pere (eds.), *Enter the Dragon: Towards a Free Trade Agreement between China and the Southern African Customs Union* (Midrand and Johannesburg: Institute for Global Dialogue and The South African Institute of International Relations, 2006); M. Power and G. Mohan, 'Good Friends and Good Partners: The "New" Face of China-African Co-operation', *Review of African Political Economy* 35(115), special issue, March 2008; S. Srinivasan, '"A Rising Great Power" Embraces Africa: Nigeria-China Relations', in A. Adebajo and R. Mustapha (eds.), *Gulliver's Troubles: Nigeria's Foreign Policy After the Cold War* (Pietermaritzburg: University of KwaZulu-Natal Press, 2008).

7. Alden, *China in Africa*, p. 4.
8. N. Okonjo-Iweala, 'Viewpoint: China Becomes Africa's Suitor' (BBC News, 24 October 2006). http://news.bbc.co.uk/1/hi/business/6079838.stm
9. See Alden, *China in Africa*, pp. 5–6.
10. Okonjo-Iweala, 'Viewpoint'; Z. Weiwei, 'The Allure of the Chinese Model', *International Herald Tribune*, 2 November 2006.
11. See E.J. Hevi, *The Dragon's Embrace: The Chinese Communists and Africa* (London: Pall Mall Press, 1967), p. 2, as quoted in Le Pere and Shelton, *China, Africa and South Africa*, p. 13.
12. See C. Jian, *Mao's China and the Cold War* (North Carolina: University of North Carolina, 2001); M.B. Yahuda, 'Chinese Foreign Policy After 1963: The Maoist Years', *The China Quarterly* (36), October–December 1968: 93–113.
13. These were first stated in the preamble to the Sino-Indian Agreement on Tibet of 30 April 1954. See J. Mackie, *Bandung 1955: Non-Alignment and Afro-Asian Solidarity* (Singapore: Editions Didier Millet, 2005), p. 59.
14. Chung-lian Jiang, 'China's African Policy', *African Geo-Politics* 23, July–September 2006: 235.
15. People's Republic of China, 'China's Africa Policy' (Beijing: PRC, 12 January 2006). http://www.fmprc.gov.cn/eng/zxxx/t230615.htm/.
16. This was 8.7 per cent of China's oil imports for 2006, compared to 36 per cent of the United Kingdom's and 33 per cent of America's. See E.S. Downs, 'The Fact or Fiction of Sino-African Energy Relations', *China Security* 3(3), 2007.
17. 'Africa-China, Atlas on Regional Integration in West Africa: Economy Series'. http://www.oecd.org/dataoecd/31/37/37944348.pdf.
18. P. Esther, 'China, Africa, Oil' (Council on Foreign Relations). http://www.cfr.org/publication/9557/.
19. Beijing Summit and Third Ministerial Conference of the Forum on China-Africa Cooperation, 'Programme for China-Africa Cooperation in Economic and Social Development' (20 September 2006). http://english.focacsummit.org/2006-09/20/content_629.htm.
20. E.M. Grioñ, 'The Political Economy of Commercial Relations: China's Engagement in Angola', in Le Pere (ed.), *China in Africa*, p. 151.
21. M. Davies, 'The Rise of China and the Commercial Consequences for Africa', in Draper and Le Pere (eds.), *Enter the Dragon*, p. 161; R. Kaplinsky 'What does the Rise of China do for Industrialisation in Sub-Saharan Africa?' *Review of African Political Economy* 115(35), March 2008.
22. 'Competition or Partnership? China, United States and Africa – An African View' (Brenthurst Discussion Paper, 2/2007), p. 2.
23. S. Naidu and M. Davies, 'China Fuels its Future with Africa's Riches', *South African Journal of International Affairs* 13(2), Summer 2006: 70.

24. See M. Davies, 'China's Development Model Comes to Africa', *Review of African Political Economy* 35(115), March 2008.
25. J. Eisenman and J. Kurlantzick, 'China's Africa Strategy', *Current History,* May 2006: 219–64.
26. According to Jian-Ye Wang, 'By the end of 2005, China Exim Bank had approved more than 50 billion yuan (US$6.5 billion) for projects in Africa, which accounted for close to 10 per cent of the bank's total approvals at the time.' See Jian-Ye Wang, 'What drives China's growing role in Africa?', IMF Working Paper WP/07/211, August 2007. Ellis notes that by mid-2006, it was estimated that the Exim Bank had approved approximately US$12.5 billion in loans for infrastructure projects in sub-Saharan Africa, while, by the beginning of September 2006, there were about 259 Exim Bank projects in 36 African countries. Ellis also estimates that 79 per cent of the bank's commitments were in the African infrastructure sector. See J.L Ellis, 'China EXIM Bank in Africa', China Environmental Forum, 22 March 2007, Woodrow Wilson Centre for Scholars.
27. There are other lenders in the African market. The Bank of China has been active in Africa since the construction of the Tanzania-Zambia Railway (TAZARA) in the late 1960s. More recently, the Industrial and Commercial Bank of China (ICBC) entered the market following its US$5.5 billion stake in South Africa's Standard Bank, which will see it increase its development financing within the continent.
28. S. Naidu, 'India's Growing Africa Strategy', *Review of African Political Economy* 35(115), March 2008.

2

The Geo-Strategic Dimensions of the Sino-African Relationship

Garth le Pere

INTRODUCTION

China's growing and dramatic role on the global stage has provoked two competing images: one of awe, the other of trepidation and paranoia. China's focus on Africa has taken on added significance since Deng Xiaoping formulated China's post-Maoist trajectory in 1978. Only astute clairvoyants at that time would have divined that this 'opening' to the world would propel China to become a formidable player in today's regional and international topography of power and influence. Hence, China in its own right is a country that merits serious study since, for good or ill, it inspires a unique sociology of the imagination. Questions thus persist whether, as a rising power, China will '. . . become a rational, peaceful, and pragmatic power or an irrational, bellicose and expansionist state'.[1] For China is a land of many complexities: it has great ethnic and linguistic variety, it draws on reverential wisdom of an ancestral past, it boasts remarkable achievements in its drive from stolid egalitarianism to dynamic modernisation, and its market-driven socialism is confronting the centrifugal effects of central control.[2]

In the great cut and thrust of Chinese history, culture and development, especially as this has played out between the portentous push of modernity and the ineluctable pull of tradition, the role that China has played in the developing world has been significant. A constant and unambiguous refrain of China's external relations has been the emphasis on its developing country pedigree and credentials: 'China presents itself as a rallying point for Third World unity and Third World efforts to receive a fair share of international power and economic benefit.'[3] This refrain often takes the form of a shared historical experience with other developing countries but there is also frequent reference to the importance of solidarity, self-reliance, shared purpose, and cooperation with other developing countries as foundational elements of its foreign policy. These values, in turn, are locked in a dialectical interplay with China's definition of its self-image, national interest and world view.

In the broad purview of China's relations with developing countries, Africa has featured prominently and strategically. The historical girders that uphold this relationship have proved enduring in defining the current norms and principles of Sino-African relations. Generally and notwithstanding, for example, the pandemic of chaos during the Cultural Revolution, which severed China's external connections, its engagement with the African continent has always formed an essential and important subtext of its foreign relations even though this was, and continues to be, steeped in controversy. Hence Emmanuel Hevi's comment of 1967 still has profound resonance today: 'Few subjects are as complicated as China's African policy and the motives behind it . . .'[4]

THE HISTORICAL CONNECTION

Contact between Africa and Asia predates the maritime forays of Western navigators who had yet to emerge from their medieval cosmology of the Earth being flat. The historical record shows that in the early days of the Ming Dynasty, a mighty armada of 62 ships crossed the China Sea, then ventured west to Ceylon, Arabia and East Africa. The fleet was under the astute charge of Zheng He, who became the embodiment of China's maritime spirit, adventure and ambition. Admiral Zheng earned the moniker 'Grand Eunuch of the Three Treasures', because three times since 1405, he and his ships had sailed to ports of Indochina, south-west India and Ceylon in search of all sorts of exotica for the Ming Court.[5] Between 1405 and 1433, Zheng launched eight great expeditions, making calls at more than 30 countries and territories, including what are today Somalia, Kenya, Tanzania and Madagascar. All this maritime activity, it must be recalled, took place about half a century before Columbus's famous voyage to America and for this reason, Zheng's expeditions have rightfully been extolled as an 'unprecedented feat in the history of navigation of mankind'.[6]

These historical precedents presage the enduring links between China and Africa. Indeed, Zheng, as envoy and commercial representative of the Ming Court, is the historical icon often referred to in terms of the traditional links and relations that have prevailed and endured, with different rhythms, ebbs and flows, depending on the era and particular periods of world politics. The organic basis of the contact has provided an ancient impetus for continuing cultural, social and economic exchanges and diplomatic ties between China and Africa. What constituted China's underlying intentions and calculations historically also remains relevant today: Zheng's explorations were not motivated by a colonial or settler project. As Philip Snow explains, '. . . the Chinese were not aggressive. Unlike the Portuguese they stormed no cities and conquered no land . . . They did not burn, as the Portuguese would, with the urge to impose their religious convictions, to lay siege to African souls. All they sought from Africans was a gesture of symbolic acquiescence in the Chinese view of the world.'[7]

THE POST-WAR PERIOD

After the Second World War and following the birth of the People's Republic of China (PRC) in 1949, China forged a new phase of relations with African countries, based mainly on political and strategic considerations: 'China sought Africa as an ally in its struggles against imperialism and hegemony.'[8] This included moral and material support for different generations of liberation and independence movements, although this was a source of great acrimony with the Soviet Union, which itself was vying for spheres of influence in Africa. Relations were further consolidated when Premier Zhou Enlai visited ten African countries in 1963 and 1964 and articulated Five Principles that would underpin the promotion of friendly Sino-African relations and Eight Principles that would inform aid.[9] Sino-African diplomacy was further consolidated by high-level visits by African leaders to China, including over 150 visits by 49 African heads of state since the founding of the PRC.[10]

Following Premier Zhou, high-level visits to Africa by the Chinese leadership have proceeded apace and have almost become 'institutionalised'. Among others, these include Premier Zhao Ziyang in 1982 and 1983; President Li Xiannian in 1986; Premier Li Peng in 1991 and 1995; President Yang Shangkun in 1992; and, most importantly, President Jiang Zhemin's visit in 1996, when he made his famous speech at the headquarters of the Organisation of African Unity (OAU) in Addis Ababa, Ethiopia, to set up what he called a 'New Historical Monument for Sino-African Friendship'. In 2004 Hu Jintao made a nine-day visit to Africa to fortify economic cooperation further, and in June 2006 both President Hu Jintao and Premier Wen Jiabao also made high-profile tours through Africa. These were again followed by important visits in early 2007 by President Hu and his then Foreign Minister Li Zhaoxing to fifteen countries. All these visits are a function of a greater strategic and diplomatic focus on Africa since Deng Xiaoping's 'opening' and extensive economic reforms in 1978.[11]

China's robust cooperation with the continent dates back to 1956, when Beijing inaugurated its official aid programme, with the establishment of diplomatic relations with Egypt – a first on the continent. A range of direct and unconditional aid projects was initiated in areas as diverse as agriculture, animal husbandry, fisheries, textiles and other light industries, energy, transportation, broadcasting and communication, water conservation, public and civil construction, education and health. Some of these flagship projects included the 1 860-km Tanzania-Zambia Railway (TAZARA);[12] the Port of Friendship in Mauritania; the 122-km Canal of Friendship in Tunisia; the International Convention Centre in Cairo; and an 80 000-capacity stadium in Kinshasa.

While its military programme remains controversial and functions under a penumbra of secrecy,[13] starting in the 1980s and then accelerating in the 1990s, China has also provided non-military technical assistance, financial aid and training to many countries in the form of:

- favourable loan framework agreements with more than 20 countries;
- cultural cooperation and exchange agreements with 42 countries;
- in-country scholarships for 5 000 students from 48 countries and the hosting of around 1 000 African students at Chinese universities;
- nineteen hospitals with 2 000 beds over the last 35 years ; and
- nearly 15 000 Chinese medical personnel in 42 African countries over the same period.[14]

The Forum on China-Africa Cooperation (FOCAC), established in 2000 in Beijing, provides a new institutional base and dialogue mechanism for consolidating and broadening this support and enhancing the frontiers and substance of cooperation.[15]

In international affairs, there has been equally close cooperation between China and Africa.[16] The most profound symbol that has further reinforced the Sino-African axis was when the PRC assumed its seat in the UN Security Council in 1971. This was a direct consequence of the 26 affirmative votes cast by African countries. China's presence on the Security Council is perceived as a vanguard for protecting developing country interests, even though the history of its voting record has been rather cautious and ambivalent in this regard. Nevertheless, the acceptance of China's leading role is reflected in the Group of 77 and China, which actually includes more than 130 countries and which, since its Havana summit in 2000, has concentrated on addressing the adverse effects of economic globalisation, improving the mechanics of South-South partnerships and bridging the North-South divide.[17] Since joining the World Trade Organisation (WTO) in December 2001 and in concert with other developing countries, China has become active in confronting the trade and market access asymmetries that exist, but it has become especially sympathetic to the marginalisation of African countries in the global trading system.[18] (This ironically takes place against the backdrop of accusations about China's neo-mercantilist inclinations and its unfair competitive advantage in the clothing and textiles sector, which has had dire and destructive economic consequences for many African countries.) The establishment of formal diplomatic ties with the new South Africa in 1998 and the launching of the South Africa-China Bi-National Commission in 2001 have further deepened and consolidated ties and provided much-needed impetus for more vigorous South-South cooperation.

This overview is meant to sketch and provide a factual account of the main features of a diverse and enduring historically grounded relationship that has helped to define the parameters of contemporary Sino-African relations. It is a relationship that has been anchored in several core principles and declaratory statements, all of which can be usefully summarised in terms of Jiang Zhemin's 'Five Point Proposal' for cooperation with Africa. These are: to promote friendship; to respect the principles of sovereign equality and non-intervention; to promote common development on the basis of mutual benefit; to increase consultation and cooperation in international affairs; and to cooperate in the creation of a more peaceful, stable, prosperous and secure global order. These principles to a large extent form a prism through which the main trajectories of Sino-African relations can be traced.

It might be useful at this point to consider how the post-Cold-War context has influenced and shaped China's conduct in international affairs and reflect on the broader systemic issues that underlie China's emergence on the global stage and its remarkable and breathtaking success in its modernisation quest.

CHINA AND THE CHANGED POST-COLD-WAR SETTING

China's opening up has made a critical difference to economic globalisation. Its global agenda is driven by three imperatives: access to raw materials, market opportunities and a greater role in international relations, in pursuit of which Africa features quite prominently.[19] China is the second largest energy consumer after the United States and oil accounts for 25 per cent of its energy needs. Based on current consumption patterns, China is expected to import 50 per cent of its petroleum requirements within the next decade. Demand for oil is forecast to more than double by 2025, to 14.2 million barrels a day from the current 7 million a day.[20] Africa supplies about 30 per cent of China's oil needs and also plays a crucial role as a strategic location for other raw materials needed to feed China's industrial machine: for example, between 1990 and 2003, China's global imports of iron ore rose from 14 million tonnes to 148 million tonnes; of aluminium from 1 million tonnes to 5.6 million tonnes; of refined copper from 20 000 tonnes to 1.3 million tonnes. Platinum imports rose from 20 000 ounces to 1.6 million ounces and China further imports an additional 40 million tonnes of steel per year to supplement its own 220 million tonnes of domestic production.[21]

The three imperatives mentioned above are, however, underpinned by developments and dynamics in China's macroeconomy. In purchasing power parity, it is the second largest economy in the world, and accounts for 12 per cent of global gross domestic product (GDP) and 7 per cent of global manufacturing production. The PRC economy has averaged growth rates in the 9 to 11 per cent range for more than a decade. Its domestic market comprises 1.3 billion people, and between 1980 and 2000 its real per capita income increased by well over 400 per cent, while its export and import volumes grew by 11 to 13 per cent, and its foreign direct investment (FDI) stock reached US$450 billion in 2002 (from US$25 billion in 1990). Equally importantly, since its opening up, some 400 million Chinese have been lifted out of extreme poverty.[22]

All this is truly exceptional and breathtaking. However, these developments must be seen in the context of China's international relations, especially with the United States. While the Chinese might have imitated much of what has made the United States economically successful, China retains an instinctive apprehension of the United States. Since the Cold War especially, China's leaders have hardly seen the United States as a benign and well-intentioned superpower and suspect that the United States is committed to systematically undermining its emerging power status and legitimacy as a major global player through various means.[23] It has been suggested that 'China's primary foreign policy goal today is to weaken American influence relatively and absolutely, while steadfastly protecting its own corner'.[24]

It is not surprising, then, that China remains suspicious of a unipolar world dominated by the United States. In a unipolar system and in theory, states that are growing and expanding economically tend to become more ambitious and dissatisfied with the status quo, more defensive about their established international interests and commitments to the point where they are prepared to disrupt the dominance of the world's major power. In such an 'anarchic' environment, a country such as China will tend to balance its position against the dominance of the hegemonic power as states become more enmeshed in what is after all a zero-sum game of winners and losers.[25] In this Darwinian race, and as an essential element of its 'opening', China has embraced globalisation and hence '. . . China's strategic choices are increasingly designed to exploit globalization as a way of making China rich and strong and simultaneously reducing fears of fast-growing Chinese material power . . . China's new foreign policy choice highlights the potential role of globalization in transforming great power politics from the unmitigated struggle for supremacy of earlier eras to a more cooperative form of interstate competition that increases prospects for China's peaceful rise.'[26]

China's economic and political development has profound implications for every region in a world of increasing interdependence. Economically, China's reform and open-door policy have exposed it on an unprecedented scale to the world of global commerce, markets, trade and investment opportunities, and the world is probably better off for its market-led growth, wide-ranging domestic economic restructuring and innovations in production.[27] The converse is that a poor and unstable China would be a huge welfare burden that the international community would not be able to cope with and hence the logic that China should rather be encouraged than contained. As has been argued: 'For economic, environmental and security reasons alike, a major priority is now to bring China into the centre of global, as well as regional governance . . . into an institutional arrangement which recognizes that, within a short space of time, China is beginning to matter as much for the rest of the world as Japan, the EU or the US.'[28]

For these and many other reasons, China needs a peaceful and stable global environment in which to advance its economic modernisation programme and to address its own myriad of domestic challenges as a developing country. It cannot be in its interests to destabilise existing regional orders or violate the letter and spirit of international regimes. Indeed, since the end of the Cold War, China has deliberately set out to develop and institutionalise cooperative relations across a broad spectrum of countries and regions. It has, for example, promoted regional economic cooperation, especially among developing countries, participated in bilateral and multilateral security dialogues in Asia, and has signed the Nuclear Non-Proliferation Treaty (NNPT). The understanding of a strong and prosperous China, therefore, needs to be more nuanced; the realist preoccupation with relative gains only perpetuates mutual suspicion. What makes more sense is an emphasis on absolute gains that encourage China and other countries to cooperate more intensively in key areas that advance global peace, stability and prosperity.[29]

Against this background, let us examine the main strategic features of the Sino-African nexus. Before doing so, a caveat is in order. The trepidation and anxiety about China's growing footprint in Africa is decidedly exaggerated. While there are legitimate and justifiable concerns about how to manage the engagement, the phobia and threat perception about China in Africa are largely products of Western-inspired hypocrisy and arrogance, which are increasingly finding echoes among Africans themselves. The historical record will show that European and American policies in Africa were characterised by a mixture of exploitation, hubris, injustice and oppression, organised mostly for economic gain, and buttressed by political expediency rather than ethical restraint. The imperative for coherent policy responses towards China by Africans must, therefore, not fall prey to lazy caricature and crude stereotyping lest we fall into a trap of moral relativism where the West is held to one set of standards and China to another.[30]

THE FORUM ON CHINA-AFRICA COOPERATION

FOCAC has become the main institutional vehicle for shaping and managing China's cooperation framework with Africa across a range of technical, economic and political platforms. FOCAC was established in October 2000 to coordinate China's activities in Africa. Its work has been significantly enhanced by the publication of China's White Paper on Africa in January 2006. The FOCAC process and the White Paper have embedded China's discourse about mutual economic benefit, development assistance, political dialogue and international cooperation and, if their statements are anything to go by, FOCAC and its outcomes are generally endorsed and accepted by African leaders. As the White Paper makes clear, China respects African countries' independent choices and paths to development; as such, it will provide and increase its assistance to African countries with no political conditions or requirements attached, except adherence to the 'One China' principle. China has diplomatic relations with every African country, except four.[31] Thus 48 countries have participated in FOCAC frameworks and processes of cooperation and meetings at ministerial level are held every three years. The second ministerial meeting took place in Addis Ababa in 2003, with 44 African countries represented. This meeting resulted in the Addis Action Plan, which proposed sixteen areas around which cooperation could be structured. It was at this meeting that Premier Wen Jiabao announced that China would cancel the debt of 31 African countries, totalling US$1.27 billion, with another US$1 billion of debt cancellation to follow in mid-2007. He also promised support for the New Partnership for Africa's Development (NEPAD) and increased Chinese participation in UN peacekeeping operations. By May 2007, there were 1 800 Chinese peacekeepers, military observers and civilian police participating in seven UN missions.[32]

The work of the first two meetings was folded into a new strategic partnership at the November 2006 FOCAC summit in Beijing, attended by 43 African heads of state and 48 delegations. At the summit, China made far-reaching commitments, which included:

- sending 100 agricultural experts to Africa;
- setting up a development fund of US$5 billion to encourage Chinese firms to invest in Africa;
- cancelling interest-free loans that were due by the end of 2005 for African countries classified as either highly indebted or least developed;
- providing US$3 billion in preferential loans, and a further US$2 billion in preferential buyer's credits to Africa over the next three years; and
- undertaking to establish three to five trade and economic cooperation zones in Africa.

Enhanced market access on the basis of zero tariffs will be provided to Africa's least developed countries (LDCs) through an increase from 190 to 440 export products.

China's Export-Import Bank (Exim) plays an important role in the practical implementation of FOCAC's financing for development commitments. The Bank is China's official credit agency, and assists with financing infrastructure required for extracting and transporting energy and mineral resources. Its loans primarily benefit state-owned enterprises, while private companies use China's informal and private lending markets. By the end of 2005, the Exim Bank had approved US$6.5 billion for 260 projects in 36 African countries. Concessional and low-interest loans for infrastructure development amounted to US$12.5 billion and more than 80 per cent of these loans are concentrated in Angola, Mozambique, Sudan and Zimbabwe. Projects in electricity generation account for 40 per cent of the loans, followed by multi-sector commitments (24 per cent), transport (20 per cent), telecommunications (12 per cent), and water projects (4 per cent). Projects at various stages of development include hydroelectric dams in Congo-Brazzaville, Ethiopia, Mozambique, Sudan and Zambia; railway lines in Angola and Sudan; copper mines in the Democratic Republic of Congo (DRC) and Zambia; and platinum mines in Zimbabwe.[33]

SUPPORT FOR SOCIAL DEVELOPMENT

Trade, investment and improved physical and communications infrastructure are but parts of the strategic calculus that defines Sino-African relations. Social development also forms an integral part.[34] From the first medical team sent to Algeria in 1963 until the end of 2005 more than 15 000 Chinese medical personnel have been active in 47 countries and over 10 000 agro-technicians have been sent to work on some 200 agricultural projects. In 2006, more than 1 000 Chinese doctors and nurses were working in 36 countries in Africa. The Chinese National Overseas Engineering Corporation has built two pharmaceutical plants in Africa for the sole purpose of manufacturing artemisinin (a synthetic derivative of the Artemisia shrub), which is very effective in treating malaria. At the 2006 FOCAC summit, President Hu Jintao also announced support for building 30 new hospitals and 30 malaria-prevention and treatment centres, and an additional US$38 million was made available for the provision of artemisinin over the next three years. By 2009, government scholarships for African students to study in China will be doubled from their present number of 2 000, and 15 000 African professionals will be trained in technical, scientific and administrative fields from 2007 to 2009. This will increase the potential pool of labour that China can draw from in its African development and business projects. And similar to the United States Peace Corps, under the Chinese Young Volunteers Serving in Africa Programme, China will send 300 Chinese youth to support education, sports, agriculture and health projects.

AREAS OF CONCERN AND CONTENTION

Most concerns about China's conduct in Africa focus on its 'no-strings-attached' approach and what are perceived as permissive policies that support and strengthen undemocratic and repressive regimes, undermine the fight against corruption and good governance and weaken social and environmental standards, and which could initiate a new cycle of debt and dependence.[35] Let us examine some examples.

The Sudan connection

Sudan is often cited as the most prominent example of China's support for an undemocratic and repressive regime and where its non-interference principle has been most criticised. China is the main investor in Sudan's oil exploration, chemical industry and rail transport network. China has also sold arms to Sudan and there are claims that these have been used to fuel the conflict in Darfur.[36] China has also supported

Sudan in the UN Security Council, threatening to use its veto against Western and Washington-inspired attempts to impose an oil embargo on Sudan. To its credit, China has, however, urged Khartoum to be more flexible in allowing UN peacekeepers into Darfur and has been publicly supportive of urging the government in Khartoum to accept an African Union/UN hybrid force, to which Khartoum has now agreed. There obviously needs to be more engagement and political dialogue at the AU level to establish how China can be more supportive of the continent's democracy, good governance and human rights agenda in a manner that does not compromise its non-interference principle. Indeed, there seems to be a creeping realisation in China that over time, non-interference could prove anathema to and collide with its deepening interests in Africa.[37]

The problem of corruption

China ratified the UN Convention against Corruption in January 2006, but this applies more to its domestic regime than its international economic and commercial activities. In October 2006, the Bribe Payers Index of Transparency International ranked Chinese companies 29th out of 30 countries, thereby suggesting that Chinese companies are more prone to graft and corrupt practices. In September 2006 and mindful of what was taking place in Angola, a task force of the AU examined Chinese investment practices. It focused on financial transparency and combating corruption as key elements of Africa's evolving partnership with China. Angola is the other country where China has come in for sharp scrutiny and where its large oil investments have allowed the government to evade international pressure to strengthen accountability and transparency in its oil sector.[38] Human Rights Watch claims, for example, that between 1997 and 2002, a startling US$4 billion in Angola's oil revenues have been skimmed from public coffers. A concessional loan of US$2 billion from China's Exim Bank gave Angola the space to ignore the clamour from donors and international financial agencies – especially the International Monetary Fund (IMF) – to improve its good governance record. The Exim Bank does not have an official policy on corruption and has no mechanism for ensuring that the projects it finances are free of corruption and financial malpractices, more so since most of these projects are closed tenders and not subject to international competitive bidding. The Organisation for Economic Cooperation and Development's (OECD) Action Statement on Bribery and Officially Supported Export Credits could be a useful model that can be examined in this regard and which the AU task force could use. China is aware of the problem and it is encouraging to note its commitment at the 2006 FOCAC summit to ensuring that its African projects are in line with international best practice and that principles of fairness, equity and transparency are adhered to.

Growing environmental concerns

The AU task force also raised concerns about China paying more attention to environmental protection in its investment practices. Concern has been raised about the Merowe Dam project in Sudan, which is one of the largest hydropower projects currently under construction, with a planned capacity of 1 250 megawatts. China's Exim Bank is providing half of the total of US$1.4 billion in multinational project financing. With a 174-km-long reservoir and a surface area of 476 km^2, the project will have severe social and environmental impacts, and already more than 50 000 people are being displaced from the fertile Nile valley to other arid desert locations.[39] In this regard, it would again be useful for China and the AU task force to examine the OECD guidelines and practices embodied in its Common Approaches to the Environment and Officially Supported Export Credits. This document contains very specific standards, benchmarks and measures for assessing projects that might have adverse environmental impacts. If China is not held to higher standards, the obvious fear is that there will be an environmental and social race to the bottom since China will finance projects that Western agencies reject because of environmental and social concerns. Conversely, Western financial institutions may use competition by Chinese banks as an excuse to lower their own standards. Nevertheless, alive to the challenge, the Action Plan adopted at the 2006 FOCAC summit commits China to giving high priority to African concerns relating to environmental protection and sustainable development. Furthermore, the White Paper refers to active China-Africa cooperation in the areas of climate change, water resources conservation, anti-desertification, biodiversity and other areas of environmental protection. In this regard, monitoring at all levels and by all concerned becomes imperative.

Challenges to China's 'image management'

Another concern is China's vertical integration formula of investment, project operation and business conduct in Africa.[40] In terms of this formula, all inputs – from management, project design and labour to materials, components and technology – originate in China, with no or little local content or participation. The dumping of cheap Chinese imports and the displacement of local products, especially clothing and textiles, has aroused growing anti-Chinese sentiment and popular resentment in many African countries. While many Africans complain that China has not encouraged domestic participation, supported local business or transferred technology and skills, the Chinese counter that they find it very difficult to identify appropriate African sources and partners for their needs, and that progress, completion and quality of projects could be compromised in such a search.

The cultural and linguistic distance also does not help matters and the charge is certainly justified that burgeoning Chinese communities across Africa have become closed enclaves, insensitive to local custom, norms and social practices. China is aware of this growing negative image and has initiated a process of establishing Confucius Institutes across Africa in an attempt to bridge the language, information and cultural divide. (Three such institutes already exist in Kenya, Rwanda and South Africa and five more are planned.) Increasing numbers of Chinese visitors also helps: with 26 African countries now being accorded 'Approved Destination Status' by China, it is projected that there will be 1 million Chinese tourists travelling to Africa by 2020, compared to 110 000 in 2005.

Chinese companies have also been urged to be more conscious of their social and corporate responsibility and there has even been a hint by Cheng Siwei, Vice-Chairman of the Standing Committee of the People's Congress, that Chinese companies will in future be held to stricter codes of conduct and could face legal penalties where they are found wanting in their social responsibility, including not adhering to labour and occupational safety standards.[41] China's National Development and Reform Commission, the Ministry of Commerce, chambers of commerce and business associations have also been tasked with giving corporate social responsibility a Chinese character and have been studying the OECD Guidelines for Multinational Enterprises. In line with this, there is a proposal that all chief executives of major Chinese companies must undertake compulsory courses in corporate social responsibility.

DEFINING CHINA'S STRATEGIC APPROACH

On the basis of all these considerations, how can the key themes and strategic factors in China's Africa involvement be defined? There are six broad areas that come together in a coherent logic, which help to shape China's approach to Africa. These can be summarised as follows:[42]

1. China's attempt to develop a strategic partnership is consistent with Beijing's global foreign policy strategy and thrust and its vision for a different kind of global order. As such, China's core national interests and its own imperatives for growth and development will increasingly bind it to Africa: it needs resources for its growth and modernisation, it needs markets to sustain its growing economy and it requires political alliances to support its global ambitions.

2. The Chinese leadership and officials believe that China's historical experience and its development model are instructive and useful for Africa and that these resonate powerfully among African governments and societies. This gives it a comparative advantage that the West does not enjoy. Over the course of its turbulent history, China has experienced colonial domination and encroachment for more than a century, and it knows the effects of internal chaos and economic hardship. Africa finds common ground with China, because, in Beijing's view, the Western development experience has been too remote and patronising, offering few transferable lessons; if anything, the legacy of Western involvement in Africa has had disastrous consequences.
3. China's history of solidarity, sincerity, friendship, respect for and assistance to Africa remain overarching values that continue to define its engagement. This goes back to the Bandung Conference in 1955. China supports principles of sovereignty and non-interference in the internal affairs of African countries in contrast to what it sees as the 'hegemonism' of the West.
4. China believes that, for the most part, Africa is on the threshold of a development takeoff. This gives China an opportunity to make a positive contribution and play a constructive role in assisting the continent with addressing its multiple challenges. In contrast to the deficit model of the West, which views Africa mostly in terms of poor governance, conflict, underdevelopment and poverty, for China, Africa represents rich diversity of culture and religion, social dynamism and popular energy, vast development synergies and great opportunities for economic cooperation.
5. China prefers the bilateral state-centred approach as the avenue for its engagement in Africa, for developing its core strengths and for defining common interests. The Beijing Action Plan of 2006 is a result of several years of political dialogue, government planning missions and high-level reciprocal visits by heads of state and senior government officials and ministers. China's policy in Africa is thus not complicated by private domestic constituencies and interest groups. In economic and business activity and transactions, China's engagement is led by state-owned or state-influenced companies. It lacks organised, independent business and civil society actors and hence the Chinese leadership and its diplomats have a relatively free hand in shaping and implementing their approach to Africa.
6. China views engagement with third parties on Africa as serving its interests but will do so on its own terms, and then only incrementally and cautiously. It is open to dialogue with the United States and other developed countries on

its approach to Africa. China is mindful that Western expertise, experience and knowledge in Africa could be useful, especially in how to relate to regional organisations, civil society and business. However, China remains very sensitive to Western criticism of its conduct in Africa. This reflects ongoing concern about the United States' domination, its overreaching power, influence and, at times, hypocritical moralising.

CONCLUSION: CRAFTING AN AFRICAN RESPONSE

FOCAC forms the basis for managing the complex relationship between China and Africa across a range of strategic dimensions and has proven its pedigree as a forum for codifying an increasingly complex and rapidly expanding cooperation agenda and development framework. As should be evident by now, increasing tensions and points of friction are emerging. An African response can, therefore, be crafted in the following five areas, which could assist in strengthening and reinforcing the essential underpinnings of the engagement:

1. There is a need for Africans to make a greater effort to overcome obstacles related to language, culture, and racial bias – the so-called 'yellow peril' stereotype. Demonising China is not helpful at all; rather, Africans themselves must become better cultural ambassadors for engaging Chinese diplomats, business people, technicians, labourers, doctors, peacekeepers and tourists. The religious and civil society interface could also be very helpful circuits since religious and civic organisations in Africa have a wide range of networks and extensive linkages within and among societies. They also exercise strong opinions in matters of public interest and debate. The non-governmental sector and civil society actors can further play an important role in socialising and sensitising China to governance and accountability imperatives in Africa. They have expertise and experience in multiple sectors, for example, election monitoring, independent media, human rights, and the empowerment of women. The non-governmental sector could become the driver behind improving the interpersonal and intersocial environment for the Chinese in Africa.[43]
2. African countries must become more involved in insisting on harmonisation of donor activity in Africa in such a manner that international and bilateral donors systematically share data and develop complementary approaches with China. China has signed the 2004 Paris Declaration on Aid Effectiveness, which, among other things, calls for improved alignment and cooperation

between donors and the development policies of aid recipients. China also increasingly refers to assisting Africa with meeting the benchmarks of the Millennium Development Goals (MDGs) and this is another arena that invites closer cooperation. There is mounting concern that Chinese unconditional lending practices undermine Western debt relief strategies, the fear being that China's lending practices may reintroduce unsustainable debt burdens in Africa. Washington is particularly concerned about Africa's borrowing patterns and the impact this may have on the long-term effectiveness of debt-relief initiatives aimed at the heavily indebted poor countries (HIPC) programme. At the continental level, the AU should insist on deepening the United States-China regional sub-dialogue, started in 2005 as a means for addressing the United States' rising concern about China's role in Africa with regard to Darfur, unconditional debt write-offs, energy competition, and relations with autocratic regimes.

3. African governments and the non-governmental sector should urge China to participate in the Extractive Industries Transparency Initiative (EITI). EITI was started in 2003 under the auspices of then British Prime Minister, Tony Blair, and aims to ensure that revenues from extractive industries contribute to sustainable development and poverty reduction. There are now 20 resource-rich countries globally that actively support and implement EITI principles and 14 of these are in Africa. EITI also enjoys the support of other Western governments, multinational companies in the extractive sector, industry associations, international organisations, non-governmental organisations (NGOs), and major multinational investors. China's participation in EITI would significantly enhance the legitimacy of its extractive activity in Africa and align it with the desire of many energy- and resource-rich African countries to fight corruption and promote greater transparency in resource management.
4. Closely linked to this is the need for African governments to improve their own regulatory frameworks and policies for business, investment, environmental protection and labour relations.[44] China is simply pursuing its national interest and is acting rationally and pragmatically in seeking business and investment opportunities where these exist in Africa. China cannot be blamed or be held accountable for the absence of or weak regulatory mechanisms and administrative systems. It is the responsibility of African governments to ensure fair and equitable business practices, for example, having in place competition laws and policies to prevent the abuses and uncompetitive behaviour of which

Chinese companies and small-medium traders are so often accused. Moreover, strategic sectors such as energy, infrastructure, communications, fisheries, forestry and mining require extra vigilance in management and governance practices. At the country level, there is therefore a growing need for African-initiated empirical research and analysis to help better understand what China is doing, to build local competencies for doing so, and to stimulate public debate.

5. It is imperative for the AU task force to explore with China the need to establish a FOCAC secretariat within the AU or a similar high-level coordinating body to guide and implement the increasingly complex mix of ambitious policy and programmatic initiatives that exist in the China-Africa cooperation agenda. Importantly, regional economic communities such as the Southern African Development Community (SADC), the East African Community (EAC) and the Economic Community of West African States (ECOWAS) must become more engaged in the exercise and must develop regionally based mechanisms that complement and support the continental strategy. In short, African ownership of the FOCAC process must be deepened and enhanced lest FOCAC be seen as a Chinese Trojan horse! This will give African leaders and civil society a greater say in shaping the level, nature and scope of China's engagement, which would help to better identify the priorities and targets in China's ambitious assistance goals and economic aspirations.[45] Moveover, it would provide greater legitimacy and transparency to Chinese policies through more regular consultations between Africans and Chinese, as well as assisting third parties with an appropriate institutional interlocutor and channel to better coordinate collaborative activities in Africa.

NOTES

1. S. Zhao, 'Chinese Foreign Policy: Pragmatism and Strategic Behaviour', in S. Zhao (ed.), *Chinese Foreign Policy: Pragmatism and Strategic Behaviour* (New York and London: M.E. Sharpe, 2004), p. 3.
2. These issues are insightfully explored in S. Zhao, *A Nation-State by Construction: Dynamics of Modern Chinese Nationalism* (Stanford, CA: Stanford University Press, 2004), pp. 8–36.
3. L.C. Harris and R.L. Worden (eds.), *China and the Third World: Champion or Challenger?* (Massachusetts: Auburn House Publishing Co, 1986), p. 5.
4. E.J. Hevi, *The Dragon's Embrace: The Chinese Communists and Africa* (London: Pall Mall Press, 1967), p. 2.

5. P. Snow, *The Star Raft: China's Encounter with Africa* (London: Weidenfeld and Nicolson, 1988), p. 21. See also J.L. Duyvendak, *China's Discovery of Africa* (London: Probsthain, 1949).
6. E. Hadingham, *Ancient Chinese Explorers* (2003), http://www.pbs.org/wgbh/nova/sultan/explorers.html.
7. Snow, *The Star Raft*, p. 29.
8. L. Anshan, 'China and Africa: Policy and Challenges', *China Security* 3(3), 2007: 73.
9. Anshan, 'China and Africa': 71.
10. See A. Hutchison, *China's African Revolution* (London: Hutchinson, 1975), p. 85.
11. G. le Pere and G. Shelton, 'Afro-Chinese Relations: An Evolving South-South Partnership', *South African Journal of International Affairs* 13(1), 2006: 37–39.
12. The financial, physical and technical challenges of TAZARA's construction are well described by G.T. Yu, 'The Tanzania-Zambia Railway: A Case Study in Chinese Economic Aid to Africa', in W. Weinstein and T.H. Henriksen (eds.), *Soviet and Chinese Aid to African Nations* (New York, Washington and London: Praeger Publishers, 1980), pp. 117–43.
13. China is Sudan's chief arms supplier and allegedly provided arms worth US$1 billion to both sides of the Ethiopia-Eritrea conflict. Other Chinese arms clients include unstable and/or autocratic regimes, such as Zimbabwe, Angola, Mali, Sierra Leone and the DRC. See C. Alden, 'China in Africa', *Survival* 47(3), 2005: 151–52.
14. See D. Brautigam, *Chinese Aid and African Development* (New York: Macmillan Press, 1997); see also Weinstein and Henriksen (eds.), *Soviet and Chinese Aid to African Nations.*
15. For an analysis of FOCAC's genesis, progress and outcomes, see G. le Pere and G. Shelton, *China, Africa and South Africa: South-South Cooperation in a Global Era* (Johannesburg: Institute for Global Dialogue, 2007), pp. 141–59.
16. B.D. Larkin, *China and Africa, 1949–1970* (Berkeley, CA: University of California Press, 1971).
17. For a critical analysis, see J. Eckl and R. Weber, 'North-South? Pitfalls of Dividing the World by Words', *Third World Quarterly* 28(1), 2007: 3–23.
18. F. Jawara and A. Kwa, *Behind the Scenes at the WTO* (London: Zed Books, 2004), pp. 118, 207.
19. See N. Lardy, *Integrating China into the Global Economy* (Washington, DC: Brookings Institution, 2002).
20. A. Vines, 'The Scramble for Resources: African Case Studies', *South African Journal of International Affairs* 13(1), 2006: 65.
21. All figures are from D. Hale, 'How China's Need for Commodities Will Change Global Politics', in P. Draper and G. le Pere (eds.), *Enter the Dragon: Towards a Free-Trade Agreement between China and the Southern African Customs Union* (Johannesburg: Institute for Global Dialogue and SAIIA, 2005).
22. R. Sally, 'China's Trade Policies and its Integration into the World Economy', in Draper and Le Pere, *Enter the Dragon*, pp. 25–26.
23. R. Foot, 'Chinese Strategies in a US-Hegemonic Global Order: Accommodating and Hedging', *International Affairs* 82(1), 2006: 80–84.
24. D. Shambaugh, 'Containment or Engagement of China? Calculating Beijing's Responses', *International Security* 21(2), 1996: 187.
25. These issues are thoroughly explored in A.I. Johnson and R.S. Ross (eds.), *Engaging China: The Management of an Emerging Power* (London and New York: Routledge, 1999).
26. Y. Deng and T.G. Moore, 'China Views Globalization: Toward a New Great-Power Politics?' *Washington Quarterly* 70(2), 1994: 261.
27. See C. Freeman, 'Regionalism, Uneven Development, and Reform in Contemporary China', in Draper and Le Pere (eds.), *Enter the Dragon*, pp. 104–09.

28. V. Cable and P. Ferdinand, 'China as an Economic Giant: Threat or Opportunity?' *International Affairs* 70(2), 1994: 261.
29. B. Schwartz, 'Managing China's Rise', *The Atlantic*, June 2007: 177–78. See also J.A. Dorn, 'Engagement or Protectionism? US Policy Towards China', *Global Dialogue* 9(1–2), 2007: 10–19.
30. See, for example, I. Taylor, 'China's Oil Diplomacy in Africa', *International Affairs* 82(5), September 2006: 951–57 and D.M. Tull, 'China's Engagement in Africa: Scope, Significance and Consequences', *The Journal of Modern African Studies* 44(3), 2006: 473–77.
31. Countries that still retain official relations with Taiwan are Burkina Faso, The Gambia, São Tomé and Príncipe and Swaziland. Significantly, in January 2008, Malawi became the latest African country to establish full diplomatic relations with China.
32. B. Gill, C. Huang and J.S. Morrison, 'Assessing China's Growing Influence in Africa', *China Security* 3(3), 2007: 5. See also E. Tjønneland (with B. Brandzaeg, A. Kolas and G. le Pere), *China in Africa: Implications for Norwegian Foreign and Domestic Policies* (Bergen, Norway: Chr Michelsen Institute, 2006).
33. See C. Alden and M. Davies, 'A Profile of the Operations of Chinese Multinationals in Africa', *South African Journal of International Affairs* 13(1), 2006: 83–96 and A. Goldstein et al., *The Rise of China and India: What's in it for Africa?* (OECD: Development Centre Studies, 2006), pp. 75–85.
34. G. le Pere, 'China and Africa: Dynamics of an Enduring Relationship', *Global Dialogue* 9(1–2), 2007: 69–78.
35. S. Marks, 'Introduction', in F. Manji and S. Marks (eds.), *African Perspectives on China in Africa* (Cape Town, Nairobi and Oxford: Fahamu and Pambazuka, 2007), pp. 1–14.
36. See A. Askouri, 'China's Investment in Sudan: Displacing Villages and Destroying Communities', in Manji and Marks (eds.), *African Perspectives on China in Africa*, pp. 74–75. For more on Sudan, see Chapter 4 in this volume.
37. B. Gill, C. Huang and J.S. Morrison, *China's Expanding Role in Africa: Implications for the United States*, a report of the CSIS delegation to China on China-Africa-US relations (28 November–1 December 2006), pp. 11–12.
38. See Vines, 'The Scramble for Resources', 70–71 and E.M. Grion, 'The Political Economy of Commercial Relations: China's Engagement in Angola', in G. le Pere (ed.), *China in Africa: Mercantilist Predator or Partner in Development?* (Johannesburg: Institute for Global Dialogue and SAIIA, 2007), pp. 141–59.
39. Askouri, 'China's Investment in Sudan', pp. 78–81. See also M. Chan-Fishel, 'Environmental Impact: More of the Same', in Manji and Marks (eds.), *African Perspectives on China in Africa*, pp. 139–52.
40. M. Davies, 'The Rise of China and the Commercial Consequences for Africa', in Draper and Le Pere, *Enter the Dragon*, pp. 154–66.
41. Quoted in *China Economic Weekly*, 29 January 2007, www.chinaview.cn.
42. This summary draws from Gill, Huang and Morrison, 'Assessing China's Growing Influence in Africa': 5–19.
43. N. Obiorah, 'Who's Afraid of China in Africa? Towards an African Civil Society Perspective on China-Africa Relations', in Manji and Marks (eds.), *African Perspectives on China in Africa*, pp. 35–55.
44. G. Shelton, 'China and Africa: Building an Economic Partnership', *South African Journal of International Affairs* 8(2), 2001.
45. D. Large, 'As the Beginning Ends: China's Return to Africa', in Manji and Marks *African Perspectives on China in Africa*, pp. 153–68.

3

The Making of Chinese Foreign Policy

Actors and Institutions

Suisheng Zhao

INTRODUCTION

The study of Chinese foreign policy-making has experienced a significant transformation in recent decades. From focusing on only a few individual leaders, it has come to include a greater mix of institutional and bureaucratic players as China's involvement in international affairs becomes more extensive and the decision-making process more complicated. Since the founding of the People's Republic of China (PRC), the study of Chinese foreign policy-making mainly focused on the role of a few leaders at the top of the political system, as a result of the centralised nature of policy-making in China. The dominant paradigm in the study of policy-making during the Mao Zedong years was the Mao-in-command model, which was aligned to Mao's changing role in and shifting views on global affairs that was critical in understanding Chinese leadership politics, as well as foreign policy-making. According to this model, the power to make important policy decisions was concentrated in the hands of one person and a few of his personal lieutenants.

After the death of Mao, China's economic and political reform has emphasised the professionalisation and institutionalisation of decision-making authorities. As a result, scholars such as Kenneth Lieberthal, Michel Oksenberg, David Lampton and Susan Shirk have adopted an institutional or bureaucratic politics approach to the study of the Chinese policy-making process. Their studies focus on the structure and process of formal government and party organisations, depicting policy-making as an outcome of competition among institutional or bureaucratic players, comparable to that of many other countries.[1] Other scholars, such as Roderick MacFarquhar and Lowell

Dittmer, however, insist that political power in Beijing is still highly personalised. Their research focuses on what they call 'informal politics', which is not governed by impersonal rules and procedures set by formal authorities. They look at policy process as determined by power contests among factional or prominent individual leaders.[2]

Indeed, foreign policy is still a domain dominated by individual political leaders. But the trends of professionalisation and institutionalisation have become important contributors to the erosion of the role of individual leaders. As Carol Lee Hamrin indicates, 'Foreign Affairs became much less manageable by a tiny elite: coordination and delegation of authority became both more necessary and more difficult.'[3] This development has expanded the numbers and kinds of actors in the foreign policy-making process to such an extent that the top leaders have struggled to contain them. At least three groups of actors have played an increasingly important role. One is the state and party bureaucratic institutions and agencies, which has been delegated more authority not only in implementing foreign policy but also in participating in the making of foreign policy, especially with respect to an increasing zone of routine decisions. The second group is foreign policy 'think tanks', which are a response to a growing demand for in-depth analyses and long-term/strategic studies of foreign policy issues. In the meantime, public opinion has gradually entered the foreign policy-making arena. As a result of the growing number of actors, foreign policy-making has become increasingly pluralised.

Professionalisation, institutionalisation and pluralisation, however, do not mean that individual leaders, their policy preferences, and their personal connections are unimportant. Nor does it mean that strategic decisions are highly participatory. With non-recurrent, crisis and strategic decisions, the personal and power dimensions remain absolutely crucial. But they have become increasingly dependent upon bureaucratic institutions and think-tank specialists to make decisions on routine and technical issues. As Lampton indicates, Chinese policy-making now presents two levels of issues with two types of policy processes. At one level, as far as major issues of strategy, the setting of broad agendas and crisis management are concerned, senior individual elites still have considerable latitude. At the next level routine issues – ranging from arms control to economic relations – have been mainly handled by an increasingly large number of bureaucratic institutional actors with multiple voices.[4] Therefore, to understand China's foreign policy-making, we have to start by examining the power structure and understanding the relationships between individual elites and bureaucratic institutions.

POWER STRUCTURE AT THE TOP: FORMAL AND INFORMAL DECISION-MAKING MECHANISMS

The ultimate decision-making power in the Chinese leadership system is controlled by a small oligarchy of individual leaders at the top-most level of the Communist Party and government. They exercise power through the command of the formal decision-making institutions, as well as through the informal functional policy coordinating mechanisms. The formal decision-making institutions at the top include the Chinese Communist Party's (CCP's) Politburo and its Standing Committee, Secretariat and Central Committee, the State Council, the Central Military Commission (CMC) and the National People's Congress (NPC) Standing Committee. In a simplified way, the most powerful individual decision-makers are three groups of leaders hierarchically located in the leadership structure: at the top, a handful of the Politburo Standing Committee members who concurrently hold the top posts in the government and military; below them are several dozen members of the Politburo and Secretariat, the State Council and the CMC; and the third-tier comprises top bureaucrats – heads of the party central committee organs, ministers of the state council agencies, top commanders in the military command structure and provincial leaders.[5]

These top leaders are in command of several million cadres in the party and government bureaucracy, as well as government-controlled organisations, which are divided into vertical, hierarchical functional systems-sectors (*xitong*), in which party organs are superior in authority to government, while government institutions are superior to non-governmental organs. Control is exercised through top-down command directives in the form of central documents, complemented by an upward flow of official reports and secret media reporting for informational feedback, and supplemented by periodic inspection tours and public opinion surveys. Vertical lines of authority and communication are the norm, and cross-sectoral coordination has been relatively weak.

The main vertical functional sectors are clustered into three key systems (*xitong*). The first is the Military and Security *xitong*, which is the coercive arm of the system. It has two sectors: the Military sector, including the CMC, the armed police and a vast defence industrial sector; and the Political and Legal sector, including public and state security, intelligence, the judiciary and procuratorate, and the NPC.

The second *xitong* comprises Party Works. It has three sectors: the Propaganda sector, including all state media, science and social science research establishments, health and sports institutions, culture and educational organisations; the Organisation and Personnel sector, which oversees all key bureaucratic structuring and personnel appointments in the party-state system (this is viewed as the most powerful sector to those in the elite, controlling the dossier system and party discipline); and the Mass Organisations and United Front sector, which are responsible for policy, administration and personnel decisions for all non-party-state social organisations, such as youth, labour, women, religious and national minority affairs, professional organisations, and especially the non-communist political parties. Thus, for example, the United Front Work Department (UFWD) of the party chooses the non-communist party representatives in both the NPC and the Chinese People's Political Consultative Conference.

The third *xitong* is Government Works. It comprises three sectors: the Financial and Economic sector, including state planning, banking, commerce, industry and communications, agriculture and forestry; the Science and Technology sector; and the Foreign Affairs sector, responsible for diplomacy, foreign economic and cultural relations, and an oversight role of the foreign presence in China through the ever-present foreign affairs bureau in each work unit.

In order for the top leaders to command such a huge bureaucracy effectively, a division of responsibility has been established through a number of informal policy-coordinating mechanisms known as leadership small groups (LSGs) organised along *xitong* and sectorial/functional administrative lines. According to scholarly studies, the problems caused by strict compartmentalisation in the party and government bureaucracy were the reasons for the creation of the LSGs. For example, there are many administrative institutions in the Political and Legal *xitong*, including the Ministry of Public Security, the Ministry of State Security, the Supreme People's Court, the Supreme People's Procuratorate, the Ministry of Justice and the Ministry of Civil Affairs, plus the organs of the NPC Standing Committee and the Military police force. Thus there was a need for a higher-level coordinating authority and the Central Political and Legal Affairs Commission (CPLAC) was set up to perform this function.

The LSGs that have been relatively stable over time include the CPLAC (internal affairs comprising public security, state security and the judiciary); the Central Propaganda Leadership Small Group; the Central Finance and Economic Work Leadership Small Group; the Central Foreign Affairs Leadership Small Group (CFELG); and the Central Taiwan Affairs Leadership Small Group. The most important functions of the LSGs are to coordinate policy actions of different agencies within each sector, implement the decisions made by the top leaders, and make decisions on certain regular policy issues. What LSGs can or cannot decide depends largely on the issue, the confidence and power of its leader, and the circumstances, such as crisis or routine situations.

LSGs are usually headed by Politburo members and, in most cases, Politburo Standing Committee members. Their membership is semi-institutional: most members are job slot representatives. For example, the CPLAC is currently headed by Wu Banguo, a member of the Politburo Standing Committee and Chairperson of the NPC. Its members consist of the Ministers of State Security, Public Security, Justice and Civil Affairs, the Chief Procurator of the Supreme Procuratorate, and the head of the Supreme People's Court. The CFELG was headed by Wen Jiabao in his capacity of Politburo Standing Committee member, as well as the Premier of the country. Its members always include the chairpersons of the State Planning Commission and the State Economic Commission (when it existed) and the Minister of Finance. Most leaders in the ministries of the economic *xitong* are also included.

Interestingly, LSGs are not part of formal institutions because their names are not generally publicised and they are not often equipped with regular staff and offices. They exist mostly as ad hoc meetings. They are composed of individuals with other formal responsibilities and institutional bases who meet together. After every LSG meeting, a memo of outcomes is usually circulated to top leaders.[6]

While LSGs are mostly informal mechanisms, using LSGs to integrate related functional systems does serve the objective of division of responsibility among the top leaders, as it allows individual leaders to control policy formulation and coordinate policy implementation, thus perpetuating the personalised style of Chinese governance. Based on the division of responsibility, an informal norm of leadership system is established, that is each leader is responsible only for his or her own functional sphere and should not be allowed to intrude into (*cashou*) the policy domain of other leaders, thus defining the leaders' duties and shaping their relationships.

Although these informal decision-making mechanisms are still significant, formal institutions have played an increasingly important role as the institutionalisation of China's leadership system is one of the most important aspects of political reform, which emphasises normative rules and procedure in the decision-making process in recent decades. The reforms started in the 1980s when Deng Xiaoping realised that the lack of effective institutions and checks on arbitrary authority had contributed to disasters under Mao Zedong's leadership. Significant reform measures have included regular party and state body meetings according to constitutional schedules, a constitutionally mandated two-term limit for the Premier and President, and a retirement age for all party and government posts, and a personnel policy emphasising youth and education. One of the most important consequences of institutionalisation is the enhancement of formal institutional authority and the decline of the informal personal authority of top leaders. By definition, personal authority revolves around individual personage and derives from the charismatic nature of strong leaders, which supersedes impersonal organisation in eliciting the personal loyalty of followers. By contrast, institutional authority derives from and is constrained by impersonal organisational rules. Ideally, such authority rests not on individual charisma but on the formal position in an institutional setting. In so far as a leader can issue commands under institutional authority, it is the function of the office he or she holds rather than of any personal quality.

For many years in PRC history, personal authority was more important than institutional authority in top-level politics. This was particularly true during the 1980s when retired senior leaders possessed great personal prestige and influence over newly promoted and younger prominent office-bearers. Institutional authority has advanced to take a more important position than personal authority since the demise of the senior revolutionary veterans in the 1990s (that completed the transition of Chinese leadership from revolutionary to post-revolutionary generations).

According to China's official account, the PRC has been led by four generations of leadership, represented respectively by Mao Zedong, Deng Xiaoping, Jiang Zhemin and Hu Jintao. While Mao and Deng belong to revolutionary generations, Jiang and Hu are members of a new generation of post-revolutionary leadership. The Jiang leadership started the transition from revolutionary to post-revolutionary generations of leadership. The rise of President Hu has completed this leadership transition. The new generations of leadership are a group of younger leaders who joined the Communist Party after the founding of the PRC and did not have any personal experience of the revolutionary war years. This is the first generation of leaders in the PRC with no significant personal memory of pre-1949 China or any wartime military experience. They are better educated than the revolutionary leadership generation with their formal education overwhelmingly concentrated in the technical and engineering fields. Their formal education was sharply attacked as pursuing a 'bourgeois white expert road' during the Cultural Revolution. One commonly shared experience is that they were all sent to factories or into the countryside for re-education by working as manual labourers during the Cultural Revolution. They had opportunities to take up professional jobs, move back to the cities and eventually advance their senior leadership positions only after Deng launched his economic modernisation programme. They thus became major beneficiaries of the post-Mao reforms.[7]

As a post-revolutionary generation, the new leadership lacks the revolutionary, charismatic authority that legitimised the rule of Mao and Deng. Fundamentally a group of civilian bureaucrats operating in an institutional context, they have to draw on broad knowledge and experience in dealing with international affairs and rely on professional policy advisers, bureaucrats and other experts to provide background information, intelligence and policy analyses. As a result of this transition, foreign affairs institutions have played a critical role in the policy-making process.

MAJOR ACTORS AND INSTITUTIONS IN THE FOREIGN POLICY-MAKING ARENA

Foreign Affairs makes up one sector of the Government Works *xitong* in the power structure of the Chinese government. A study of the role of political elites and institutions in the foreign policy arena reveals three types of actors in this sector: paramount leaders; the foreign policy LSG; and major foreign policy bureaucrats.[8]

The paramount leader resides at the apex of the party leadership system and plays a special role in setting the national agenda and determining China's national security policy. The paramount leader is usually actively involved in setting guidelines for overall foreign policy, particularly policy toward the United States and other major powers, and in addressing urgent regional crises. The paramount leader may or may not hold the top government or party positions as the Chairperson/President of the state or general secretary of the party in order to be involved in foreign policy-making. During most of the 1980s and early 1990s, Deng Xiaoping was the paramount leader without formally holding top office. Jiang Zhemin has tried to play the same role since his retirement from the top positions of the party and government in 2002 but he has not been as successful because he has come up against the institutionalisation of Chinese leadership politics in recent years.[9]

The CCP central foreign affairs LSG, which consists of a head, one or two deputy heads and ministerial officials from various foreign affairs bureaucracies, is the main organ that takes overall charge of foreign affairs. It provides a forum for the members of the central leadership in charge of foreign affairs to meet face-to-face with the senior bureaucrats of various party, government and military foreign affairs institutions. Although the foreign affairs LSG is not a decision-making body, its policy preferences and recommendations are likely to have a significant impact on the final outcome of the decision-making process. The ratification of these decisions by the central leadership is sometimes simply a formality.

In addition to the paramount leaders and the informal LSG mechanism, specialised institutions have played an increasingly important role in the foreign policy-making process due to the trend towards a high level of specialised knowledge among Chinese foreign policy decision-makers, the proliferation of expert-based bureaucracies in the decision-making process, and the increased reliance by decision-makers on information provided by specialised bureaucracies. There are many agencies in charge of foreign affairs in the government, party and military. The major government agencies include the Ministry of Foreign Affairs (MFA), the Ministry of Foreign Trade and Economic Relations/Ministry of Commerce, the Ministry of State Security (counter-intelligence, as well as intelligence collection and analysis), the Foreign Affairs Committee of the NPC, the Foreign Affairs Office of the State Council, and the Xinhua News Agency. On the party side, the International Liaison Department of the CCP's Central Committee handles the contacts between the CCP and foreign political parties. It used to deal only with foreign communist and nationalist parties but has in recent decades expanded to include other political parties, both those in power and the opposition.

The authority over strategic foreign policy decisions is highly centralised and rests with the Politburo and the foreign affairs LSG, with limited power being delegated to the MFA and other specialised agencies. The jurisdiction of these institutions in the foreign affairs sector is also significantly circumscribed to policy implementation or information gathering/analysis. The Foreign Affairs Committee of the NPC does not have foreign policy-making power; it has largely served as an international liaison office of the NPC's Standing Committee. The Foreign Affairs Office of the State Council is largely an administrative set-up without any policy discretion. Its function is to supervise the local foreign affairs office and coordinate mostly routine matters involving foreign affairs for the top leaders.[10]

Let's look at the example of the MFA in order to understand the policy role of specialised agencies. The MFA is an agency under the State Council handling foreign affairs. It is not a policy-making institution but purely a specialised agency responsible for foreign policy implementation and recommendation. The MFA is composed of three parts. First, there are regional departments such as Asian, West Asian and North African, African, Eastern European and Central Asia, Western European and American and Oceanic affairs, where the staff is divided into political analysts for situation evaluation and policy recommendation, and general practitioners for diplomatic operations and case handling. Second, there are functional departments that deal with protocol, information, consular, international organisations, and international laws and treaties. Third, there are special departments such as Taiwan affairs, Hong Kong-Macao affairs, and affairs of the provincial and local foreign affairs offices.[11]

Professionalism has been the hallmark of the MFA. While the make-up of the ministry's personnel has undergone a marked change, any sizeable transfer of middle-ranked officials from other ministries or provincial governments to the MFA has not taken place since the mid-1960s. The new recruits are mostly college graduates who have majored in foreign languages or international relations. Thus foreign affairs professionals with relatively narrow experience dominate in the MFA. Those who currently hold senior posts in the MFA are career professionals who have worked their way up from the bottom over a period of more than 25 years. It has become a pattern that the retired foreign minister is promoted to the position of a Vice-Premier or State Councillor in charge of foreign affairs. Li Zhaoxing has been the only exception as he was not promoted to a State Council position after his retirement from the foreign minister's post in 2007.

The military agencies within the jurisdiction of foreign affairs are the CMC and the People's Liberation Army (PLA) general staff. The PLA retains a powerful voice at the highest levels of the country's decision-making process, especially in defence and security arenas. A study of the CMC illustrates the role of the PLA in shaping China's strategic disposition. According to this study, acting as the nexus between the military and civilian decision-making apparatuses, the CMC has played a prominent role in areas that have a major impact on the country's defence and security postures, especially related to safeguarding the country's sovereignty and territorial integrity. These areas include arms exports, cross-Strait Taiwan relations, strategic engagements with major powers and maritime sovereignty disputes.[12]

Military leaders are represented in the policy-making meetings of two key leading groups of the party. One is the foreign affairs LSG, the other is the Taiwan affairs LSG. The military delegates also form an important bloc at the annual sessions of the NPC. Throughout the broader foreign and national security bureaucracies, the military role in the policy-making system, however, has become increasingly institutionalised and bureaucratic. Although personal factors occasionally play an important role in shaping policies, they are generally no longer of great significance. The military interaction with the party has steadily diminished due to the party's focus on professionalism and its reluctance to become entangled in domestic affairs. With regard to relations between the military and state decision-making apparatuses, the state CMC and the Ministry of National Defence (MND) serve as the formal links. However, the state CMC exists simply for symbolic purposes. The MND's primary role is to liaise with foreign military establishments and it has a small administrative staff, including a foreign affairs bureau.

In addition, although the PLA's influence in the national policy-making process remains strong, its ability to be heard at the very top levels of the political leadership cannot be taken for granted except during major crises.[13] The military chiefs have to rely on institutionalised channels of communication to pass their views on to the senior political leadership. Moreover, professional military interests have largely shaped the PLA's involvement in national security and foreign policy decision-making, which has focused on safeguarding China's sovereignty and territorial integrity. Although the CMC has paid more attention to the external security environment, its involvement in the mainstream foreign policy arena appears to have diminished. In its domain, the military is powerful, but its influence in this sector no longer translates into equal influence in other realms of policy. This has allowed the civilian foreign policy establishment, especially the MFA and the Ministry of Commerce, to become more assertive in advancing its own diplomatic and economic interests and expanding its areas of responsibility. The MFA, for example, has assumed a leading role in international arms-control negotiations.[14]

BEYOND THE ELITE AND BUREAUCRACY: FOREIGN POLICY THINK TANKS AND PUBLIC OPINION

Although foreign policy-making is still an arena monopolised largely by the political elite, there has been a trend towards pluralisation due to the expansion of the numbers and kinds of individuals and institutions in foreign affairs over the past decade. Pluralisation means the proliferation of organisations, groups and sometimes opinions from the general public in the policy-making process. The policy-making system, in this case, has become more consultative over time, with an increased role being played by the specialists and the involved public outside the decision-making elites. Lampton calls this trend 'corporate pluralisation' because almost all of the central actors are 'licensed' in corporatist fashion to participate; their numbers are still comparatively small and their participation contingent upon elite decisions. China's growing place in the international economy and the increasing impact of international developments on domestic interests has mobilised new groups in the foreign policy-making process.[15]

The trend towards pluralisation has occurred simultaneously with two developments in recent decades. One is the decentralisation of power in the bureaucratic hierarchy, a reflection of an increase in the number of stakeholders, and the growing complexity of foreign policy decision-making. Decentralisation has multiplied the points of initiatives within the Chinese system. The second development is China's increased interaction abroad, which has boosted the prospects for widespread learning from China's participation in world affairs. As China becomes more involved in international affairs, there has been a proliferation of complicated policy issues, such as military trade, science and technology, education and culture, foreign expertise, intelligence and information, foreign publicity, trade and technology transfer, that require long-term research and follow-up.

One important result of the pluralisation is that China's foreign affairs have become much less managed by a few elites. Chinese leaders have found a greater need for improved information about and insights into international affairs from specialists in foreign policy think tanks and even non-governmental academic institutions. They have increasingly turned to these think-tank specialists and academics for policy research and advice. Many policy issues have been debated among these specialists in widely circulated publications before and even after policy decisions are made. As a result, these think tanks and academics have played an increasingly influential role in providing information and policy analyses for the foreign policy-makers.[16]

Almost all the important foreign policy think tanks have operated within the state bureaucratic hierarchies. Many of them are directly affiliated to the State Council ministries in Beijing. The most important international strategic studies think tank is the China Institute of Contemporary International Relations (CICIR), which is affiliated to the State Council Foreign Affairs Office and the State Security Ministry. Established in the 1980s and upgraded in 2003, it consists of seven institutes, three research divisions and ten research centres with a combined staff of 380 people. Its website indicates that CICIR's research work includes world strategic, political, economic and security studies, country and regional studies, and China's relations with other countries. The research findings are submitted to relevant government departments either as reports or as articles published in academic journals. The China Institute of International Studies (CIIS) is another important foreign policy think tank, which is affiliated to the MFA. It consists of seven research divisions: International Politics, World Economy, American Studies, Asian-Pacific Studies, Western European Studies, South Asian, Middle Eastern and African Studies, and East European, Central Asian and Russian Studies. On the international economic policy front, the most important think tank is the Chinese Academy of International Trade and Economic Cooperation (CAITEC). Affiliated to the Ministry of Commerce, CAITEC is a conglomerate integrating various functions such as research, information, consultation, publishing and training. It has more than 600 staff members.

Some of China's academic institutions have also been active in providing policy research analyses and advice to the government. Among them are many international/area studies institutes under the Chinese Academy of Social Sciences, including: the Institute of World Economics and Politics; the American Institute; the Western Europe Institute; the Latin American Institute; the Asia-Pacific Institute; the Japan Institute;

the Russian and Eastern European Institute; the Western Asia and African Institute; and the Taiwan Research Institute.

Many international/area studies schools and centres have also been established at major universities to enable staff and students to engage in foreign policy analyses in addition to their theoretical research and teaching responsibilities. The influences of these academic institutions, however, vary considerably depending on the connections of the institutional heads and individual scholars with foreign policy-making institutions and top leaders.

Another important development related to pluralisation is that public opinion has become more important in foreign policy-making.[17] This is evident in the occasional references to the constraints that 'public opinion' places upon Chinese leaders. Chinese leaders have not only made reference to public opinion to resist foreign entreaties and make their own policy positions more credible to foreigners but they have also been constrained increasingly by public pressure on certain foreign policy issues. For example, in response to more than 20 million Chinese signatures being gathered on the Internet to oppose Japan's bid to join the UN Security Council, and thousands of Chinese protesters marching through major Chinese cities protesting against Japan's approval of history textbooks that they say whitewashed Japanese wartime atrocities, visiting Chinese Vice-Minister Wu Yi had to dramatically cancel her meeting with Japanese Prime Minister Junichiro Koizumi at the last minute in May 2005. The public demonstration plunged relations between Beijing and Tokyo to a perilous low during 2005 and 2006. The high-level meeting was halted for more than a year until Japan's newly elected Prime Minister Shinzo Abe decided to undertake his first official overseas trip to Beijing in October 2006.[18]

Pluralisation can enhance system legitimacy and compliance with decisions in so far as organisations and individuals come to feel that their interests are being taken into account. It also increases the chances that decision-makers will have heard a greater number of the considerations that will affect policy viability and, finally, it offers new opportunities for Beijing to bring its practice more in line with international norms.

CONCLUSION

The mechanism of China's foreign policy-making has evolved toward institutionalisation and professionalisation in recent years. Although foreign policy-making in China is still highly centralised, the process of foreign policy information-processing, deliberation and decision-making, and the management of foreign relations, are no longer the prerogative of a handful of individual leaders. While specialised government institutions have become more active in the making of Chinese foreign policy and the routine management of China's foreign relations, foreign policy think tanks, social groups and public opinion have become increasingly important in China's foreign policy-making process. Growing professionalisation, mounting specialisation, a more complex bureaucracy, and more information have created a setting in which persuasion is an increasingly important tool of leadership, and compulsion has correspondingly retreated as a leadership instrument.[19]

NOTES

1. K. Lieberthal and M. Oksenberg, *Policy Making in China: Leaders, Structures, and Process* (Princeton, NJ: Princeton University Press, 1988); S. Shirk, *The Political Logic of Economic Reform in China* (Berkeley, CA: University of California Press, 1993); D.M. Lampton, *The Making of Chinese Foreign and Security Policy* (Stanford, CA: Stanford University Press, 2001).
2. R. MacFarquhar, *Origins of the Cultural Revolution* (Cambridge, MA: Oelgeschlager, Gun and Hain, 1981); L. Dittmer, H. Fukui and P.N.S. Lee, *Informal Politics in East Asia* (Cambridge: Cambridge University Press, 2000).
3. C.L. Hamrin, 'Elite Politics and the Development of China's Foreign Relations', in T.W. Robinson and D. Shambaugh (eds.), *Chinese Foreign Policy: Theory and Practice* (Oxford: Clarendon Press, 1994) p. 89.
4. D.M. Lampton, 'China's Foreign and National Security Policy-Making Process: Is it Changing and does it Matter?' in Lampton, *The Making of Chinese Foreign and Security Policy*, p. 2.
5. S. Zhao, 'The Structure of Authority and Decision-Making: A Theoretical Framework', in C.L. Hamrin and S. Zhao (eds.), *Decision-Making in Deng's China: Perspectives from Insiders* (Armonk, NY: M.E. Sharpe, 1995), pp. 233–45.
6. Carol Lee Hamrin was among the first Western scholars who revealed the operation of the LSG. See C.L. Hamrin, 'The Party Leadership System', in K.G. Lieberthal and D.M. Lampton (eds.), *Bureaucracy, Politics, and Decision-Making in Post-Mao China* (Berkeley, CA: University of California Press, 1992).
7. S. Zhao, 'The New Generation of Leadership and the Direction of Political Reform after the 16th Party Congress', in Y. Chu, C. Lo and R.H. Myers (eds.), *The New Chinese Leadership: Challenges and Opportunities after the 16th Party Congress* (Cambridge: Cambridge University Press, 2004), pp. 10–32.
8. L. Ning, 'The Central Leadership, Supraministry Coordinating Bodies, State Council Ministries, and Party Departments', in Lampton, *The Making of Chinese Foreign and Security Policy*, p. 40.
9. S. Zhao, 'Toward a Rule of Law Regime: Political Reform under China's Fourth Generation of Leadership', in S. Zhao (ed.), *Debating Political Reform in China, Rule of Law vs Democratization* (Armonk, NY: M.E. Sharpe, 2006), pp. 230–33.
10. One insider's account of the top foreign policy-making institutions is L. Ning, *The Dynamics of Foreign-Policy Decision-Making in China* (Boulder, CO: Westview Press, 1997).

11. G. Yang, 'Mechanism of Foreign Policy-Making and Implementation in the Ministry of Foreign Affairs', in Hamrin and Zhao (eds.), *Decision-Making in Deng's China*, pp. 91–100.
12. T.M. Cheung, 'The Influence of the Gun: China's Central Military Commission and its Relationship with the Military, Party, and State Decision-Making Systems', in Lampton, *The Making of Chinese Foreign and Security Policy*, pp. 61–90.
13. M. Swaine, T. Zhang and D. Cohen, *Managing Sino-American Crises: Case Studies and Analysis* (Washington, DC: Carnegie Endowment for International Peace, 2004).
14. J. Yuan, 'China's Pragmatic Approach to Non-Proliferation Policy in the Post-Cold-War Era', in S. Zhao (ed.), *Chinese Foreign Policy, Pragmatism and Strategic Behaviour* (Armonk, NY: M.E. Sharpe, 2004) pp. 151–78.
15. Lampton, 'China's Foreign and National Security Policy-Making Process', p. 12.
16. D. Shambaugh, 'China's International Relations Think Tanks: Evolving Structure and Process', *China Quarterly* 171, 2002: 575.
17. J. Fewsmith and S. Rosen, 'The Domestic Context of Chinese Foreign Policy: Does Public Opinion Matter?' in Lampton, *The Making of Chinese Foreign and Security Policy*, pp. 151–90.
18. S. Zhao, 'China's Pragmatic Nationalism: Is it Manageable?' *Washington Quarterly* (Winter, 2005–2006): 131.
19. H.L. Miller and L. Xiaohong, 'The Foreign Policy Outlook of China's Third Generation Elite', in Lampton, *The Making of Chinese Foreign and Security Policy*, pp. 129–39.

PART 2

Country Case Studies

4

A Marriage Less Convenient

China, Sudan and Darfur

Sharath Srinivasan

INTRODUCTION

Extensive oil investments, large infrastructure projects and obscure arms deals in a country fraught with conflict have always suggested that Sino-Sudanese relations would feature prominently in debates on the China-Africa 'phenomenon'. But intense scrutiny of China's role in efforts to address the conflict in Darfur leading up to the 2008 Olympic Games ensured that what began as Beijing's marriage of convenience with Khartoum would undoubtedly test the durability of China's evolving foreign policy towards Africa. The Darfur dimension of Sino-Sudanese relations is the focus of this chapter. Sudan's internal crises and its poor relationship with the West introduce a complex backdrop to the fast-growing economic, strategic and political relationship between Beijing and Khartoum. The chapter begins by introducing this wider context of Sudan's relations with China. China has emerged as Sudan's most important trading partner and, arguably, its most important international friend, but as the Darfur crisis protracted, the two countries were no longer able to conduct their affairs quietly.

This chapter argues that Darfur exemplifies challenges for China's foreign policy that have emerged from two categorical changes in the nature of its presence in Africa. First, China's direct commercial interests in Sudan have required different calculations to be made in its foreign policy-making than was previously the case. Blithe references to non-interference, anti-hegemony and 'business is business' fail to mask real concerns that its investments and strategic interests could be adversely affected by the 'internal' situation in the country. Second, the nature and extent of China's interests in Sudan specifically, as well as in Africa more generally, correlate with the fact of China's prominence and its political leverage: Beijing has become a major player in African affairs whether it recognises it or not. As China emerges as a global power, Beijing's relations with governments such as Khartoum and its response to situations such as Darfur represent a test of China's claim to be a 'responsible great power' and its self-proclaimed trajectory of a 'peaceful rise' or, more recently, 'peaceful development'.

CHINA AND AFRICA: SINO-SUDANESE RELATIONS IN CONTEXT

The overarching purpose of this chapter is to glean from contemporary Sino-Sudanese relations, and the Darfur experience in particular, insights into how the wider Sino-African context is evolving and to provide some suggestions as to its future direction. Considering the burgeoning literature on China's growing presence in Africa, some important issues nevertheless need to be raised.[1]

Historically, and based on its own domestic experience, China has emphasised anti-imperialist cooperation in its foreign policy dealings with Africa, which is based on respect for sovereignty and non-interference in the internal affairs of its partners. While the inconsistency in the past between this rhetoric and the reality of Sino-African relations has been analysed,[2] today, China's significant *direct* material interest in Africa means that the difference is more visible and of greater consequence. China's 'peaceful rise' to great power status is proving to be at odds with South-South solidarity.

The challenges for China in transforming itself from an inward-looking and autarchic country to an outwardly engaged, interdependent and emerging global power are well exemplified in Africa. To keep its 'peaceful rise' on track, China's global foreign policy finds itself facing two choices: 'bandwagoning' with an American-led international order, i.e. 'balancing' against the 'hyperpower', or pushing for a more transitory and prudent policy of 'hedging'.[3] Sudan, and in particular the crisis in Darfur, illustrates this dilemma well. China has been required to manage this broader international agenda whilst effectively protecting short- and long-term energy and commercial interests secured through a South-South cooperation-inspired 'no conditions plus incentives' proposition to Khartoum.

It is clear that in its dealings with countries such as Sudan, China has benefited from combining principles of non-interference and respect for sovereignty with a commercial opportunism that meets its expanding economic interests. However, apprehensions in Africa and the West as to Beijing's intentions have perhaps assumed the worst, failing to grasp fully the implications of the foreign policy dilemmas that China faces in this new era. Even before the case of Darfur rose to prominence in 2006 and 2007, Western commentary and public debate was rife with suspicion over

China's intentions and modes of operation in Africa.[4] In July 2005, the chairperson of the US Congress House Sub-Committee on Africa, Chris Smith, warned, 'China is playing an increasingly influential role on the continent of Africa and there is concern that the Chinese intend to aid and abet African dictators, gain a stranglehold on precious African natural resources, and undo much of the progress that has been made on democracy and governance in the last 15 years.'[5] Conversely, also in 2005, a lead architect of China's 'peaceful rise' concept, Zheng Bijian, stated in *Foreign Affairs* that 'China does not seek hegemony or predominance in world affairs . . . China's development depends on world peace – a peace that its development will in turn advance.'[6]

Neither accusations against Beijing of harbouring malevolent or purposefully disruptive intentions in Africa, nor causal assumptions that China's 'peaceful development' or 'peaceful rise' automatically depends upon and contributes to 'world peace', stands up to scrutiny. On the one hand, Beijing's enhanced new presence on the continent should not be conflated with a strategic interest in emerging as a triumphant global power that is pursuing ideological expansion combatively against the West. On the other hand, China's increased presence and influence in Africa necessarily has an impact on the often volatile and violent political economy of its societies, and not always for the better.

Assessments of China's role in Africa must necessarily incorporate the tension between China's direct material interests and concerns about state sovereignty and non-interference, and Beijing's longer-term desire to be recognised as a responsible great power in a world that it increasingly accepts as comprising interdependent states. Beijing is reinterpreting and reshaping China's core foreign policy principles (see Chapter 3). This is taking place in an era in which the multipolar international system that Beijing promotes in turn requires it, on account of its enhanced influence, to make a contribution, whether in multilateral fora or in its bilateral dealings, to managing global order and defining and pursuing collective interests.[7] In Africa, Beijing's support for continental institutions and leadership, above all the African Union (AU) and the New Partnership for Africa's Development (NEPAD), is being put to the test. Beijing's experience with Sudan's conflict in Darfur gives insight into the emerging contours and parameters of these new directions in China's African foreign policy. On account of its extensive oil, military and commercial dealings with the Sudanese government, China became, however reluctantly, central to international policy and debate on how to address the catastrophe in Darfur. By mid-2007, Lord Mark Malloch-Brown, the former UN Deputy Secretary-General and the new United Kingdom Minister for

Africa, Asia and the UN, reflects on China's importance: 'Trying to move on Darfur without the active involvement of China was kind of like pushing a very big rock up an extremely steep mountain, you just couldn't do it.'[8]

CHINA AND SUDAN: AN OVERVIEW

A brief overview of Sino-Sudanese relations begins, saliently, in the common historic figure of General Charles Gordon. To the British, he was an 'eminent Victorian'[9] who led imperial forces during the Opium Wars in China and later served as the Egyptian Khedive's representative in Khartoum, where he sought to bring an end to slavery. 'Chinese Gordon' – 'Gordon Pasha' to the Sudanese – has provided a lasting symbolic bridge between the two countries, testifying to their mutual experience of colonial oppression and, in Sudan's case, successful resistance.[10] It is said that Chinese officials visiting Khartoum have toured the site of Gordon's death and that one official expressed gratitude to the Sudanese for 'killing Chinese Gordon'.[11]

With their common history of Gordon, Beijing's diplomatic overtures of South-South solidarity and resistance to neo-imperialism were grounded tangibly in its relations with Sudan. Since 1959, when a recently independent Sudan became only the fourth African country to recognise the People's Republic of China (PRC), the two countries have enjoyed stable relations. Notwithstanding its active support for wars of liberation elsewhere in sub-Saharan Africa, China did not get involved in Sudan's first civil war (1955–72). Sudan's early recognition of Beijing and its unwavering 'One China' stance laid strong foundations for China's non-interference.

Cooperation spiked in the 1970s when Beijing supplied the socialist dictatorship of Jafar Nimairi with arms, development aid and technical assistance, and was responsible for the construction of high-profile government buildings (most notably Khartoum's Friendship Hall conference centre in 1976). This prompted an assessment of what some Sudanese considered an 'infatuation' with their Chinese friends.[12] The infatuation, if that was what it was, was short-lived. In the late 1970s, Nimairi's struggling socialist one-party state was forced to build a coalition that embraced a more Arab-Islamic identity, just as China under Deng Xiaoping focused its efforts on internal transformation and away from the Third World. Two-way trade between the countries, which stood at a modest but not insignificant US$100 million in 1980, fell to a low US$20 million in the mid-1980s (see Figure 4.1). By this time, Sudan was in the grip of its second civil war between the government in Khartoum and the Sudan People's Liberation Army (SPLA) based in the country's south.

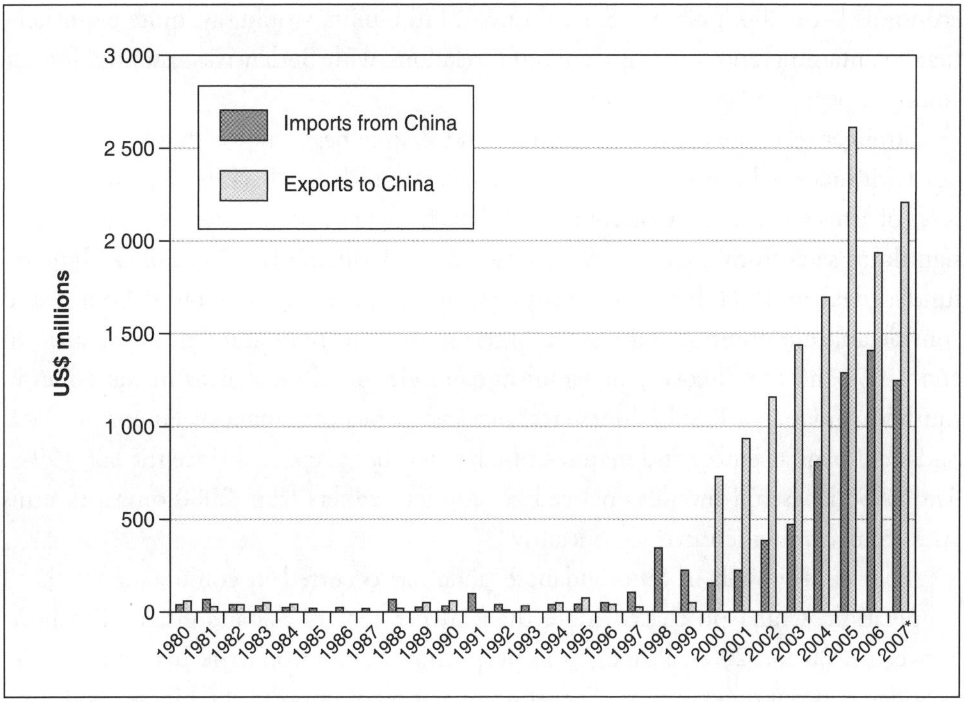

Figure 4.1 Sino-Sudanese trade 1980–2007.

* 2007 figures are annualised from 1st quarter

Source: IMF Direction of Trade Statistics (DOTS)

June 1989 was an important juncture in the history of both countries. On 4 June, the world's attention was focused on the crackdown in Tiananmen Square in Beijing. On 30 June, a military coup orchestrated and backed by the National Islamic Front (NIF) quietly brought a new regime to power in Khartoum. By the time Sudanese President Omar al-Bashir visited Beijing in November 1990 entreating aid from China, both countries were subject to heavy Western scrutiny. Al-Bashir's government was throwing its support behind Saddam Hussein in the lead-up to the 1991 Gulf War and Sudan, having already largely lost the aid support from the United States that had bank-rolled Khartoum in the 1970s and 1980s, faced increasing isolation from Western countries – as well as from many Arab nations.[13] In Beijing, the two countries signed separate agreements on economic and technical cooperation and cultural exchanges, but China was reluctant to give more than symbolic aid. China approached the new regime in Sudan cautiously, with President Jiang Zhemin reportedly advising al-Bashir that 'without political stability and unity, it is impossible to push forward the economy'.[14] By 2007, China's Special Envoy, Liu Guijin, would say, quite oppositely, that maintaining and growing economic relations with Sudan was essential for the country's peace and political stability.

Stronger relations between Khartoum and Beijing began not with oil exploration, but with increased arms sales, a field of cooperation dating back to the early 1970s. Sales of arms are difficult to account for exhaustively; however, various reviews suggest significant sales from the early 1990s onwards, including: a US$300 million Iranian-funded deal in 1991 for two helicopters, one hundred 1 000-pound bombs and considerable ammunition; sales of troop transport helicopters and fighter jets in 1996 and 1997; and the discovery of significant supplies of Chinese arms in war zones in southern Sudan in 1998.[15] Chinese technical assistance and financial support for local Sudanese arms assembly and manufacture has also been reported since the late 1990s. And as Sudanese oil revenues buoyed government coffers from 2000 onwards, arms sales from China increased significantly.[16]

The rapid growth in Sino-Sudanese trade has occurred in conjunction with oil cooperation. China purchased more than 80 per cent of Sudan's crude oil exports between 2000 and 2004, although this proportion would drop to 40 per cent by 2007 as Sudan's output quickly grew. The substantial level of imports of Chinese goods into Sudan should also not be ignored (see Figure 4.1). In 2006, imports from China were close to US$1.5 billion, more than 20 per cent of Sudan's total imports. The composition of Chinese imports varies significantly from year to year, but major items include heavy and specialised machinery, electronics, consumer goods and textiles, and transport equipment.

China's investments and operations in the Sudanese oil sector date back to the mid-1990s. As such, the activities of its National Oil Corporations (NOCs) – in Sudan, China National Petroleum Corporation (CNPC) and Sinopec – slightly pre-date Beijing's formal adoption in 1997 of its 'going out strategy' to meet its energy needs. This relates to an important and often overlooked point in assessments of China's 'oil diplomacy'. Although there is undoubtedly significant cooperation and relations between the NOCs and the Chinese government, since Beijing clearly supports their overseas commercial activities through diplomatic means, it is misleading to equate the two entirely.[17]

CNPC is the major Chinese oil company in Sudan. It has a 40 per cent holding in the Greater Nile Petroleum Operating Company (GNPOC) established in 1997 to develop oil field blocks 1, 2 and 4, which began producing oil in 1999 (Malaysia's Petronas holds 30 per cent and India's ONGC Videsh holds 25 per cent). It also has a

41 per cent holding in the Petrodar Operating Company (PDOC) set up in October 2001 to develop oil field blocks 3 and 7, a major reserve that began producing oil in 2005–06 (Petronas holds 40 per cent). CNPC owns 95 per cent of block 6, which has been in production since 2004. All of the aforementioned blocks straddle Sudan's contested north-south border except block 6, which extends into Darfur. CNPC has also taken a 35 per cent stake in the Red Sea Petroleum Operating Company (RSPOC), which owns the partly offshore block 15. In June 2007, CNPC also entered into a joint venture and production sharing agreement to explore the offshore block 13. CNPC has a 50 per cent stake in the Khartoum oil refinery, which it helped to build in 1997 and subsequently expanded in 2006. GNPOC also constructed a 1 600-km pipeline from the oil fields in block 2 to the Red Sea export facility. Sinopec, the second Chinese oil company in Sudan, owns a 6 per cent stake in PDOC.

Today, Sudan is one of five countries in Africa – after Libya, Nigeria, Algeria and Angola – that together produce 80 per cent of the continent's oil and hold 90 per cent of its reserves.[18] Nevertheless, it is not yet a major petroleum exporter in international terms. Given China's fast-growing reliance on energy imports – from energy self-sufficiency in 1993, it is now the world's second largest importer of oil and accounted for 40 per cent of global growth in oil demand between 2002 and 2005 – Sudan will not easily retain its high position as a major source of crude oil for China. In the short to medium term, however, supplies of crude from Sudan will continue to be buoyant. Chinese oil imports reached new heights amidst the international scrutiny surrounding Beijing's policy on Darfur. China reportedly purchased over 200 000 barrels per day from Sudan in 2007, a 40 per cent increase on 2006. This secured Sudan's position as the world's sixth largest supplier of crude oil to China and left it within 'striking distance' of the fifth largest supplier, Oman.[19]

Importantly, Africa remains a major source of oil and energy security for China; Angola, Sudan, Congo-Brazzaville, Gabon, Equatorial Guinea, Chad and Nigeria supplied close to one-third of China's crude imports in 2005. Significant new investments by China in Nigeria and North African countries such as Libya and Algeria will ensure this remains the case. Sudan, which in 2002 provided China with 40 per cent of its crude imports from Africa, is perhaps best understood as having been a 'bridgehead for China into the African oil market'.[20] In Sudan, Chinese oil companies successfully completed their first foreign non-market vertically integrated oil production project. CNPC reportedly employed 10 000 Chinese workers to build the pipeline linking the oil fields to the refinery in Khartoum and the Red Sea terminal near Port Sudan (the refinery and export terminal were also Chinese projects). On the back of oil, but also of significant imports of Chinese goods into Sudan, two-way Sino-Sudanese trade is the third highest in Africa, behind only South Africa and Angola (see Figure 4.2). Again, as China's trade with wealthier countries and larger energy suppliers, such as Nigeria, Libya and Algeria grows rapidly, it is probable that Sudan will slip from this prominent place.

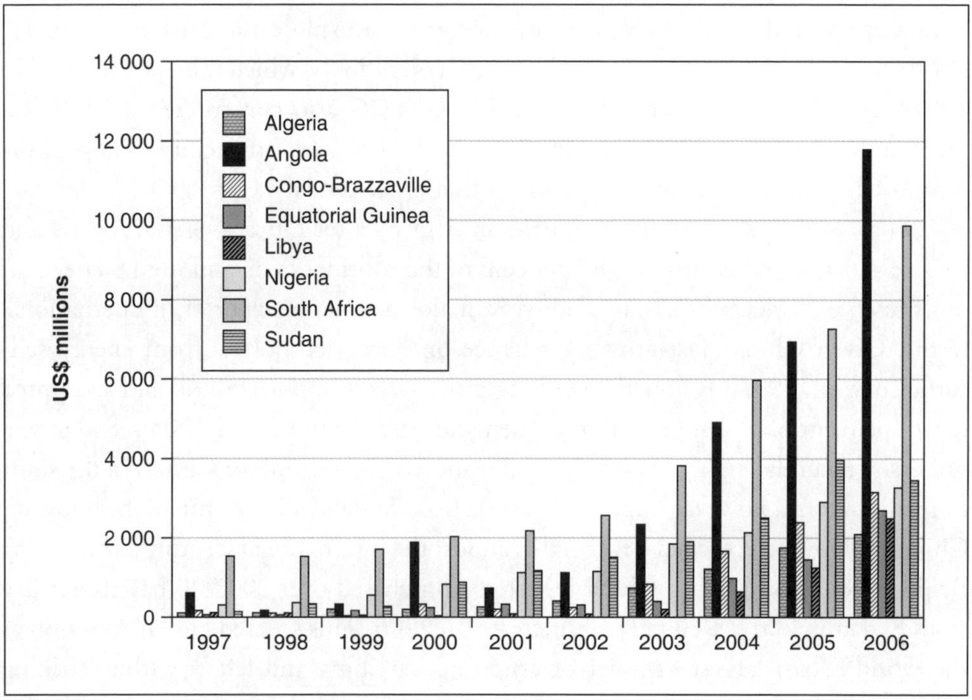

Figure 4.2 Major African trade partners 1997–2006.
Source: IMF Direction of Trade Statistics (DOTS)

China's oil investments occurred during a time of Sudan's isolation and heavy pressure on Western oil companies to exit the country given Khartoum's human rights' record, as well as the specific role oil played in the war in central and southern Sudan which exacted a heavy toll on civilians. Forced displacement in the oil-field regions, the recruitment and arming of ethnic militias in these areas, and the use of oil revenues by Khartoum to prosecute the war more ruthlessly: these represent some of the evidence used by activists to put pressure on Western governments and oil companies.[21] US lawmakers proposed capital market sanctions on companies operating in Sudan. The most high-profile result of this pressure was the forced exit of the Canadian company Talisman in 2003.

Nevertheless, the opportunity presented by the development of Sudan's oil fields played a role in greater rapprochement between Khartoum and the West – with the exception of the United States. With many European companies operating in the oil sector and related industries, the European Union (EU) chose a policy of 'constructive engagement' with Khartoum in 1999 and in effect provided support to Sudan when challenged on its human rights' record in international arenas.[22] UN sanctions on Sudan were lifted in 2001. While China's investments in Sudan's oil industry would ultimately dwarf those of other foreign actors, one would be mistaken to think that China was a lone rebel against all others. Moreover, some analysts took the view in the years immediately following the production of oil that this could contribute to a stalemate in the civil war.[23] The government's military capacity would soon be insurmountable for the SPLA, yet insufficient to defeat a guerrilla war in the 'bush'. And both sides had an interest in using oil revenues to buttress their authority and develop the economy of their constituents. In this view, oil production contributed to the 'ripeness' of the conflict for negotiated settlement and oil revenue sharing was a central feature of negotiations and the final agreement (the Comprehensive Peace Agreement [CPA] signed between the Khartoum government and the SPLA in January 2005). While this is true in part, it must also be noted that oil continues to divide the two partners to the CPA, as well as communities across southern and central Sudan, and the CPA did not provide a sufficient basis for addressing other grievances and areas of conflict elsewhere in Sudan.

In 2005, Sudan was Africa's largest recipient of Chinese foreign direct investment. According to the UN Conference on Trade and Development (UNCTAD), Sudan received US$351.5 million, making it Beijing's ninth largest target for such flows worldwide.[24] Information on the destination of this investment is not readily available. While much of it no doubt flows into oil projects, a great proportion flows into a less publicised but major dimension of Sino-Sudanese cooperation: infrastructure projects. Chinese corporations have been heavily involved in recent years in the construction of highways, railways, bridges, dams and power projects across northern Sudan. In 2004, Chinese contractors secured their then biggest international contract to build the US$650 million Merowe Dam, 350 km north of Khartoum. Beijing's Exim Bank had already provided Khartoum with a US$530 million loan for the US$1,8 billion project. The dam has proved highly controversial within Sudan, with over 55 000 people likely to be displaced and concerns raised over its environmental impact. However, the associated hydroelectric project is expected to meet a great proportion of Khartoum's – and much of northern Sudan's – electricity needs. Notwithstanding considerable attention being directed towards China's involvement in the project, European companies are also significantly involved. Contracts worth approximately US$400 million include those granted to Germany's Lahmeyer International, France's Alstom and Switzerland's ABB.

The El Gaili Power Station project contracted to China's Harbin Power Engineering Company is another major Sino-Sudanese venture. A large gas- and oil-fired power plant, the power station is to be built in four phases. The first phase went into service in August 2004, delivering 200 000 kilowatts to Sudan's grid, which was one-third of Sudan's national supply at the time. Phase II was due for completion at the time of writing. According to the state-backed Xinhua News Agency, 'local people lovingly refer to Chinese and Sudanese workers taking part in the project as "bringers of light" '.[25] In early 2007, two Chinese companies, Transtech and China Railway Engineering Corporation, won a US$1 billion contract to build a railway linking Port Sudan and Khartoum. And as a sign of the depth of collaboration that has been built up over the last decade, in August 2007, a Sudanese company, Danfodio Holdings, and Transtech agreed with the Mauritanian government to build a US$634 million railway line linking Mauritania's capital Nouakchott to Bofal, a phosphate deposit site 430 km away.[26]

It is with an understanding of this multifaceted and extensive nature of Sino-Sudanese relations during the past decade that the situation in Darfur, and Beijing's response, must be assessed. China's commercial relations with Sudan have been mutually beneficial for both Khartoum and Beijing. That all Sudanese do not experience the benefits flowing to Sudan, and that the benefits flowing to Khartoum are actually detrimental to specific sections of the population, is an issue that had already arisen in the context of oil extraction and the war in central and southern Sudan.

Notwithstanding pre-existing fears and insecurities concerning Beijing's activities and intentions in Sudan, it is the Darfur experience that has decisively shortened China's honeymoon period in this recent chapter of rejuvenated Sino-African relations. In a sense, this was Beijing's bad luck, as the policy crisis emerged for reasons that were not immediately of China's making. In a situation of no conflict in Darfur, Sudan may have consolidated its path towards peace under the CPA, the government of Sudan could by now have been on a more certain trajectory of political reform, and the country on course to social and economic recovery. In such a scenario, China may have been even better rewarded for its tactical foray into the country in the 1990s when Sudan was an international pariah and its nascent oil sector a risky and morally problematic venture.

Specialists on politics and conflict in Sudan would rightly argue that such a scenario denies the complex socio-political reality of the country. The conflict between the SPLA and the government in Khartoum, the extraction of oil and the boon of oil revenues, inequitable and uneven development across Sudan, an exclusive and bilateral peace process and, in turn, conflict in Darfur (not to mention the east and other areas in the country) are deeply interconnected. To the extent that an understanding such as this is arrived at in Beijing, it might necessitate a more rigorous assessment of the political economy effects of its engagement in Sudan and Africa and the role it can and must play in minimising adverse impacts and contributing to security and well-being on the continent. As it turned out, Beijing was required to respond to consequences, not mitigate causes. On account of China's importance to Sudan, the conflict in Darfur drew Beijing into engaging with a grave humanitarian catastrophe and fraught international political crisis whether it, or anyone else, wanted China to be involved or not.

CHINA AND DARFUR

The conflict in Darfur in western Sudan, which began in early 2003 and continues to this day, has confounded the policy-makers of all foreign actors engaged with Sudan. In this predicament, China is not alone. Darfur has necessitated awkward trade-offs of competing priorities and led, in hindsight, to some serious miscalculations. That China has emerged in recent debate and discussion as *the* 'thorn in the side' of an adequate international response to the human tragedy in the Darfur region is simplistic and biased. This is little comfort for Beijing, which has been required to respond to scrutiny and criticism in ways that have tested and augmented some fundamental precepts of its foreign policy principles and modes of operation in Africa. As Daniel Large has noted, Darfur has 'internationalized' China's relations with Sudan to an unprecedented degree.[27] The point could perhaps be taken further. Just as Darfur has proven seminal in testing the range and reach of the emerging 'Responsibility to Protect' (R2P) doctrine advocated by liberal interventionist actors,[28] it is arguably a defining case for analysing China's evolving foreign policy of active engagement in Africa.

China's historic freedom of manoeuvre and seemingly unproblematic use of rhetorical device in its African dealings has proven impossible in its Darfur experience. The very fact that China matters considerably to international engagement with Sudan derives from an appreciation of Beijing's relations of power with Khartoum, borne of an incontrovertible commercial reality. The empirical reality inhibits a great proportion of any claims of non-interference. This is not necessarily interference out of choice, but a necessity born of fact. China's policy actions have had to come down from well-tested positions of general principle in the high echelons of the UN Security Council in New York to the grubby politics of persuasion in Khartoum. However, the evolution of China's policy regarding Darfur shows us that what matters is not whether China recognises the inevitable fact of its influence and thus its capacity for interference in Africa; Beijing clearly does. Nor is the appropriate measure of China's apparent departure from strict non-interference the extent to which it agrees with other – especially Western – norms and specific policy priorities. The Darfur case indicates areas of possible reshaping and reformulation in China's foreign policy and suggests some new parameters for engagement that are being tested. These are discussed at the end of this chapter. The following sections trace the evolution of China's policy on Darfur across three periods: opposition to active political engagement and protection of its commercial interests between 2004 and mid-2006; responding to international scrutiny and seeking to bring to bear its influence on Khartoum up to early 2007; and, for the rest of 2007, publicising its more active efforts, while reasserting its core foreign policy principles and rejecting ongoing criticism of its role.

'BUSINESS IS BUSINESS'

In early 2003, when a long period of waves of unrest and violence in Darfur finally escalated into full-scale armed rebellion against the government, most foreign actors engaged with Sudan looked the other way. Many feared jeopardising the delicately poised peace negotiations between the SPLA and the government of Sudan, hosted and directed by the Inter-Governmental Authority for Development (IGAD), the regional organisation in the Horn and East Africa. The international response to Darfur began to change in early to mid-2004, when the scale of the humanitarian crisis and impact of war on the civilian population was too large to ignore. Darfur became headline news when then UN Secretary-General, Kofi Annan, marking the tenth anniversary of the Rwandan genocide on 7 April 2004, expressed his fears that a similar tragedy could happen in Sudan. By late May 2004, the key protocols of the peace agreement between Khartoum and the SPLA were signed. International pressure on Khartoum over the situation in Darfur rapidly increased. To the shame of the international community, the violence – especially Khartoum's unrestrained counter-insurgency – had already resulted in the greater proportion of death than the conflict would inflict in its five-year history.

In early September 2004, the United States declared that 'genocide' was occurring in Darfur and pushed for a full international investigation, as well as a threat of sanctions if Khartoum did not fulfil its 'international obligations'.[29] The priorities and trade-offs made by other (mostly Western) actors engaged in Sudan that allowed for a shift from near-silence that verged on complicity in 2003 to condemnation and confrontation by mid-2004 were not those made by China. But we should note plainly the fact that there were policy judgements of questionable humanitarian credentials from various sides.[30]

From mid-2004 onwards, it was Beijing that was seen by many to be foot-dragging and obstructing on the Darfur issue. In August 2004, responding to criticisms of its seeming indifference to Sudan's poor human rights' record, deputy Chinese foreign minister, Zhou Wenzhong replied, 'business is business. We try to separate politics from business . . . the internal situation in Sudan is an internal affair, we are not in a position to impose upon them.'[31] Howard French assessed China's approach in Africa as 'all trade with no political baggage', but the very fact of such an assessment was politically relevant in itself, as the baggage weighing Beijing down in the following two years would prove. China was increasingly seen to be in a *key* position to impose upon Khartoum, and by 2007, it would appear to have acknowledged that it was acting with such an understanding of its power in mind.

In September 2004, China abstained from voting on a resolution of the UN Security Council that authorised the establishment of an international commission of inquiry into crimes committed in Darfur. Resolution 1564 also expressed the Security Council's intent, in the event of Khartoum's failure to fulfil requirements made of it, to '*consider* taking additional measures as contemplated in article 41 of the Charter of the UN, *such as actions to affect Sudan's petroleum sector* [emphasis added]'.[32] Wielding its veto card, Beijing had succeeded in ensuring that the threat of oil trading sanctions against Khartoum was significantly weakened. The United States had already revised the text twice to water down the provision on sanctions.[33] China did not relent, and its UN ambassador, Wang Guangya, served notice he would veto any future resolution that would impose sanctions.[34]

Commentators at the time suggested that China, not wanting to disrupt its oil supply, shared a common interest with other members of the international community in defusing the crisis in Sudan and postulated that China could be either a 'productive partner' or a 'road block' on Sudan for the Bush administration, depending on whether its interests were protected.[35] Tellingly, as frustrations with Khartoum grew towards 2007, wholesale oil sanctions were taken off the table, seemingly in deference or surrender to China's concerns. Nevertheless, Beijing did subsequently urge Khartoum to comply with the two UN Security Council resolutions on Darfur up to that point, indicating a willingness not to be wholly silent on the matter. It also chose to abstain rather than exercise its veto on the Security Council resolution of March 2005 that authorised the International Criminal Court (ICC) to investigate alleged international crimes and human rights violations in Sudan.

As the conflict extended into 2005, China's engagement did not evolve beyond having quiet words with Khartoum and in effect shielded Sudan from a growing international consensus for tougher action. The former head of the Sudanese intelligence and government party heavyweight, Qutbi Mahdi, iterated as much in March 2005: 'If it were not for China's involvement with us, all these punishments [including sanctions] proposed by the American delegation would [have been] passed.'[36] Again, questions were asked about the limits of this marriage of convenience between Beijing and Khartoum. China, with extensive resource and infrastructure investments in Sudan, had no interest in ongoing instability and conflict in the country. It perhaps expected Khartoum to deal with the conflict swiftly and decisively, arguably just as Western countries had expected or hoped in 2003. But as the Darfur crisis gained the label of a 'genocide' and rose to prominence in the United States as the major crisis in Africa of the day, questions were also asked about the impact of China's stance on Washington-Beijing relations. As one Western diplomat noted: 'It can put a brake on the Security Council, but China also has a special interest with the US and, if the US were to put Sudan on the China/US agenda, things could change.'[37] For the time being, however, senior officials in Beijing sought to explain China's position as that of a reliable and engaged partner in Sudan whose oil projects were a 'part of our policy of long-term cooperation that helps both sides'.[38]

There were hopes in many quarters that the signing of the CPA in January 2005 would lay the foundation for a speedy political resolution of the Darfur conflict. However, this was dealt a massive blow by the untimely death in August 2005 of the lynchpin in this plan, SPLA leader and newly appointed first vice-president of Sudan, John Garang. Subsequent concern to keep the CPA process on track paralleled ineffective efforts to resolve the Darfur conflict by the AU and the international community. Meanwhile, the conflict increased in complexity and intractability through 2005 and into 2006 as rebel groups splintered and violence spread across the border to Chad and the Central African Republic.

As discussed in the previous section, during this period and into 2006 and 2007, Sino-Sudanese relations were further strengthened at many levels. These included military cooperation and new investments in the oil sector. Activists on Darfur began to consider how best to pressurise Beijing to use its presence in Sudan and influence on Khartoum to achieve their aims. In an early but lasting Western critique of China's role, in April 2006, Nicholas Kristoff of *The New York Times* argued that China, through its dealings with Khartoum, was 'underwriting its second genocide in three decades' (the first being Cambodia).[39]

INTERFERENCE 'LIGHT'? THE RELUCTANT POLITICS OF 'INFLUENCE'

The critical period in analysing Beijing's Darfur policy and its implications for Chinese engagement in Africa began after the failure of the Darfur Peace Agreement (DPA) to bring about an end either to conflict in the region or to the humanitarian crisis. The government of Sudan and only one of then three rebel movements in Darfur signed the DPA in Abuja, Nigeria, on 5 May 2006. Initially, there remained hope that pressure on the non-signatory rebel groups would result in their acceding to the agreement. And in mid-May, China joined in the unanimous UN Security Council Resolution 1679, paving the way for transition of the beleaguered, poorly mandated and inadequately resourced African Union Mission in Sudan (AMIS) peacekeeping force to the UN by the beginning of 2007. This transition, tabled by the AU's Peace and Security Council as early as January 2006, was to be effected by extending the remit and presence of the UN Mission in Sudan (UNMIS), the peacekeeping force already deployed elsewhere in Sudan as part of the CPA. However, in the associated Security Council debate, Beijing made clear its insistence on the 'basic principle and precondition' of peacekeeping operations that the consent and cooperation of the relevant country must be obtained prior to any deployment.[40] In the months following, violence in Darfur increased dramatically. It became apparent the non-signatories would not accept the DPA and that Khartoum would return to pursuing earnestly its counter-insurgency. In such a context, it was highly unlikely to consent to any expanded international peacekeeping force.

The failure of the DPA and the subsequent surge in violence led the United States, the United Kingdom and then UN Secretary-General Annan to reprioritise the humanitarian situation and civilian security, and to move urgently for a more robust UN-backed peacekeeping force to be deployed as soon as possible. Again, Beijing backed the initiative in principle, but repeated its requirement that troop deployment required Khartoum's consent. Khartoum made clear that it rejected replacing AMIS with UN peacekeepers. Washington once again threatened sanctions. When UN Security Council Resolution 1706 was adopted on 31 August 2006, 'invit[ing] the consent of the [Sudanese] government' to the deployment of a 17 700-strong UN force (and up to 3 300 civilian policemen) in Darfur 'no later than 31 December 2006', China abstained from voting (together with Russia and Qatar).[41] Beijing's position was that while it agreed to 'almost all the contents of the resolution' (including that the force required a strong mandate under Chapter VII of the UN Charter), the consent of the Sudanese government had to be obtained, not merely 'invited', ideally prior to the council vote and certainly prior to any deployment of a force, and that a vote on the resolution should have therefore been delayed.[42] The abstentions raised the ire of Washington and London and emboldened Khartoum, which promptly rejected Resolution 1706 as 'violat[ing] its sovereignty' by seeking to deploy a force having 'colonial' ambitions.[43]

In hindsight, however, it was after this juncture that Beijing and Khartoum began to see less than eye-to-eye. Resolution 1706 (and 1679 before it) *had* been adopted, the urgent need for a UN force had been recognised and Beijing's stated sole concern was achieving Khartoum's consent. In September, China's ambassador to the UN, Wang Guangya entreated that Beijing had 'sent a message to [the Sudanese government] that we feel the UN taking over is a good idea, but it is up to them to agree to that. We are not imposing upon them. We need to have them consider it and agree to it.'[44] China's viewpoint, and the resolution, was dismissed by Khartoum. In a letter to diplomatic missions in early October 2006, Sudan's UN mission in New York delivered the country's 'total rejection' of Resolution 1706 and determined that any nations' 'volunteering to provide peacekeeping troops to Darfur will be considered as a hostile act, a prelude to an invasion of a member country of the UN'.[45]

Khartoum's increasingly recalcitrant position and disregard for the international consensus that UN peacekeeping was required in Darfur led to fingers being pointed at the countries that had abstained from voting on Resolution 1706, above all China. Khartoum could not have easily maintained its position without tacit support from Beijing. Annan's focus on achieving agreement on the peacekeeping force in the last months of his ten-year tenure as UN Secretary-General threatened to make Beijing look even more unhelpful, unless it showed its commitment to being part of a solution.

Meanwhile, China's 'Year of Africa' and the lead-up to the high-profile November 2006 African Heads of State and Government (AHSG) Summit in Beijing (as part of the triennial Forum on China-Africa Cooperation, or FOCAC) coincided with a new level of international scrutiny of China's Africa relations. In June 2006, during a whistle-stop seven-nation African tour, premier Wen Jiabao responded to critics and decried concerns of a 'Chinese threat' in Africa as inaccurate and irresponsible.[46] He explained that 'in cooperating with Africa, China is not looking for selfish gains. We are committed to two principles: equality . . . and the non-interference in internal African affairs.'[47] A report released the same month by the human rights' organisation, Amnesty International, entitled 'China: Sustaining Conflict and Human Rights Abuses' gave specific attention to Beijing's arms supplies to Sudan and its impact in Darfur.[48] As the FOCAC Summit meeting opened in Beijing on 2 November 2006, Human Rights Watch lobbied, 'China insists that it will not "interfere" in other countries' domestic affairs, but it also claims to be great friend of the African people and a responsible major power. But that doesn't square with staying silent while mass killings go on in Darfur.'[49]

China was, however, better than silent. In addition to Beijing's communications with Khartoum in September 2006, Ambassador Wang Guangya reportedly played an important diplomatic role in Addis Ababa in mid-November when Sudan finally joined the AU's High Level Consultation on the Situation in Darfur. His efforts assisted in building support for the 'three-phase' plan Annan had devised for the establishment of a compromise 'hybrid' UN-AU peacekeeping force.[50] The US President's Special Envoy to Sudan, Andrew Natsios, would later report that Ambassador Wang's efforts were 'vital and constructive' in obtaining Sudan's agreement to the plan.[51]

Beijing, however, remained behind the pace in the public relations stakes, and on 14 December 2006, *The Washington Post* ran a piece entitled 'China and Darfur – the Genocide Olympics?' in which it argued: 'China seeks acceptance at the world's diplomatic top table – and this cause is unlikely to be advanced if China is perceived to be complicit in genocide. Imagine the newspaper ads leading up to the Beijing Games in 2008: Human rights campaigners will call on the world to boycott the Genocide Olympics.'[52] The week before, Hollywood actors George Clooney and Don Cheadle, together with two Olympic athletes, were in Beijing on a mission to 'simply ask questions and hopefully find answers about Darfur'.[53]

Even if all this seemed 'unfair' (as China's new Special Envoy to Africa, Liu Guijin, would later complain), Khartoum, too, wasn't being very helpful to Beijing's predicament. In January 2007, ahead of President Hu Jintao's February visit to Sudan, Khartoum was stalling again, maintaining that it had only agreed 'in principle' to the Annan plan in November 2006 and that there was no need for UN troops in Darfur. At his meeting with President al-Bashir in Khartoum, President Hu reportedly 'broke with his country's traditional policy of non-interference in a nation's internal affairs' by telling Sudan's leader that he should accept fully the Annan proposal.[54] Back in New York, Ambassador Wang publicised this development: 'Usually China doesn't send messages, but this time they did. It was a clear strong message that the proposal from Kofi Annan is a good one and Sudan has to accept it.' Wang was quick to add that China 'never twists arms', while assuring that Sudan 'got the message'.[55]

It became apparent that not only was the Sudanese president's arm far from twisted but that the message had, again, not been received as Beijing would have liked. In March 2007, al-Bashir wrote to the new UN Secretary-General, Ban Ki-moon, reportedly making scant reference to the November agreement reached in Addis Ababa, obstructing the phase two UN 'heavy support package' for AMIS that awaited Khartoum's agreement, and rejecting the large hybrid UN-AU force previously agreed for phase three. This prompted Ambassador Wang to affirm the Addis Ababa agreement, postulate 'miscommunications and misunderstandings' from Khartoum and to seek 'some explanation' from the Sudanese about their position.[56] For a country loath to interfere, this appeared as something close to a public stand-off.

Khartoum's intransigence once again left Beijing in a bind: it was already responding in ways considerably outside its comfort zone, beginning to publicise this to a frustrated and increasingly hostile international community, and yet seemingly still providing Sudan with the international disaccord so helpful for its manoeuvring. When Ban Ki-moon refused to accept Sudan's own rejection of the Annan plan, Washington and London once again called for sanctions. A wrong-footed Ambassador Wang replied that China understood Khartoum to have agreed to the Addis Ababa communiqué but opposed sanctions, arguing somewhat generously that 'as a sovereign state and also as an equal partner in the international efforts to address [Darfur, Sudan has] the right and [is] entitled to have reservations'.[57] Al-Bashir's response, Wang added nevertheless, was not 'what we expect at the Council'. China's aspiration for being a responsible power pursuing peaceful development in a multipolar world was as much threatened by Khartoum's disregard for the pre-eminent world body as by what appeared to Beijing as over-zealous and counter-productive interventionism by its Western colleagues.

Meanwhile, the Western (mostly in the United States) public pressure campaign on Beijing linking its stance on Darfur to the 2008 Olympics reached new levels of intensity, including a widely read opinion piece by actress and UN Children's Fund (UNICEF) Ambassador Mia Farrow in *The Wall Street Journal* in late March 2007.[58] The pressure campaign forced an analysis upon Beijing far more blunt than debates in the Security Council corridors: Beijing's stance allows Khartoum to resist sanction and intervention and to prosecute a war that continues to kill civilians; for this, China will be shamed in the harshest possible way. Sudan's cooperation and consent was a matter of steadily increasing importance to Beijing. It was left to determine how and to what extent Beijing could prevail upon Khartoum, whilst looking after its bilateral relationship and still holding fast to a veneer of non-interference.

ENOUGH IS ENOUGH: BEIJING EMBRACES 'INFLUENCE' AND REBUFFS CRITICS

In early April 2007, only days after Farrow's opinion piece, Beijing dispatched Assistant Foreign Minister Zhai Jun to Khartoum where he urged President al-Bashir to be 'more flexible' on the Annan plan. He then took the opportunity to label the linking of Darfur and the 2008 Olympics as 'ridiculous' and 'either ignorant or ill natured'.[59] In May, Beijing appointed its first Special Envoy to Africa, Liu Guijin, with a foreign ministry spokeswoman noting, 'since the situation in Darfur has drawn significant international attention the work of the special representative will focus on the Darfur issue'.[60] Beijing was charting new territory, especially with regard to its foreign relations with Africa. In the same week, China committed an engineering unit as part of UN support to AMIS in Darfur. And away from the public hue and cry of the 'Save Darfur Coalition' and the 'Olympic Dream for Darfur' campaigns, Darfur increasingly presented opportunities for dialogue and degrees of understanding between China and the West. Washington and London welcomed China's redoubled efforts, appeared to appreciate somewhat its predicament, while also urging China to use its leverage more forcefully to change Khartoum's behaviour.[61]

Yet China remained on a 'diplomatic high wire' and playing a 'delicate game' in the public spotlight, which now had a momentum all its own. In early May 2007, *The Boston Globe* ran another editorial stating: '. . . [T]he best way to deter China's rulers from being the principal enablers of genocide in Darfur . . . is to name them and shame them as often as possible. The last thing China's rulers want is to have the 2008 Olympic Games in Beijing branded with the name that many are trying to apply: the Genocide Olympics.'[62] On 9 May 2007, a day before China appointed its Special Envoy, an open letter signed by 106 members of the US Congress to President Hu warned of a public relations disaster for Beijing if it did not use its influence over Khartoum to help curtail the violence. It went further than the 2008 Olympics, cautioning President Hu that 'history will judge your government as having bankrolled a genocide'.[63] A major divestment campaign across the United States led Fidelity Investments, the second largest investor in PetroChina (a subsidiary of CNPC), to divest 91 per cent of its American Depository Receipts.[64] The campaign also put pressure on one of the United States's wealthiest individuals, Warren Buffett, and his investment group Berkshire Hathaway to do the same.[65]

In June 2007, the US House of Representatives passed a non-binding resolution urging China to suspend economic and military ties with Khartoum until the latter complied with UN Security Council resolutions. In the same month, the Olympic Dream for Darfur campaign launched a torch relay through historic genocide sites around the world to 'prod China to use its considerable clout with Sudan to stop the killings there'. Farrow explained to reporters, 'there is one thing that China holds more dear than its unfettered access to Sudanese oil and that is their successful staging of the 2008 Olympic Games. That desire does present a point of unique leverage with a country that has thus far been impervious to criticism.'[66] China's responsiveness to criticism was far more complex, but the allegation that Beijing was again 'underwriting genocide'[67] invited Beijing to be unreceptive. Rubbing salt into the wound, in June the Japanese Prime Minister, Shinzo Abe, commented publicly that China had 'failed to show sensitivity to the international calls and unanimous international pressure on Sudan'.[68] And in late July, on the eve of the UN Security Council vote on the hybrid peacekeeping force, film director Steven Spielberg (under pressure from Farrow and other activists, and having already called on President Hu to use greater influence on Khartoum in March), threatened to quit as artistic director of the Beijing Olympics 'unless China takes a tougher stance against Sudan'.[69] Eventually, in February 2008, Spielberg formally resigned.

Already by late May 2007, Beijing appeared increasingly frustrated by its invidious position: the lack of cooperation from Khartoum and the lack of appreciation elsewhere for the efforts it had made. Returning from a visit to Darfur (which he subsequently described as 'basically stable'), Envoy Liu rebutted criticisms linking China's oil interests to its stance on Darfur and Khartoum's actions: 'Oil drilling in a country is a normal business activity,' he argued, 'China opposes "politicising" and playing up normal cooperation in the energy field.' Opposite to the message once delivered by former President Jiang to an entreating al-Bashir in 1990, the envoy explained: 'China's oil cooperation helps Sudan develop its economy and fundamentally address the country's chaos caused by war and its unrest.'[70] And following the US House of Representatives resolution in early June, a Chinese official responded angrily that 'disregarding China's constructive efforts over the Darfur issue, the resolution condemned China without reason, tries to link the issue [to] the Beijing Olympics and wantonly interfered with China's internal affairs'.[71]

A week later, Liu Guijin explained that Beijing had again privately exerted pressure on Khartoum using 'very direct language'. China's ties with Sudan had nevertheless been 'unnecessarily politicised', added Envoy Liu, which was 'unfair and irrational'.[72] He reiterated that Beijing had 'tried to advise the Sudanese government to be more flexible' regarding the Annan plan. In July, Envoy Liu again dismissed the claim that the Olympics should be linked to China's policy on Darfur as 'sheer nonsense' and evidence of poor knowledge of China's role in Darfur, or that some of its critics 'harbour a Cold-War mentality and take a distorted view'.[73] Reports suggested China was now gathering intelligence on anti-Olympics activists.[74] In late July, referring to critical statements by Democratic presidential hopefuls regarding Beijing's stance on Darfur, Liu assessed that 'certain US politicians like to play up Darfur to show that they are standing on a higher moral ground'.[75]

The appointment of Envoy Liu and his engagement with the Darfur situation heralded a clear diplomatic offensive by China in which it sought to put an end to the game of catch-up it had started to play from late 2006. Liu sought to turn the tables on the debate, making clear Beijing's 'very direct language' towards Khartoum had contributed significantly to the latter's accepting 'without condition' the third phase of the Annan plan.[76] China's policy on the Darfur issue, he argued, had been recognised by the world's leading powers and, particularly, by the African and developing countries. When Sudan's first vice-president and leader of southern Sudan, Salva Kiir, visited Beijing, China also publicised its willingness to work with the international community to 'push for the early and proper settlement of the Darfur issue'.[77] Significantly, this suggested China saw itself playing a role in conflict resolution and peacemaking.

Whether African countries and the AU were satisfied with China's efforts for the eighteen-month period since the AU had called for AMIS's replacement with UN peacekeepers is not entirely clear.[78] Darfur had dominated the agenda of the regional body for four years; African troops deployed there were under enormous strain; the AU's inaugural peacekeeping mission had been assessed unfavourably; and Khartoum had given limited credence to the decisions taken by the AU's nascent Peace and Security Council, including those relating to the hybrid force. Nevertheless, for African states, just as for the wider international community, if China had now helped convince Khartoum to yield on the hybrid force, there would be few objectors. Never mind that Khartoum's stalling until this time had been greatly helped by the buffer provided by Beijing's position.

The verdict in Western quarters on Beijing's redoubled efforts up to July was something akin to 'much welcomed; necessary, but not sufficient'. *The Economist*, though cognisant and supportive of Chinese cooperation with the West on Sudan, noted that while China had 'boasted of putting pressure on the [Khartoum] regime' leading to its acceptance of the hybrid peacekeeping force, this 'new tactic' was 'hardly a sacrifice for the common good' because Sudan was anyway too isolated to lose its crucial international partner.[79] In any case, more work needed to be done to establish the hybrid force, beginning with an authorising resolution of the UN Security Council.

The unanimous adoption of UN Security Council Resolution 1769, establishing the hybrid peacekeeping force, United Nations-African Union Mission in Darfur (UNAMID), on 31 July 2007 ended, in policy-decision terms, the long period of delays and obstructions facing the pre-eminent world body since early 2006.[80] Beijing had been important in pressuring Khartoum to come on board, but it also sought to influence the content of the resolution to keep Khartoum contented. Above all, Khartoum objected to the resolution invoking Chapter VII of the UN Charter as its authority. Given the many previous resolutions on peacekeeping in Sudan and specifically Darfur that referred to Chapter VII, the argument was difficult to make.

In the days leading up to the vote, a leading Darfur activist in the United States, Eric Reeves, laid down the gauntlet: 'The moment of truth is at hand. Beijing's actions going forward must be judged in the context of a present decision about Chapter VII authority.'[81] In a telling remark to the official *China Daily*, Envoy Liu explained Beijing's approach: 'China insists on using influence without interference, and we know respect for all parties is vital to finding a solution.'[82] Resolution 1769, agreed by the Security Council under the presidency of the Chinese ambassador, invoked Chapter VII, notwithstanding Khartoum's reservations, and this was heralded as a breakthrough. But it also made concessions to Sudan, omitting any mandate for UNAMID to seize weapons brought to Darfur in violation of the embargo or to prevent aerial bombardments in the region.

Activists such as Reeves welcomed the resolution cautiously and considered China's 'feigned support' insufficient unless it advanced the resolution's actual implementation.[83] Talk of the 'Genocide Olympics' continued to be heard on 8 August 2007, the day marking the one-year countdown to the opening ceremony in Beijing.

IMPLICATIONS FROM DARFUR FOR SUDAN-CHINA AND AFRICA-CHINA RELATIONS

What can be learned about the direction of Sino-African relations and Chinese foreign policy from the Dafur case? One must be wary of generalising too much from a situation that involved a motley mix of oil, assessments of 'genocide', Hollywood actors and directors, a country formerly on the United States terror list, the Olympics, the world's wealthiest individuals, and the world's emerging great power already under scrutiny for its forays in Africa.

However, it remains worthwhile to examine some of the major developments that occurred during the last three or so years with regard to Darfur and to then observe whether or not they might shape Chinese foreign policy and Beijing's Sino-African dealings in the future. With Darfur, Beijing's policy calculations weighed up several competing factors:

1) the desire to maintain a flourishing and deepening commercial relationship with Khartoum that nevertheless faced new challenges from other players including India, Malaysia, Indonesia, the Gulf states and European companies;
2) the risks to its existing and future investments presented by increased instability in Sudan, especially if Darfur jeopardised the north-south accord;
3) the adherence to cardinal and core foreign policy principles of non-interference and respect for state sovereignty, manifesting specifically in the issue of obtaining Khartoum's consent to any international peacekeeping deployment and opposition to sanctions; and
4) the desire to enhance Beijing's international standing and respect, in the short term by minimising the harm and damage to high-profile interests such as the 2008 Olympics, and, in the long term, by displaying that it is and would be a responsible power in international affairs with a contribution to make to multilateral efforts in pursuit of collective interests.

First and foremost, Darfur compels us to reassess anew that core principle of China's foreign policy: non-interference in the internal affairs of another country. As this chapter has argued, from the outset the very fact of China's substantial direct material interests in Sudan equated to economic and strategic significance to Khartoum. When Khartoum mattered to international policy debates, Beijing also mattered. Whatever action Beijing took, including inaction, had real effects. This may not be 'interference' in the strict sense, especially where no action was taken without the consent of Khartoum. Nor, conversely, is it non-involvement. Further, the focus of all interested parties – whether Khartoum, Washington or activists such as Reeves and the like – on Beijing's conduct brought China into play as a pivotal force.

In balancing the competing factors outlined above, Beijing sought to work with international efforts on Darfur but maintain its bilateral relations and core foreign policy principles. Beijing sought to have it both ways – achieve the international action it supported but without sanctions being required to persuade Khartoum to come on board. This proved difficult, as Beijing, through this stance, had also become Khartoum's main defence against more concerted international action. The very fact that Beijing, given its importance, sought Khartoum's consent strengthened Khartoum's ability to obstruct and stall. Again, non-interference was far from non-involvement, and requiring consent squarely undermined the urgent outcome that Beijing and the international community sought.

As others have noted, President Hu's pronouncement of 'four principles' to address Darfur in Khartoum in February 2007 attested to this contradiction in reaffirming non-interference but noting the 'imperative to improve the situation in Darfur and living conditions of local people'.[84] Within these competing priorities lay China's empirical position on the emerging doctrine of a 'Responsibility to Protect' (R2P). The threshold for a sovereign state's displaying a 'manifest failure' to protect its citizens from 'genocide, war crimes, ethnic cleansing and crimes against humanity', and thus triggering an international responsibility to act, had not been met in Beijing's view.[85]

Whether it wanted to be involved politically or not, Beijing's earlier positions on Darfur delivered a lose-lose outcome: the ire of Western actors, the undermining of multilateral authority, and the lack of cooperation from its bilateral counter-party on a response that it supported in substance. In moving from a 'business is business' rhetorical stance to one of embracing and publicising 'influence not interference', Beijing charted new waters. In using political influence that derives its power significantly from an economic relationship, China is calling into question the veracity of its 'no political conditions' value proposition to African states. While it responded to its invidious position using informal power with Khartoum that did not explicitly jeopardise its core foreign policy principles or its lucrative dealings, the reality all the same was one of China's active engagement in Sudan's political affairs.

The appointment of a special envoy and the use of 'very direct language' occurred at a time of unprecedented international scrutiny. Beijing's willingness to publicise its efforts, but its refusal to see this as a response to the international politicisation of its relations with Sudan is hard to sustain logically. If Beijing can and will use its influence, but chooses to do so only on an ad hoc basis, then others will seek to give Beijing reason to exert influence when and in the way they would like it to. The Olympics presented a rare and unique opportunity to put pressure on Beijing, but it is not impossible to imagine there may be others in the future. The threshold levels for Beijing deciding to use its influence, and the levers of control it uses in different circumstances, are issues that will require close examination in the future.

It should also be noted that Beijing is concerned to distinguish influence from interference partly in order to protect its domestic interests. To the extent that the primary motivation for China's strict rhetorical insistence on non-interference is its perceived vulnerability to interference in its own domestic affairs at home, this vulnerability will inevitably diminish as China rises as a global power. No doubt the spectre of the United States's hyper-power status will always motivate a defensive posture, but just as China's interdependence with the world grows, so grows the world's, and especially that of the United States, with China. As this occurs, we may be correct to expect Beijing to be quite comfortable with a progressive expansion in the scope and depth of its use of influence that increasingly crosses over into interference as and when China's interests demand.

Away from the hysteria of the public pressure campaigns there is a clear realisation among Western governments that China now matters greatly to African affairs, and needs to be actively engaged as a partner. In 2005, Princeton Lyman queried whether there were 'more areas of win-win situations in Africa for both the United States and China?' He added that 'it is better to explore these possibilities than to start down the path of trying to limit Chinese influence, for the odds are against that happening any time soon'.[86] The Darfur situation has not been a 'win-win' matter in this regard, but it has allowed for a new level of dialogue, interaction and collaboration on Africa between the UN, London, Brussels, Washington and Beijing.

Putting aside concerns about its international reputation, a growing argument for China's deeper engagement in Africa's politics and development rests on the way Beijing understands the nexus between its economic opportunities (whether energy security, returns on its investments or markets for its goods and services) and political stability and development on the continent. *The Economist*, in entreating President Hu to use his leverage with Khartoum in February 2007, remarked 'as China's economic interests and dependencies spread, it is going to have to learn the need to invest in peace as well as pipelines. Sometimes that will require it to put unwelcome pressure on its trading partners.'[87] With Darfur, this lesson is being heeded to some extent. In addition to using its influence on Khartoum regarding the UNAMID hybrid force in Sudan, China has made important troop and personnel contributions to UNAMID, provided a not inconsiderable amount of humanitarian and development assistance (notably in water and power) to communities in Darfur, and has even waded in to support international efforts to reach a political solution to the crisis. Taken together, China's engagement in Sudan's Darfur crisis is unprecedented in Africa in recent years. However, this appeared to many as wholly insufficient compared to Beijing's relative importance, or even completely undermined by Beijing's ongoing sales of arms to Khartoum.[88]

In any case, what *The Economist* failed to address is the connection between China's investments in 'pipelines' in weak and unstable states in Africa and the role that inequitable processes of extraction play in profiting unaccountable elites and exacerbating political violence and civil war. This is a problem that China does not face alone. However, between former President Jiang's advice to Sudan's al-Bashir in 1990 and the opposite argument by Envoy Liu in 2007 lies the necessity for China to better understand the political economy consequences of its dealings in Africa. This necessity has already arisen in the case of Sudan, not only with Darfur. As the country's fragile north-south peace comes under increasing strain, key issues include allocation of oil revenues to the southern regional government and demarcation of borders in the oil regions straddling north and south.

During his August 2007 trip to Beijing, Salva Kiir, as president of the government of southern Sudan, reportedly made the case to Beijing that the vast majority of Sudan's oil is in the south. Beijing has since made an effort to be more actively engaged in the south, including indicating a willingness to provide substantial support for the region's recovery. Merely winning friends cannot be sufficient for the long haul. In April 2007, responding to a question regarding risks from insecurity to China's oil investments in Sudan, Envoy Liu stated: 'as with any investor in any country it is logical that the investor hopes to have a more stable, more peaceful situation . . . That is something quite natural. But currently we do not see imminent danger'.[89] By 2008, threats to the CPA, and consequential dangers associated with the oil fields that may either bind or betray Sudan's quest for peace, had become ever more real. Looking forward, the prospects for Sino-Sudanese relations are entwined with, and therefore as complex and uncertain as, Sudan's prospects for peace, stability and development.

CONCLUSION

During the countdown to the 2008 Beijing Olympics, the games' official motto 'One World, One Dream' was, from China's perspective, under considerable strain. In early 2008, as the Sudanese government once again stalled on the deployment of peacekeepers in Darfur, Assistant Foreign Minister Zhai Jun reportedly warned Sudan 'not to do things that [would] cause the international community to impose sanctions on them' explaining that 'the world [was] running out of patience over [what was] going on in Darfur'.[90] A far cry from Mao's strident autarchy in the late 1960s, the China of the new century now appeared willing to speak on behalf of the world. And, with the world, Beijing was confronting Khartoum with more than non-interference. Despite this, many in the West – such as Steven Spielberg, who resigned from his Olympics' role in February 2008 – had run out of patience with Beijing.

The Darfur case may prove to be an important chapter in China's arrival as a status quo global power. Faced with unprecedented scrutiny of its Sino-African relations, Darfur evidences an evolution in Chinese foreign policy from a value proposition of 'no political conditions' to a pragmatic acceptance of the need to use its growing influence, if and when the situation demands. Through its actions, if not its words, China's self-perception and approach to its foreign relations in Africa are noticeably shifting. That the Darfur situation demanded, and saw, such a distinct shift may be an exception rather than the rule in the short term, owing to a unique confluence of circumstances peculiar to the Darfur situation. With Darfur, Beijing ultimately calculated that Khartoum's submission to its publicised influence would be worth more than strict non-interference. This calculation was swayed significantly by the ability of activists to play on Beijing's pride, shame and desire for recognition in the run-up to the Olympics. Yet in the eyes of many, China's 'positive influence' on Khartoum was only sporadically effective and ultimately frustrating. This was as much due to Khartoum's defiance as to the real limitations of a brand of influence that stops short of any material consequence. Looking ahead, Beijing's own assessment of the results of its foray into 'positive influence' in Sudan is certain to influence future Chinese engagement in the political affairs of African countries. That Beijing's experience in Sudan could noticeably change how China decides and manages its commercial investments and its arms deals in Africa is a more naïve speculation. Khartoum, at least, understands this only too well.

NOTES

1. This section draws on analysis by the author in S. Srinivasan, '"A Rising Great Power" Embraces Africa: Nigeria-China Relations', in A. Adebajo and R. Mustapha (eds.), *Gulliver's Troubles: Nigeria's Foreign Policy after the Cold War* (Pietermaritzburg: University of KwaZulu-Natal Press, 2008).
2. On China's relations with Africa before the late 1990s, see especially: P. Snow, 'China and Africa: Consensus and Camouflage', in T.W. Robinson and D.L. Shambaugh (eds.), *Chinese Foreign Policy: Theory and Practice* (Oxford: Clarendon Press, 1994); P. Snow, *The Star Raft: China's Encounter with Africa* (London: Weidenfeld and Nicolson, 1988); I. Taylor, 'China's Foreign Policy towards Africa in the 1990s', *Journal of Modern African Studies* 36(3), 1998: 443–60; P. van Ness, 'China and the Third World: Patterns of Engagement and Indifference', in Samuel S. Kim (ed.), *China and the World: Chinese Foreign Policy Faces the New Millennium.* (Boulder, CO: Westview Press, 1998).
3. R. Foot, 'Chinese Strategies in a US-Hegemonic Global Order: Accommodating and Hedging', *International Affairs* 82(1), 2006: 77–94.

4. See, for example, S. Giry, 'China's Africa Strategy: Out of Beijing', *The New Republic*, 15 November 2004 (pp. 19–23).
5. J. Fisher-Thompson, 'China No Threat to United States in Africa, US Official Says', US State Department Information Service, 28 July 2005. http://www.usinfo.state.gov/eap/Archive/2005/Jul/29-550683.html.
6. Z. Bijian, 'China's "Peaceful Rise" to Great-Power Status', *Foreign Affairs* 84(5), 2005: 18–24. It should be noted that 'peaceful rise' soon fell out of favour with leaders in the Chinese Communist Party and they instead opted for the term 'peaceful development', which was seen as less threatening.
7. Foot, 'Chinese Strategies'.
8. J. Pomfret, 'British Minister Urges China to Help on Darfur', Reuters, 28 August 2007.
9. Gordon was considered a hero of Empire and his story recorded famously in L. Strachey, *Eminent Victorians* (Harmondsworth: Penguin Books, 1986).
10. See P.M. Holt, *The Mahdist State in the Sudan: 1881–1898: A Study of its Origins, Development and Overthrow*, 2nd ed. (Oxford: Oxford University Press, 1979).
11. The latter anecdote was related by a Sudanese official to a Western diplomat in Khartoum, who related it to the author in 2004.
12. See A. Abdalla Ali, 'EU, China and Africa: The Sudanese Experience', *Sudan Tribune*, 10 July 2007. http://www.sudantribune.com/spip.php?page=imprimableandid_article=22783.
13. Khartoum's international isolation increased during the 1990s, especially following its alleged role in the attempted assassination of Egyptian President Hosni Mubarak in 1995 and Sudan's hosting of Osama Bin Laden.
14. See L.C. Harris, *China Considers the Middle East* (London: Tauris), quoted in D. Large, 'China's Role in Armed Conflict and Post-War Reconstruction in Africa: Sudan in Comparative Context' (unpublished conference paper, January 2007).
15. See D. Large, 'Arms, Oil, and Darfur: The Evolution of Relations between China and Sudan', in 'Human Security Baseline Assessment: Sudan Issue Brief' (Geneva: Small Arms Survey, Graduate Institute of International Studies, 2007), citing Y. Shichor, 'Sudan: China's Outpost in Africa', *China Brief* 5(21), 2005.
16. See Amnesty International, *People's Republic of China: Sustaining Conflict and Human Rights Abuses* (London: Amnesty International, 2006).
17. See detailed discussion in S.W. Lewis, *Chinese NOCs and World Energy Markets: CNPC, Sinopec and CNOOC* (Houston, TX: The James A Baker III Institute for Public Policy, Rice University, 2007). Lewis concludes: 'The NOCs and the Chinese central government will continue to face obstacles in reconciling their competing political and economic goals in "going abroad" and in developing strategies [sic] ties to resource providing nations in particular. The role of Chinese NOCs in world energy markets is thus one very much in transition, with NOC commercial interests and strategies mediated by the evolving geopolitical strategies of their principal owner, the Chinese government.'
18. See E.N. Tjønneland, B. Brandtzæg, Å. Kolås and G. le Pere, *China in Africa: Implications for Norwegian Foreign and Development Policies* (Bergen: Chr Michelsen Institute, 2006).
19. Reuters, 'Sudan Doubles Crude Exports to China in 2007', *Sudan Tribune*, 28 January 2008. http://www.sudantribune.com/spip.php?article25671.
20. Large, 'Arms, Oil, and Darfur', p. 2.
21. See, for example, J. Rone and Human Rights Watch, *Sudan, Oil, and Human Rights* (New York: Human Rights Watch, 2003).
22. See Rone and Human Rights Watch, *Sudan, Oil, and Human Rights*, pp. 673–87.

23. See, for example, extensive analysis in International Crisis Group, *God, Oil and Country: Changing the Logic of War in the Sudan* (Brussels: International Crisis Group, January 2002).
24. L. MacInnis, 'Sudan Top Target for Chinese Investment in Africa', Reuters, 28 March 2007. http://www.africa.reuters.com/business/news/usnBAN822386.html.
25. Xinhua News Agency, 'Sudan Oil Minister Says Energy Cooperation with China Fruitful', *Sudan Tribune*, translated by British Broadcasting Corporation Monitoring Service (BBCMS), 15 July 2007. http://www.sudantribune. com/spip.php?article22865.
26. Reuters, 'Sudan, China to Build US$630 million Mauritania Railway', *Sudan Tribune*, 4 August 2007. http://www.sudantribune.com/spip.php?page=imprimableandid_article=23140.
27. Large, 'Arms, Oil, and Darfur', p. 7.
28. See, for example, A.J. Bellamy, 'Responsibility to Protect or Trojan Horse? The Crisis in Darfur and Humanitarian Intervention After Iraq', *Ethics and International Affairs* 19(2), 2005: 31–54.
29. C.L. Powell, 'The Crisis in Darfur', testimony before the Senate Foreign Relations Committee, 9 September 2004 (Washington, DC: US Department of State).
30. See discussion in S. Srinivasan, *Minority Rights, Early Warning and Conflict Prevention: Lessons from Darfur* (London: Minority Rights Group International, 2006); H. Slim, 'Dithering over Darfur? A Preliminary Review of the International Response', *International Affairs* 80(5), 2004: 811–28.
31. H. French, 'China in Africa: All Trade, with No Political Baggage', *The New York Times*, 8 August 2004.
32. UN Security Council Resolution S/RES/1564, 18 September 2004. Russia, Pakistan and Algeria also abstained.
33. Bloomberg, 'China Threatens to Veto UN Darfur Resolution over Oil Sanctions', *Sudan Tribune*, 18 September 2004. http://www.sudantribune.com/spip.php?page=imprimableandid_article=5500.
34. 'UN Adopts Resolution on Sudan's Darfur', *China Daily*, 19 September 2004. http://www.chinadaily.com .cn/english/doc/2004-09/19/content_375722.htm.
35. D. Thompson, 'Darfur Complications: Disaccord on Sudan Could Poison China-US Ties', *International Herald Tribune*, 18 November 2004.
36. A. England, 'Beijing and Sudan Reap Benefits from Marriage of Convenience', *Financial Times*, 22 March 2005.
37. England, 'Beijing and Sudan Reap Benefits'.
38. Li Xiaobing, a senior Africa official at China's Ministry of Commerce, in K. Leggett, 'China Flexes Economic Muscle throughout Burgeoning Africa', *The Wall Street Journal*, 29 March 2005.
39. N.D. Kristoff, 'China and Sudan, Blood and Oil', *The New York Times*, 23 April 2006.
40. United Nations, *Security Council Endorses African Union Decision on Need for Concrete Steps in Transition to United Nations Operation in Darfur* (New York: United Nations Department of Public Information, 2006).
41. United Nations, *Security Council Expands Mandate of UN Mission in Sudan to Include Darfur, Adopting Resolution 1706 by Vote of 12 in Favour, with 3 Abstaining* (New York: United Nations Department of Public Information, 31 August 2006).
42. United Nations, *Security Council Expands Mandate of UN Mission in Sudan.*
43. BBC News, 'Sudan Rejects Darfur Resolution', 31 August 2006. http://www.news.bbc.co.uk/2/hi/africa/5304160.stm.
44. Reuters, 'China Pushes Sudan to Let UN Troops into Darfur', 14 September 2006.
45. Agence France-Presse (AFP), 'Sudan – Participation in Darfur is a Hostile Act', 4 October 2006. Sudan appeared to soon back down from this extreme position following outrage at the Security Council: see W.M. Reilly, 'Analysis: Extend Sudan UN Mission', *United Press International (UPI)*, 9 October 2006.

46. G. Stamp, 'China Defends its Africa Relations', BBC News, 26 June 2006. http://www.news.bbc.co.uk/2/hi/business/5114980.stm.
47. IRIN, 'China and Africa – For Better or For Worse?', 27 June 2006.
48. Amnesty International, *People's Republic of China*.
49. S. Richardson, 'China-Africa Summit: Focus on Human Rights, Not Just Trade' (New York: Human Rights Watch, 2 November 2006).
50. African Union Peace and Security Council, *Communiqué of the 66th Meeting of the Peace and Security Council PSC/AHG/Comm (LXVI) on the Situation in Darfur (the Sudan), 30 November 2006* (Addis Ababa: African Union).
51. A. Natsios, 'Statement of the President's Special Envoy to Sudan to the Senate Foreign Relations Committee' (Washington, DC: United States Senate, 11 April 2007).
52. 'China and Darfur: "The Genocide Olympics?"', *The Washington Post*, 14 December 2006.
53. Associated Press, 'George Clooney Campaigns in China and Egypt to Raise Awareness over Darfur Conflict', 13 December 2006.
54. B. Varner, 'China, Breaking Tradition, Told Sudan to Adopt UN's Darfur Plan', Bloomberg, 6 February 2007. During his visit to Khartoum, President Hu also unveiled a package that included an interest-free loan of approximately US$13 million for a new presidential palace, as well as debt cancellation of up to US$70 million.
55. Varner, 'China, Breaking Tradition'.
56. Associated Press, 'China Seeks Explanation of Sudan Letter Challenging UN Darfur Plan', 12 March 2007.
57. W. Ali, 'China Voices Opposition to Sanctions on Sudan', *Sudan Tribune*, 18 March 2007. http://www.sudantribune.com/spip.php?page=imprimableandid_article=20853.
58. R. Farrow and M. Farrow, 'The Genocide Olympics', *The Wall Street Journal*, 28 March 2007. See also K. Cullen, 'Genocide Games', *The Boston Globe*, 25 March 2007.
59. See H. Cooper, 'Darfur Collides with Olympics, and China Yields', *International Herald Tribune*, 12 April 2007; 'China Dismisses "Genocide Olympics" Tag', *Independent Online*, 11 April 2007. http://www.int.iol.co.za/index.php?set_id=1andclick_id=126andart_id=nw20070411125843199C839238.
60. Associated Press, 'China Appoints Special Representative to Focus on Darfur Crisis', 10 May 2007.
61. See C. Buckley, 'Analysis: China on Diplomatic Highwire over Darfur', Reuters, 24 April 2007. See also B. Gill, C. Huang and J.S. Morrison, 'Assessing China's Growing Influence in Africa', *China Security* 3(3), 2007. In early May, *The Economist* applauded China's 'shift' of position in seeking more publicly to pressure Khartoum as 'the kind of commitment to Darfur that the West has been urging on China for years'. 'Sudan: A Hopeful Wind of Change', *The Economist*, 10 May 2007.
62. 'Chinese Shadows', *The Boston Globe*, 8 May 2007.
63. Associated Press, 'China Appoints Special Representative'. See also C. Buckley, 'China Defends Darfur Role, Deflects Olympic Warning', Reuters, 10 May 2007.
64. AFX News Limited, 'Activists Urge Berkshire Hathaway to Engage with PetroChina, Beijing on Darfur', in *Forbes Online*, 5 May 2007. http://www.forbes.com/markets/feeds/afx/2007/05/22/afx3748899.html.
65. AFX News Limited, 'Activists Urge Berkshire Hathaway '. Regarding Berkshire Hathaway's investment in PetroChina, and the connection to the Gates Foundation through Buffett's endowment, see C. Piller, 'Berkshire Wealth Clashes with Gates Mission in Sudan', *Los Angeles Times*, 4 May 2007.
66. Reuters, 'Darfur Campaign Rejects China Olympics Boycott', *Sudan Tribune*, 13 June 2007. http://www.sudantribune.com/spip.php?page=imprimableandid_article=22371.

67. See testimony of Darfur analyst and activist, E. Reeves, *China in Sudan: Underwriting Genocide*. Paper presented at 'China's Role in the World: Is China a Responsible Stakeholder?' (US-China Economic and Security Review Commission, Washington DC: 3 April 2007).
68. Agence France-Presse (AFP), 'Japan's PM Faults China over Darfur', 13 June 2007.
69. BBC News, 'Spielberg May Quit Olympic Role', 27 July 2007. http://www.news.bbc.co.uk/2/hi/entertainment/6919010.stm.
70. Xinhua News Agency, 'China Opposes "Politicizing" Oil Cooperation with Sudan', *Sudan Tribune*, 30 May 2007 (translated by BBCMS). http://www.sudantribune.com/spip.php?article22141.
71. Associated Press, 'China Says Strongly Opposed to US House Resolution on Darfur', *Sudan Tribune*, 8 June 2007. http://www.sudantribune.com/spip.php?page=imprimableandid_article=22284.
72. A. Russell and W. Wallis, 'China Puts Private Pressure on Sudan', *Financial Times*, 19 June 2007.
73. Xinhua News Agency, 'China Censures Linking between Darfur and Olympic Games', *Sudan Tribune*, 6 July 2007. http://www.sudantribune.com/spip.php?page=imprimableandid_article=22717.
74. Associated Press, 'China Gathering Intelligence on Activists it Thinks Might Disrupt 2008 Olympics', *International Herald Tribune*, 23 July 2007.
75. *People's Daily*, 'Confrontation over Darfur "Will Lead Us Nowhere" ', 27 July 2007. http://www.china.org.cn/english/darfur/218776.htm.
76. *People's Daily*, 'Confrontation over Darfur'.
77. Vice-President Zeng Qinghong, see Xinhua News Agency, 'China Willing to Help Resolve Darfur Issue as Sudan's VP Visits Beijing', 18 July 2007. http://news.xinhuanet.com/english/2007-07/19/content_6399052.htm.
78. Gill, Huang and Morrison, 'Assessing China's Growing Influence in Africa'.
79. 'China Winks at the West, *The Economist*, 3 July 2007. http://www.economist.com/world/asia/displaystory.cfm?story_id=9431307.
80. UN Security Council Resolution 1769: UN Doc S/RES/1769, 31 July 2007.
81. C. Buckley, 'China Defends Darfur Stance as Pressure Grows', Reuters, 27 July 2007.
82. Buckley, 'China Defends Darfur Stance'.
83. E. Reeves, 'China's Feigned Support for Darfur Unresolved', *The New Republic* (TNR Online), 2 August 2007. https://ssl.tnr.com/p/docsub.mhtml?i=w070730ands=reeves080207.
84. Gill, Huang and Morrison, 'Assessing China's Growing Influence in Africa'.
85. China (with Russia, the United States and states in the Non-Aligned Movement) had already influenced the dilution of the 2005 UN World Summit Outcome Document's wording on the R2P, including the phrase 'manifest failure' rather than the lower threshold of 'unwilling or unable': see A.J. Bellamy, 'Whither the Responsibility to Protect? Humanitarian Intervention and the 2005 World Summit', *Ethics and International Affairs* 20(2): 143–69.
86. P. Lyman, *China's Rising Role in Africa*. Presentation to the US-China Economic and Security Review Commission (Washington, DC, 21 July 2005).
87. 'Sudan and China: Mr Hu's Mission to Khartoum', *The Economist*, 3 February 2007.
88. See UPI, 'China Sells Arms to Sudan', *Sudan Tribune*, 15 February 2008. http://www.sudantribune.com/spip.php?article2599.
89. Russell and Wallis, 'China Puts Private Pressure on Sudan'.
90. 'China Issues a Warning to Sudan over Darfur Crisis', *Sudan Tribune*, 30 January 2008. http://www.sudantribune.com/spip.php?article25753.

5

Partner or Predator in the Heart of Africa?

Chinese Engagement with the DRC

Devon Curtis

Today, the reconstruction of our country begins, let's celebrate the collaboration with China.

Congolese Minister of Infrastructure, Public Works and Reconstruction, Pierre Lumbi Okongo, 28 January 2008[1]

If we can take the Congo, we can have all of Africa.

Attributed to Zedong, 1964[2]

China has long recognised the importance of the Congo (Zaire),[3] but the above quotations illustrate two very different ways of interpreting this relationship. The first quotation, from the current Congolese Minister of Infrastructure, Public Works and Reconstruction, Pierre Lumbi Okongo, followed the signing of two important agreements between the Democratic Republic of Congo (DRC) and China in January 2008, including a preferential loan to the Congolese government from China's Export-Import (Exim) Bank. This occurred in the wake of a monumental US$8 billion draft agreement signed in September 2007, in which some of the DRC's mineral resources are exchanged for the financing of infrastructure projects.

The second quotation highlights a very different kind of relationship. The quote is attributed to Mao in 1964, in reference to the possibility of Chinese-style 'revolutions' spreading through Africa.[4] The ambassador designate to Burundi at the time was told by a Chinese foreign ministry official to concentrate on the Congo, since this was the key to Chinese influence in the continent. The Congo was discussed as a possible site for a socialist alternative. This initiative failed, as the Congo's position as a firm Western ally became entrenched, and relations between China and the Congo were subsumed to larger Cold-War politics. Levels of trade and diplomatic activity between the two countries were irregular.

Has the DRC-China relationship thus changed from one defined by ideological pressure and competition, to one marked today by mutually beneficial economic arrangements? This chapter will argue that such a view is flawed. Both China and the DRC have undergone enormous changes in the last 50 years, but today's dominant views of China as either a mutually beneficial partner or a strategic predator in the DRC mask the complexities that characterise the past and present relationship between the two countries.

Contemporary relations between China and the DRC have many elements in common with relations between China and other resource-rich African countries, which are too complex to subsume under predator-versus-partner labels. However, the Congo has not occupied a privileged place in the recent flood of books and articles that focus on the China-Africa relationship. Until 2007, China-DRC trade, investment and economic development assistance figures were relatively low compared to other resource-rich African countries. The DRC was not one of the top ten African importers from or exporters to China and neither was it one of the African countries China identified in the mid-1990s as a centre of commerce and investment.

This changed dramatically in September 2007 with the announcement that China planned to invest more than US$8 billion in the DRC. Relative to the DRC's current earnings, the deal was China's most significant single commitment in Africa so far. At least US$3 billion was to be invested in mining projects, and more than US$5 billion was committed to financing infrastructural development, including a 3 200 km railway, a 3 200 km road, and many hospitals and clinics. Since 2007, there has been a flood of visits between China and the DRC, and several follow-up agreements have been signed.[5]

The September 2007 agreement catapulted the DRC to centre stage in China-Africa cooperation. Reaction to the news was mixed. The announcement left some Western donors and diplomats reeling, particularly since it was made just as an International Monetary Fund (IMF) delegation had arrived in Kinshasa to review progress towards the resumption of budgetary support for the DRC. Congolese and Chinese officials, however, spoke enthusiastically of partnership, win-win development and new opportunities.

This chapter situates this recent agreement within the broader context of Chinese-Congolese relations. It first provides an account of the historical underpinnings of the

China-DRC relationship, since the legacies of the earlier period resurface in numerous ways in contemporary politics. The chapter then turns to China's role during the Congolese civil wars (1996–2003) and the transitional period (2003–06), including China's contribution to the Mission des Nations Unies en République Démocratique du Congo (MONUC), the United Nations (UN) peacekeeping mission in the country. Finally, the chapter focuses on the recent loan agreement and its possible implications for the DRC.

In uncovering different facets of the China-DRC relationship and the unsuitability of the partner-versus-predator framework, this chapter makes three interrelated points. First, the DRC looms large in the Western imagination. Western understandings of the Congo rely upon earlier powerful images and representations of the Congo as the 'Heart of Darkness',[6] as a place of greed, violence, backwardness and disorder. This representation has endured through to the contemporary period, and the DRC is often constructed in one of two ways: either as a place where external (usually Western) actors need to speak for it, help it and save it from itself, or alternatively, as a place where external actors have brazenly contributed to the chaos and violence. The 'darkened' representation of the Congo has facilitated the simplified categorisations of the role of outside actors, including China, and has contributed to the frequent misreading of Congolese realities.

Second, understanding the China-DRC relationship as one of either predation or partnership ignores the way in which *both* exploitation and cooperation are simultaneous features of that relationship. Furthermore, China itself is changing through its experiences in the DRC and elsewhere in Africa. Viewing China as either a predator or as an alternative kind of partner in solidarity with the Congolese fails to capture how China is taking on new and different roles. For instance, although overshadowed by larger African, European and American commitments, China has contributed to multilateral peace initiatives in the DRC, even as it endeavours to pursue its bilateral relations with the country.

Third, unsurprisingly, there exists a sense of disillusionment in the DRC towards Western donors and diplomats and the development/peace package and post-conflict/post-transition models that they promote and encourage. As such, declarations about emulating the 'Chinese model', together with the enormous influx of money for infrastructural development, have generated considerable excitement and attention among the Congolese political class. The recent China-DRC loan is remarkable in its magnitude and will certainly bring important infrastructural improvements to the country. At the same time, however, the current transition from war in the DRC is firmly anchored in principles and programmes emanating from the Congo's traditional European and American donors, and it is still not clear what the 'Chinese model' means to the Congolese. The extent to which China is able to play its cards as both a new and responsible global power, as well as a southern friend in solidarity with a different approach to development, is yet to be seen in the DRC. The Chinese deal is likely to strengthen some members of the Congolese political class, particularly President Joseph Kabila. It will bring new opportunities for this class and will benefit key actors, but it is unlikely to lead to new patterns of governance and political authority, nor to any fundamental transformation in the nature of politics and development in the DRC. Ultimately, much depends on how the Congolese respond to their circumstances and to renewed Chinese engagement.

EARLIER ENCOUNTERS

Those who champion contemporary Chinese involvement in the continent, including the Chinese government, point to historical connections between China and Africa and emphasise solidarity due to a shared history of underdevelopment and exploitation. China played a different role than Western colonial powers and thus Chinese-African partnerships have different historical contexts. In the 1950s and 1960s, China supported a number of African countries in their liberation struggles and provided educational opportunities and healthcare. Yet the Congolese-Chinese historical relationship has been deeply ambiguous, and Congolese-Chinese friendship has been discontinuous and fragmented.

Upon attaining its independence in 1960, the Congo was deeply caught up in the internecine feud of the Cold-War powers. A badly managed independence process in the Congo, including reprehensible involvement by foreign countries, meant that there was considerable disruption and instability in the country. Both the Soviet Union and China saw this instability as an opportunity to spread their influence.[7]

The Congo's elected prime minister, Patrice Lumumba, received support from both the Soviet Union (USSR) and China. Faced with a Belgian-backed secessionist rebellion in the mineral-rich Katanga province, Lumumba appealed to the UN for help. Initially, the USSR supported this call to the UN, but subsequently both the USSR and China criticised the UN as a vehicle of US imperialism. Chiding the Soviet Union, China's official newspaper, *People's Daily*, stated that 'some naïve people were inclined to believe that the UN intervention could help the Congolese people . . . They did not realize that the US has always used the UN as an instrument for aggression, and that inviting in the UN means letting in US imperialism.'[8]

In September 1960, President Joseph Kasavubu dismissed Prime Minister Lumumba. Lumumba was assassinated in January 1961 and his deputy, Antoine Gizenga, set up a rival government in Stanleyville (now Kisangani) and appealed to China for support.[9] Although China did send financial assistance (£1 million), it did not respond to Gizenga's request for troops and equipment. In essence, while China hoped that a revolutionary base might be established in the Congo, there was a sharp contrast in its publicly declared support for Gizenga and his government, and China's own private expectations. Apparently, Beijing had modest expectations for the Lumumba-Gizenga group, as demonstrated in an official Chinese document: 'The struggle of the Congo people is extensive, severe and heroic, but at present there is no core guidance organized by the workers' class.'[10] All the same, China did recognise Gizenga's government in Stanleyville, and sent representatives to it along with the USSR.

Cooperation between the USSR and China in their support of Gizenga's government was, however, short-lived. This was partly because, despite Chinese disapproval, the USSR convinced Gizenga to join the new moderate government in Leopoldville (Kinshasa). In the event, China withdrew its mission to Stanleyville only two months after it had been set up. At the same time, Beijing refused to establish diplomatic relations with the government in Leopoldville because the government recognised Taiwan, against the One-China policy. As Sino-Soviet relations became tenuous, the two countries denounced each other's policies in the Congo. The Chinese criticised the revolutionary 'lukewarmness of the Soviet Union' and challenged the Soviet idea of peaceful coexistence.[11]

Meanwhile, Congolese politicians continued to vie for control of the country with the help of different external actors. The central Congolese government was very weak and fractured, but after Gizenga's co-option to Leopoldville, China could not find a suitable opposition movement to support.[12] This changed in 1963 when Pierre Mulele, who had spent time in China and who had been education minister in the Lumumba government, launched a guerrilla operation. Mulele based his rebellion on Chinese Maoist principles, and China provided training and supplies from Brazzaville, Burundi and Tanzania. By August 1964, groups of semi-independent movements led by Mulele, Gaston Soumialot and Christophe Gbenye had captured Stanleyville and set up a rebel government there, but ultimately this failed.

At the same time, another opposition group made up of politicians who had been close to Gizenga, as well as dissatisfied politicians in Leopoldville and provincial leaders, set up a government-in-exile in Brazzaville. This group was supported to some extent by both China and the USSR, but it split into factions. China trained some of the Congolese rebels in Congo-Brazzaville, but never fully recognised the government-in-exile.[13]

So, although China was involved in the Congo, its involvement was quite restrained. Its assistance to the rebels was secretive and limited. Why was this the case? Official Chinese statements saw the Congo as a highly promising revolutionary situation, at the forefront of the world struggle against imperialism. If there could be a successful revolution in the Congo, it could also occur elsewhere in Africa. Yet China did not want to embarrass the governments to which it gave its aid and support.[14] Furthermore, China may have been waiting to see if the rebels were capable of being successful before giving further help. It also insisted that revolution could not be exported.[15]

In any case, this early post-independence period showed that there were significant contradictions in China's relations with the Congo. While it employed a language of support and solidarity, this was not matched with any significant commitment. By 1965, China was paying less and less attention to the Congolese rebels. Success in establishing a socialist alternative was not looking very likely, and China had been thrown out of Burundi, which had previously been one of its bases for supporting Congolese rebels.[16] In November 1965, Mobutu Sese Seko seized power in the Congo with the help of the American Central Intelligence Agency (CIA).

The Mobutu period

Relations between the Congo and China went through a number of transformations during the Mobutu period. Connections were initially very cool but evolved alongside changes in the international context. Increasingly, the Congo looked to China as an alternative development model, and China took more and more notice of opportunities in the Congo. The Chinese-Congolese relationship therefore shifted and changed through this period depending on strategic calculations, ideological concerns, international rivalries and alliances, and evolving ideas about appropriate development strategy.[17]

When Mobutu became President of the Congo (renamed Zaire under the new leader), the stage was set for a period of frosty relations between Zaire and China. The Chinese described Mobutu as 'a running dog of imperialism'.[18] Mobutu distrusted China and the USSR due in part to their support of Lumumba in 1960 and the rebels in 1963–65. Nevertheless, some members of Mobutu's administration pushed for normalisation of relations with the USSR and China in order to project an anti-imperialist and non-aligned image. Consequently, the USSR opened an embassy in

Zaire in 1968, but relations remained strained and Mobutu never travelled to the USSR.[19]

In contrast with the continued taut relations between Zaire and the USSR, relations between Zaire and China improved in the 1970s. Propelled by improved relations between Washington and Beijing, Mobutu started to view China as an opportunity to buttress his questionable non-aligned credentials.[20] From the Chinese vantage point, improved relations with Kinshasa were attractive because they had recently lost favour with the authorities in Congo-Brazzaville.[21] Thus, China and Zaire established full diplomatic ties in 1972 and Mobutu made his first state visit to China in January 1973. He subsequently visited China four more times (in 1974, 1980, 1982 and 1994).

Mobutu returned from his first trip in 1973 with a commitment of US$100 million in economic aid for agricultural development and pledges of arms for the Angolan liberation movement that he supported. During his second trip to China in 1974, he was apparently deeply impressed by the contrast between the problems in Zaire and the 'revolutionary discipline' in China and North Korea.[22] The official Congolese press launched attacks on the bourgeoisie, economic liberalism and consumerist society. The Chinese ambassador to Kinshasa received privileged access to Mobutu and he became a trusted diplomatic confidant. These links played an important role in improving Mobutu's image as a Third World leader.[23] By 1975, however, relations between China and Zaire were scaled down, not least because of Zaire's role in the United States's covert operation in the Angolan civil war.[24] Nevertheless, several projects were initiated in this period, including the Chinese-financed construction of the massive National Assembly and Senate building, the Palais du Peuple (Palace of the People).[25]

Zaire-Chinese relations during the Mobutu period were never as important as the strategic relationship between Zaire and Western powers, and Mobutu was careful not to stray too far into areas that were at odds with Western interests. Nonetheless, relations with China did help Mobutu project himself as a Third World leader, and opened the Congolese imagination to the idea that alternative development visions were possible. This is a theme that has been skilfully repackaged in the contemporary context, and is very much present in today's discourse on Chinese-DRC relations. Yet even in this earlier period, Chinese involvement shows a number of different tendencies and ambiguities that are more complicated than the language of external manipulation and exploitation, or mutual solidarity would suggest.

THE CONGOLESE WARS AND THE TRANSITION PERIOD

Congolese-Chinese relations evolved again in the late 1990s, reflecting enormous changes in the two countries. Politics in the DRC during this period was precarious and violent. Following a successful rebellion backed by Rwanda and Uganda, Laurent Kabila took power from Mobutu in May 1997. Kabila had a long relationship with China. He had attended military school in China and had participated in Marxist uprisings in the Congo in the 1960s.[26] In December 1997, President Kabila paid a state visit to China and the two countries signed an agreement on mutual interests and the encouragement of investment.[27]

A new government in the DRC did not mean an end to violent conflict. A second Congolese war was launched in 1998, which eventually involved the armies of eight African countries. Although a peace agreement was signed in Lusaka in 1999, fighting continued in many parts of the country. A UN peacekeeping mission (MONUC) was established and remains in place today.

President Laurent Kabila was assassinated in 2001. His son, Joseph Kabila, succeeded him as president and reinvigorated the peace process, bringing the various Congolese parties involved in the conflict into the negotiations. This eventually led to the signing of a new peace agreement and the establishment of Congolese transitional institutions. With massive support from international donors, the Congo held democratic elections in 2006, in which the incumbent, Joseph Kabila, won the presidency. This marked the official end of the transitional period, but Congolese politics remain extremely tense and volatile.

China was a relatively minor player in the DRC during the wars and transitional period, but its influence and interests continually expanded. China's economy, of course, was growing rapidly in the late 1990s and it searched for resources to fuel its growth. The DRC was notoriously unstable politically, but it also possessed vast quantities of mineral deposits that had long attracted the attention of international, regional and local companies. China thus joined a long list of countries and companies with their eyes on the DRC's resources. Even though there is an argument that Chinese firms tend to be more willing than Western ones to take risks in volatile environments, African, Western and Chinese firms have all shown themselves to be willing to take risks in the DRC, given the attractive potential rewards.

Conflict, commodities and the arms trade in the DRC

Much has been written about the role of natural resources in civil war and the DRC is often used as an illustration of the connections between natural resource extraction, rebel financing, globalisation, the arms trade and the continuation of conflict.[28] For instance, one well-publicised example of the relationship between conflict and natural resources in the DRC was the nature of the coltan trade. The DRC has the world's largest reserves, concentrated in the eastern part of the country. At the time the DRC was engulfed in conflict, there was a boom in the international price of coltan. During this period, Rwandan and Ugandan military and political officials entered into suspect coltan business deals with Western and Chinese companies, usually through a web of subsidiaries and shadowy import-export companies and cover firms.[29] These deals helped to finance the war and enrich key belligerents. Economic motivations for the continuation of conflict became difficult to separate from political ones.

It could, therefore, be argued that Chinese commercial interests helped fuel the Congolese war, but China was by no means alone. Other international, regional and local commercial interests were heavily involved. In fact, a UN report on the illegal exploitation of resources in the Congo mentioned only one Chinese company as being in violation of the Organisation for Economic Cooperation and Development (OECD) guidelines for multinational enterprises, along with 84 non-Chinese companies.[30] In this instance, Chinese business behaviour in the DRC did not seem to be very different from its European and American counterparts. Furthermore, the internationalised nature of trade and exchange in the DRC means that it is very difficult to make meaningful distinctions between various companies and individuals who profited from conflict in the DRC.

China's role in arming various belligerents in the Congolese conflict is a subject of much attention and speculation. The government of Zimbabwe said that China was its main arms supplier in its 1998 war effort in support of Laurent Kabila.[31] More recently however, it appears that Chinese involvement in the arms trade in the DRC has been primarily a business venture, rather than fulfilling any larger political aims. Companies that have arms agreements with the DRC include firms based in China, as well as in the Czech Republic, Bulgaria, Georgia, Ukraine and Zimbabwe.[32] Although a UN arms embargo against all foreign and Congolese armed groups and militias operating in the Kivu provinces and Ituri was put in place in July 2003,[33] it was discovered in November 2005 that the majority of the Kalashnikov assault rifles surrendered by armed groups in Ituri were made in China. Control Arms researchers who visited compounds in Bunia (Ituri) in September 2006 also found Chinese-made assault rifles.[34] It is, however, not known how these arms arrived in eastern Congo, and it is likely that they took a circuitous route.

During the Congolese wars, the responses of the West were heavily informed by perceptions that the Congolese had returned to a prehistoric condition marked by savagery, anarchy and tribalism. At the same time, the image of the Congo as an untapped source of riches was also mobilised. This allowed for relative political disengagement from the Congo (with a loss of confidence in the ability to 'save' Congo) but continued economic extraction.[35] Increasingly though, foreign economic involvement, in which China was a growing participant, was seen in one of two ways. Either, foreign business interests were understood to be operating in a challenging environment but working to unleash the Congo's potential in the name of development, or they were understood to be complicit in predation and exploitation, undermining the efforts of the Congolese to reap the rewards from their own resources. These two views remain very much at play today.

China as peacekeeper and political partner?

During the war, therefore, Chinese business interests behaved in similar ways to their European, American and South African counterparts. What is perhaps more striking was China's political role in the DRC's transitional period, and its willingness to send peacekeeping troops to the UN mission in the DRC (MONUC).

The cornerstones of China's political relationships with African countries are support for sovereignty, non-intervention and South-South bilateral cooperation. In this context, China's participation in the UN peacekeeping mission in the DRC may appear surprising. Indeed, China's role as peacekeeper underlines the complexities and different tendencies that shape Chinese actions on the continent. Despite its emphasis on bilateral relations, as an emerging power, China is eager to enhance its prestige at the global level, and interestingly it has chosen to work within the UN in the DRC on some issues. China has over 1 800 personnel serving in UN peacekeeping missions across the world.[36] Its contribution to MONUC can therefore be seen as part of a wider Chinese effort to show that the country is a responsible member of global society not averse to multilateral action.

China's initial contribution to MONUC was one of its earliest contributions to UN peacekeeping mission operations. In April 2003, China sent 228 military personnel to the DRC as part of MONUC, including 219 troops and 9 military observers. This was a significant number for China, as it only had a total of 323 military personnel serving in UN missions at the time.[37] Since then, China's contribution to MONUC has remained fairly constant (approximately 250 troops) but it has sent even larger numbers of peacekeepers to other UN missions in Africa.[38]

Not only has China sent troops to MONUC, it has also participated in multilateral diplomatic efforts assisting the DRC's transition. China was not a lead player in facilitating the Congo's transition, but it did play a limited role. By virtue of its status as a permanent member of the Security Council, China was a member of the International Committee in Support of the Transition (CIAT) along with the United States, France, the United Kingdom, Belgium, South Africa, Angola, Canada, Russia, the AU and the European Union. The CIAT was chaired by the special representative of the Secretary-General and met on a weekly basis during the transition, sometimes more frequently in periods of crisis. The CIAT's mandate was to assist the transition, including the promotion of democracy and support for the electoral process. Although China did not engage in democracy promotion activities in the DRC, it was a reasonably active member of this committee; it was also a supporter of international standards in the DRC, such as the Millennium Development Goals (MDGs).

China has been criticised for not taking a stronger stance against corruption in the DRC. Critics point to the fact that when the then UN Secretary-General, Kofi Annan, asked the donor community to take a harder stand on corruption in the DRC, this initiative was blocked by Russia, China and Tanzania.[39] Nonetheless, this kind of criticism is disingenuous. Corruption in the DRC has involved countless Western-based firms, some of which are very close to their home governments. Despite the heavy pro-democracy and anti-corruption rhetoric of some of the members of the CIAT, most were very reluctant to confront Kabila in the lead-up to the elections in the DRC. The International Crisis Group (ICG) alleges that CIAT members were anxious to promote their economic interests and even helped companies obtain mining contracts and state tenders from the presidency. One ICG report notes that the United States, Belgium, South Africa and Canada sought control of minerals and tried to restrict China's access.[40] Even though they advocate governance reforms in the DRC, Western countries tend to tread carefully, not least because they want to protect their interests and maintain special relations with President Kabila.

Economic relations in the transitional period

During the transitional period, economic links between China and the DRC grew quickly. Yet in this period, the DRC was not one of China's biggest African trading partners, nor was it one of the top ten African recipients of Chinese aid. Trade data between the DRC and China is unreliable,[41] but according to IMF statistics until 2006, the DRC was a middle-sized African trading partner for China. Official imports rose from US$35 million in 2004 to US$75 million in 2006. Official figures for exports from the DRC to China made a bigger jump. Export figures hovered around the US$1 million mark for much of the 1990s, but started increasing exponentially every year from 2001. Export figures were US$6.6 million in 2001. This increased to US$83 million in 2004 and then to US$334 million in 2006.[42] Compared with trade between China and other African countries (particularly oil-exporting countries), these figures are relatively small. Yet considering that the DRC is not a major oil exporter and that over 50 per cent of China's imports from Africa are oil imports (and that much of the remaining exports come from South Africa), non-oil exports from the DRC to China are significant, and are rising quickly.[43]

Furthermore, when compared with the DRC's traditional trading partners, China is rapidly establishing prominence in the country. According to IMF figures, exports from the DRC to the United States in 2006 were strikingly less than those to China (US$78 million and US$334 million respectively). Exports from the DRC to the European Union were double the amount to China (US$725 compared to US$334 million), and exports to South Africa were also significant (US$400 million).[44] Yet official exports to China are rising at a rapid rate, and there is also a considerable amount of unrecorded unofficial trade.

During the transition, Congolese President, Joseph Kabila, was aware of the opportunities presented by China. In President Kabila's second visit to China – a four-day trip in March 2005 – he reaffirmed his country's support for the One-China policy and for China's anti-secession law. The two countries pledged to enhance bilateral cooperation, including collaboration between their two militaries. At around that time, Beijing-based company Cobec discussed with Eugene Dongala, the Minister of Mines, plans to rehabilitate the Kamatanda copper and cobalt mines and three copper processing plants in Katanga for US$27.5 million.[45]

In April 2005, Feza Mining, a joint venture between the Chinese company Wambao Resources and the Congolese firm COMIDE (with close ties to Kabila), opened a plant in Likasi with production capacity of 4 000 tonnes of cobalt-copper alloys. Chinese expertise also helped to equip the Congolese Sodimico Co. with a furnace to process cobalt and copper.[46] This is in addition to a mine near Lwiswishi (outside Lubumbashi) that produces 4 500 tonnes of cobalt annually (but only employs less than 400 local workers). Nanjing Hanrui Cobalt Co. Ltd, a large conglomerate in China, and one of the top three cobalt powder producers in the world, purchased three high-grade copper-cobalt mines in Lubumbashi in 2006.[47] It is assumed that in order to meet China's voracious demand, the DRC might have to produce an extra 20 000 tonnes of cobalt per year.[48]

It is worth noting that the DRC currently has 40 per cent of the world share in cobalt (used in magnetic alloys for products such as turbines, batteries and steel, as well as inks, paints and varnish). Demand for copper, used in wires, electromagnets and circuit boards, is also likely to continue and some of it may well end up in illicit or unaccounted trading, which was widespread during the Congolese conflict.[49]

Congo-China economic relations were intensifying in other sectors as well. In May 2005, Chinese corporation Sinohydro International put in a tender to build a second power line to stretch 350 km between Inga dam and Kinshasa. Another priority sector is telecommunications. In 2000, China Zhongxing Telecommunications Co. Ltd and the Congolese government used preferential loans from China's Exim Bank to set up the China Telecommunications Co. Ltd in the Congo.[50]

Chinese activities during the Congo wars and transitional period underscore China's growing economic interest in the DRC's natural resources, as well as China's increased tendency to act multilaterally on some issues. The Congolese leadership was receptive to this growing attention from Chinese interests, but China had certainly not displaced or altered the established patterns and practices of traditional donors and international business.

THE CHINESE-DRC SEPTEMBER 2007 AGREEMENT

The September 2007 announcement of the US$8 billion draft agreement between China and the DRC signalled that the DRC was on the verge of becoming one of China's main partners in Africa.[51] Yet while the scale of China's proposed involvement was unprecedented, the nature of that involvement echoed Chinese initiatives elsewhere on the continent. The agreement followed the model of 'infrastructure development resources backed finance' (IDRF) where Chinese infrastructure financing would be provided in return for resources.

The September agreement was conducted between the government of the DRC on the one hand, and a group of Chinese state-owned enterprises (SOEs) on the other (including China's Exim Bank, the China Railway Engineering Company [CREC] and Sinohydro). Essentially, the agreements allow for a US$3 billion loan for mining development, along with other loans from China's Exim Bank to the Chinese companies CREC and Sinohydro, to finance over US$5 billion in infrastructure projects.

CREC will build railway lines and roads, including a 3 200 km railway from Matadi in Bas-Congo to Sakania in Katanga and a 3 200 km road from Kisangani in Orientale province to Kasumbalesa on the border of Zambia. Sinohydro will build power lines and power plants, as well as distribution centres supplying water. More than 30 hospitals will be built, along with 145 health centres, 4 universities, and more than 20 000 housing units.

In return, a Congolese-Chinese joint venture will be created called Socomin (Société Congolaise Minière), headquartered in Beijing. The large state-owned Congolese mining company Gécamines (La Générale des Carrières et des Mines) will hold 32 per cent of the shares of this joint venture company and the Chinese SOEs (CREC and Sinohydro) will hold 68 per cent.[52] These firms will invest US$3 billion in mining. In the first phase, the profits from the new mines will be used to repay the initial US$3 billion mining investment. In the second phase, 66 per cent of the profits will go towards paying off the loans from the Chinese for the first set of infrastructure projects (estimated at US$3 billion). The remaining 34 per cent will be distributed to the shareholders. During these first two phases, the joint venture will not be taxed. In the third phase – the commercial exploitation phase – the joint venture will be taxed according to the Congolese law.[53] During the repayment period, therefore, the joint venture will be exempt from the payment of fees and taxes. It has the right to freely choose equipment providers and to hire qualified personnel.

Advance teams of engineers arrived in the DRC in April 2008, and work on the infrastructural projects was scheduled to begin in June 2008. According to some Congolese mining officials, it could be another three years before the US$3 billion investment into Katanga's mineral reserves will begin,[54] but the CEO of Gécamines, Paul Fortin, believes that work will start in 2008.

Reaction to the agreement has varied. Chinese and Congolese officials spoke of a new era of cooperation and partnership. Others were more cautious, especially given the timing of the September announcement. The agreement was announced when the IMF had arrived in Kinshasa for negotiations to renew budgetary support and to assess the Congolese government's attempt at fiscal and monetary reform.[55] When President Kabila had outlined his economic programme at his inauguration in December 2006, more than half the cost of the 2007–11 programme (US$7.4 billion out of a total of US$14.3 billion) was to come from donors. The IMF's review of the Congolese economy in March 2007 noted that the government had not achieved the macroeconomic targets set in the consolidated programme, so it suspended its payments under the Poverty Reduction and Growth Facility. As a result, many aid infrastructure projects were stalled.[56] While the Congolese transitional government had finalised a Poverty Reduction Strategy Paper (PRSP) before leaving office, implementation was poor and the World Bank and IMF required the PRSP to be implemented for one year before the country qualified for debt relief.[57] The September 2007 loan agreement with China took place in this context.[58] This context helps explain why dealing with China is so appealing to Joseph Kabila's government and other Congolese elites. It also helps explain why the September 2007 agreement generated some concern among Western donors and international financial institutions.

The World Bank, IMF and African Development Bank scrambled to respond to the news of the deal. A headline in the *Financial Times* captured the 'Alarm over China's Congo Deal',[59] and Western embassies in Kinshasa showed great interest and muted concern.[60] Although the Congolese Minister of Mines intimated that the Chinese deal would not affect existing joint ventures, several companies were nervous about the deal in light of the ongoing review of 60 contracts signed during the Congo's civil war.

Possible implications

Does the agreement herald a new era of hope for the DRC? The answer is a cautious yes. On the one hand, the size and scale of the infrastructural projects are enormous, and China has shown that it is committed to starting quickly. Some of these projects are likely to greatly improve the lives of many Congolese, and this is not a negligible point. On the other hand, China will possibly encounter problems as it intensifies its relationship with the DRC. Not surprisingly, some aspects of Chinese involvement in the DRC are already controversial among the Congolese. For instance, the Congo's main textile plant, Utexafrica, was sold in 2004 to a Chinese corporation, and some Congolese consultants believe that this was done in order to undermine the domestic industry and allow Chinese products to flood the country.[61] In addition, there has been an increase in smuggled textile products from China, which some people worry may destroy local production.

Furthermore, many of the details of the various agreements remain unclear. Some Congolese complain about the lack of transparency and the lack of information about the September 2007 deal and follow-up agreements. For instance, there is some debate as to how much Chinese labour will be brought to the DRC for the infrastructure projects. According to one report, only one in five workers can be Chinese,[62] but this has not been publicly confirmed.

This new agreement is not the harbinger of the arrival of a more dangerous predator in the DRC. Yet it is also unlikely to bring about the large-scale transformation proclaimed by some advocates. Chinese-DRC economic exchanges take place in distinctive economic and political national and international contexts. The economic sector is highly personalised and closely linked to politics and security issues. The DRC's banking sector is unreliable, the judiciary is not independent, and key local, regional and international actors benefit from continued uncertainty and insecurity. Congolese patterns of political authority and networks are notoriously resilient, and there are no signs that Chinese involvement is going to have a transformative impact on the nature of the Congolese state.

There are, nonetheless, several possible implications of this landmark agreement. First, it is likely that the intensification of Chinese-Congolese ties and the building of infrastructural projects will strengthen ruling Congolese elites, particularly President Kabila. It will therefore buttress current patterns of political authority in the DRC, rather than transforming or re-centring them. Since the disputed elections in 2006, progress on the reform of the Congolese armed forces has been slow, violent conflict continues in the Kivu provinces in the eastern part of the country, and the President is deeply unpopular in some parts of the country, especially around Kinshasa. Chinese-backed infrastructural development could give the President a much-needed boost in the run-up towards elections in three years' time. As such, Chinese involvement will strengthen President Kabila and other key government figures vis-à-vis opposition members and critics.

Second, the agreement may have consequences for China. Aside from the obvious economic benefits that will accrue from the investments, involvement in the DRC may contribute to changes in China as a global power. China's official development assistance policy is deliberately non-prescriptive. It emphasises equality, mutual benefit, non-intervention and draws on the shared history of China and its African partners as 'Southern' countries. For China, business and economics are separate from politics. Yet any kind of involvement in a country such as the Congo is bound to be political; and despite Chinese claims to the contrary, business (including profit-making business) is deeply political. Similarly, China's involvement in the DRC underscores a willingness to work with multilateral partners, even if the bulk of its links are bilateral ones. In July 2007, when a large group of potential Chinese investors arrived in Kinshasa for talks with government ministers, they came in a delegation with officials from the China-Africa group, as well as officials from the UN who wanted to discuss investment in environmental protection. China may find itself working increasingly closely with the UN and traditional Western (and South African) interests in the DRC. This inevitably will affect how China views itself and the world, and how others view China.

Conclusions

After the second round of elections in the DRC, Joseph Kabila declared that he was inspired by the Chinese success story (and the economic achievements of the other East Asian countries) to launch a Congolese economic take-off. Following his return from the assembly of the African Development Bank held in Shanghai in May 2007, Minister of Finance, Athanase Matenda Kyelu, also added his voice to the debate, arguing that the DRC can 'learn from certain elements within the Chinese development model with a view to increasing growth and reducing poverty'.[63]

Why is the idea of a Chinese development model so appealing to Congolese politicians? First, the image of an imminent Congolese economic take-off is intrinsically attractive. Second, a Chinese model is imbued with a legitimacy that comes from China's own spectacular economic record. Third, there is a strong disenchantment with the West. There is a sense that the West has failed in the DRC and that a Chinese alternative can deliver in its place.

There are, however, several problems with this optimistic view. China itself emphasises the specificity of each case and argues against the universalism of Western liberal democratic models. In any case, according to China, foreigners cannot develop other countries, and certainly not by imposing their own model. It is unclear which aspects of the Chinese development path can be replicated, and at what costs.[64]

The DRC currently faces a myriad of challenges, which have arisen in part from its historical experiences and interactions with outsiders. Democracy is a veneer and despite the show of multiparty elections, the government has retained strong authoritarian tendencies and executive power. Security is elusive, with major fighting in the east and violent tensions in the south. Resentment towards the government is very strong in Kinshasa. Army integration is proceeding slowly and tensions remain high. Resource management in general and mining contracts in particular are opaque and contested.

This is the context into which China has entered as an increasingly important actor. The September US$8 billion agreement is a landmark event for the DRC, and will significantly shape the DRC's economic landscape for years to come. Western donors largely reacted to the agreement with public approval but private concern. Congolese officials largely reacted positively and declared a new period of Congolese growth and reconstruction. Is China a particularly menacing actor due to its enormous need for mineral resources and its reluctance to address governance issues in the DRC? Or, is China a hopeful example of southern solidarity; one which offers a realistic alternative to the long history of devastation, poverty and violence in the DRC? This chapter has argued that both of these views are fatally flawed. The first assumes that other powers in the DRC have behaved benevolently, or at least more benevolently than a resource-thirsty China. The second assumes that resource considerations are secondary to political-humanitarian concerns for China. On the contrary, this chapter has shown that the present and the past are characterised by a range of motives and considerations governing the nature and type of Chinese-Congolese engagement, which cannot be neatly categorised and ranked alongside equally complex Western motives.

The DRC has long suffered from the inequities of the global system and the hypocrisy surrounding much of the discourse on development. China is now a full member of the global economy, and part of its concerns focus on maintaining favourable systems of exchange, as well as enhancing its prestige. Although China has extricated itself from the burden of a 'civilising mission', there is no reason to believe that this has freed it from exploitative practices. In the DRC, exploitation has often been couched in alluring messages of solidarity and humanitarian concern.[65]

This is not, however, to say that China is a menacing predator and the DRC a passive victim. Increased Chinese activity in the DRC will be embedded in a well-anchored, resilient system of personalised political exchange. Chinese engagement in the Congo has the possibility of benefiting some Congolese, but also the possibility of perpetuating harmful practices and networks established by European and American forerunners. Despite improvements in infrastructure, Chinese money may contribute to the resilience of the links between external capital and a disregard for the population in the DRC. Yet this is not inevitable, and while it would be a mistake to assume that China and other outside powers will be the catalysts for progressive change, one must hope that they will not thwart any Congolese effort to engage in a different kind of politics.

NOTES

1. Quoted in P.M Wete, *L'Observateur RDC*, 29 January 2008.
2. Quoted in B.D. Larkin, *China and Africa, 1949–1970: The Foreign Policy of the People's Republic of China* (Berkeley, CA: University of California Press, 1970), p. 72 and A. Hutchison, *China's African Revolution* (London: Hutchinson, 1975), p. 111.
3. The Democratic Republic of Congo has changed its name several times. Following independence in 1960, it was called Republic of Congo. This changed to Democratic Republic of Congo in 1964 to distinguish it from its neighbour (Republic of Congo-Brazzaville). President Mobutu renamed the country in 1971 to Zaire. Laurent Kabila reverted the country name back to the Democratic Republic of Congo when he became President in 1997.
4. There is, however, no independent confirmation of this quote from Mao Zedong.
5. For instance, on 11 October 2007, a protocol agreement (for an unfixed amount of money) on financing development and co-operation was signed with the Chinese Development Bank. One of the first planned

projects is the construction of a highway linking the airport to downtown Kinshasa. Subsequent phases will focus on agriculture and telecommunications. On 28 January 2008, a preferential loan agreement for US$35 million was signed for the modernisation of the Office Congolais des Postes et des Télécommunications. At the same time, a convention of collaboration between the Congolese Ministry of Infrastructure, Public Works and Reconstruction and three Chinese companies was signed, drawing on the September 2007 draft agreement.

6. This is the title of a famous novel by Joseph Conrad, first published in *Blackwood's Magazine*, 1899.
7. Hutchison, *China's African Revolution*, p. 29.
8. *People's Daily,* 25 November 1960, quoted in Hutchison, *China's African Revolution*, p. 30.
9. The resilience of the political class in the DRC is witnessed by the fact that 82-year-old Antoine Gizenga is currently the prime minister of the DRC. He was appointed by President Joseph Kabila in December 2006.
10. Larkin, *China and Africa*, pp. 55–56.
11. Hutchison, *China's African Revolution*, pp. 31–33.
12. Hutchison, *China's African Revolution*, p. 111.
13. Document of the Quartier Général de l'Armée Nationale Congolaise, March 1965 (Congo 1965) p. 283. This document says that there were over 100 Chinese in Congo-Brazzaville (50 at the embassy), including some specialised instructors.
14. This is suggested by Hutchison, *China's African Revolution*, pp. 110–11.
15. Larkin, *China and Africa*, p. 73.
16. China was thrown out of Burundi in January 1965 after being accused of supporting the Republican Trade Union Movement in that country.
17. For instance, the China-United States rivalry and China-USSR rivalry continued to have consequences for Chinese engagement in Africa. China believed that both the United States and the USSR were the root causes of Africa's blight. G. Yu, 'China and the Third World', *Asian Survey* 17(11), 1977: 1041.
18. Congo 1965, p. 455, quoted in C. Young and T. Turner, *The Rise and Decline of the Zairian State* (Madison: University of Wisconsin Press, 1985), p. 57 fn. 22.
19. A trip was planned in 1974, but Mobutu went to China instead.
20. Young and Turner, *The Rise and Decline of the Zairian State*, p. 370. United States President, Richard Nixon, visited China that year, so Congolese relations with China would no longer arouse hostility on the part of the Americans.
21. In late 1972, Chinese authorities had been involved in the Diawara conspiracy in Congo-Brazzaville.
22. When he returned from his trip, Mobutu announced the adoption of a ten-point radicalisation programme. He discussed ten plagues afflicting Zairian society and the corresponding remedies. For instance, one 'plague' was the agricultural crisis and the remedy was to raise food output. Another 'plague' was social problems and the remedy was to abolish the Ministry of Social Affairs and assign all social functions to his wife. Young and Turner, *The Rise and Decline of the Zairian State*, pp. 350–53.
23. Young and Turner, *The Rise and Decline of the Zairian State*, p. 371.
24. When the MPLA was installed in Angola, this was a defeat for Zaire and its aspirations to be a regional power. It was also a defeat for China.
25. This was built between 1975 and 1979 at a cost of $US42 million. Other Chinese projects in Zaire at this time included rice production schemes, cattle projects and Chinese medical teams. See G. Eadie and D.M. Grizzell, 'China's Foreign Aid, 1975–1978', *The China Quarterly* 77, March 1979: 217–34.
26. In 1967, Kabila founded the People's Revolutionary Army in South Kivu province and received arms and

financial support from China. He stayed in South Kivu until 1988 and later returned in 1996 to conduct the rebellion against Mobutu's forces.

27. Yet several of the ambitious Chinese projects that were announced when Laurent Kabila was sworn in never materialised during his presidency, such as the construction of a network of highways throughout the Congo. SouthScan, 'China Scoops up Minerals, Infrastructure Contracts' (London: 30 June 2005).
28. See, for instance, P. le Billon, 'The Geopolitical Economy of Resource Wars', *Geopolitics* 9(1), 2004; D. Renton, D. Seddon, and L. Zeiling, *The Congo: Plunder and Resistance* (London: Zed Books, 2007); M. Duffield, 'Transborder Trade and War Economies', in M. Berdal and D. Malone (eds.), *Greed and Grievance: Economic Agendas in Civil Wars* (Boulder, CO: Lynne Rienner, 2001); I. Samset, 'Conflict of Interests or Interests in Conflict?: Diamonds and the War in the DRC', *Review of African Political Economy* 29(93), 2002: 4.
29. See B. Aust and W. Jaspers, *From Resource War to 'Violent Peace': Transition in the Democratic Republic of Congo (DRC)* (Bonn: Bonn International Centre for Conversion, 2006), p. 93. See also J. Cuvelier and T. Raeymaekers, *European Companies and the Coltan Trade* (Antwerp: International Peace Information Service, 2002).
30. United Nations, 'Final Report of the Panel of Experts on the Illegal Exploitation of Natural Resources and Other Forms of Wealth in the Democratic Republic of Congo', 16 October 2002, paragraphs 79–82. The report says that a company called Eagle Wings (based in Rwanda, but a subsidiary of Trinitech International of Ohio) sold coltan to Ningxia Non-Ferrous Metals Smeltery processing plant in China. A number of brokers trading in coltan confirmed that coltan from the area did go to the Chinese plant, even though the Chinese firm denied the allegations. Yet Ningxia's public relations' staff said that the reason their price was so low was because they received low-cost coltan from central Africa.
31. BBC News, 'Zimbabwe Names Backers in Congo War', 7 January 1999.
32. Amnesty International, International Action Network on Small Arms and Oxfam International, *Control Arms: The Call for Tough Arms Controls, Voices from the Democratic Republic of Congo*, January 2006.
33. This did not include the armed forces of the Congolese government (UN Security Council Resolution 1493).
34. There were also other small arms and bullets from Greece, Russia, South Africa, Serbia and the United States. Oxfam Press Release, 16 October 2006; see also D. Fruchart, 'United Nations Arms Embargoes: Their Impact on Arms Flows and Target Behaviour: Case Study: Democratic Republic of Congo 2003–2006' (Stockholm: Stockholm International Peace Research Institute, 2007) and K. Mwanawavene, B. Bahete and Nasibu-Bilali, *Trafics d'Armes: Enquête de Terrain au Kivu (RDC)* (Brussels: GRIP, 2006).
35. For an excellent discussion of these processes, see K. Dunn, *Imagining the Congo: The International Relations of Identity* (New York: Palgrave Macmillan, 2003). See also D. Johnson and C. Kayser, 'Democratic Republic of Congo: Shadow Economies in the "Heart of Darkness"' in M. Basedau and A. Mehler (eds.), *Resource Politics in Sub-Saharan Africa* (Hamburg: Institute for African Affairs, 2005).
36. All peacekeeping contribution figures come from http://www.un.org (accessed on 10 September 2007).
37. This number included 65 Chinese civilian police to UNMISET in East Timor (Timor Lente).
38. For instance, in March 2008, China had 218 troops and 16 military observers as part of MONUC.
39. Nineteenth report of the Secretary-General on the United Nations Organisation Mission in the Democratic Republic of the Congo, UNSC S/2005/603, 26 September 2005. See also International Crisis Group, 'A Congo Action Plan', *Africa Briefing* 34 (19 October 2005) and Aust and Jaspers, *From Resource War to 'Violent Peace'*, p. 48.
40. International Crisis Group, 'Congo: Consolidating the Peace', *Africa Report* 128, 5 July 2007: 3.

41. There is enormous discrepancy in the figures for trade between China and the DRC. One example of the unreliability of statistics is that, according to the International Crisis Group, official Congolese export and Chinese import statistics in the cobalt and copper trade in April and May 2004 show a tenfold difference, probably due to customs fraud. International Crisis Group, 'Katanga: Congo's Forgotten Crisis', *Africa Report* 128, 9 January 2006: 9.
42. International Monetary Fund (IMF), Direction of Trade Statistics (DOTS) 2007, ESDS International, (MIMAS) University of Manchester.
43. The most significant oil and gas finds in the DRC have been offshore, but these are limited and do not involve oil exports to China. For a list of companies, see Mbendi profile, http://www.mbendi.co.za/indy/oilg/af/zr/p0005.htm.
44. All figures are from the International Monetary Fund (IMF), Direction of Trade Statistics (DOTS) 2007, ESDS International, (MIMAS) University of Manchester.
45. SouthScan, 'China Scoops up Minerals, Infrastructure Contracts'.
46. SouthScan, 'China Scoops up Minerals, Infrastructure Contracts'.
47. M. Chan-Fishel, 'Environmental Impact: More of the Same?' *Pambazuka News*, 14 December 2006.
48. BBC News, 'Chinese Demand Boosts DR Congo Mines', 16 March 2005.
49. One report showed how artisan miners for cobalt sell to middlemen who then sell to foreigners, mostly from China and India, who have furnaces in nearby towns in Katanga. These are apparently exported to China through South Africa or Zambia. According to a 2005 BBC report, the Congolese Ministry of Mines says that monthly exports of copper and cobalt range from 5 500–9 000 tonnes, but one transport operator says that trucks overloaded with raw and concentrated copper and cobalt leave every day. The transport operator said that 65 per cent of those trucks were loaded by Chinese businessmen (BBC News, 'Chinese Demand Boosts DR Congo Mines').
50. Congo-China Telecom (of which China owns 51 per cent) now plans to install a new Internet network. V. Niquet, '*La Stratégie Africaine de la Chine*', *Politique Etrangère* 2, 2006.
51. The text was signed on 17 September 2007. This was followed by additional negotiations in November and December 2007. After a visit by the governor of the Exim Bank in January 2008, a further agreement was signed (D. Munsala Buakasa, *L'Observateur RDC*, 29 January 2008).
52. Article 4, *Texte du Contrat entre la République Démocratique du Congo et la Chine, Ministère des Infrastructure, Travaux Publics et Reconstruction*, 17 September 2007.
53. Articles 5 and 6, *Texte du Contrat entre la République Démocratique du Congo et la Chine*.
54. 'Checking the Assets', *Africa-Asia Confidential* 1(3), January 2008: 1.
55. The donors' conference that had been scheduled for March 2007 was postponed until October 2007.
56. 'The Bashing of Bemba', *Africa Confidential*, 13 April 2007: 8–9.
57. International debt servicing constitutes nearly one-third of government expenditure.
58. Part of the problem was that Kabila's government has been democratically elected, so it is no longer classed as 'emerging from conflict' and it is, therefore, expected to maintain high governance standards. When the DRC was previously classed as 'emerging from conflict', qualifications for aid and credit from Western donors had been less stringent ('More Fighting, More Aid', *Africa Confidential*, 7 September 2007: 3).
59. W. Wallis and R. Bream, 'Alarm over China's Congo Deal', *Financial Times*, 19 September 2007.
60. *Africa-Asia Confidential* 1(1), 2 November 2007, reported that all of the European Union embassies were asked to produce strategy papers on the likely effect of the proposed Chinese investment.
61. SouthScan, 'China Scoops up Minerals, Infrastructure Contracts'.

62. J. Vandaele, 'China Outdoes Europeans in Congo', Interpress Service, 8 February 2008.
63. Xinhua News Agency, 21 May 2007.
64. At least one author attributes this to racist beliefs and thinks that the absence of a Chinese 'civilising mission' is because access to Chinese civilisation (for barbarians) is unthinkable. See Niquet, '*La Stratégie Africaine de la Chine*', *Politique Etrangère* 2: 364.
65. King Leopold's 'project' immediately comes to mind.

6

All's Fair in Loans and War

The Development of China-Angola Relations

Lucy Corkin

INTRODUCTION

In 2005, Angola experienced difficulties in securing public financing as a result of being disqualified by international financial institutions (IFIs) due to poor standards of governance and transparency. In the event, China was regarded as a welcome alternative loan source to a country desperately in need of the financial means to rebuild a war-torn economy. For China's part, cultivating relations with Angola, the second largest African oil-producing country after Nigeria, was particularly important in terms of potential oil exploration contracts to ensure energy security. Suffice to say, as China increases its diplomatic and commercial presence on the African landscape, one of the most strategic Sino-African partnerships to have emerged has been the strengthening ties between China and Angola.

Unsurprisingly, the rapid entry of China's state-owned enterprises (SOEs) into several key sectors of the Angolan economy has met with increasing criticism, as it is feared that the closed-door nature of such bilateral negotiation will do little to encourage accountability and will erode what little leverage Western donors possess vis-à-vis engaging the Angolan government. Recent developments, however, such as the collapse of negotiations on the proposed Sinopec-Sonangol joint venture to build a US$3 billion oil refinery in Lobito, and Angola's ascension to the Organisation of Petroleum Exporting Countries (OPEC) as a fully fledged member, suggest that Angola is enjoying a new-found sense of political and economic leverage, as a result of the rising global demand for oil. What follows suggests that while the Angolan government is a long way from ensuring the transparent management of the country's natural resources, it seems that the potential for economic self-determination has been realised, setting a potential precedent for Africa's future engagement with China in particular and the global economy in general.

AN OVERVIEW OF CHINA-ANGOLA RELATIONS

Prior to the establishment of official diplomatic ties between the People's Republic of China (PRC) and the Republic of Angola in 1983, China and Angola had a long political association. After initially supporting the Popular Movement for the Liberation of Angola (MPLA) in the 1960s and 1970s, when China sought to export its 'people's revolution', Beijing switched its support to the National Union for the Total Independence of Angola (UNITA) during the Angolan civil war. This occurred after Moscow-Beijing relations soured and China embarked on an effort to counter the Soviet Union's strong influence in Angola through its support of the MPLA.

This particular African foray proved somewhat embarrassing for China, as it ended up backing the same side as sworn Cold-War enemies, the United States and apartheid South Africa.[1] It is likely this led to the delayed establishment of official diplomatic ties between Angola and China.[2] Eventually, the Joint Communiqué on the Establishment of Diplomatic Relations between the Government of the People's Republic of China and the Government of the Republic of Angola was ratified on 12 January 1983, although the Chinese embassy was not opened until the late 1980s, and for many years was kept at arm's length by the Angolan government.

Evidently in defiance of Beijing's One-China policy, but possibly due in part to Angola's desperate need for external funding following a dip in global oil prices, Luanda made efforts to establish diplomatic relations with Taiwan in the early 1990s. It sent several diplomatic missions to the island – to no avail. That this initiative failed may be partly due to the increased diplomatic efforts by the PRC towards Angola, for it was around this time that oil imports became one of China's economic imperatives, since it became a net oil importer in 1993. With increased commercial cooperation between Angola and China, Taiwanese diplomatic efforts towards Angola have disappeared.

The oil-backed loan agreement

On 21 March 2004, China's Export-Import (Exim) Bank extended an oil-backed US$2 billion credit line to the Angolan government. The first tranche was payable in September 2004 and the second in March 2005.[3] The loan was doubled to US$4 billion on 20 June 2006,[4] rendering China the biggest player in Angola's post-war reconstruction process.

In May 2007, an additional US$500 million was negotiated to assist with 'complementary actions'. This, according to a representative of the Angolan Ministry of Finance, encompasses further incidental expenditures that will facilitate the integration of the newly built infrastructural projects into the national economy. This includes, for example, the purchase of school buses to transport children to the newly constructed schools planned for the interior provinces.[5]

Overall, the loan is intended to assist Angola in the rebuilding of vital infrastructure and is managed by the Angolan Ministry of Finance. The loan, which operates like a current account held in China under the name of the Angolan government, is paid directly to the Chinese companies responsible for the construction work. As may be expected, the loan has placed China in a favourable position with the Angolan government, especially as a much smaller amount of oil must be put up for collateral, as compared to traditional, expensive oil-backed loans.[6]

This agreement is significant, particularly because Angola had been experiencing difficulties securing capital from international financial institutions, such as the Paris Club and the International Monetary Fund (IMF). Although negotiating from a rather weak position, Angola was loath to submit to external pressure regarding good governance and transparency, particularly as the Angolan government felt that these preconditions for financial assistance were unreasonable. After all, its present circumstances differ from those of the early 1990s, when oil prices were ebbing and the Dos Santos regime was slightly more vulnerable to external pressure. By contrast, however, in 2004, global oil prices were on the rise, due in part to China's increasing demand. This placed Angola's government in a stronger position vis-à-vis the IFIs, particularly when the prospect of financing from an alternative source emerged.

However, tied to China's Exim Bank loan is the agreement that 70 per cent of the public tenders for the construction and civil engineering contracts tabled for Angola's reconstruction will be awarded to Chinese enterprises approved by Beijing.[7] The remaining 30 per cent has been allocated to the Angolan private sector to encourage local participation in the reconstruction process. In exchange for the loan, payable at Libor plus 1.5 per cent over seventeen years, including a grace period of five years, China has secured 10 000 barrels of oil per day from Angola. The price of the oil is also the spot market price of the day, which, in the current oil climate, assists with Angola's debt amortisation.

As the loan is a government-to-government initiative, it is not classified as private investment. Consequently, Chinese companies tendering for contracts financed by China's Exim Bank loan do not have to register with the Angolan National Agency for

Private Investment (ANIP). Instead, the projects financed by the loan fall under a Programme of Public Investments (PIP) in the sectors of public works, health, energy and water, agriculture, telecommunications, the fishing industry, and education.

According to the Angolan Ministry of Finance, the projects allocated to each sector are managed by their respective ministries, while the Ministry of Finance coordinates the process of fund allocation. Consequently, applications for projects to be financed by the loan are submitted by the various ministries under the guidance of the Presidency. According to the Chinese Economic Counsellor in Angola, Chang Hexi, the fund is managed through a cooperation agreement between the Angolan Ministry of Finance and the Chinese Ministry of Foreign and Commercial Affairs (MOFCOM). Nevertheless, projects are determined by the Angolan government, which must then present a proposal to the joint committee of MOFCOM and the Angolan Ministry of Finance before it can be put out to tender. According to various observers from civil society, however, the Presidency has the overriding power regarding where the money is allocated.

China's Exim Bank has increased the amount for the oil-backed loan to Angola several times, as a result of which, the Angolan Ministry of Finance is currently managing a US$4 billion loan package from Beijing. According to the Organisation for Economic Cooperation and Development (OECD), US$1.8 billion of the original US$2 billion loan from China's Exim Bank had been spent by April 2006.[8] Additional loans from the China International Fund Ltd (CIF), a Hong-Kong-based fund management company, have been placed under the auspices of the Gabinete de Reconstrucção Nacional (GRN),[9] headed by General Helder Vieira Dias 'Kopelipa'. Kopelipa is also Minister-in-Chief of the Presidency. The GRN was created specially to manage the Chinese credit line and the large construction projects it was to finance. The result of such a structure is that the funds from the PRC loan are centrally controlled by the Angolan Presidency. Thus the non-governmental organisation (NGO), Global Witness, has raised concerns about the transparency of the procurement process of construction tenders managed by GRN.[10] It is worth noting that the loans managed by GRN were speculated to be in excess of US$9 billion,[11] spurring the Angolan Ministry of Finance in October 2007 to publicly declare that the loans from the CIF amounted to only US$2.9 billion.[12]

Because the China-Angola financial agreement takes the form of an oil-backed loan, Chinese involvement in the Angolan economy is not direct investment in the traditional sense. However, a representative from the Angolan Chamber of Commerce and Industry suggested that the loan still involves capital risk through the potential for loan defaulting, as it is a sizeable sum that is being made available to a developing African country. Apparently, China is also the only country to have made such amounts of money available to the Angolan government. Nonetheless, the Chinese loan provides the means and the momentum for Angola to finance the rebuilding of its infrastructure, which can be seen as a long-term investment in terms of business facilitation, especially where the improvement of transport networks is concerned.

In this way China is beginning to encroach on the IFIs' traditional domain of influence and their potential control of domestic policy and affairs of debtor nations. Evidently, the nature of the loan, with its very low interest rate and policy of domestic non-interference, makes the Chinese government an attractive lender; it also has implications for the donor community and its diminishing leverage on enforcing policies of governmental transparency. Basically, the traditional sources of loans, the World Bank and the IMF, have been less than forthcoming with large-scale, long-term loans, as the Angolan government has not fulfilled the prerequisites of transparency and practices of good governance. Angola, albeit through lack of political will, is still struggling to implement the governance practices that are deemed necessary by Western donors before such loans are granted. The emergence of China as an alternative source of funding has been particularly welcome, considering the paucity of options available to the Angolan government and the urgent need for such funds.[13] In view of this, China is increasingly being viewed as an important strategic ally, as the credit line, unlike other financing from the World Bank and IMF, has no political conditions. Furthermore, since the funds from this loan do not enter the Angolan banking system, access to the transactions and the participation of third parties is very limited.

Further illustrating the consolidation of Sino-Angolan commercial engagement, Angola briefly became the primary source of crude oil imports to China in March 2006, having shipped 2.12 million tonnes of crude to China in February, surpassing Saudi Arabia, the global leader in crude oil exports.[14] Angola again cursorily returned to its position as China's main oil producer after its exports increased 40 per cent in May 2006.[15] Forty-five per cent of Angola's oil exports are destined for China, supplying 15 per cent of China's total oil imports.[16]

On 21 June 2006, during an official state visit by PRC Premier Wen Jiabao to Angola, the two countries further cemented political and economic relations, issuing a joint communiqué detailing the signing of additional agreements and legal documents on bilateral cooperation in the economic, technological, judicial, health and agricultural sectors. Premier Wen was accompanied by the president of China's Exim Bank, Li Ruogu, to discuss the allocation of the loaned funds and to review the infrastructural projects already completed by the Chinese companies at the time of Premier Wen's visit. In September 2007, Li Ruogu visited Angola again in order to assess the progress on the projects financed by the bank's loan. In a meeting with Angolan President, Eduardo dos Santos, the Exim Bank president concluded a further loan agreement of US$2 billion, to be used in additional large-scale infrastructural projects in Angola.[17]

CHINA AND ANGOLA'S GROWING COMMERCIAL TIES

As represented in Figure 6.1, the two countries' bilateral trade has seen a significant increase in recent years. The trade volume between Angola and China in 2006 was US$11.8 billion, of which China's exports to Angola were US$894 million, while Angola exported resources to the value of US$10.9 billion to China, of which 99.9 per cent was crude oil. These figures render Angola China's largest trading partner in Africa, representing roughly one-fifth of China's trade with the African continent.[18]

China is generally favoured for goods and services, construction and electronics, according to ANIP,[19] yet despite a leap in Chinese exports to Angola, China has

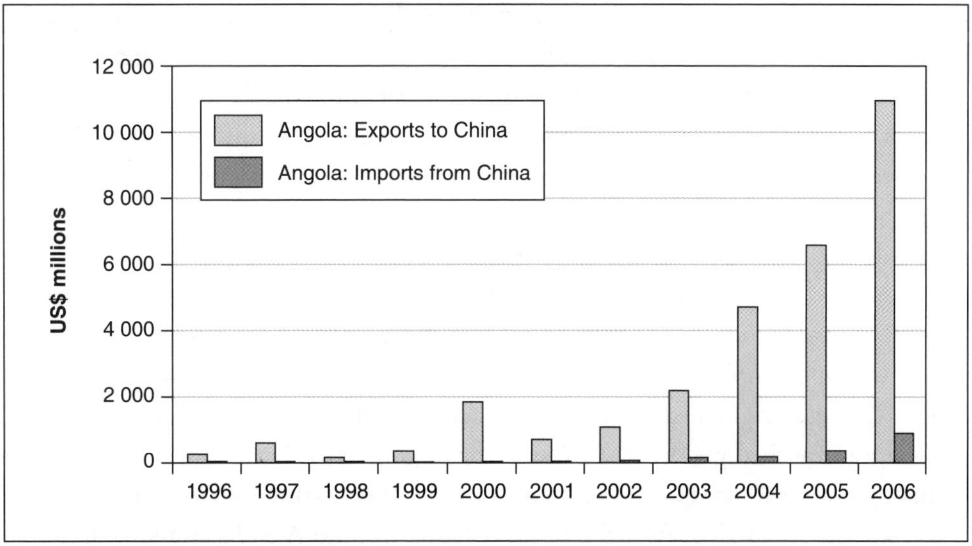

Figure 6.1 Angola: Value of trade with China, 1996–2006.

continued to run a considerable trade deficit with Angola, due to the rapidly rising rate of oil importation from the African country. It is instructive to note that Angola is one of the few countries in Africa to enjoy a trade surplus with China.

Angola carries a growing trade surplus with China, not only due to increasing oil exports but also because only a small percentage of its imports originate from China (8.5 per cent), relative to Chinese import levels in other African countries.[20] While Asian partners have increasingly become large sources of imports since 2007, it is South Korea, and not China, that is a favoured import origin.[21] Nevertheless, as mentioned previously, while China's absolute share of imports is small, the growth in these imports is considerable. In 2006, imports from China reportedly grew 139 per cent from 2005 levels, which may soon render China one of Angola's largest import partners; if import growth levels continue at such a rate, they will supersede import growth from Portugal.[22]

Connected to this is the development of trader communities on Angola's borders, such as that in Oshikango, in northern Namibia, which is a phenomenon not unique to Angola. Chinese traders have for years been trading out of relatively secure Uganda in order to access the potentially lucrative markets in the Democratic Republic of Congo (DRC) and Sudan, which, like Angola, have limited transport networks due to civil conflict. Essentially, poor transport infrastructure isolated areas outside Luanda from the domestic market and import supply chains, providing a niche for cross-border trade between Namibia and Angola that functions like a duty-free zone.[23] The tightening up of customs regulations and the weakening dollar have reportedly since dampened such trade.[24] Consequently, it is possible that Chinese entrepreneurs who previously traded over the border have since relocated to Angola itself. Furthermore, anecdotal evidence suggests that 'under the radar trade' in the informal economy has increased in terms of micro-enterprise Chinese retail stores. Previously only concerned with wholesale on Angola's borders, it seems that Chinese traders are involved in both wholesale and retail in Angola: more research is, however, required to ascertain the trend and development of their supply networks. Much of this trade is not regulated. Indeed, official figures do not seem to capture the increase in the quantity of Chinese products. For example, there is no data tracing the importation of goods that come from a Chinese original equipment manufacturer (OEM) that have been repackaged as European finished goods. The same is true of goods that have been imported from China by European companies and redirected to Angola, thus possibly distorting the reality of import origins. As a result, an increase in Sino-Angolan trade in terms of Chinese imports does not reflect an increase in Chinese imports to Angola. What is evident is an instance of more direct trade, cutting out trading middlemen in Dubai, South Africa or Europe so that Chinese imports come straight from Chinese ports to Angolan markets.

Investments and joint ventures

According to an estimate by a senior official at ANIP, 99 per cent of Chinese companies' activity is state-owned and directed by the Chinese credit line. As such, the Chinese government's credit line, despite being the reason for much Chinese commercial activity in Angola, does not constitute direct investment in the conventional sense. Despite a paucity of private Chinese investment, ANIP is confident that this will grow over the short term, with private Chinese firms being attracted to the high activity of other Chinese firms in Angola due to the credit line.

Indeed, it is already occurring: companies that entered Angola on the Chinese credit line have returned following the completion of their projects to register formally with ANIP. China Jiangsu International, one of only two Chinese companies registered with ANIP, entered the Angolan market through the Chinese credit line. The company, currently engaged in constructing the Palacio de Justiço and housing projects in Cabinda through the Chinese credit line, is now looking for private-sector contracts. Thus, while the Chinese credit line does not circulate in the Angolan financial system – preventing any knock-on effect for Angolan banks – it is estimated that in time, the credit line that has spearheaded Chinese entry will allow an estimated US$2 billion of private investment into the Angolan economy.[25]

Chinese investment in Angola is primarily located in the telecommunications infrastructure and extractive industry sectors, particularly oil. In the telecommunications sector, Mundo Startel, the Angolan fixed-line telecommunications utility, has signed a framework agreement with the Chinese company, ZTE Corporation International, for the purchase of telecommunications equipment. The agreement signalled the start of new business operations in Angola, as Mundo Startel began constructing the physical infrastructure for its network, which was launched in 2006. ZTE Corporation is to invest US$400 million in the Angolan telecommunications industry. This investment will be used for the construction of Angola Telecom's network; improvements to Angola's military telecommunications system; the construction of a mobile telephone factory; the creation of a telecommunications institute for the training of Angolan staff; and the creation of a telecommunications research laboratory. This deal seems to be the only concrete form of military cooperation between China and Angola.[26]

The most important and tangible form of China-Angola commercial cooperation is a joint venture between Sinopec and Sonangol to form Sonangol-Sinopec International (SSI). This joint venture is currently the largest and clearest example of foreign direct investment (FDI) as most of the Chinese construction companies that have won tenders have yet to carry out their expressed intentions to establish joint ventures with local partners.[27] The joint-venture holding, announced in March 2006, reported that Sonangol's share was 45 per cent and Sinopec's 55 per cent.

The joint venture owns 20 per cent of Angola's block 15. SSI made the largest bid in May 2006 to develop Angola's oil blocks 17 and 18,[28] with collective reserves of approximately four billion barrels totalling at least US$2.4 billion, including US$1.1 billion in signature bonuses for each block and US$100 million in 'social projects'. In June 2006, it was announced that SSI had secured stakes in blocks 17 and 18, financed by a consortium of banks, including the Agricultural Bank of China, Bank of China, China Construction Bank and Exim Bank, Bayerische Landesbank, BNP Paribas, Calyon, ING Groep, KBC Groep, Natexis, Banques Populaires, Societé Generale and Standard Chartered. According to expectations, oil production was boosted by 100 000 barrels per day after they came on stream in 2007. Through SSI, Sinopec thus acquired the stakes of 27.5 per cent, 40 per cent and 20 per cent in the offshore blocks 17, 18 and 15 respectively through its joint venture with Sonangol.[29]

In addition to oil exploration, SSI intended to develop a new refinery at Lobito, requiring a total investment of US$3.5 billion. Sonangol held 70 per cent shares in this project, while Sinopec held the remaining 30 per cent. Work on the refinery, Angola's second such refinery, was supposed to begin before the end of 2007. The project, named Sonaref, was estimated to have a total capacity of approximately 240 000 barrels per day when on full stream, almost tripling the capacity of Angola's current refinery. SSI planned to take on the entire capital of each of the new concessions and proposed to drill ten test wells but this did not materialise. The announcement in March 2007 that the negotiations around the construction of the Sonaref-SSI joint venture had collapsed poses some interesting questions regarding the developing dynamics surrounding Angola's oil reserves, and particularly Angola's burgeoning relationship with China. Apparently, SSI talks unravelled over a disagreement regarding the target markets for the proposed Sonaref refinery's products,[30] 80 per cent of which the Chinese partner wanted to go to the export market. Meanwhile, Angola's domestic market regularly suffers shortages of oil by-products, not least because there is a refining capacity shortage in Angola, as only 40 000 of the 1.4 million barrels Angola produces per day can be refined by Angola's current refinery. As such, Angola imports 70 per cent of its derivatives needs. In addition, the chemical composition of products exported to China is different to that of products consumed locally, rendering inflexible the refinery's proportional output of export and local market consumption.

Sonangol has since announced that it will develop the refinery alone and has stepped up plans to 'Angolanise' the extractive sector by encouraging local companies to become more involved in the oil industry.[31] To maximise the objectives of the project, Angola plans to sell to the rest of Africa – not to an entirely overseas market. At any rate, many potential investors have doubted the project's financial viability and raised concerns about the risks that the project exposes the investor to, in view of threats of oil price fluctuations.

In essence, the dynamics of these negotiations point to the fact that Sino-Angolan relations are directed by commercial imperatives, and that contrary to popular opinion Chinese investors are risk averse, and will only invest in projects that they believe will show returns, albeit on a longer-term basis than typical multinational oil majors. With regard to the Angolan government, on the other hand, the indications are that the Dos Santos Presidency will go to some length to preserve a sense of national sovereignty. In other words, the Angolan government does not, it seems, feel obligated to China and refuses to relinquish strategic control over its oil resources to a foreign owner. The collapse of the planned Lobito refinery project, for example, is indicative of the fact that Sonangol refused to concede to the (at the time) majority foreign-owned stakeholder, Sinopec.[32] This has to be seen in the context of the fact that the Lobito refinery was a long-term dream of the Angolan government and that it was reported to have experienced difficulty in finding sufficient financing for the project.[33]

THE IMPACT OF CHINA'S ENGAGEMENT WITH ANGOLA

The economic impact of Chinese engagement

Concerns have been expressed that there is insufficient Angolan participation in the steadily growing number of projects funded by the Chinese. The 30 per cent provision of the Chinese government credit line for Angolan contractors is supposed to address this, but this is possibly not adequately enforced. This is particularly salient considering the reluctance of Chinese companies to enter into joint ventures with their Angolan counterparts.[34] While there are some Sino-Angolan commercial partnerships, it seems that the majority of these are with *empresas de confiança*,[35] so that the Chinese company can benefit from the former's political connections, which does little to encourage bottom-up growth. Questions have also been raised about the employment opportunities created by these ventures for Angolan workers. There are concerns, for example, that Angolan labourers are employed only on a casual basis to avoid the country's inflexible labour-law regime. As a new tranche of credit is being negotiated, it seems that the Angolan government may attempt to re-emphasise the need to build local capacity in the construction industry. Without doubt, the leverage Angola has gained as a major oil supplier to China could be used to strengthen their negotiating position.

Interestingly, however, according to ANIP, it appears that even Angolan companies are keen to import and use Chinese labour, because it is considered to be more productive than its local counterpart, which suffers from a lack of skills due to the civil war and paucity in education facilities and spending. Angola, however, also has an extremely inflexible labour regime, skewed in favour of the worker. This includes a mandated three days' sick leave per month and an allowance of two weeks off for bereavement, which are open to abuse by workers. As a result, employers often have to recruit extra workers to complete the tasks of a single worker (this is compounded by the fact that dismissing a permanent staff member is extremely difficult). Understandably, this discourages employers from contracting permanent staff and does nothing to help the high unemployment rate. Furthermore, with regard to projects financed by China's Exim Bank credit, at least 50 per cent of the procurement materials must originate from China,[36] which reduces the potential positive spin-offs of private-sector development that Chinese engagement in Angola could have.

Despite the reservations of several NGOs about China's presence in Angola, the Chinese line of credit is recognised as an opportunity to rehabilitate and improve on much-needed transport and telecommunications infrastructure. On the other hand, several of the Portuguese construction firms that have been present in Angola for several decades have a reputation for overpriced and shoddy work and the Chinese companies' competition may provide an incentive to improve the standards of construction work. Consequently, the resultant upgrading of the roads leading from Luanda to other provinces, which Chinese, Portuguese and Brazilian firms are working on, has markedly improved internal communication and may prove vital in terms of market access for agricultural goods when this sector is developed.

In addition, at a macroeconomic level, the cheaper Chinese products may have mitigated inflation in Angola. Chinese companies' entry into the Angolan oil sector has, however, caused the prices of oil blocks to soar, particularly the signature bonuses, with Sinopec having offered an unprecedented US$1.1 billion signature bonus for each of the blocks 17 and 18 in May 2006. Furthermore, the Luanda harbour is becoming increasingly congested and does not have the capacity to deal with rising import volumes. This creates delays in the delivery of materials and also impedes access to the harbour, preventing the entry of other goods, including food, thus pushing prices up further. In an attempt to mitigate the problem, in mid-2007, a number of other areas were approved for use as harbours – including Lobito, Namibe and the Sonils base – but the situation remains dire.

For the embryonic Angolan private sector, therefore, Chinese entry into the Angolan economy is something of a mixed blessing. Despite being a competitor that is rapidly cornering market share, the work of Chinese construction companies may help to improve Angola's business environment through infrastructural rehabilitation. What is clear, however, is that policies need to be implemented to foster the growth of local businesses in the face of such competition, particularly in the non-extractive sectors. With regard to the informal economy, however, there is, as yet, little perceived impact on the influx of Chinese imports, as the informal economy has traditionally always relied on imported goods. According to 2006 Angolan customs figures, China is Angola's fourth largest source of imports, accounting for 8.5 per cent, behind Portugal (17.1 per cent), the United States (9.8 per cent) and Brazil (8.6 per cent) and ahead of South Africa (8 per cent).[37] While the percentage of Chinese imports to Angola is relatively small, it should be noted that it has more than doubled since 2004.[38]

CONCLUSION: IMPLICATIONS FOR SINO-ANGOLAN RELATIONS

China has been a favoured diplomatic ally in Africa as its loans, in the spirit of China's policy of non-interference, come with few conditions. This is especially attractive for Angola, given that it was a proxy war zone during the Cold War. What is concerning, however, is that as the credit line is linked to oil, a non-renewable resource, Angola's leverage to negotiate such credit lines is finite. This fuels the perception that the Angolan government has not yet formulated a long-term strategy regarding the operationalisation of the Chinese credit line.

In the meantime, the growing relationship between China and Angola is being closely observed. The IFIs have, together with international donors, expressed concern at the lack of transparency of bilateral negotiations between Chinese and Angolan leaders, particularly those that are oil-backed.[39] The Paris Club and the IMF fear that the little leverage they have over Angola will be further eroded by high oil revenues.[40] Correspondingly, American policy hawks are worried about the expanding sphere of influence that China is strategically building around Africa's second largest oil producer.[41] These concerns, while not unreasonable, are perhaps somewhat exaggerated.

Luanda, for strategic reasons of its own, has no intention of aligning itself solely with Beijing since it is pursuing a home-grown version of non-alignment in favour of its nationalist resource policy. Indeed, in contrast to neighbouring Zimbabwe's 'Look East Policy' and despite warm relations between Zimbabwe's President Mugabe and Angolan President Dos Santos, Beijing is seen by Angola as an important ally – albeit not a unitary strategic partner – who is helping Angola to diversify its sources of aid and concessional loans.[42]

In addition, while particularly hostile to foreign agencies such as the World Bank and the IMF for their attempt to influence domestic economic and fiscal policy, Angola has no intention of alienating the international community completely. On the contrary, it eagerly wants international recognition as a regional and possibly a global player.[43] For this reason, Angola's accession to the OPEC cartel in January 2007 has been particularly significant; it demonstrates Angola's interest in engaging with the global economy in an effort to increase its international standing.

Interestingly, aside from Angola's fundamental reluctance to be beholden to any one foreign partner, there have been recent signs that Sino-Angolan relations are not as cordial as originally presumed. With the upcoming presidential elections in 2009, the Chinese credit line was viewed as an opportunity by the MPLA for a quick fix to service delivery and infrastructure problems. Most of the projects were due to be completed well before the elections, thus adding prestige to and bolstering the MPLA government's delivery credentials. Unfortunately, owing to procurement bottlenecks, corruption and other unforeseen problems, many of the Chinese projects have been delayed or completed in a substandard fashion. The heavy rains in Luanda that brought the city to a complete standstill served only to underline the massive deficiencies in basic service infrastructure. If, as it is believed, the Chinese credit line was viewed as a political helpline that would assist with much-needed national infrastructure reconstruction and, subsequently, service delivery, it is highly conceivable that some MPLA cadres may feel that they have been let down by the Chinese companies' failure to deliver. There are, after all, concerns that the elections, already further delayed from an initial target date in 2007, will once more be delayed in order to allow the infrastructure projects to be completed before the electorate takes to the polls.[44]

Perhaps further indicating his disillusionment, President Dos Santos did not attend the Forum on China-African Cooperation (FOCAC) summit in November 2006 – a minister was sent instead.[45] While this may not necessarily have political overtones, it could undoubtedly have been seen as a snub by the Chinese. On the other hand, it may have been Dos Santos's way of avoiding 'paying homage' to the Chinese president as one of 48 African heads of state in attendance at the FOCAC summit. Notably, however, President Hu Jintao did not visit Angola on his African tour in February 2007. At any rate, signs of discontent among the Angolan political elite with regard to China does not mean a permanent souring of relations, but merely that the initial headiness of Sino-Angolan commercial engagement has worn off and both countries can now attend to business.[46] China and Angola's respective political elites have undoubtedly recognised complementarities within their economies and national interests. The rapid market entry of Chinese state-owned enterprises into the Angolan economy and a number of high-level cooperative oil deals over a short period of time are evidence of this.

As the general development of infrastructure is a national priority to sustain economic growth and encourage FDI, it is worth noting that Chinese companies have made, broadly, a positive contribution towards the development efforts of Angola. Of concern, however, are the challenges posed by a lack of institutional framework and government capacity to monitor and encourage direct investment in terms of local skills development and technology transfer. Linked to this is the issue of whether enough is being done to cultivate and harness the development of the local private sector. An additional challenge is the question of whether the Angolan government has ownership of the reconstruction process. This is pertinent since at least 70 per cent of the contracts funded by the loan money goes to Chinese companies, in addition to the original loan, which will also be paid back to China's Exim Bank. Furthermore, once these large-scale projects have been completed, the question of maintaining them arises. Either the Chinese companies must be kept on at additional expense or the project will be handed over to the local authorities, with the risk of the projects falling into disuse over time through a lack of funds and/or skills and technological know-how.

Ultimately, it is of supreme importance how the Angolan government invests the revenue the country receives from the oil exports to diversify the economy into manufacturing and services. Basically, revenue from Chinese purchases of Angola's oil provides an excellent opportunity for Angola to invest in economic diversification away from extractive industries. In the event, although the Angolan government is a long way from ensuring the transparent management of the country's natural resources, it seems that the potential for economic self-determination has been created, setting a potential precedent for Africa's future engagement with China and with the global economy. The government must harness this opportunity to become a developmental, as opposed to a predatory, state apparatus.

NOTES

1. I. Taylor, 'PRC Relations with Angola', in I. Taylor, *China and Africa: Engagement and Compromise* (London: Routledge, 2006), p. 80.
2. Taylor 'PRC Relations with Angola', p. 87; Chatham House, 'Angola: Drivers of Change', Position Paper 2: Politics (London: Royal Institute of International Affairs, April 2005).
3. A. Vines, 'The Scramble for Resources: African Case Studies', *South African Journal of International Affairs* 13(1), 2006: 71.
4. Angolan Ministry of Finance Press Liaison, 'Ministry of Finance Denies Misuse of Chinese Loans', 17 October 2007.
5. According to *Agora* (6 May 2007), Chinese companies have been contracted to construct a total of 53 schools across Angola.
6. Chatham House 'Angola: Drivers of Change'.
7. This refers to 70 per cent of the total value of the contracts financed by the Chinese Exim Bank loan.
8. R. Aguilar and A. Goldstein, 'The Asian Drivers and Angola', draft paper, OECD Development Centre, 2007, p. 13.
9. National Office for Reconstruction.
10. Integrated Regional Information Network, 'Angola: Oil-Backed Loan Will Finance Recovery Projects', 11 February 2005. http://www.irinnews.org/report.aspx?reportid=53112.
11. Interview with a director of a foreign investment bank in Luanda, 7 June 2006.
12. Angolan Ministry of Finance, 'Ministry of Finance Denies Misuse of Chinese Loans'. Due to CIF encountering difficulties in raising the funding, the Angolan Ministry of Finance issued treasury bonds to raise US$3.5 billion.
13. This statement refers to the fact that the World Bank and the IMF have been reluctant donors to Angola, as the Angolan government failed to comply with the necessary preconditions of good governance and transparency.
14. 'Angola Becomes Oil-Hungry China's Top Source of Crude', *Mail & Guardian*, 30 March 2006. http://www.mg.co.za/articlePage.aspx?articleid=268099andarea=/breaking_news/breaking_news_business/.
15. 'China in Line for Nigerian Oil', *International Business Times*, 20 August 2007. http://www.ibtimes.com/articles/20061106/china-nigeria-oil.htm.
16. P. Hare, 'China in Angola: An Emerging Energy Partnership', *Jamestown Foundation China Brief*, 8 November 2006. http://www.jamestown.org/news_details.php?news_id=205.
17. Angola Press Agency, 'Angola: Head of State Analyses Bilateral Cooperation with China Exim Bank Chief', 28 September 2007. http://allafrica.com/stories/200709281104.html; '*Governo e Banco Chinês Assinam Acordo de 2 Biliões de Dólares*', statement by Angolan Ministry of Finance, 29 September 2007. http://www. minfin.gv.ao/press/news_104.htm.
18. L. Horta, 'China and Angola Strengthen Bilateral Relationship', *Power and Interest News Report*, 23 June 2006. http://www.pinr.com/report.php?ac=view_reportandreport_id=516andlanguage_id=1.
19. Interview with ANIP representative, 22 May 2007, Luanda.
20. 'Portuguese Investment Projects in Angola Double in 2006', *Macauhub*, 10 July 2007. http://www.macauhub.com.mo/en/news.php?ID=3647.
21. Economist Intelligence Unit, 'Angola Report (2007)', p. 5.
22. 'Main Exporters to Angola See Sharp Rise in Sales', *Macauhub*, 8 October 2007. http://www.macauhub.com.mo/en/news.php?ID=4154.
23. G. Dobler, 'South-South Business Relations in Practice: Chinese Merchants in Oshikango, Nambia', draft paper prepared for the Asian Drivers programme, 2005.

24. Dobler, 'South-South Business Relations in Practice'.
25. Interview, 28 May 2007, Luanda.
26. Indeed, particularly due to the Soviet Union's support of the MPLA government during the civil war, China kept its distance. Following the strengthening of relations between Luanda and Beijing, China is reported to have supplied Angola with light armoured vehicles and equipment. China and Angola were also to have signed an agreement whereby China would supply equipment to the Angolan Armed Forces (AAF) early in 2007.
27. It is possible that the current Angolan skills base is too low for joint ventures with Chinese firms, which are, therefore, not a viable proposal over the short term.
28. Interestingly, although the SSI joint venture holds majority stakes in the lucrative block 18, as neither investor possessed the technology or expertise required to operate deep and ultra-deep oil extraction, the block 18 is in fact to be operated by Brazilian oil company, Petrobras.
29. 'China's Sinopec Buys New Stakes in Angolan Oil Fields', *Macauhub*, 14 June 2006. http://www.macauhub.com.mo/en/news.php?ID=1471.
30. 'Beijing Plays Down End of Partnership Between Sonangol and Sinopec', *Macauhub*, 9 March 2007. http://www.macauhub.com.mo/en/news.php?ID=2971.
31. Chatham House, 'Angola: Drivers of Change'.
32. Although Sonangol was the major investor in the proposed Sonaref project in a 70–30 per cent share split, Sinopec is the majority shareholder in the joint venture, with a shareholding of 55 per cent.
33. 'Angola: Oil's New Power', *Africa Confidential* 48(7): 10.
34. C. Burke and L. Corkin, 'China's Interest and Activity in Africa's Construction and Infrastructure Sectors'. A research undertaking evaluating China's involvement in Africa's construction and infrastructure sector prepared for the Department for International Development (DFID) (Stellenbosch University: Centre for Chinese Studies, 2006), p. 17.
35. *Empresas de confiança* is the term used to describe firms and businesses that are owned by politically connected elites in Angola, thus enjoying the protection and special privileges of such connections in an unregulated environment.
36. This is a condition of Chinese Government Concessional Loans as stipulated on the Chinese Exim Bank website: http://www.english.eximbank.gov.cn/business/government.jsp.
37. 'Portuguese Investment Projects in Angola Double in 2006'.
38. Aguilar and Goldstein 'The Asian Drivers and Angola', p. 4.
39. Chatham House, 'Angola: Drivers of Change'; Vines, 'The Scramble for Resources'.
40. Chatham House, *All Party Parliamentary Group on Angola Report* (London: Chatham House, 2006), p. 23. http://www.chathamhouse.org.uk/research/africa/papers/view/-/id/429/.
41. A. Wolfe, 'The Increasing Importance of African Oil', *Power and Interest News Report*, 20 March 2006. http://www.pinr.com/report.php?ac=view_printableandreport_id=460andlanguage_id=1.
42. A. Vines et al., *Angola – Driver of Change: An Overview* (London: Chatham House, 2005).
43. Chatham House, 'Angola: Drivers of Change', Position Paper 1: Economic Change and Reform (London: Royal Institute of International Affairs, April 2005); Chatham House, 'Angola: Drivers of Change', Position Paper 3: Civil Society (London: Royal Institute of International Affairs, April 2005).
44. As an indication of their lack of faith in the government and the electoral process, less than half of the population had registered by the end of May 2007, the scheduled end of the registration period.
45. Hare, 'China in Angola'.
46. 'Angola: Oil's New Power'.

7

Crouching Tiger, Hidden Agenda?

Zimbabwe-China Relations

Lloyd Sachikonye

We have turned east where the sun rises, and given our backs to the West where the sun sets.

Robert Mugabe, 2005[1]

The country has been mortgaged to the Chinese. How can we violently remove Zimbabweans from our flea markets to make way for the Chinese?

Morgan Tsvangirai, 2005[2]

INTRODUCTION

At the end of August 2007, Zimbabwe, one of China's closest allies on the African continent, notched a distinguished world record hyperinflation of 7 600 per cent. An estimated 25 per cent of Zimbabwe's population of 12 million people had migrated to neighbouring countries and overseas for economic and political reasons. Authoritarianism continued to deepen, with little prospect for reform, at least in the short term. Yet relations between Zimbabwe and China have never been closer and materially substantive since the liberation-war era and independence. While relations between some African countries and China are of a recent vintage, that with Zimbabwe spans about 40 years dating back to Chinese ideological and material support to ZANU (Zimbabwe African National Union), which eventually became the dominant ruling party as ZANU-PF (Patriotic Front) at independence in 1980. This may be interpreted as a long-term political investment, which is bearing fruit for the Chinese a generation later.

This chapter assesses the relationship between Zimbabwe and China, especially in the post-2000 period although the earlier historical foundations form an important backdrop. Indeed, those foundations have conditioned the present era of the relationship. The economic and political dimensions of the relationship are examined in the context of China's preoccupation with extraction of natural resources, particularly minerals, and its tolerance of authoritarian repression in Africa. The military dimension is then explored against the background of an arms embargo on Zimbabwe by the West, and the refurbishment of the state coercive apparatus against the opposition movement and civil society. The Zimbabwe case may be exceptional in terms of consecutive economic contraction in the past seven years but the Chinese approach to resource extraction bears resemblance to that in other African countries. The same pattern is evident in Chinese export of manufactured items such as textiles, toys and buses to Zimbabwe, which has contributed to de-industrialisation in these sectors since the late 1990s. In addition, the Zimbabwe case is also one that is illustrative of China's emphasis on personal ties with regimes and elites, which are necessary for its economic and political advantage and manipulation. The chapter is generally sceptical on whether Zimbabwe would be capable of extracting tangible benefits – beyond an immediate lifeline to buy time against the reform tide – out of a seemingly one-sided relationship. As one analyst observed, whether the Zimbabwe-China relationship turns out to be 'a win-win one will depend much on how effectively Zimbabwe can build institutional and bureaucratic capacity to harness Chinese funds and investment for the benefit of the country'.[3] The indications from the accelerated economic melt-down in 2007 have not inspired confidence.

FROM FRATERNAL SOLIDARITY TO A BILATERAL PARTNERSHIP

As we observed above, the relationship between the ruling ZANU-PF party and China was nurtured in the 1960s in the context of the Cold War, as well as Sino-Soviet ideological rivalry. Following the split in the Zimbabwean nationalist movement, the two splinter parties of ZANU and ZAPU (Zimbabwe African People's Union) were aligned separately to China and the Soviet Union respectively. The parties drew their ideological inspiration from the communist parties of the latter states. The figures and teachings of Lenin and Mao were drawn upon respectively by ZAPU under Joshua Nkomo and ZANU, first under Ndabaningi Sithole and later under Robert Mugabe. ZANU cadres closely studied Chairman Mao's writings on guerrilla strategy and political education ('indoctrination') techniques. During the phase of intensified liberation struggle in the 1970s, they toyed with the idea of establishing an ideological college called the 'Whampoa Academy'.[4] After independence, there was an intention to set up an academy to be called the Chitepo Ideological College to train ZANU-PF party cadres, but this did not materialise. The Chinese clearly backed the 'right horse' with ZANU-PF having won the majority of seats in Parliament and with the Soviet-backed ZAPU invited into government in 1980 as a junior partner. Although it became fashionable to de-emphasise 'socialism', otherwise also termed 'Marxism-Leninism-Maoism', as an ideology in the 1980s leading up to the fall of the Berlin Wall, ZANU-PF had once described itself as a socialist party.

China began to reap the political capital that it had invested in the 1960s when it was invited to construct stadiums and hospitals in the 1980s. Confronted by its domestic challenges in the 1980s, China did not enter into major commercial projects. However, party-to-party relations remained close. They would become more significant when Zimbabwe experienced a rupture in relations with the West in the post-2000 period.

AUTHORITARIANISM AND ISOLATION

Zimbabwe's slide into authoritarianism from 2000 has been extensively documented.[5] It has been characterised by political violence, human rights' violations and election rigging. In addition, repressive media laws have resulted in the closure of several independent newspapers and radio stations. In short, democratic space has been severely circumscribed. The turning point in this authoritarian process was a government defeat in a referendum on a new Constitution in February 2000, a defeat that was followed by a widely disputed general election result of that year. Instead of seeking a compromise with the opposition Movement for Democratic Change (MDC), state strategy was to undermine it through repression, attrition and a rigged electoral process. The international response to these authoritarian measures was condemnation and isolation especially by the West. In 2000, most of Zimbabwe's trade was with neighbouring countries and with the West. Most of the investments, loans and grants were from the West, as was trade in arms and military cooperation.

It was anticipated by the West, especially by the European Union (EU) and United States, that by isolating the Zimbabwe government and its leadership, there would be a change of heart over the issue of authoritarianism. The punitive measures of travel restrictions on members of the leadership and elite were accompanied by investment, loan and grant restrictions. The latter had an immediate impact on the country's balance of payments, foreign exchange reserves and capacity to maintain basic social services. International financial institutions such as the International Monetary Fund (IMF) and World Bank stopped lending but demanded loan repayments. In addition, a hastily implemented land reform programme contributed to a significant decline in production in an economy in which agriculture is still a vital sector. The steady decline in the country's gross domestic product (GDP) dates from that period and continues in the present. This was the context in which the Mugabe government had little alternative but to 'look east' for economic infusions and survival. Perhaps this political and economic conjuncture is what distinguishes the imperatives behind the immediate context of the bilateral relationship between Zimbabwe and China in comparison with other African countries. While the economic dimension is important, that of ideological affinity and solidarity also plays a part. Like Zimbabwe, the nature of China's political system receives profound attention in terms of criticisms levelled against what is seen as Beijing's repressive nature especially in the areas of human rights and civil liberties. Despite China's successful developmentalist programme, its tough image was symbolised by its crushing of the student protests in Tianamen Square in 1989. The major difference is, however, that while the authoritarian model has been accompanied by impressive growth in China, in Zimbabwe it has contributed to significant economic decline.

Of course, the stalemate in Zimbabwe has lasted for much longer than the government authorities and the West anticipated. Their original strategies, if there were any, misfired. The high rates of emigration from Zimbabwe and of hyperinflation speak for themselves. It is within this contextualised landscape that China has entered Zimbabwe's economic space to become a significant player.

ECONOMIC RELATIONS AND RESOURCE EXTRACTION

There is empirical evidence that China has become the second biggest investor and trading partner of Zimbabwe in direct competition with South Africa. By the end of 2004, Chinese investments amounted to an estimated US$600 million. The surge in investment began in the post-2000 period and coincided with the deterioration in Zimbabwe's relations with the European Union and the international financial institutions (IFIs), such as the World Bank and the IMF. Chinese investments have largely been concentrated in extractive sectors, such as mining, infrastructure and utilities.

As its industrialisation programme broadens, China's demand for raw materials, such as copper, platinum and chrome, along with other commodities, increases exponentially.

Mining

China has been particularly interested in the extraction of chrome, platinum, nickel and copper, as well as in the processing of iron and steel. Significantly, Zimbabwe has the second largest reserves of platinum in the world, and substantial reserves of chrome. Although there were initial hopes that Chinese investments in the mining and processing sectors would be immediate and substantially high, the major investment to date has been in the ferrochrome industry. In September 2007, Sinosteel, China's second largest iron dealer, signed an investment agreement with the ZIMASCO firm.[6] Once the world's fifth largest ferrochrome producer with a production of 210 000 tonnes a year, ZIMASCO produced about 5 per cent of the global output. Sinosteel's investment has been interpreted as an extension of China's expanding interest in African metals as the Asian giant seeks to feed the voracious appetite of its booming economy. It is noteworthy that China is now the world's largest steelmaker and consumer. This is the broad context in which global ferrochrome demand is projected to rise by about 5 per cent a year for the next few years on the back of soaring Chinese demand for stainless steel for infrastructure development and consumer products. In a related development, a Chinese company, Bunday Technical Mining, has indicated an interest in setting up a chrome-processing plant at Lalapanzi in the Midlands province.

Another major development was a leading investment in 2003 by the Shanghai Baosteel Group in the mining and metals sector. It invested US$300 million in the sector, creating 2 000 jobs in the process. Furthermore, the Metallurgical Corporation of China (MCC), the biggest steel manufacturer in China, has been assessing prospects of investing in Zimbabwe's iron- and steel-processing industry. In November 2006, it reportedly made a bid for a substantial stake of 60 per cent in the Zimbabwe Iron and Steel Corporation (ZISCO), the state-owned manufacturer.[7] However, the bid was not successful, partly because the state appeared to have been reluctant to cede such a substantial stake in what is considered to be a strategic industry. While the prospects of investment in mining might have been attractive to foreign capital, including Chinese finance, a new mining law now requires 51 per cent state ownership. This has made both foreign and domestic capital nervous and placed the sector under a cloud of uncertainty. The law does not make any exceptions, and unless it is reviewed, it will have an adverse impact on foreign investment in the mining sector.

Agriculture

There has been a spectacular surge in Zimbabwean agricultural exports to China, as well as substantial imports of agricultural inputs and equipment from the latter. These exports consist largely of tobacco and cotton, with China becoming the largest consumer of Zimbabwean tobacco. However, it is important to observe that, in the short term at least, Chinese credit remains a significant contributor to the fortunes of Zimbabwe's agriculture, a sector that has experienced a serious crisis and decline following the hastily implemented land-reform programme in 2000–03. With the contraction of the manufacturing and agro-industrial sectors in the past seven years, supplies of key inputs such as fertilisers, agrochemicals and seeds have become erratic. A Chinese credit facility of US$200 million dollars has enabled Zimbabwe to import these inputs for its agricultural sector in the past two years. Chinese credit has thus been a critical lifeline for the sector and indeed for the economy as a whole.[8] Until the refurbishment of Zimbabwe's own fertiliser plants is complete, the dependence on Chinese credit and fertiliser imports is likely to continue in the near future.

Significantly, China has reportedly bought some commercial farmland in the prime agricultural Mashonaland provinces. However, it is still unclear whether Chinese companies have commenced production on these farms. The intention behind the purchase of the farms is to utilise local labour to produce commodities for export to China. However, the obstacles to production include endemic shortages of inputs, such as fuel, electricity and seed, which are linked to the ongoing economic crisis.

Infrastructure and utilities

As elsewhere in Africa, Chinese corporations have invested in infrastructure and in utilities in Zimbabwe, with the main emphasis on the railway and telecommunications sectors, electricity generation, as well as water and irrigation. For example, the Chinese have provided equipment for the state railway network, National Railways of Zimbabwe (NRZ), which urgently needed to refurbish and upgrade its transport and haulage services. Chinese corporations have also signed two agreements with local phone networks. The first is with the main fixed-line network Tel One, worth US$288 million, for the expansion and growth of its subscriber base, and the second, valued at US$40 million, is with the largest mobile phone operator Net One. In addition, Chinese telecommunications equipment has been imported by other mobile phone operators, such as Econet and Telecel, and the Chinese have provided training to Zimbabwean telecommunications personnel.

The Chinese have also signed agreements with a major Zimbabwean coal corporation for the construction of thermal power stations to generate electricity supplies. In the past four years, power supplies have become increasingly erratic and the projects that were commissioned involved the construction of three such stations at Hwange, a coal-mining centre, and at Dande in the Mashonaland Central province.

Significantly, some of the agreements have not been followed up and financed. This was also the case with a major dam construction project at Kunzvi, which was aimed at augmenting Harare's water supply.

Retail sector

The Chinese have been steadily making inroads in the retail sector with an increasing number of Chinese traders receiving business and trading licences. As one analyst observed, in addition to 35 Chinese companies, the government has been issuing business permits to Chinese shopkeepers and street traders 'like confetti'.[9] This has reinforced competition with local traders and created some resentment towards the Chinese newcomers. To complicate matters, Operation Murambatsvina largely spared the Chinese, while local traders suffered substantial losses as a consequence of that 'clean up' in 2005.[10] One interpretation of the state's draconian Operation was that it was partly aimed at clearing the ground for Chinese retailers. This stemmed from the fact that Chinese shops and flea markets were spared during the Operation in which indigenous small traders lost goods and property, worth billions of Zimbabwean dollars. This prompted condemnation from the UN after an enquiry was carried out under Anna Tibaijuka.[11] Indeed, in an environment of high unemployment and difficult economic conditions resulting from the economic crisis, there is a thinly veiled envy and hostility among local businesses and trade unions towards Chinese traders. Although relatively cheap, Chinese goods tend to be of a questionable quality and are derisively termed *zhing zhong*.

Trade

After South Africa, China has become Zimbabwe's second largest trading partner. The deterioration in Zimbabwe's economic fortunes has not discouraged the Chinese juggernaut. While the trade was initially skewed in favour of Zimbabwe, this appears to be changing. For instance, there is a notable decline in Zimbabwe's exports and a steep rise in imports from China in the form of tractors, ploughs, fertilisers and other agricultural equipment, and textiles and clothing. Since 2000, clothing, textile and footwear imports from China have doubled, largely a reflection of the contraction of Zimbabwe's manufacturing base during this period.

Chinese exports to Zimbabwe increased by nearly 10 per cent from US$125 million in 2005 to US$136 million in 2006. However, in the first half of 2007, Chinese exports surged to US$187 million while Zimbabwe's exports were a paltry US$16 million.[12] The overall value of bilateral trade between the two countries was expected to reach US$400 million by the end of 2007. It would appear that there has been a significant increase of Chinese exports, especially of agricultural and industrial equipment, as Zimbabwe, like other countries assessed in this volume, become more exposed to Chinese credit lines.

However, the bilateral trade figures do not fully capture the increasing level of 'barter trade' between the two countries. Some commodities like tobacco and beef, chrome, copper and platinum have been exported to China under barter trade arrangements. Zimbabwean tobacco and cotton exports were utilised as repayment for a loan worth US$100 million from the China National Aero Technology Import and Export Corporation, which was lent to the national power utility, the Zimbabwe Electricity Supply Authority (ZESA) in 2005.[13] It is difficult to make precise estimates of this seemingly expanding form of trade. Yet, barter trade has not been without critics. It has been argued, for instance, that Zimbabwe is ultimately a loser because it has to forgo future foreign currency earnings as a result of the barter system.[14] In the final analysis, however, an increase in bilateral trade would only become more sustainable when conditions of political and economic stability improve.

In an assessment of both investment and trade relations between China and Zimbabwe, the role of Chinese state-owned enterprises (SOEs) needs to be highlighted. Beijing's assistance to counter a complete collapse of Zimbabwe's economy through cash injections, credit lines and other support have granted Chinese SOEs access to a number of projects in Zimbabwe, as noted earlier. The enterprises are able to take on the high-risk environment because in the event of the situation worsening, Beijing is likely to bail them out. The Chinese government thus has the ability to influence its SOEs to invest in Zimbabwe spurred by the good relations between the two countries.[15]

Sustainable surge in investment and trade?

Is the upsurge in bilateral trade and investment between Zimbabwe and China sustainable? This question becomes more resonant and urgent against the background of a desperate hyperinflationary environment in the last quarter of 2007. While the official figure put it at 8 000 per cent in November 2007, unofficial estimates were double this figure. In January 2008, the figure climbed to 100 580 per cent.[16] And as of May 2008, it is estimated to be more than 355 000 per cent. Already burdened with the highest inflation in the world, the economic crisis in Zimbabwe has been compounded by shortages of fuel and other key inputs, as well as by frequent power outages. These shortages reflect low levels of foreign exchange reserves and indebtedness to electricity suppliers in Mozambique, the Democratic Republic of Congo (DRC) and South Africa. Most industries operate below capacity as a result of these conditions. And it has been no different for Chinese investors who have not been spared the erratic electricity, fuel and water supply interruptions and shortages. Indeed, the Chinese have conceded that the deterioration of economic conditions in 2007 will affect trade and investment relations. As one senior Chinese diplomat noted, 'in the past, China provided substantial aid. Now with devaluation of the currency and the deterioration of the economic situation, the outlook for this aid is not very good.'[17] Indeed, in spite of official denials, there has been speculation that the Chinese have been reviewing their economic relations with Zimbabwe.

Zimbabwe's own ranking as an export destination of Chinese goods declined from the 24th to 28th position in 2006.[18] In the larger canvas of international economic relations, Zimbabwe may not be a very attractive destination for Chinese business, at least in the short term. This would explain why the appeals for large bail-out loans such as the US$2 billion that Zimbabwe sought in 2006 have not been forthcoming. Instead China made available a US$3 million grant in cash. The Chinese appear to be wary of committing large sums of money in Zimbabwe in the present conjuncture of economic crisis. It is also against this background that one can explain why Chinese President Hu Jintao avoided visiting Harare during his African visit in the first quarter of 2007. Having gained a significant foothold in Zimbabwe's economy as a result of Mugabe's 'Look East Policy', the security and growth of Chinese investment and trade relations will, ironically, in future depend on the restoration of macroeconomic and political stability, as well as the normalisation of international relations, including with the West. China's non-interference and respect for sovereignty response is being managed in a more responsible manner by Beijing, which is especially relevant in the current atmosphere of the global setting where the 2008 Olympic Games are being threatened by political considerations about Darfur and Tibet. As the host of this prestigious international sporting event, China is becoming more aware of its international image and what this means for its future global position. This has definitely prompted China to circumvent any embarrassing situations and become a more responsible proto-superpower. As in the case of Sudan (see Chapter 4), China's engagements with Khartoum reflect these significant shifts in China's Africa policy, where Beijing is becoming more involved through the appointment of its Special Envoy. Perhaps this lack of appreciation of the subtle changes in how China perceives its peaceful rise does, indeed, indicate that being seen to have close association with regimes that have been ostracised in various international fora indicates a new thinking in China's foreign policy, which is often overlooked within contemporary discourse.

DE-INDUSTRIALISATION

Some analysts credit China for 'thinking strategically through taking advantage of Zimbabwe's decline to secure mining concessions and trading opportunities at knock-down prices and getting loans repaid in kind with badly needed commodities'.[19] The mercantilist instincts of China are fairly obvious in how it has sought advantage in access to agricultural and mineral commodities. However, a significant aspect of its trade relations consists of exports of textiles, clothing and leather goods, which compete directly with Zimbabwe's own fledgling industries. The combination of structural adjustment measures, which facilitated hasty trade liberalisation in the 1990s, and Chinese inroads have almost decimated Zimbabwe's clothing and textile sector. Derisively termed *zhing zhong*, cheap Chinese goods have contributed to more than 50 per cent of job losses in this sector, and certainly affected job levels in the shoe, toy and electrical industries. It is estimated that overall, clothing, textile and footwear imports from China have more than doubled since 2000. This process has resulted in considerable de-industrialisation.

In sum, the pattern of Zimbabwe-Chinese trade has adversely affected the fortunes of a manufacturing and retail sector that were already weakening at the beginning of the decade. As observed above, the agro-industrial sector, which supplied inputs to agriculture, has been undermined by imports such as fertiliser and tractors from China. The sector entered a phase of decline following the contraction of commercial agriculture, particularly between 2000 and 2003. The wider repercussions of agricultural decline include substantial loss of foreign earnings and limited capacity to import inputs for manufacturing. The same has happened with the imports of bus and vehicle parts, which used to be produced and assembled locally. It is difficult to comprehend the Zimbabwean state's acquiescence in this process of de-industrialisation. One explanation is political short-termism. The availability of cheap consumer goods, *zhing zhong* or *fong kong*, buys the ZANU-PF government political time despite strident criticism from affected industries and labour unions.

When it comes to Chinese investment and aid to African countries, the Zimbabwean experience is no exception to the general trend, which is highlighted throughout this volume. However, this analysis tends to downgrade the strings attached to that investment and aid. The conditions include that the aid's availability is restricted solely to investment in Chinese enterprises and projects, and that 70 per cent of the contracts are set aside for Chinese companies.[20] It is the remainder that goes to African businesses, many of whom already work with Chinese enterprises.[21]

POLITICAL AND MILITARY TIES

China has sought to project itself as a power that respects the national sovereignty of countries with which it has relations. It stresses the principle of non-interference, even where human rights' violations are rampant. Where Western powers are perceived to be reluctant to engage with a country on account of its corruption and authoritarianism, China is seen as less reticent about such engagement.

In the Zimbabwean case, China cannot claim to be adhering to the principle of non-interference. First, there are close party-to-party relations between the ZANU-PF party and the Chinese Communist Party, and these relations have been cemented by bilateral visits by high-ranking officials. The ruling elite in Zimbabwe has been a beneficiary of and accessory to Chinese investment in infrastructure projects and barter trade. Second, China has taken sides in the struggle over media freedom between the Zimbabwean government and the opposition. It has exported equipment to jam radio broadcasts aimed at giving 'voice' to the opposition, which is denied space on the state media. When the new law to monitor electronic mail, Internet traffic and other forms of communication was introduced, it was widely believed that Chinese expertise in this field would be drawn upon. Chinese proximity to the ruling elite might be an asset, as long as the latter is in power, but if political change occurred, this would lose its currency. Perhaps the more recent example of China's support for ZANU-PF is a loan that Beijing reportedly extended to Harare for agricultural equipment just before the 2008 Presidential and Parliamentary elections.

Third, the Chinese stance of non-interference is undermined by its significant contribution to the process of militarisation in Africa. It has been observed that it has built several arms factories in Sudan, sold arms worth about US$1 billion to Ethiopia and Eritrea during their war in 1998–2000, and has supplied various armaments to countries such as Mali and Angola.[22] Similarly, China has become a significant military supplier to Zimbabwe. In recent years, it has exported twelve fighter jets, as well as army trucks to the country. Although precise details are difficult to obtain, Chinese military supplies have become more crucial as a result of the Western military embargo. The combination of political and military support and cooperation makes it difficult for China to claim to be upholding the principle of non-interference in the case of Zimbabwe.

CONCLUDING REMARKS

Although Zimbabwe's authoritarian mode and stand-off with the West has created economic and political windows of opportunity for Beijing, there are nevertheless some risks inherent in the relationship. One risk is the continued economic melt-down in the country. It is a melt-down that threatens economic activity – constant power cuts, fuel shortages, transport bottlenecks, utilities and infrastructure breakdown – which represent a threat to commercial operations that range from agriculture and mining to manufacturing and retailing. Chinese operations cannot remain unscathed. Another risk is the insolvency of those interests that have borrowed Chinese capital, including state institutions and parastatals. There have been reports of unpaid loans for aircraft purchase and for construction projects that have led to the suspension of work.[23] The concern is that if Zimbabwe continues to borrow heavily from China without repaying consistently, it may be forced to mortgage more of its natural and national resources such as land, platinum and gold mines, amongst other assets. The current relationship is not one of equals despite the rhetoric. The risk for Zimbabwe in its current position of weakness is that it could become a dependent state in its relations with China. This would present both costs and opportunities to this emerging East Asian power.

During the second half of 2007, China appeared to be reviewing its relations with Zimbabwe. This reflected some sensitivity, as host of the forthcoming 2008 Olympics, to charges that it was consorting with African despots in Zimbabwe and Sudan. As one analyst has observed:

> 2007 may mark a watershed in the relationship between the two countries. Whereas Mugabe may continue to 'look east' to survive, China does not seem to be willing to return the gaze directly. Rather China is becoming increasingly concerned about how it appears to the West. What is lost to Mugabe and other African leaders is that even the Chinese would admit that they would not be an emerging giant without Western technology and markets . . . African leaders should be wary of simply looking East. They should heed Kwame Nkrumah's admonition that Africa needs to look forward rather than east or west for its development . . .[24]

Finally, China is likely to become more cautious in its relations with Zimbabwe despite the continued rhetoric of solidarity on both sides. While the strategic and economic value of a non-oil-producing country such as Zimbabwe to China is much more limited, it would be interesting to see if China invests in a diplomatic initiative in Zimbabwe, as it has done in Sudan. China would be more likely to watch how the 2007 Southern African Development Community (SADC) initiative on Inter-Party Dialogue plays out, and whether the outcome of the 2008 election in Zimbabwe would be legitimate enough to encourage political and economic engagement with the international community, including the West. As this chapter is being written, any indications toward this scenario remain uncertain, as the outcome of the 2008 elections is being hijacked by the gerrymandering of the Mugabe regime. Although there exist undercurrents of tension with respect to relations and competition between domestic and Chinese capital, the latter does not have such a critical mass that overt hostility would break out in the short term. However, this possibility is surely a source of worry to both the Zimbabwean and Chinese governments. And more pertinently, depending what outcome emerges from the current stalemate between the MDC and ZANU-PF following the calamitous 2008 elections, China will have to decide whether it wants to continue its own version of quiet diplomacy that it has shown ZANU-PF or to demonstrate to the rest of the world that it is assessing its engagements with objectionable governments in a more measured and responsible manner.

NOTES

1. Robert Mugabe, 'Speech Marking the 25th Anniversary of Zimbabwe's Independence', delivered at the National Sports Stadium, 18 April 2005. Quoted in Andrew Meldrum, 'Mugabe Turns Back on West and Looks East', *The Guardian*, 19 April 2005.
2. Quoted in Roger Bate, 'Zimbabwe's New Colonialists', *Weekly Standard*, 25 May 2005.
3. J.B. Karumbidza, 'Win-Win Economic Cooperation: Can China Save the Zimbabwean Economy?', in F. Manji and S. Marks (eds.), *African Perspectives on China* (Oxford and Nairobi: FAHAMU, 2007).
4. F. Chung, *Reliving the Second Chimurenga* (Uppsala: NAI, 2006).
5. D. Harold-Barry (ed.), *The Past is the Future* (Harare: Weaver Press, 2004); B. Raftopoulos and Tyrone Savage (eds.), *Zimbabwe: Injustice and Political Reconciliation* (Cape Town: One World Books, 2005); L.M. Sachikonye et al., *Consolidating Democratic Governance in Southern Africa: The Case of Zimbabwe* (Johannesburg: EISA, 2007).
6. 'Zimbabwe: Look East or Look Chinese?', *Financial Gazette* (Zimbabwe), 25 October 2007.
7. *Herald* (Zimbabwe), 27 November 2006.
8. *Zimbabwe Independent*, 13 September 2007.
9. O. Matahwa, 'China and Zimbabwe: Is There a Future?' *Africa Files at Issue Ezine* 6(4), August–November 2007.
10. Operation Murambatsvina (Restore Order) was a large government urban 'clean-up' operation conducted by the police and security services in 2005. It affected about a million people and resulted in the destruction of informal settlements, housing and small shops in most of the country's cities and towns. The destruction of property and goods ran into billions of dollars.

11. A. Tibaijuka, 'Report of the Fact-Finding Mission to Zimbabwe to Assess the Scope and Impact of Operation *Murambatsvina* by the UN Special Envoy on Human Settlements Issues in Zimbabwe' (Harare: Ledriz, 2005); 'The Impact of Operation *Murambatsvina* on Workers and [the] Informal Sector' (Harare: Ledriz, 2006).
12. T. Munda, 'Zimbabwe Posts a Huge Deficit against China', *Zimbabwe Online*, 28 September 2007.
13. L. Hilsum, 'Re-Enter the Dragon: China's New Mission in Africa', *Review of African Political Economy* 32(104/105), June/September 2005: 419–25.
14. Matahwa, 'China and Zimbawe'.
15. C. Burke and H. Edinger, 'AERC Scoping Studies on China-Africa Relations: A Research Report on Zimbabwe', University of Stellenbosch, 2007.
16. *Zimbabwe Independent*, 22 February 2008.
17. As quoted in Munda, 'Zimbabwe Posts a Huge Deficit against China'.
18. Burke and Edinger, 'AERC Scoping Studies on China-Africa Relations'.
19. Hilsum, 'Re-Enter the Dragon'.
20. M. Deibert, 'Concern Greeting China's Growing Prominence in Africa', Inter-Press Service, 2007.
21. Deibert, 'Concern Greeting China's Growing Prominence in Africa'.
22. M.C. Lee, 'The 21st Century Scramble for Africa', *Journal of Contemporary African Studies* 24(3), 2006: 303–30.
23. Karumbidza, 'Win-Win Economic Cooperation'.
24. Matahwa, 'China and Zimbawe'.

8

Chinese Investments in Africa
A Case Study of Zambia

Muna Ndulo

INTRODUCTION

China's resurgent interest in Africa has spawned a perplexing variety of worldwide reaction and, as some of the contributors to this volume show, the response of the West has generally been negative, warning Africa of exploitation and a new form of colonialism. On the other hand, the African reactions have been sanguine, precisely because China's investments in the region run the gamut of oil infrastructure in large oil-exporting countries, such as Nigeria, Angola and Algeria to building railroads, dams, power stations and landing giant contracts in several African countries.[1] Effectively, China's surging interest in Africa has helped bring about what some Africans believe is the most important change in international relations since the end of the Cold War. For example, in Zambia alone, China plans to invest US$800 million in the next few years in one of the five economic zones it intends to establish in Africa.[2]

In the overall assessment of China's global economic initiatives, the World Bank classifies Chinese investment in Africa into three categories: (a) investments aimed at supplying China with natural resources and processed raw materials; (b) investments that target African domestic markets, which could get a boost via effective regional integration; and (c) investments aimed at supplying the international markets, such as the European Union and the United States, motivated mostly by low labour costs plus favourable trade access given to African countries in those markets.[3] Chinese investment in Zambia is spread in all these three categories.

This chapter focuses on the challenges of development in Zambia, the role that Chinese investments are playing in the Zambian economy, the areas of tension, and it concludes by making some recommendations aimed at ensuring that the relationship between China and Zambia is beneficial to both countries. The chapter takes the view that China's investment in Africa, and in Zambia, specifically, is an evolution that should not be viewed with suspicion, but instead be explored for challenges and opportunities.

Relations between Zambia and China have their origins in the southern African liberation wars of the 1960s to 1980s, during which China played a significant role in training and arming liberation movements. Further, the relationship flourished as it revolved around solidarity with several socialist countries in the region, namely Zambia, Tanzania, Zimbabwe and Mozambique, among others. A major boost in China-Zambia relations was the construction of the Tanzania-Zambia Railway (TAZARA) between Dar es Salaam and Kapiri-Mposhi that was built with Chinese financial and technical assistance.[4] When Tanzania and Zambia failed to obtain Western support for the construction of the rail line, they turned to China for help. China agreed to build the railway, confounding Western states, which had doubts about its ability to deliver on such a huge project, by completing it in 1976.

As pointed out in Chapter 2 by Garth le Pere, the People's Republic of China (PRC) has always had an interest in Africa. What has changed is the unprecedented level of interest by China in African affairs, a level of interest that is concomitant with its rising importance in the world economy.[5] In its relationship with African states, China has adopted a different approach from that which is associated with the West. The West often stereotypes Africa as a global backwater plagued by poverty, disease, ethnicity, conflict and corruption.[6] The result is an approach based on paternalism and cultural superiority. In essence, as a Western analyst has noted, China has 'increasingly regarded Africa as an opportunity, while Europe has long regarded Africa as a burden'.[7] The central issue that arises is whether this major interest is beneficial to Africa.

The increasing importance of Africa for China is clearly evident in the intensified Chinese diplomatic activity in recent years. More significant is the extensive Chinese government initiative towards greater investment in Africa, which is clearly stated in the China-Africa policy document.[8] On the eve of the Forum on China-Africa Cooperation (FOCAC), China's state council issued 'Nine Principles to Encourage and Standardise Enterprises Overseas Investment'. These require Chinese-owned companies to: (a) abide by local laws; (b) bid for contracts on the basis of transparency and equality; (c) protect labour rights of local employers; (d) protect the environment; and (e) implement corporate responsibilities.

China can also be an African ally on the development front as Chinese investments can help Zambia, as well as other African countries, to alleviate poverty. A 2007 World

Bank report observed that, compared to the rest of the world, Africa has been losing the battle against poverty.[9] With the continent hosting 10 per cent of the world's population, but a staggering 30 per cent of the world's poor, the challenges facing the region are enormous but not insurmountable, according to the report. It further observed that African countries missed out on two decades of global growth and that, while other countries have made strides in addressing poverty, the reverse has occurred in Africa.[10] In addition, the report explained that Asian countries' growth has not only been meteoric but steady. By contrast, each country in Africa has had spurts of rapid growth (in the 1960s and 1970s), and then between 1975 and 1995 many of them decelerated. The percentage of the population classified as living in extreme poverty was 36 per cent in 1970 but reached 50 per cent by the end of the century. Poverty, as the report concludes, is increasingly assuming an Africa face, and eradicating it has become a predominantly African challenge.[11]

CHINESE INVESTMENT IN THE ZAMBIAN ECONOMY

Zambia is one of the leading copper-producing countries in the world and its economy is largely mineral-based; effectively, the mining industry is the most important sector of the economy. Fortunately, copper output, which had suffered a steep decline in the 1990s, has increased steadily since 2004, due to higher prices and the opening of new mines, like the Kansanshi copper mine.[12] Most copper in Zambia is mined on what has come to be known as the Copperbelt, an undulating area, roughly 114 km in length by 48 km in width. New copper mines are being developed in Solwezi, an area that is, due to its potential mineral production, poised to outstrip that of the present Copperbelt, and is already being called the new Copperbelt. Zambia also produces zinc, lead, silver and cobalt, but to a lesser extent than copper. Large nickel deposits are being developed in the Munali prospecting area south of Lusaka, while iron ore deposits are common and widely distributed throughout Zambia. However, Zambia needs huge investments to develop its mineral resources and diversify its economy, as it is only through such development that it can provide employment and improve the living standards of its people. As the indicators show, 70 per cent of the 11 million Zambians live below the poverty line and most have not felt the benefits of recent macroeconomic improvements.[13] In 2007, Zambia ranked 165th out of 177 countries in terms of human development.[14] Consequently, Zambia must make additional efforts to ensure that the mining sector, boosted by copper production, has a favourable impact on ordinary Zambians.[15]

Given the abundance of the above-mentioned natural resources in the country, tremendous opportunity exists for Chinese investment in Zambia, not least because China's economic growth is dependent on these raw materials. The real issue, however, is whether Zambia's need for investment and China's need for raw materials can work for both countries to bring about economic development and alleviate poverty in both countries, a matter that is not wholly dependent on China alone. To a large extent, it will depend on the strategies for development adopted by Zambia and the extent to which it uses its mineral revenue to improve and sustain the national infrastructure, education, technology and manufacturing capacity.

MAJOR CHALLENGES OF DEVELOPMENT IN THE ZAMBIAN ECONOMY

One of the factors affecting development in Zambia, as elsewhere in Africa, is the availability of capital. Economic development is achieved through the productive employment of labour and the full utilisation of natural resources. The productive employment of labour requires capital and presupposes an increase in the general level of education and the acquisition of technical skills, as well as the formation of a body of capable administrators and entrepreneurs. For the utilisation of natural resources, a number of basic facilities are needed, such as roads, railways, harnessing of electric power and other forms of energy. For example, several countries in Africa, including Zambia, are facing serious power shortages, partly because they are beginning to experience modest economic growth, which increases the demand for electricity. Despite this, there has been no investment in building generating capacity. A recent *New York Times* article observed that the gravity of sub-Saharan power shortage is all the more apparent considering how little electricity sub-Saharan Africa has to begin with. Excluding South Africa, whose economy and power consumption dwarfs other nations, the region's remaining 700 million citizens have access to roughly as much electricity as do 38 million citizens of Poland. In order to reverse this situation, a huge injection of external capital in the energy sector is required. Foreign capital has played a significant role in countries that have made tremendous achievements in economic development and there is no reason why China cannot play a similar role in Africa.

The role of Chinese investments in the Zambian economy

Zambia attracts less foreign investments than most of the Southern African Development Community (SADC) countries – including Botswana, Tanzania, Namibia and Angola – a fact that underlines the scarcity of capital in Zambia. According to the

World Bank's 2007 African Competitiveness Report, Zambia ranks 117 out of 128 countries in its Global Competitiveness Index. As such, a report on foreign direct investment by local economists, states that investment from China, especially in the mining sector, is in line with Zambia's development agenda.[16]

Since China and Zambia established diplomatic relations 44 years ago, 200 Chinese companies have set up businesses in Zambia, ranging from mining, textile, construction, banking, agriculture, to medical clinics and restaurants.[17] Some of these companies, such as China's Non-Ferrous Africa Mining Plc (NFC-Africa) and Zambia China Mulungusi Textile Company, are large-sized and play an important role in the county's economy. In recent years, Chinese investment in Zambia has witnessed a significant growth, making China Zambia's third largest investor, after South Africa and the United Kingdom. China and Zambia have also experienced a rapid trade boom in recent years. Bilateral trade in the early 1990s was only US$20 million, but in 2006 it hit US$300 million.[18]

During the Beijing summit of FOCAC in November 2006, the Chinese and Zambian governments signed an agreement to build a copper smelter worth about US$200 million which will be constructed by NFC-Africa. Zambia Electricity Supply Corporation (ZESCO) has also signed a US$243 million power contract with Sinohydro Corporation of China to extend the Kariba North Bank power station in a bid to forestall the looming power shortage due to increased demand.

Other Chinese investments in Zambia include: the Chambishi Copper Mine, which China purchased during the privatisation of the Zambian copper mines in the 1990s; the Mulungushi textile factory; several farming ventures; construction firms; and the Kabwe General Hospital. Additionally, a Chinese manufacturing company that specialises in agricultural tractors is setting up an assembly plant to serve the southern African region. Zambia and China have also agreed to extablish the Zambia-China Chambishi Trade and Economic Zone. In the zone, Zambia will exempt Chinese firms from import duties and value added taxes. The creation of the zone in Chambishi is expected to bring a total of US$800 million in Chinese investments into Zambia.[19] It is forecast that 60 Chinese firms will launch manufacturing operations in the zone and create thousands of jobs for Zambians in the next three years. China is also involved in the construction industry and has developed modern markets, using the build, operate and transfer approach. Last but not least, Zambia has asked Chinese companies to help it to meet its targeted investment, amounting to US$3 billion, into the Zambian economy next year. [20] As Trade and Industry Minister, Felix Mutati, has noted, with the injection of US$3 billion into the Zambian economy next year, Zambia hopes to create 100 000 jobs.[21]

Zambia-China cooperation also includes tariff-free access for Zambian products into the Chinese market: suffice to say, the number of tariff-free products currently stands at 452, and Zambian citizens now have access to the Bank of China, with a commercial branch in Lusaka, for finance and manufacturing operations needed to export to China. In addition to investments, China has cancelled Zambian debt and is providing assistance in the form of agricultural training and educational scholarships.

Chinese investment in Zambia is a positive and welcome development. For one thing, China's strong economic growth and its hunger for raw materials, such as copper, iron ore and aluminum, have provided the foundations for sharp rises in commodities prices over the past five years. These increments have resulted in increased revenues for Zambia and, as a result, the country's mining sector grew by an average of 9 per cent between 2002 and 2005.[22] Another positive factor is the message from mining executives to the effect that neither the shortages of metals nor China's demand for them is likely to change anytime soon. Furthermore, the growth of India will provide additional support for commodities prices;[23] and meanwhile, the demand for minerals by China has led to increased investment in mining exploration and exploitation. The resulting high metal prices have meant that ores that were deemed uneconomical to mine in the 1970s, 1980s and 1990s are now economical and being investigated.

As noted earlier, the Chinese investments are in line with the objective of the mining sector under the Zambian Fifth National Development Plan (FNDP), which aims to promote investment in the mining sector in order to increase its contribution to the national economy. For example, investments by China's NFC-Africa in Chambishi mines has led to increased production and hence contributed to the economy in terms of new jobs and income.[24] These investments have also had positive effects on the local industries' downstream operations, making it possible for these industries to develop and to supply mining operations with intermediate goods.

The major issue that arises in the context of Chinese investments in Zambia is whether the two countries can work constructively together to ensure that this is a win-win situation for both and what policies and mechanisms can be put in place to ensure this result. Research by the World Bank suggests that part of the solution lies in African countries such as Zambia developing their capacity to trade and developing linkages between trade capacity and Chinese investment.[25] At the same time, Zambians must remember that foreign investment will only come to a country that provides an economic and political climate that is conducive to investment and in which it is relatively easy to conduct business. To create such a climate means addressing the constraints that discourage investments, such as the issue of efficiency in the economy.

Ultimately, however, the critical responsibility for both China and Zambia is to ensure that their relationship is based on mutual respect, so that it brings about joint prosperity, and is free of the overtones of exploitation and paternalism that critics worldwide say have governed much of the West's post-colonial relationship with Africa.

CHINESE INVESTMENTS IN ZAMBIA: AREAS OF TENSION

As mentioned previously, there are problems associated with foreign direct investment in Zambia by both China and Western countries. It is alleged that the Chinese, in their dealings with Africa, bypass multilateral institutions like the World Bank and the International Monetary Fund and flout many of their lending criteria, including minimum standards of transparency, open bidding for contracts, environmental impact studies and assessments of overall debt and fiscal policies.

The risks and threats posed by Chinese investments in Zambia range from: (a) potential for corruption and patrimonialism; (b) Dutch disease effect on the economy;[26] (c) environmental degradation; (d) safety and health issues; and (e) low wages and poor labour relations. Some ask whether China's willingness to spend whatever it needs in Africa without regard to fiscal prudence, democracy, honest business practices and human rights produces a replay of past booms, enriching local elites but leaving the continent poorer, its environment despoiled and its natural resources depleted. An auditor-general's report over a 20-year period estimates that about K348 244 billion of public money is either misappropriated, stolen or grossly mismanaged every year in Zambia.[27] In addition, Zambia ranks 123rd out of 179 countries on the Tranparency International Corruption Index.[28]

With regard to China's investment initiatives in Zambia, major complaints have emerged in the field of labour relations. Chinese enterprises are often accused of exploiting workers through the payment of low wages and unsatisfactory working conditions, such as those relating to the health and safety of workers. A coal mine in Maamba, southern Zambia, was closed down after reports that workers were being sent underground without protective clothing. More importantly, one of the worst mining disasters in Zambian mining history occurred in 2006 at the Chinese-owned Chambishi mine where 46 miners were killed. The accident was blamed on lax safety standards. Other concerns include increased environmental degradation and investment in sectors that do not add value to the raw materials obtained in the country. Chinese companies are further accused of importing Chinese labour for jobs that could be done by Zambians, especially in the construction industries, and of exporting low-quality goods to Zambia. These are, however, common problems that arise regardless of the race or origins of the investor and they are matters on which governments can take legislative measures.

The issues raised are therefore pertinent for the conduct of enterprises from other countries as well – not only the emerging capital-exporting countries (Brazil, India, Malaysia), but also the Organisation for Economic Cooperation and Development (OECD) countries. They demand that Zambia strengthens the legislative framework and the monitoring capacity of government institutions such as the Environmental Council, Bureau of Standards, the Labour Department and the Factory Safety Inspections Units to enable them to deal with these problems effectively and proactively. The importance of good governance in economic management cannot be over-emphasised. Governance is central to all issues relating to the efficiency affecting government operations and economic development. Investors are not philanthropists driven by a moral code. They are typically large organisations, each with its own set of goals and objectives, motivated by profit and strategic interests, both national and corporate. It is the Zambian government that must put in place a framework to ensure the pursuit of profit is carried out in the context of respect for worker's rights and the protection of the environment. The Zambian government has put in place institutions that are beginning to address the conduct of investors; for example, in partnership with the International Labour Organisation, it has completed the Zambia Decent Work Programme that caters for improved working conditions and social protection for workers.[29] Consequently, in a recent case in the town of Kabwe, a Chinese-owned factory, Fine Street Manufacturing Company, was closed down by the government on the orders of a factory inspector on the grounds that the Chinese firm failed to comply with safety regulations. Following the inspection of the factory, it was discovered that the environment at the plant was unsafe as it constituted a threat to the health and safety of the workers. Among other risks was exposure of workers to dust, which could cause respiratory diseases, high temperatures in the working areas, unguarded machinery, inadequate personal protective clothing and equipment, as well as poor sanitary conditions. The Chinese company complied and met all the requirements demanded by the inspectors.[30] Meanwhile, the accusation that China is underwriting oppression by investing in rogue regimes is difficult to sustain because dictatorships in Sudan, the Congo and Zimbabwe existed long before there was any significant Chinese investment in those territories.

Chinese investment in Zambia became a political issue in the 2006 Zambian Presidential elections. One opposition leader, Michael Sata, of the Patriotic Front Party, campaigned on an anti-China platform and promised to expel the Chinese if elected to office and to break diplomatic relations with China and instead establish relations with Taiwan.[31] Sata accused Chinese enterprises of exploiting workers through the payment of low wages; unsatisfactory working conditions, such as those relating to health and the safety of workers; and of importing Chinese labour, instead of hiring Zambians.[32] Early in 2008, a strike and subsequent sackings at Chambishi Copper Smelter attracted widespread media attention. The smelter is a joint venture between China Nonferrous Metal Mining (CNMN) and Yunnan Copper Industry (YNCIG). The German company, Norddeutsche, and an Australian company, Ord River Resources, also have a stake in the venture.[33] Workers constructing a smelter rioted and destroyed company property in protest at what they said were low wages. The workers were fired but many of them were subsequently reinstated. The strike action was, however, later found to have been caused by an unfounded rumour that while wage negotiations were going on with union officials, the Chinese managers at Chambishi were planning to go on holiday. The leadership of the trade union to which the workers belonged denounced the strike and disassociated themselves from it. During the general elections, China, ill advisedly, reacted to Sata's public attacks on Chinese investors and threatened to halt all investments to Zambia if Sata was elected president. This was perceived as an unnecessary interference in Zambian internal politics.

While Sata's stance has received much publicity abroad, opposing views have not been as widely covered. The Zambian government has continued to welcome Chinese investment. The Zambian deputy-minister of finance has stated: 'There is no doubt that China has been good for Zambia, why should we have a bad attitude toward the Chinese when they are doing all the right things? They are bringing investment, world class technology, jobs, value addition. What more can you ask for?'[34] Other sectors of Zambian society have voiced their support for Chinese investments, for example, the Zambia Consumer Association. The chairperson of the Association stated: 'We are in support of Chinese investment in Zambia, the country needs a lot of investment, people need jobs.'[35] Church leaders have spoken out in opposition to Sata's campaign against Chinese investors. Bishop Chihana of the International Fellowship of Christian Churches of Zambia (IFCC) claimed: 'It's wrong and unethical to do what Mr Sata is doing . . . government should ensure that the investment climate is conducive not only for the Chinese but other nationalities as well.'[36] Further, two opposition parties, the United Liberal Party (ULP) and the United Party for National Development

(UPND), have also condemned Sata's blanket condemnation of Chinese nationals:[37] 'Like anywhere, you find good and bad people and so it is not fair to label all Chinese as crooks. We have a duty as leaders to promote and attract foreign investors. We have to ensure that investors come to Zambia and create jobs for our people.'[38] In addition, business associations in Zambia have generally welcomed Chinese investments.[39] They have, however, asked the government to assist Zambian entrepreneurs to capture the foreign direct investment through partnerships. Therefore, while there are areas of tension and ethical concerns with respect to Chinese investments in Zambia, it is clear that the reaction of Zambians to Chinese investments is complex, but on the whole, welcomed. There is also consensus that the government should take measures to regulate and ensure that Chinese investment will have the greatest possible development impact on the country.

CONCLUSIONS AND RECOMMENDATIONS

Foreign investment is desperately needed in Zambia to address the capital deficit in the country. Zambia is not attracting the much-needed investment despite the existence of lucrative investment opportunities in the country because its investment climate is riddled with rigidities that need to be addressed. The final criterion of an investment climate depends primarily on the political and legal security of the country. There is a need to convince investors that there is little or no possibility of the creation of an unfavourable legal situation at a later date that will be harmful to their investments.[40] In general, the responsibility of the government is to create a conducive business and political climate and to perpetuate an atmosphere of trust between itself and investors. It can only achieve this by committing itself to the future and by promising with reasonable credibility that arbitrary measures are not going to be taken once an investor has established his or her operations. Also, the government needs to reassure foreign investors that existing measures and agreements will continue to be respected or that should changes be desired, investors will be compensated for any loss due to such changes. In short, investors have to be assured that they will receive, both today and in the future, legally defined and controlled treatment. However, as the Zambian government encourages investment, it should also implement measures that promote corporate governance. These measures should ensure the respect of workers' rights, the protection of the environment and the efficient management of investments. The state should also design systems that require accepted accounting and auditing practices and maintain standards of responsibility that ensure the continuous monitoring of operations and full documentation of all transactions.

Zambia should strategically structure itself to benefit from the emerging Sino-Africa relations and investment collaborations. It must focus on the development of education, technology, science, energy and infrastructure as the method to drive economic growth, and it must direct Chinese investment in these areas. These forms of investment would help the country to escape its dependence on commodities and low-skill manufacturing. Furthermore, it will assist in building capacity, which will enable it to escape its current role as a raw materials exporter. As President Thabo Mbeki of South Africa has rightly observed, if Africa just exported raw materials to China while importing Chinese manufactured goods, the African continent could be condemned to underdevelopment,[41] which would simply mean a replication of Africa's historical relationship with its former colonial powers.[42] From the Chinese perspective, however, Zambia's level of development and resource endowment make the exploitation of natural resources an appropriate development strategy. Thus, it is up to Zambia to use the resources that these exports generate wisely to take it to the next level of developmental progress. It is also worth noting that China and a number of other Asian countries have accumulated huge reserves, which Zambia and other African countries can tap as a source of much needed investments (China – US$1.3 trillion; Hong Kong – US$136.3 billion; India – US$211.7 billion).

It is prudent to note here that even the much-heralded commodity boom and increased investment in mining are partly a result of increased demand from China. For example, China has now surpassed the United States as the world's leading importer of copper. This symbiotic relationship, if managed properly, can be beneficial for both China and Zambia. Consequently, there is a need to change the current mindset about China to one that is more embracing and one in which Africans determine the terms of engagement. China is one major source of much-needed capital, which in partnership with African states might very well turn the tables of development in Africa. In addition, China's own development experience is phenomenal and has some positive lessons for Africa, not least because of its strategic emphasis on infrastructure development. It has reduced poverty by the greatest margins in recent times. Essentially, Zambia must learn from the example of China's development strategies, and form a long-term partnership that will benefit both countries. It is only through the development of Zambian infrastructure, the implementation of structural reforms to increase Zambia's competitiveness and the formation of a credible investment climate, that Zambia will achieve higher levels of development and provide increased standards of living for its citizens.[43]

In order for Zambia to benefit effectively from its engagement with China, several steps must be taken. Zambia needs to (a) collect comprehensive data on the financial, commercial, social and environmental impact of Chinese investment; (b) establish clear development objectives and identify priorities; (c) identify mechanisms to meet the objectives; (d) provide the institutional arrangements to implement the mechanisms; and (e) include all relevant local stakeholders, especially the poor, in the policy-formulation process.[44] These steps would allow Zambia to (a) attract foreign (including Chinese) investment, which is essential to reducing its capital deficit; (b) invest heavily in infrastructure with particular emphasis on transportation and energy; and (c) improve competitiveness of Zambian goods and add value to raw materials produced in Zambia. A key to increasing Zambian competitiveness in a global knowledge-based economy is to further develop innovations through the applications of and advances in science and technology and investment in higher education and research.

NOTES

1. H.G. Broadman, *Africa's Silk Road: China and India's New Economic Frontier* (Washington, DC: The World Bank, 2007), p. 100.
2. L. Polgreen and W. French. 'China's Trade in Africa Carries a Price Tag', *The New York Times*, 21 August 2007. http://www.nytimes.com (accessed on 21 December 2007).
3. A. Geda, 'The Impact of China and India on Africa: Trade, FFDI and the African Manufacturing Sector: Issues and Challenges', AERC project, September 2006.
4. J.M. Mwanakatwe, *End of Kaunda Era* (Lusaka: Multimedia Publications, 1993), p. 72.
5. M. Ayogu, 'Impact of China and India on Politics and Governance in SSA: Issues and Challenges', framework paper on politics and governance (EETC Project on SSA-Asian Drivers), February 2007.
6. See article by M. Gunther, 'IBM's Next Big Thing: Africa'. http://cnnmoney.printthis.clickability.com/pt/cpt (accessed on 9 December 2007). Gunther states that while all eyes are on India and China, the technology giant sees business opportunity in the expanding economy of the world's poorest continent.
7. B. Berger, 'China Outwits the EU in Africa', *Asia Times*, 13 December 2007. http://www.atimes.com (accessed on 21 December 2007).
8. China's Africa Policy, January 2006. In the paragraph on investments, it states: 'The Chinese Government encourages and supports Chinese enterprise's investment and business in Africa, and will continue to provide preferential loans and buyer credits to this end.' http://www.gov.cn/misc/2006-01/12/content_156490.htm
9. B.J. Ndulu et al., *Challenges of African Growth: Opportunities, Constraits, and Strategic Directions* (Washington, DC: The World Bank, 2007), p. 4.
10. Ndulu et al., *Challenges of African Growth.*
11. Ndulu et al., *Challenges of African Growth.*

12. Central Intelligence Agency, 'The World Factbook: Zambia' (2007). http://www.cia.gov/library/publications/the-world-factbook (accessed on 21 December 2007).
13. African Development Bank, 'African Economic Outlook 2007', African Development Bank/Organisation for Economic Cooperation and Development, 2007, pp. 500–600.
14. United Nations Development Programme, 'Human Development Report: Zambia' (2007). http://www.undp.org (accessed on 21 December 2007).
15. African Development Bank, 'African Economic Outlook 2007'.
16. 'Chinese Investment Helps Zambia's Economy', Xinhua News Agency, 1 November 2007. htpp://www.china.org.cn (accessed on 21 December 2007).
17. 'China, Zambia Witness Booming Economic Cooperation', *People's Daily Online*. http://english.peopledaily.com.cn/200702/02 (accessed on 1 February 2008).
18. 'China, Zambia Witness Booming Economic Cooperation'.
19. 'Zambia President Hails Zambia-China Trade Co-op', *People's Daily Online*, 19 December 2007. http://english.poeple.com.cn (accessed on 21 December 2007).
20. 'Zambia: State Seeks Chinese Investment to Meet $3 billion Target', *The Times of Zambia*, 21 December 2007.
21. 'Zambia: State Seeks Chinese Investment to Meet $3 billion Target'.
22. African Development Bank/African Development Fund, 'Zambia: 2002–2004. Country Strategy Paper: 2006 Update', pp. 4–5.
23. 'Mining Groups are Emboldened by Notions of a Super-Cycle', *Financial Times*, 20 July 20 2007.
24. 'Asian Mining Investment Swells', *Times of Zambia*, 10 March 2007. http://www.times co.ZM/news/viewnews.cgi (accessed on 31 October 2007).
25. Broadman, *Africa's Silk Road*, p. 34 ff.
26. Dutch disease refers to the movement of resources from tradable sectors to the commodity (mining) sector, creating problems for a country to diversify its economy.
27. G. Neumann, 'TI Zambia Launches its New Publication "Show me the Money!"' *Transparency International*, 27 March 2007. http://www.transparency.org (accessed on 22 December 2007).
28. 'Corruption Perception Index', *Transparency International* (2007). http://www.transparency.org (accessed on 22 December 2007).
29. 'State Forms Labor Task Force', Zambia Communications Systems Ltd. http://www.Zamnet.ZM/newssys/news/viewnews.cgi (accessed on 21 November, 2007).
30. 'Shut Chinese Firm Set to Resume Operations', *Times of Zambia*, 26 November 2007. http://www.times.co.zm/news/views.cgi (accessed on 26 November 2007).
31. L. Polgreen and H. French, 'In Africa, China is Both Benefactor and Competitor', *The New York Times*, 13 September 2007. http://www. Nytimes.com/2007/08/20/africa/20cnd-zambia.html?.
32. Mr Sata repeated his allegations at a Harvard seminar, see B. Phiri, 'Zambia Has Fallen Prey to Unscrupulous Chinese Investors – Sata', 25 October 2007, http://maravi.blogsport.com/207/10/zambiahas-fallen-preyto unscrupulous.html (accessed on 20 April 2008).
33. *Times of Zambia*, 10 March 2008.
34. Polgreen and French, 'In Africa, China is Both Benefactor and Competitor'.
35. 'Consumer Watchdog Supports Chinese Investment', *Daily Mail*, 29 October 2007. http://www.dailmail.co.zm/press/news/viewnews.cgi?category (accessed on 20 April 2008).
36. 'Opposition Censures Sata', *Times of Zambia*, 29 October 2007. http://www.times.co.zm/news/vienews.cgi? Category+2andid (accessed on 20 April 2008).
37. 'Opposition Censures Sata'.

38. 'Opposition Censures Sata'.
39. G. Kaimana, 'Zambians Prodded to Enter into Partnerships', *Times of Zambia*, 26 November 2007. http://www.times.co.zm/news/vienews.cgi?category+11andid (accessed on 20 April 2008).
40. A primary mode of securing investment through law is by the constitutional protection of private property. Article 16(1) of the Zambian Constitution protects the right to property subject to a number of exceptions.
41. T. Mbeki (interview, *Financial Times*), 1 April 2007.
42. T. Mbeki (interview, *Financial Times*), 1 April 1007.
43. See also 'Memorandum of the President of the International Development Association to the Executive Directors on a Country Assistance Strategy for the Republic of Zambia' (World Bank, March 2004), p. 16. http://www.worldbank.org (accessed on 21 December 2007).
44. On how mineral-based economies like Zambia can use the mining sector to alleviate poverty and spur development, see M. Weber-Fahr et al., 'Mining', in *A Sourcebook for Poverty Reduction Strategies* (Washington, DC: The World Bank, n.d.) pp. 439–68. http://www.worldbank.org (accessed on 21 December 2001).

9

The Three Faces of the Dragon

Tanzania-China Relations in Historical Perspective

Mwesiga Baregu

INTRODUCTION

Unlike many African countries that have developed close relations with China only in the last ten years, Tanzania has had a much longer relationship with the Middle Kingdom, dating back to the early 1960s. Indeed, it could be said that Tanzania played something of a pioneering role in establishing Sino-African relations. This relationship has undergone a number of twists and turns resulting from, inter alia, Tanzania and China's changing ideological orientations; changes in the international power environment; Tanzania's economic decline and the resulting pressures from international financial institutions (IFIs), especially in relation to the country's macroeconomic policies. The relationship was also affected by the developments leading to major political and economic changes in China itself in the 1970s and 1980s. In line with these parameters, therefore, the relationship between the two countries has gone through roughly three phases:

- The initial phase, which lasted from the early 1960s to the end of the 1970s, could be labelled 'the dragon's embrace'. It stressed a time when Sino-Tanzanian relations were characterised by a strong component of 'proletarian internationalism' where China gave economic assistance to newly independent African states and shared solidarity with African movements engaged in liberation struggles. In Tanzania, China's political and economic support complemented a period of relatively fast growth in manufacturing and infrastructure construction.

- The second phase, which has its roots in the early 1980s to the early 1990s, is generally characterised by the internal power struggles and economic reforms in China that saw the relative disengagement from external commitments by the Deng Xiaoping leadership. In Tanzania, this was also a time of severe economic stress, marked by substantial declines in industry and agriculture and forcing the country to submit to structural adjustment programmes under the World Bank and the International Monetary Fund (IMF).
- The third and current phase began in the mid-1990s and continues to this day. This period has witnessed renewed vigour in Sino-Tanzanian relations with emphasis on trade and investment. China has increased investments in energy, construction work and timber, while Tanzania has imported a significant share of consumer goods, rather than industrial equipment.

This chapter reviews the three phases of Sino-Tanzanian relations in order to map out the changes and continuities in Dar es Salaam's engagement with Beijing. This is followed by an assessment of the relationship by observing significant trends in Sino-Tanzanian ties and the implications this has for deepening these relations in the future.

THE DRAGON'S EMBRACE: COMRADES-IN-ARMS

The first period in Tanzania's ties with China from the early 1960s is considered to be the halcyon days of Chinese support for Tanzania's economy, ideology and leadership in the construction of socialism and self-reliance at home and solidarity with the liberation struggles in southern Africa. It was also the period of Tanzania's shared vision with China's struggle for recognition of the One-China policy, as well as its admission into the United Nations in 1971, with strong African support, to replace Taiwan in the Security Council. At the same time Chairman Mao Zedong was actively seeking international support against United States aggression and Soviet 'social imperialism'. These expositions partly inspired Tanzania's adoption of the ideology of *ujamaa* – a type of socialism and self-reliance modelled along the lines of China's development strategy, which at that time stressed rural production through the establishment of local communes.

In short, this period signified the ideological convergence between Tanzania and China. Tanzanian leader, Julius Nyerere, was seeking to diversify his ideological alliances in a quest for an alternative development strategy to the British colonial model inherited at independence. China was reaching out to Africa and other countries in an attempt to attenuate its isolation and extend its ideological influence under Chairman Mao Zedong's theory of the Three Worlds. In this schema, most of Asia including China, as well as Africa and Latin America were part of the Third World; the European countries were in the Second World, and the Soviet Union and the United States were the First World superpowers.

At this time, Tanzania went through considerable primary industrialisation, which included, among other things, textiles, farm implements, large-scale rice farming and coal and steel mining. Most of this was undertaken with Chinese capital and technical assistance. It was probably the only time in Tanzania's history that such a high level of industrial employment has been reached. Owing to the labour intensity of Chinese technology and the close cooperation with Chinese technicians, Tanzanian workers acquired remarkable technical skills. In some of the factories, workers became so innovative that local technicians employed in the Friendship Textile Mill in Tanzania's capital, Dar es Salaam, were reported to have invented and forged new parts for the textile machinery. Industrial production was vibrant, with clear efforts being made to create forward and backward linkages, particularly in the cotton textile industry. Building manufacturing capacity became the strategic manifestation of the policy of self-reliance and the bridgehead to basic industry. In agriculture, the distinct formation of *ujamaa* villages was somewhat akin to Chinese communes.

Tanzania became arguably the largest and earliest recipient of Chinese assistance in Africa. This was after Nyerere paid his first visit to China in 1965 and signed the 'Friendship Treaty'. On his return, Nyerere commented in his state-of-the-nation address:

> I learned one important thing. China is a huge country with a population of more than six hundred million people. And the Chinese government is one of those which is making money and technicians available to Tanzania to help us with our Development Plan. But they are able to do this only because they are frugal people; they husband their resources very carefully indeed, and only spend money on things which are absolutely essential. This is true both of individuals and of the government. There are hardly any private cars in China; people go to work by bus or on bicycles. The government officials too, use cars only when it is really necessary for their job – and then the cars are small and cheap ones.[1]

Many other agreements followed in the wake of this visit. These resulted in the construction of the TAZARA Railway, Friendship Textile Mill, Mbarali Rice Farm, Kiwira Coal Mine (on the mainland) and Mahonda Sugarcane Factory in Zanzibar. The TAZARA Railway, in particular, was the largest and most visible project and was undertaken as part of China's support to the liberation struggle against imperialism and colonialism of the superpowers and the destabilising influence of the racist regimes of South Africa and southern Rhodesia.[2]

It needs to be stressed that Tanzania and Zambia first approached the Western countries and the then Soviet Union for the same project, but were turned down. Indeed, China's initial offer to undertake the project was intended to trigger a knee-jerk Western response to do it in the context of the Cold War. But the West continued to reject the project, favouring a road project that was eventually undertaken by the United States at the same time as the railway construction.

Arguably the largest Chinese aid project in Africa, the TAZARA Railway – popularly known as the Uhuru (freedom) railway – took nearly six years to construct. The project was colossal and involved complicated engineering techniques. Construction was carried out under the most difficult conditions resulting in the deaths of both Chinese and Tanzanian workers. Beijing provided an interest-free loan of US$450 million to finance the project. During this period, China also assisted Tanzania in establishing the Keko Pharmaceuticals factory, and the Ubungo Farm Implements factory in Dar es Salaam. China also supported the Mangula Mechanical Workshop (an offshoot of the TAZARA Railway construction project). All of these undertakings entailed interest-free loans, which, on maturity in 1999, totalled US$19.2 million in Tanzanian debt to China. In 2001, however, China signed an agreement with Tanzania in which Beijing unconditionally cancelled one-third of this debt '. . . with the view to supporting Tanzania to develop its national economy and reduce its debt burden'.[3]

China became the largest single external donor to Tanzania in the 1960s and 1970s, with aid transfers totalling US$4 000 million. It should be stressed that a significant part of this aid included the provision of Chinese medical teams, which became an important part of the provision of free medical services by the government.

China's model of rural socialism, known as Chinese agricultural communes, also appealed to the Nyerere government. In 1967, Tanzania declared a policy of 'socialism and self-reliance' and launched a programme of creating communal villages known as *ujamaa* villages. This programme entailed forced removals and the relocation of a large section of the country's rural population. It resulted in the disruption of traditional subsistence agricultural production, without establishing a more efficient and reliable system. This led to food shortages and, in many cases, the deepening of poverty among the rural population. It must be noted, however, that China was not directly involved in this programme.

Apart from projects such as the TAZARA Railway, China also engaged in different forms of military cooperation with a number of African countries. In Tanzania, military cooperation took the form of training and supplying the armed forces. By the 1980s, however, China itself was undergoing significant political changes and was in the process of shedding its ideological orientation in favour of a trade or business orientation in its relations with Africa. As Ai Ping argues: 'Before 1979, China's foreign aid was based more on the notion of "proletarian internationalism" and had a strong element of "idealism". Its efforts since the 1980s have become more realistic, with stress on "equality and mutual benefit emphasizing actual results, with different forms and aimed at mutual development"'.[4]

On aggregate during the *ujamaa* period, Tanzania tried to maintain a balanced relationship between the East and the West under the general rubric of non-alignment. Progressively, however, with the adoption of *ujamaa* policies in 1967 and in the context of collaboration in the liberation struggles in southern Africa, Tanzania and China grew closer in political, economic and even military terms. This was to change radically in the early 1980s with the adoption of structural adjustment policies and the gradual abandonment of the *ujamaa* policies. This change, which saw China's relative disengagement from Africa, was also a result of the onset of China's inward-looking policies under the 'Four Modernisations Programme' (in agriculture, industry, science and technology, and national defence), notwithstanding the political turmoil that ensued in the wake of Mao Zedong's death (see Chapter 2), which heralded the second phase of Sino-Tanzanian relations.

THE DRAGON RECOILS: ONE STEP BACKWARDS

In the early 1980s, the Tanzanian economy came under severe stress in the wake of the oil shocks of the mid-1970s and the persistent economic decline that followed. During the 1980s, Tanzania's attention was on short-term economic survival issues and Dar es Salaam did not pay much attention to long-term economic growth. It was during this period that the gains made in industrial production with Chinese cooperation were lost, along with the manufacturing momentum that had been stimulated. Industrial capacity became chronically under-utilised, resulting in a precipitous decline in industrial output. The maintenance of plants and machinery, as well as the replacement of parts, became difficult and plant shutdowns became commonplace. Public spending on education, health and water also became negligible, gross domestic product (GDP) growth was estimated at 2 per cent; while industrial production, mostly in state enterprises, declined to 1 per cent per annum.

All of this was happening under the structural adjustment programmes negotiated with the major IFIs (i.e. the World Bank and the IMF). The austerity measures of the programmes stressed privatisation, which led to most parastatal companies either being privatised or simply abandoned, including those formed with Chinese assistance. Whereas, the Friendship Textile Mill was privatised under a joint venture agreement, for example, the Ubungo Farm Implements factory was virtually abandoned by Nyerere. By the end of the 1980s and the beginning of the early 1990s, all pretence to socialism and self-reliance had been abandoned in favour of liberalisation and privatisation policies. This was marked by the Presidential Parastatal Sector Reform Commission, which was formed specifically to liquidate state-owned enterprises. By this time, Chinese industrial (production-oriented) cooperation had also become eclipsed by growing trade relations. It is significant to note that in this period, China was looking inward, focusing its attention on its 'modernisation' programme. This second period characterised the lowest interaction between China and Tanzania.

THE DRAGON'S RETURN: STRATEGIC PARTNERSHIP OR SELF-INTEREST?

The beginning of the 1990s signalled a renewal of Sino-Tanzanian ties where liberalisation became Tanzania's official policy framework, while China embarked on a new phase of aggressive economic expansion. The re-emergence of China in Tanzania was part of Beijing's overall strategy of pursuing new economic relations across the African continent.

This third phase also marks the time when Nyerere relinquished the position of party chairperson, which he had held since retiring from the Presidency in 1985. Nyerere's resignation in 1987 was directly linked to the changes in the political ideology and economic policy of the country, with Tanzania's metamorphosis from a largely statist, socialist and self-reliance-seeking economy, into a private-sector driven, quasi-capitalist and open economy.

Nyerere's departure from power also marked the end of the old ideological relationship between Tanzania and China and ushered in the beginning of a new one, which focused primarily on trade and resource extraction. Under the neo-liberal influence, Tanzania's economic policy has shifted from a focus on microeconomic dynamism to macroeconomic stability. Hence, economic resources have steadily shifted from production to commerce, leading to a general decline in industrial output. What used to be factories are now *go-downs* stocked with foreign imports. Moreover, industrial production has continued to decline as a proportion of national output, while imports have increased. It is this demand for imports that has fuelled the rapidly growing trade in largely consumer goods from China. However, as long as the demand for imports is not matched by export earnings, Tanzania is bound to face a growing balance of payments problem with China. This could force Dar es Salaam to engage in some detrimental forms of resource-based barter trade arrangements with Beijing to meet its obligations.

It is important to note that during this period, Tanzania-China relations gradually entered a new phase marked by three dominant trends: declining investment in manufacturing and growing export trade; diminished interest in ideological issues; and increasing investment in raw materials and infrastructure construction.

INVESTMENT

Patterns of Chinese investment and trade in Tanzania are still emerging and therefore difficult to profile in a definite manner. What is clear, however, is that over the last 40 years or so, the Chinese investment presence in Tanzania presents a mixed picture. Unlike the *ujamaa* years, during which Chinese investment largely assumed the form of loans, normally accompanied by technical personnel, extended to capitalise state-owned enterprises, from the 1990s, direct investment from China has seen the entrance of Chinese companies in almost all sectors of Tanzania's economy. Areas of investment range from mineral extraction (such as coal mining) to sugarcane farming, textile manufacturing and fishing. By 2006, China had 134 projects in Tanzania, which accounted for 8 per cent of the total foreign projects; this ranked China fourth among the top investors in Tanzania. The value of the projects amounted to US$833.23 million, and China is ranked sixth among the total value of FDI flows in Tanzania. Currently, it is estimated that about 147 Chinese companies have invested in Tanzania in a variety of sectors.

Table 9.1 Breakdown of investment of Chinese companies in the Tanzanian economy, 1990–2006.

Sector	Companies	Jobs	Investment value (US$ millions)
Agriculture	5	928	42.45
Construction	11	1 398	14.83
Manufacturing	110	45 969	317.19
Natural resources	6	691	7.12
Transport	4	190	2.91
Services	5	123	3.26
Tourism	6	318	7.03

Source: Compiled from the Tanzanian Investment Centre.

In Table 9.1, the overall picture that emerges from the size of capital invested is that total investment stands at US$398 790 million. In terms of sector dominance, Chinese investment is primarily concentrated in manufacturing, followed by agriculture and construction. Natural resources come fourth, followed closely by tourism. Most Chinese companies in Tanzania, however, hold less than US$1 million in investment. Out of the 147 companies, only 22 hold portfolios in excess of this amount. There are only three companies that have capital investments above this figure: one that has invested in building materials to the value of US$17 170 million, and the other two companies have investments over US$159 000 million in sugarcane farming. Other areas of visible Chinese investment include Chinese traditional medical practices. Whereas Chinese doctors in government hospitals were a regular feature of the aid programme of the 1970s, the new migrants are '. . . private entrepreneurs, many ill trained and some operating in the gray zones of legality'[5] and their numbers are growing.

An interesting and emerging aspect of China's investment in Tanzania is the forging of partnerships between Chinese corporates and other foreign companies. A Canadian company, Tanzania Royalty Exploration Corporation, recently announced that it had entered into negotiations with a Chinese company for thirteen prospecting licences in Tanzania. The licences include gold properties in the Ushirombo, Lunguya, and Nyanzaga area of Tanzania and nickel licences in the Kagera/Kabanga nickel belt. Tanzania Royalty chairperson, James Sinclair, has argued that his company's timely '. . . acquisition of its diverse asset base in one of the world's great mineral producing regions – along with [China's] political capital build up in Tanzania over the years bodes well for its future'.[6] He concludes that few would dispute the proposition that China is the partner of choice in today's mineral industry.

From a manufacturing point of view, China and Tanzania have reached an advanced stage in negotiations for one of the three to five special economic zones (SEZ) proposed by the Forum on China-Africa Cooperation (FOCAC) summit in November 2006. The first SEZ is a metals hub, which has already been launched in Zambia's Copperbelt region, with the Chambisi Copper Smelter as the core enterprise (see Chapter 8). Others countries that are being considered are Mauritius (trading hub), Nigeria (manufacturing hub) and Egypt. The Dar es Salaam SEZ is designed to be a trans-shipment hub for commodities mined in the Copperbelt. This will be linked to the TAZARA Railway terminal to Kapirimposhi, which, in turn, links up with the Benguela railway to Angola, creating '. . . for the first time . . . a functioning east-west infrastructure corridor across the continent'.[7] Although China presents the zones as development cooperation initiatives, they are actually intended to strengthen the 'Going Out' strategy of Chinese public and private enterprises in China's eleventh Five-Year Plan period.

TRADE

Trade between Tanzania and China has been growing rapidly since 2003 in the wake of the domestic open-market policy. The volume of trade increased from 124 722 million Tanzanian schillings in 2003 to 347 237 million in 2005. By 2005, China ranked third among Dar es Salaam's trading partners, constituting 6.7 per cent of Tanzania's total trade volume. However, this growth in trade has entailed imbalances. Chinese exports to Tanzania have been growing at a higher rate than Tanzanian exports to China. According to Tanzanian figures, the value of trade between the two countries more than doubled from US$124 million in 2003 to US$347 million in 2007, with Chinese exports accounting for a greater share of the trade volume.

Although in June 2007, it was reported that Beijing had allowed 442 commodities into the Chinese market duty free, this had not had a significant impact on Tanzanian exports to China. At the same time, Chinese exports were eroding the local market in Tanzania for domestically produced goods. A local company in Tanzania producing flip-flops (rubber sandals), for example, used to employ 3 000 workers, but by 2006, was employing only 1 000 people and finding it difficult to compete with Chinese imports (see Figures 9.1 and 9.2).

Between 1998 and 2002, the trade imbalance between Tanzania and China grew from 46.38 per cent to 78.23 per cent. According to Chinese sources, in 2005, total trade between the two countries reached US$474.3 million, of which China's exports to Tanzania equalled US$303.59 million, while imports from Tanzania stood at US$170.71 million. The composition of Chinese exports to Tanzania includes foodstuffs, vehicles, textiles, light industrial products, chemical products, mechanical equipment, electrical appliances and steel. Tanzania, for its part, exports fresh and dried seafood, raw leather, coarse copper, wooden handcrafts, cotton, paper yarn, woven fabrics, glassware, timber, iron, steel, coffee, edible fruits and nuts. Major imports to Tanzania from China include: articles of iron and steel, vehicles, nuclear reactors, boilers, machinery, mechanical appliances, electrical machinery equipment parts, and leather goods.[8]

Apart from the manufacturing sector, the footprint of Chinese companies can also be seen in the construction and telecommunications sectors, timber and other wood products. Unfortunately trade has been marred by illegal activity, resulting in an estimated annual loss of nearly US$58 million between 2001 and 2005 as a result of poor governance and corruption.[9]

Table 9.2 Tanzania-China trade statistics (in millions of Tanzanian shillings).

Year	1999	2000	2001	2002	2003	2004	2005
Exports Imports	90 43 213	483 54 453	620 61 830	688 76 335	3 886 120 836	76 742 186 806	101 838 245 399
Balance of trade	(43 123)	(53 970)	(61 210)	(75 647)	(116 950)	(110 064)	(14 356)
Volume of trade	43 303	54 936	62 450	77 023	124 722	263 548	347 237
Tanzania total trade	1 641 628	1 750 394	2 190 391	2 481 830	3 402 534	4 186 429	5 204 459
% of volume to total trade	2.64	2.14	2.85	1.84	3.67	7.75	6.67
Ranking: Exports Imports	 66 10	 48 7	 48 8	 49 8	 30 6	 5 5	 3 2

Source: Tanzania Revenue Authority (TRA) 2007

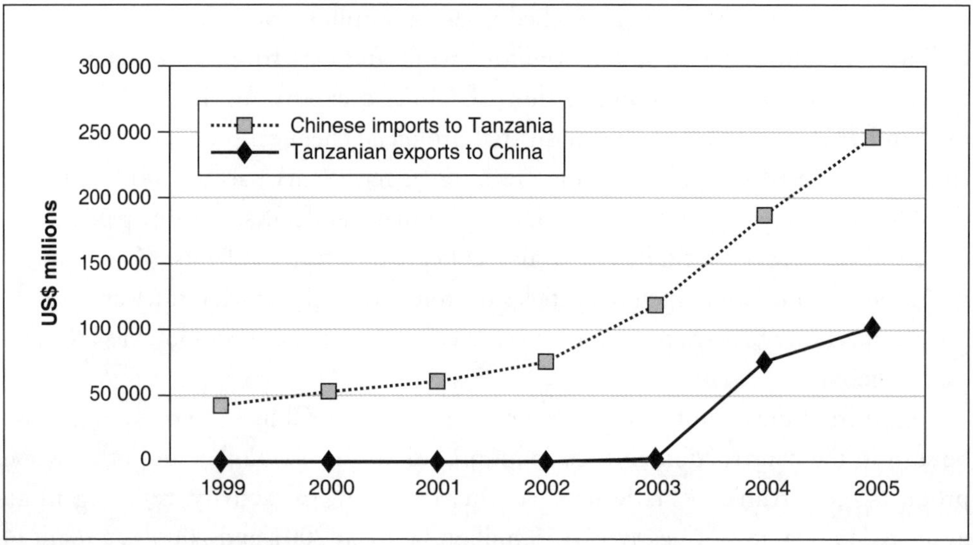

Figure 9.1 Exports-imports graph: Tanzania and China.

Source: TRA 2007

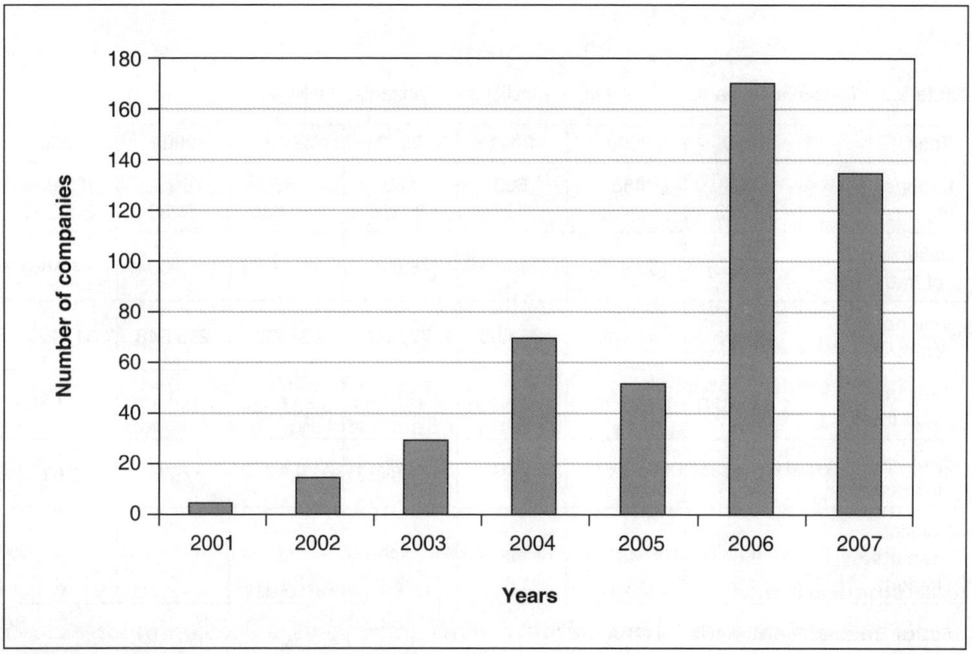

Figure 9.2 Tanzanian companies trading with China, 2001–07.

Source: http://www.made-in-china.com/global-company-index

CONCLUSION: WHO'S AFRAID OF THE EASTERN DRAGON?

China's renewed and growing engagement with Tanzania will remain rather enigmatic for a while, as is the case in most African countries. This is because Beijing's emerging policy towards Africa, in general terms, is progressively acquiring a realistic feature in which China's interests will be the major driving force. This does not mean, however, that the interests of China and Tanzania are diametrically opposed. These can be mutually reinforcing, so that the 'win-win' outcomes espoused by China's policy statements are achievable. This will, however, depend much more on objective conditions of demand and supply, rather than on subjective conditions of narrow interests. Bilateral relations will also be shaped by the level of political will, as well as the marketing and negotiation skills from the Tanzanian side.

Nevertheless, China represents more of an opportunity than a threat to Dar es Salaam, if Tanzania and other African countries act as a collective group in their engagement with Beijing. Dealing with China separately will not only weaken African countries, but may also deny Africa large-scale projects that can only be undertaken on a continental scale. That China took the initiative to create FOCAC is some indication that, unlike Western countries, China prefers to interact with Africa as a whole. Through FOCAC and the African Union (AU), African countries have an opportunity to form their own strategic teams to deal with China and to negotiate as a group. Moreover, African countries such as Tanzania now have an opportunity to present China with projects that straddle borders of individual countries, such as hydroelectricity projects or trans-Africa communication systems. This is something that already appears to be taking place, despite the nature of China's bilateral engagements with individual African states. The trans-shipment SEZ hub that is to be set up in Dar es Salaam is a case in point of a regional transport corridor that traverses three African countries (Angola, Tanzania and Zambia).

China certainly presents Tanzania with more coherent and fresh opportunities than the New Partnership for Africa's Development (NEPAD), which was created in 2001 to promote economic development in Africa, or the EU-ACP Cotonou Agreement's Economic Partnership Agreements (EPAs) (see Chapter 15). Tanzania, like the rest of Africa, needs to make a clear decision on whether to continue to hinge its economic fortunes on its traditional Western markets or to diversify steadily towards deeper engagement with China. In order to maximise gains, a decision to forge closer relations with China must be collectively undertaken, preferably under the umbrella of the AU.

The objective conditions facing Tanzania and Africa, as a whole, include, but are not confined to, the practical circumstances or imperatives that necessitate a positive-sum game. Five of these conditions include:

1. Tanzania and China have a relationship that spans a 40-year history in which attempts were made to set up a manufacturing sector linked to a basic industry sector in coal mining and iron smelting. The two countries were roughly at the same level of development until recently, when China made an economic leap forward. Dar es Salaam can capitalise on its long-term relationship with Beijing to forge a new link, as long as it has clear aims and objectives to learn from China's path and Beijing is keen to share its experience through training opportunities in Tanzania and in China.
2. China's growing demand for resources can be turned into an industrialisation opportunity for Africa. Tanzania can take a lead in this process by drawing upon its experience with China to organise other countries to negotiate large-scale technology-transfer projects. China's level of technology, particularly the labour intensity in its industrial production, is certainly more appropriate for Africa. This can create added employment and opportunities for artisan-miners, for example.
3. Technology transfer can also be achieved through resource-for-technology barter exchanges, bypassing the conventional international trade with hard currency, which is in short supply in Tanzania.
4. China offers Tanzania an opportunity to expand its market for traditional commodities such as cashew nuts, coffee and cotton and to diversify the composition of its production output in manufacturing and agriculture using its massive market size. A division of labour can be created between both countries.
5. China needs Africa as an ally in the struggle against the hegemony of the United States (see Chapters 13 and 14). Beijing, therefore, has a vested interest in strengthening the continent. A stronger Tanzania – one less subservient to the United States – is more likely to stand by China. This has particular relevance since the collapse of the Soviet Union and the rise of America's 'War on Terrorism'.

In conclusion, the subjective conditions of this relationship revolve around what Tanzania, in particular, must fulfil to realise its aspirations in the relationship. Four of these key factors include:

1. Political will, which is well grounded in the recognition of, and commitment to, mutual interests and trust between Tanzania and China. Since political will is a function of national interests, it will be necessary for Tanzania and China to identify and negotiate their interests openly and honestly, particularly with a view to promote trade that will lead to industrial transformation in Tanzania.
2. The capacity to take risks. The pragmatism that Tanzania exhibited during the *ujamaa* years demonstrates a risk-aversion when it comes to braving the frontiers and pursuing policies that are in the interests of the Tanzanian people. Dar es Salaam must return to this pragmatism, as well as diversifying its economies away from traditional patterns of trade and investment. Whereas it is clear that the adoption of the Washington Consensus has not brought prosperity to Tanzania, it remains less clear whether what some have described as China's Beijing Consensus offers a unique opportunity to transform Tanzania's economy and break away from structural dependence. Dar es Salaam must not feel uncomfortable taking advantage of its long historical relationship with Beijing to pursue its material interests.
3. Tanzania should develop a 'resource nationalism', as is the case with the Hugo Chavez regime in Venezuela, in response to its own economic transformation needs and China's resource hunger. This must also be beneficial to the overall African strategic partnership with Beijing. In this regard, Dar es Salaam needs to participate in the preparation of an African comprehensive resource survey, exploitation and utilisation plan. Such a plan should link the resources of different countries by resource regions akin to the plan proposed by Cheik Anta Diop[10] in the early 1970s. Tanzania, along with larger African groupings, should negotiate partnership agreements with China, rather than the traditional concessions that tend to disadvantage the host country.
4. Tanzania must participate in a collective African effort to marshall strategic economic information on global traditional and emerging markets, particularly for natural resources and agricultural products. Such an exercise should map out Africa's current position and role in the international division of labour. This initiative should also seek to carve out a new economic space that will reposition Africa in the emerging post-Cold-War international division of labour.

NOTES

1. Quoted in N.O. Ndeskoi, 'Mwalimu JK Nyerere is Kicking himself in his Grave'. http://www.raceandhistory.com.
2. Ministry of Foreign Affairs of the PRC, 'China's Assistance in the Construction of the Tanzania-Zambia Railway', 17 November 2000. http://www.fmprc.gov.cn/eng.
3. 'China Agrees to Cancel Part of Tanzania's Debt', *China View*, 12 October 2001.
4. A. Ping, 'From Proletarian Internationalism to Mutual Development: China's Cooperation with Tanzania: 1965–95', in G. Hyden and R. Mukandala (eds.), *Agencies in Foreign Aid: Comparing China, Sweden and the United States in Tanzania* (Basingstoke: Macmillan, 1999). See also http://www.fmprc.gov.cn/eng.
5. E. Hsu, 'Medicine as a Business: Chinese Medicine in Tanzania', Institute for Social and Cultural Anthropology, University of Oxford. http://www.ascleiden.nl/Pdf/paper.
6. 'Tanzania Royalty Enters into Contract Negotiations for Mineral Licenses with Company from PRC', 9 August 2007. http://www.bizyahoo.com.
7. M. Davies, 'China's Development Model Comes to Africa', *Review of African Political Economy* 115(35), 2008.
8. R. Canter, 'Guilty Imports in Tanzania', 25 November 2006. http://www.rachelcanter.blogspot.com.
9. E. Barclay, 'China Spurring Illegal Timber Trade in Tanzania', *National Geographic News*, 21 December 2007.
10. C.A. Diop, *Black Africa: The Economic and Cultural Basis for a Federated Republic* (Westport, Connecticut: Lawrence Hill and Co, 1974).

10

Balancing a Strategic Partnership?

South Africa-China Relations

Sanusha Naidu

INTRODUCTION

This chapter is based on an earlier article that appeared in the 2005–06 *State of the Nation* publication.[1] In the period since that chapter was written, relations between China and South Africa have deepened. This has seen significant increases in official visits from both sides, a reaffirmation of the commitment to reform the international system in order to create a fairer and more equitable global order, as well as growing bilateral cooperation in politics, the economy, trade and investment, technology, education, human resource development and tourism. At the 2007 meeting of the Bi-National Commission (BNC) in Beijing, South Africa's Deputy-President, Phumzile Mlambo-Ngucka, applauded the relationship for its win-win approach. As one analyst commented: 'engaging with China politically and recalibrating our economic policies towards her are absolute necessities' for the South African government.[2]

Likewise, China places a high premium on relations with Pretoria. In fact, South Africa is perceived as a strategic ally, given its economic strength and position vis-à-vis the southern African region and the continent more broadly, its reputable international status, and not least because of its influence and position in advancing a multilateral global order aligned to Africa's reintegration into the global economy. Pretoria's own expression of South-South cooperation and increasing the voice of the economically marginalised and less developed reinforces Beijing's aims of global harmony and common prosperity for all.

But relations between South Africa and China are still in the embryonic stage. As suggested in the earlier article, the Mandela Presidency faced one of the more critical tests in its foreign policy, namely debating the Two-China policy. Deliberating whether to remain with Taipei or to follow the international consensus and formally recognise Beijing posed a challenge for the newly elected government, given the high premium it placed on human rights in its foreign-policy formulation, at least in its early years.

Even if the Mandela Presidency were to stand by this universal approach to foreign policy, it could ill afford to ignore Beijing, which was fast becoming an alternative centre of power in an otherwise unilateral post-Cold-War world order. And with both governments demonstrating resounding synergies in their global outlook this, indeed, made them likely allies in the context of a highly unequal world.

Ten years later, it would appear that establishing diplomatic relations with Beijing has proved fruitful, or so the rhetoric seems to indicate. The engagement has indeed shifted to the next level, with 2008 marking the tenth anniversary of Sino-South African relations and the BNC providing the institutional vehicle through which these relations are formalised. While the first ten years heralded the dawning of a new chapter in Sino-South African relations, the second decade of engagement represents an augmentation of such ties by concretising the commitments made at the 2006 Forum on China-Africa Cooperation (FOCAC) summit and the 2007 BNC meeting in Beijing. This takes the form of increased two-way trade; more investment by Chinese companies in the South African market and vice versa; more cultural exchanges; increased scholarships for South African students to study in China; and greater development assistance for South Africa's human resources and technical skills base.

In so doing, China is emerging as a valuable partner, along with other traditional powers from the West. But is this rhetoric as positive as we are led to believe? And why is it that not everyone is as optimistic about the Chinese engagement? On aggregate, what appears to be a strategic partnership, in theory, comes with inherent contradictions. This chapter assesses to what extent South Africa's engagement with China represents a strategic partnership. It analyses the following set of questions: What is meant by 'strategic partnership'? Is it a relationship borne out of political expediency? Or is it crafted out of economic pragmatism? Where do the lines of complementarity lie and what are the divisions? Do Pretoria and Beijing speak with one voice when it comes to the South, especially regarding African issues? Or is it a case of differing agendas? Answers to these questions as well as the above concerns are discussed in the latter part of this chapter. But first a brief analysis will be provided of the Two-China dilemma that confronted the Mandela Presidency, including the political and economic dimensions of the relationship.

THE TWO-CHINA DILEMMA

Since April 1994, South Africa's foreign policy-making has frustrated commentators who have complained about its incoherence and contradictory nature. What perturbs them most is Pretoria's vacillation between 'realist' and 'moral' internationalism.[3] It was within this context of obfuscation that the Two-China dilemma tested Pretoria's ambitious – albeit ambiguous – international relations.

That the newly democratic South Africa would extend relations with Beijing was never in doubt, though what interested Pretoria's new leadership and the foreign-policy fraternity was how this relationship would be expressed in diplomatic terms. On the one hand, there were the extensive trade and investment linkages with Taiwan to consider, while, on the other hand, mainland China's increasing political and economic global footprint could not be ignored. As part of this debate, Greg Mills outlined three possible scenarios.[4] The first scenario called for the maintenance of the status quo. This option meant that Pretoria could wait and see whether the issue of recognition could rectify itself through the developments in the People's Republic of China (PRC) and Taiwan before making its own choice, while at the same time, continuing economic relations with Taiwan and procuring gains by being courted by both sides.

The second scenario – an attempt at dual recognition – meant that Pretoria could avail itself of its universal approach to international relations and seek to establish diplomatic ties with the PRC, while still retaining official linkages with Taiwan. This stance would have aligned Pretoria with the UN Charter on the principle of universality and international law on statehood, for which Taiwan fulfils most of the requirements. This position would also have dovetailed with the UN's 'model of parallel representation of divided countries', such as the two Koreas and the former East and West Germany. Whereas option one would have meant exclusive recognition of Taiwan, option two was irreconcilable with Beijing's One-China policy.[5]

The third scenario – downgrade relations with Taiwan in favour of the PRC – flowed from international consensus. This was primarily based on China's rapidly growing economic influence and the opportunities this opened up for South African business.

But the Two-China dilemma forced the Mandela Presidency to realise that arriving at a decision was fraught with internal contradictions. First, forging ties with Beijing would send out a confused message about the South African government's own values, in terms of democratic and human rights norms, especially after the Tiananmen Square crisis. Second, if the leadership sought to switch ties to Beijing, it had to reconcile itself with the loss of the financial inducements it received from Taipei as part of the latter's cheque-book diplomacy, which was designed precisely to encourage Pretoria to retain the status quo.[6] In the early 1990s, Taipei announced increased investments in South Africa through a series of loans and contracts to Eskom, MacSteel and the Development Bank of Southern Africa, while making commitments – on paper at least – to undertake projects valued at over R1 billion linked to the Reconstruction and Development Programme (RDP).[7] Such commitments compelled the Mandela government to evaluate the implications that Taiwan disinvestments would have for the South African economy and other cultural and educational exchanges if diplomatic ties were switched to the mainland. However, what concerned the Mandela Presidency most was whether the comparatively small amount of PRC investment in the country would be increased to match that of the Taiwanese, especially in terms of financing the RDP.

The Hong Kong factor was another consideration. With Hong Kong destined to return to Chinese rule in 1997, Pretoria had to consider the implications this would have for its economic linkages with the island, which was South Africa's fifth largest trading partner at the time. Since there were no formal ties between the PRC and Pretoria, South Africa's economic interests and political status on the island were not protected by basic law. This meant that the status of its mission, the air-service agreements, as well as duties on goods entering the market would be at the discretion of the PRC and determined by whether or not Pretoria afforded Beijing diplomatic recognition. Against this, the dynamism of Hong Kong being included into China's economy and the rising living standards on the mainland would open up new opportunities for South African goods, which could well surpass those offered by maintaining relations with Taiwan.

Even before coming to power, there were signs that the African National Congress (ANC) was wavering. During a visit to Taipei in 1993, Nelson Mandela appeased the Taiwanese government's anxieties by noting that 'a democratic South Africa will not abandon its long-term friend who assisted the ANC during its worst time'.[8] Yet, in the following year, after the elections, indications from the newly elected ANC government were that it was willing to enter into diplomatic relations with China, although it would not consider severing ties with Taiwan. Meanwhile, senior members of the ANC, such as Deputy-President, Thabo Mbeki, who were more clear-sighted about South Africa's engagement with PRC, stated as early as 1993 that normal diplomatic relations would be pursued with Beijing.[9] In part, the uncertainty surrounding the Two-China issue reflected the determination of the Mandela government to assert its sovereignty, while simultaneously attempting to promote South Africa's rapid reintegration into the world community. In the end, Pretoria could not ignore the rise of China in the global system and the attendant benefits that establishing formal ties with Beijing would bring, especially with regard to the new regime's aspirations in the reformed UN Security Council and in the context of South-South cooperation. That South Africa dragged its feet in making its choice may well have reflected the new government's recollection of Beijing's initial inability to commit wholly to the ANC's anti-apartheid struggle, as well as clandestine trading with the apartheid regime.[10] In the end, however, pragmatism prevailed, and scenario three was implemented.

The logic of formalising relations with the PRC was the anticipation that it would have the following spin-offs:

- allow access to a burgeoning consumer market;
- establish a strategic partnership for promoting the interests of the emerging markets of the developing world;
- facilitate sharing of the common task of development and the advocacy of a multipolar, rather than a unipolar world system; and
- promote a common agenda for the reform of the global political and economic system.

FORMAL RELATIONS

After reaching agreement on relevant issues, the two countries signed a Joint Communiqué on the Establishment of Diplomatic Relations in December 1997. Under the agreement, the South African government affirmed that it would adhere to the One-China position. On 1 January 1998, the two countries formally established diplomatic relations and opened a new chapter in their relations.[11]

Since then, bilateral cooperation has burgeoned, and there has been a flurry of high-level visits and exchanges on both sides. During his state visit to South Africa in April 2000, President Jiang Zhemin joined President Mbeki in signing the Pretoria Declaration, marking the formal establishment of 'partnership' between the two countries. In the document, the two sides announced the founding of a high-level BNC in order to further enhance the partnership and to promote cooperation in political, economic and other fields. In turn, President Mbeki officially inaugurated the BNC during his return state visit to China in December 2001, and together the two heads of state presided over the first plenary session of the BNC.

Separate talks on cooperation in relevant areas were held between leading members of both countries' ministries and departments of foreign affairs, economic cooperation and trade, public security, justice, science-technology, energy and tourism. Subsequently, four sectoral committees on foreign affairs, economy and trade, science-technology and national defence have been established, while various other government departments have also set up channels of communication at different levels and stayed in regular working contact.

In June 2004, the second South Africa-PRC BNC issued a communiqué that indicated that the two countries had reached broad consensus on and reaffirmed commitments to the following:

- promoting peace, stability and development in Africa through the Addis Ababa Action Plan and FOCAC;
- mutual support for the New Partnership for Africa's Development (NEPAD);
- the launch of the Southern African Customs Union (SACU)-China free trade agreement negotiations;
- South Africa's recognition of China's market economy status;
- the inauguration of the sectoral committee on education for further cooperation and the confirmation and establishment of the Centre for Chinese Studies at the University of Stellenbosch;
- the need to advocate multilateralism and equality in addressing and resolving international issues, such as the reformation of the trading regime, the 'War on Terrorism', and so forth;
- confirmation of their position as important partners in the pursuit of a new international political and economic order based on peace, stability, justice and equality;
- strengthening their cooperative South-South relationship; and
- commitment to the One-China policy.

This second meeting of the BNC concluded with:

- an agreement on education cooperation;
- an exchange of letters regarding grant aid for human resources' projects in South Africa;
- an agreement on the administration of quality supervision, inspection and quarantine;
- an understanding on a sanitary and phytosanitary consultation mechanism; and
- signing of the protocol of phytosanitary requirements in June 2004 for the export of citrus fruits from South Africa to China.

The third meeting of the BNC in 2007 was preceded by the FOCAC summit held in Beijing, November 2006, and President Hu Jintao's visit in February 2007. Following the FOCAC summit, President Mbeki conducted an official visit to China during which he re-emphasised South Africa's commitment to solidifying the strategic partnership and highlighted that engagement with China could assist with South Africa's skills shortage. He also urged South African companies to take advantage of the US$5 billion China-Africa Development Fund to access opportunities in the Chinese markets. Moreover, President Mbeki cautioned that the trade deficit between China and South Africa should be addressed so that South Africa would not remain mainly a supplier of primary commodities to China. In fact, he urged China to source manufactured goods from the South African market, which he argued was in keeping with the development agenda of NEPAD.

In February 2007, President Hu visited South Africa as part of his eight-nation Africa tour to set in motion the 2006 FOCAC commitments. During the visit to South Africa, seven agreements were signed:

- protocol on phytosanitary requirements for the export of pear fruits from China to South Africa;
- protocol on phytosanitary requirements for the export of table grapes from South Africa to China;
- protocol on phytosanitary requirements for the export of apple fruit from China to South Africa;
- protocol on phytosanitary requirements for the export of tobacco leaf from China to South Africa;
- agreement between South Africa and the PRC on cooperation in the Minerals and Energy Sector;
- agreement between South Africa and the PRC on cooperation in the Minerals and Energy Sectoral Cooperation Committee; and
- agreement on economic and technical cooperation between South Africa and the PRC.

President Hu also reiterated that the future of the BNC was significant to the future of the strategic partnership between the two countries.

In September 2007, Deputy-President Mlambo-Ngucka led the South African delegation to Beijing for the third meeting of the BNC. During the discussions, President Hu introduced a three-point proposal to push forward the strategic partnership: maintain the frequent exchanges of high-level visits and strengthen the dialogue and consultation on major issues; realise and promote the agreements on human resources and agricultural cooperation; and, lastly, to take advantage of the BNC to explore new areas for cooperation. Both governments agreed that over the next three years, the BNC should focus on poverty, human development, commerce and people-to-people relationships.

From the South African side, the government delegation pushed for greater expansion of trade and investment and recommitted itself to the One-China policy. Deputy-President Mlambo-Ngucka also expressed appreciation to the Chinese government for supporting the Joint Initiative for Priority Skills Acquisition (JIPSA) programme that will assist South Africa's skills development. During her stay in China. the Deputy-President gave a speech at Tsinghua University where she made renewed calls for the strategic partnership between the respective countries to be elevated to academic exchanges, especially towards skills transfer. At the conclusion of the BNC, two agreements on cooperation were signed in Education and Minerals and Energy, as was a memorandum of understanding (MOU) in Human Resources Development and Public Administration.

Relations have been strengthened further by the signing of an MOU between the South African Parliament and the National People's Congress to further cooperation within the legislative sphere.

The tenth anniversary of the BNC in 2008 signals that relations are moving in a steady and predictable manner, essentially because the commitments sustained under the BNC do not deviate substantially from the substance and rhetoric of China's broader Africa policy. It also aligns increasingly with what was recognised as a new type of strategic partnership with Africa during the FOCAC summit in November 2006.

ECONOMIC RELATIONS

Trade dynamics

It was in the early 1990s that China and South Africa started to open commercial exchanges. The volume of bilateral trade in 1991 was US$14 million and in 1997, over US$1.5 billion. Since the establishment of diplomatic ties, bilateral trade has grown rapidly. It stood at US$2.58 billion in 2002, of which China's imports amounted to US$1.269 billion and exports US$1.311 billion. By the end of the first half of 2004, the volume of China-South Africa trade had grown substantially to US$2.75 billion, a 64 per cent increase over the same period.

At present, South Africa is China's second largest trading partner in Africa, after Angola. The trade volume between the two countries accounts for 20 per cent of the total trade volume between China and Africa.

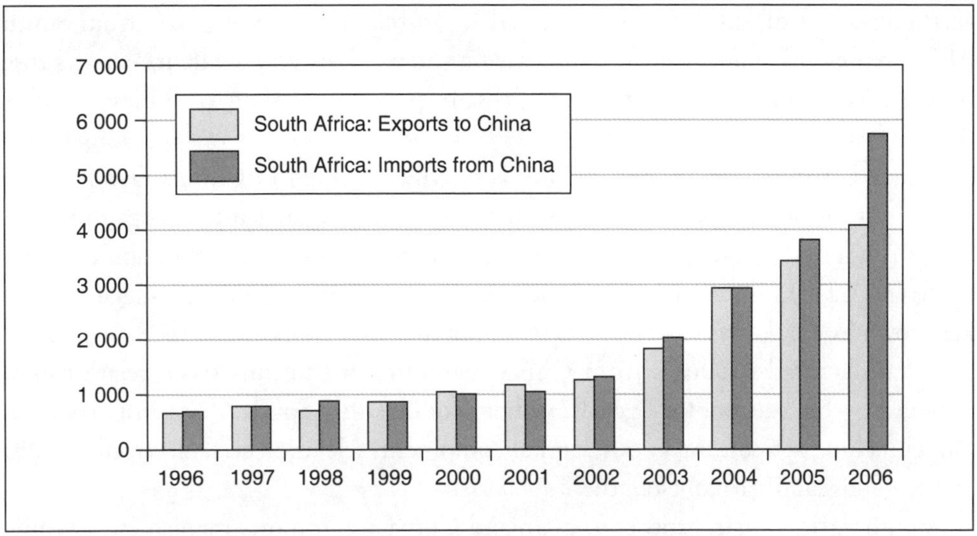

Figure 10.1 South Africa's value of trade with the PRC, 1996–2006 (US$ millions).

Source: World Trade Atlas Data

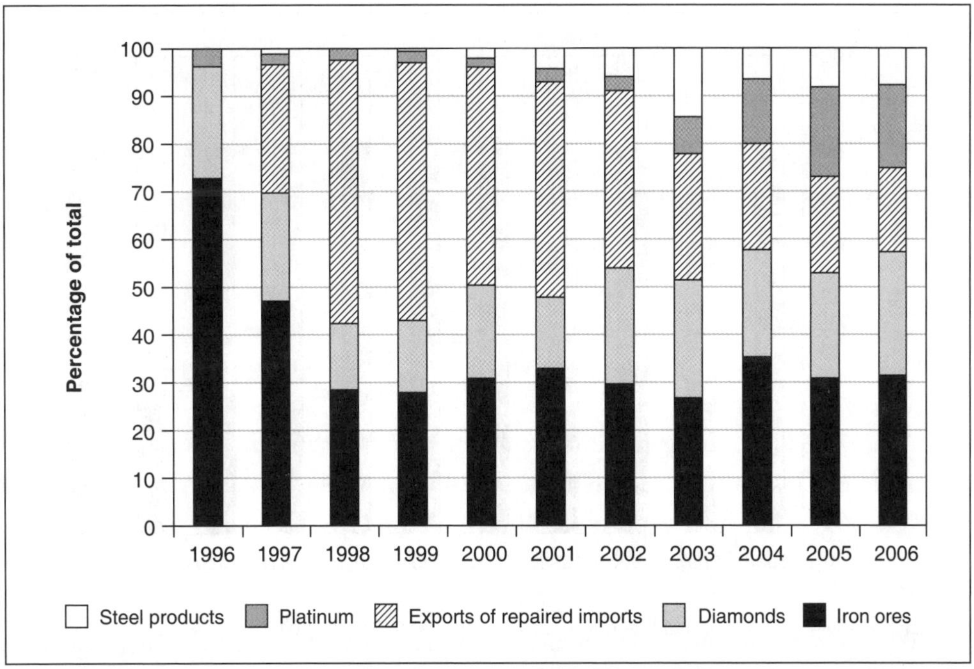

Figure 10.2 South Africa's top five exports to China, 1996–2006.

Source: World Trade Atlas Data

In the first half of 2007, China imported US$3 billion worth of goods from South Africa, representing a 65 per cent increase on the previous year, while its exports rose by 40 per cent to US$3.2 billion during the same period, according to Chinese customs data.

Trade between Pretoria and Beijing is heavily weighted in China's favour. With trade growing rapidly, South Africa is experiencing a trade deficit that began to spike in 2002. Chinese figures put the total value of trade at almost US$9.9 billion in 2006, up from US$1.3 billion in 1995, while the South African government suggests trade has grown from approximately US$770 million to US$8.7 billion over the same period.

Manufactured products from China mainly dominate this trade relationship, followed by high-technology goods. Other products that South Africa imports from China include agricultural goods, capital equipment, television sets, electronic goods, 'white goods' and garments/textiles.

South Africa's main exports to mainland China are iron ore, manganese, chrome ore, tobacco, wool, granite, gold, copper, aluminium and auto components, thereby making South Africa a net supplier of raw materials to the Chinese market.

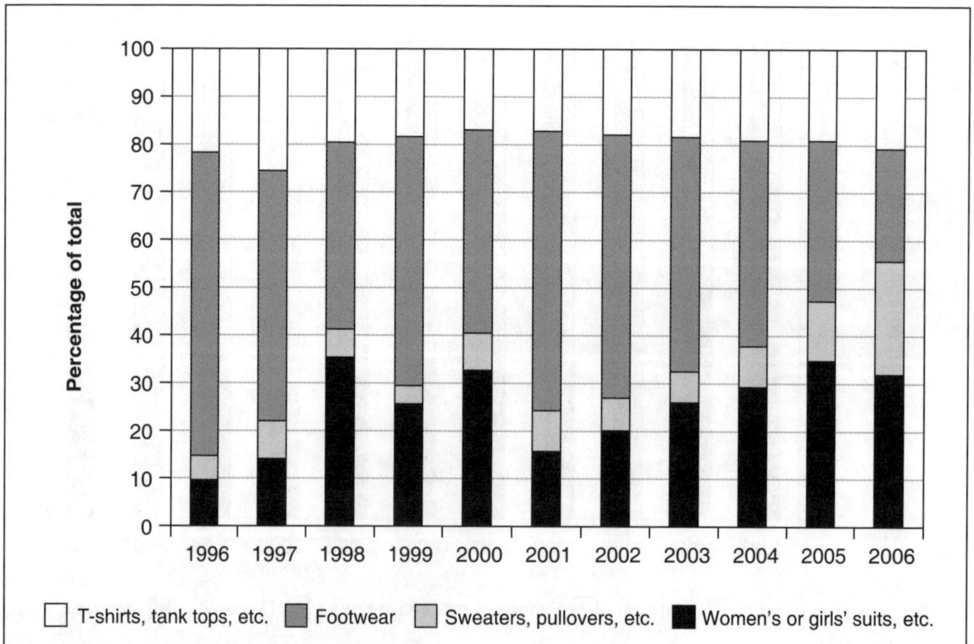

Figure 10.3 South Africa's top five imports from China, 1996–2006.
Source: World Trade Atlas Data

Moreover, South Africa has granted China market economy status, which is a much sought-after status for Beijing, even if this is a politically motivated decision, rather than commercially driven. This is because under the World Trade Organisation (WTO) accord, China must be granted market economy status by 2015 and with Europe and the United States still classifying the PRC as a 'non-market' economy, it has begun to lobby developing country economies to meet the requirement. Market economy status is important for Beijing because it is a precursor of free trade negotiations.

Investment trajectory: Into South Africa

Two-way investment has been slow, although in recent years, there has been a steady increase. In comparison to other African countries, Chinese investment in South Africa has been relatively small. Out of the total investment of US$11.7 billion across the continent by Chinese corporates at the end of 2006, it is estimated that only US$200 million had been channelled to South Africa. A senior diplomat at the PRC embassy in Pretoria, however, put this figure at a much higher value of US$600 million.

In South Africa, by the end of 2002, 98 projects by Chinese enterprises in the fields of agriculture, textiles, electronics, mining, banking, transportation and communications were underway, while South African enterprises had invested in 206 projects in China. Chinese companies are also beginning to use the South African market as a springboard into the rest of the continent. Companies such as the Chinese Construction Bank, Huawei Technologies, Zhongxing Commmunications (ZTE) and the Chinese Central Bank all have offices in the economic hub of the country, Gauteng. This enables Chinese companies to have a greater nexus to the African market in the search for investment opportunities as part of the 'going-out' strategy. Also, South Africa's fairly developed infrastructure and robust economy facilitates this entry-point into Africa.

Apart from the large-scale corporates, there are also small-scale entrepreneurs that are investing in 'mom-and-pop' industries across the South Africa market. These investors are largely located in the service and retail industry and form part of the 'going-out' strategy, albeit at a grassroots level, which has taken off in the last ten years. It remains unclear how much these investors are contributing to China's overall investment into the country.

The presence of Chinese firms in the South African market is a relatively new phenomenon. Unlike in other African markets, the South African market posed certain structural challenges to Chinese companies wanting to invest. First, it was difficult to compete with local industries, especially in the construction sector, given their dominance and structural strength in the domestic market. Second, with South Africa undergoing a political and economic transformation, there were increasing regulations and investment codes relating to black economic empowerment (BEE). Whereas, initially, these factors tended to sway Chinese investors into neighbouring economies, investors are now bucking the trend and breaking into the South African market:

- Hi-Sense entered South Africa in 1997 with the procurement of the Daewoo electronics factory. The company produces hi-tech electronic goods, such as television sets, DVDs, Hi-Fi's and VCRs. It exports its products to more than ten countries in the region, including Namibia, Lesotho, Mozambique and Botswana. The company is currently planning a US$19 million expansion that will see it boosting its production base. Its sales and profit growth has averaged between 20 and 30 per cent, and in 2006, the South African branch registered a profit of US$1.26 million from an income of US$47 million.[12]
- Sinoprima Investment and Manufacturing South Africa, a subsidiary of Xiamen Overseas Chinese Electronic Co. Ltd (XOCECO), set up operations in South Africa in 1998 as a manufacturer and distributor of consumer electronics, specialising in CRT TV, Plasma and LCDTV.[13]
- First Automotive Works (FAW) Vehicle Manufacturer (Pty) Ltd has been set up to manufacture heavy vehicles and assemble component parts of trucks and cars at its plant in Kempton Park, Gauteng. There are 25 dealerships selling FAW trucks across South Africa and the company is hoping to expand its operations into the sub-Saharan region.
- Zijin Mining recently acquired a 20 per cent share in South African platinium producer, Ridge Mining. The company invested approximately R120 million, which Ridge Mining hopes will help to assist in building the necessary infrastructure, such as a smelter or refinery to boost the company's output.
- Sinosteel bought a 50 per cent stake in Samancor Chrome's Tatse Smelter and the Tweefontein chrome mine and has entered into a joint venture with the Limpopo Economic Development Enterprise in ASA metals in which it has a 60 per cent stake.
- Jisco, a steel producer, bought 29.1 per cent of International Ferro Metals and agreed to purchase half of the mine's production after the new expansion project is complete.
- China Minmetals Development Company, the Shanghai-listed arm of Chinese state-owned trading firm, the China Minmetals Group, is to enter into agreements with Mission Point and Versatex of South Africa to buy the exploration rights to a South African ferrochrome deposit for R45.7 million.

- China Overseas Engineering Company (COVEC) won a US$61 million contract for the civil engineering component of the US$357 million Vaal River Eastern Sub-System Augmentation Project (VRESAP).
- In 2005, CITIC Arc was awarded a R455-million contract to demolish and rebuild a portion of the Mittal Steel Newcastle coke battery project, as well as upgrade a gas-cleaning plant.
- Three Chinese companies have entered into a consortium with a BEE firm, which won the R2 billion tender from Portnet for a dry-dock facility in Richards Bay.

In addition, Beijing is also expanding its interests in the South African market to include technologies in mining, electricity supply and power stations, water management, solar energy, pollution control, and military and nuclear research. Clearly, with a population of more than one billion people, the Chinese government needs to boost alternative sources of energy supply, while it also has major concerns about water. This has resulted in a MOU being signed between South Africa's pebble-bed modular reactor (PBMR) company and China's Chinergy to cooperate in the development of the PBMR. China's interest in the PBMR is based on expanding its electricity capacity, although the nuclear component of the PBMR has caused concern that China could have other designs in mind.[14]

Investment trajectory: Out of South Africa

South Africa is the only African country that has a notable corporate profile in China. There are around 20 South African-based businesses with offices in China. Several of these companies (see Table 10.1) have significant proportions of their investment listed in third countries and Hong Kong. Few of these firms have invested more than US$5 to 10 million – with the exception of SABMiller, which is by far the single largest investor and, according to one senior representative of the company, has a total investment of between US$500 million and US$1 billion.[15]

The list of South African companies already investing in China is impressive; they include a basket of resource, mining and financial conglomerates that anchor the South African economy. The total investment by South African companies in the Chinese market is estimated to be around US$500 million.[16] But some industry analysts put the figure higher, at between US$1.2 billion and US$1.5 billion, with a possibility of it reaching US$2 billion if offshore listings are included.[17] The Chinese embassy in

Table 10.1 Major South African companies operating in China.

Company	Sector
Naspers/MIH	Media
Metspan	Manufacturing
Freeplay	Manufacturing
Beijing Axis	Consultancy/research
Kumba Resources	Mining/metals
AngloGold Ashanti	Mining
AngloCoal	Mining
Anglo American	Mining
Goldfields	Mining
Old Mutual	Financial
Standard Bank	Financial
First Rand Bank	Financial
Sasol	Energy
SABMiller	Beverages
African Explosives Limited (AEL)	Engineering
Bateman	Engineering
Landpac	Engineering
Spur	Hospitality/restaurant

Pretoria disputes this figure as being excessive. A senior diplomat at the embassy believed that figures from the Ministry of Commerce in Beijing reflected a more sober assessment, which put the total figure at between US$600 and US$800 million.[18]

The discrepancy over investment figures notwithstanding, South African companies have proved particularly successful in China. This, it has been suggested, has to do with South African corporate experience in Africa, where these companies have shown a penchant to underwrite risk.

Over the last two years, there has been a 65 per cent growth in trade in mining equipment and transport from South Africa to China. In addition, Sasol has signed a MOU with the Combined Chinese Working Team, on the one hand, and with Shenhua Coal Liquefaction Corporation and Ningxia Coal Group Company, on the other hand, in order to develop two plants in the coal-rich western part of China. The purpose is to convert coal into liquid fuels in the Ningxia Autonomous region and Shaanxi province, with the aim of becoming operational before the end of 2012.[19] The projects are expected to cost about US$3 billion each and, if economically viable, they will have a combined annual production of 60 million tonnes of oil.[20] Sasol further deepened its presence in China by opening an office in Shanghai towards the latter half of 2007. The office, operating under the name Sasol Chemicals Shanghai Co. Ltd, will 'initially market products from the global Sasol Business' into the Chinese economy.[21]

In the telecommunication sector, MIH, a subsidiary of media giant, Naspers, invested up to US$45 million to become the biggest single foreign media investor in the listing of the Chinese newspaper group, Beijing Media Corporation, in December 2007.[22] Naspers took a 9.9 per cent stake in Beijing Media, which gives the group a foothold in China's potentially huge print and television markets. The group also has an interest in Tencent Holdings Ltd, a telecommunications company that is a leading provider of Internet and mobile services in China, while it also holds an 87 per cent interest in Sportscn.com, which is one of the principal suppliers of sports news and results via its mobile phone and fixed-line platforms.[23]

In addition, there are local companies such as Leitch Chance, a property specialist agency, which has launched a service to find and manage offshore property investments for South African clients with surplus capital from the domestic property boom. Its first project is Talent Studios, being built in China's fast-growing city, Shanghai. The project, which is being developed by Shanghai Fudan Science Park, will be used for accommodation for workers at the Science Park and MBA students from Fudan University.[24]

Furthermore, investment is also facilitated through provincial and city twinning agreements. Several are currently in existence between Bloemfontein and Xi'an, the Western Cape and Shandong provincial governments, and the Gauteng government and Beijing. The Gauteng Economic Development Agency (GEDA) has established a virtual mining initiative with China whereby if a Chinese company needs mining equipment or has any other mining needs, a request can be made to GEDA, which will, in turn, facilitate contact with appropriate Gauteng-based suppliers. A recent deal concluded under this initiative saw China's largest manufacturer of gas-detection devices, which supplies 80 per cent of mines in China, enter into a venture with a Gauteng-based gas-detection manufacturer. GEDA has also led a South African business delegation to China, where new partnerships and business deals were discussed.[25]

The examples above illustrate that China has become a pivotal focus for South African corporates. Clearly, if South African companies are going to have a global presence, it would seem that the Chinese market would be the first step in this direction, since it is considered one of the core economies of the global economic architecture.

There is a natural synergy between South Africa and China in terms of gold production. This is particularly so due to a growing demand for gold products from China's rapidly growing middle class. However, the concern is that South Africa remains a primary exporter of gold and needs to transform this advantage into value-added manufactured products destined for the Chinese market – a challenge that has not yet been met. At the end of 2007, China emerged as the largest gold producer, surpassing South Africa. This came as no surprise as gold production in South Africa has been declining over the years. Although this did not have any significant reaction in the South African market, it does have important considerations for the South African government in terms of taking advantage of being a strategic supplier of gold products to the Chinese market.

Meanwhile, South Africa became the first sub-Saharan African country to be granted approved destination status by the Chinese government, a milestone reached in 2002. The South African authorities see this as an important benefit in boosting the tourism and service industry. More than 33 000 tourists from China visited South Africa in 2003 and they are becoming one of the fastest-growing groups of visitors to the country.

The volume of air cargo between the two nations has also increased dramatically. With the introduction of the Airbus by South African Airways (SAA) on the Hong Kong route, the volume of inbound cargo from the Far East escalated by 86 per cent in 2004. On the other hand, exports flown by SAA Cargo to the Far East grew by 35 per cent and tended to include mostly mining equipment, telecommunications materials and large consignments of Chinese favourites: abalone and lobster.[26]

Trade between the two countries is likely to increase with the pending SACU-China free trade agreement (FTA), which is expected to act as a stimulus to all sectors of the South African economy, in terms of exports and employment, and boost South-South trade, especially in agricultural products, such as fruit, vegetable and beef products. There are also political concerns that Swaziland's diplomatic ties with Taiwan could delay the negotiations on the FTA, as is the case with Lesotho, which provides incentives to Taiwan based on the African Growth and Opportunity Act (AGOA).[27] However, to date, negotiations on the FTA remain slow and protracted with the India-South Africa FTA moving ahead more rapidly.

Tensions in the market

a) The clothing and textile issue

Unfortunately the debacle surrounding the clothing and textile sector has had a negative effect on relations between the South African government and the unions. The garment industry has already suffered as a result of the influx of cheap Chinese imports into the market, due to China's cheap labour and undervalued currency. In South Africa, Chinese imports account for 74 per cent of all apparel imports into the country. The phasing out of the Multi-Fibre Agreement on 1 January 2005 has posed significant structural problems for the sector in terms of competitiveness locally and internationally. The effect has been a massive loss in jobs for workers across the industry and although the precise figures are difficult to calculate, estimates range from 23 000 to 85 000.

According to the WTO, member countries can adopt certain measures, such as curbs on exports, in cases where the entire market could be disrupted. In 2006, labour and manufacturers successfully lobbied the South African government to initiate discussions on an import limitation with China. As a founding member of the General Agreement on Tariffs and Trade (GATT) and the WTO, the South African government is bound by their agreements. This resulted in a request to implement 'safeguard measures', which the Chinese government accepted. Consequently, China agreed to place voluntary restrictions on 31 categories of export products for a two-year period to allow the clothing and textile sector to restructure and prepare itself for direct competition. While initially it appeared that Pretoria seemed to be moving cautiously on the clothing and textile issue, this move signalled that the union had put significant pressure on government to do something. It also illustrated that China could be engaged on the issue. As one senior Chinese diplomat noted, the decision to accept the voluntary export restraint was a political decision to further strengthen ties and promote goodwill between Pretoria and Beijing.[28]

But this stop-gap measure has done little to improve the industry. A number of South African wholesalers continue to import Chinese garments beyond the limits of the quota through third countries such as Dubai, while other Asian countries, such as Vietnam, Bangladesh and India have stepped in to fill the void.

b) Steel

Other concerns relate to unfair trading practice in the steel industry, issues of reciprocity and symmetrical versus asymmetrical reduction in trade tariffs. China has opposed South Africa's proposal for an asymmetrical reduction in trade tariffs because it does not believe that the South African economy needs to be protected from Chinese competition since Pretoria is a signatory to the WTO rules on open trade.

c) Construction

There are also concerns regarding increased competition from Chinese companies in the local construction industry. As more Chinese companies enter the construction market, they realise that they have to employ local labour. While they have accepted the rules of the local market, the shortage of skills has meant that labour has had to be brought in from China. This has created some tensions between the unions, government and big business. The contract awarded to a Chinese consortium, CITIC-ARCE, by steelmaker Ispat Iscor has raised eyebrows in the industry and the media.[29] The controversy surrounding the contract relates to the fact that Chinese workers are to be brought in to work on the construction of a coke-oven battery and gas-plant at the steelmaker's Newcastle plant. Ispat Iscor defended its decision, arguing that local expertise did not exist. Industry experts are worried that this move could set a precedent in the domestic market for a preference for Chinese companies, which can provide cheap labour. It has also set a precedent for domestic industries such as Sasol to argue that it would have to import about 2 000 qualified artisans, mainly from Asia, due to shortages in the domestic economy.[30]

d) The motor industry

Meanwhile, the automotive industry is another sector in which China poses a challenge, for many of the major global automotive component manufacturers have already established operations in China, and may drain investment away from South Africa.[31]

Despite these concerns, China and South Africa have signed a series of government agreements on the protection of investments, trade, economic and technical cooperation, the avoidance of double taxation, civil air transport, maritime transport, and so forth. With the Sectoral Committee on Economy and Trade under the BNC serving as a contact channel, the relevant government departments have stayed in close consultation on matters concerning China-South Africa cooperation in the WTO, the protection of intellectual property rights and NEPAD, as well as on specific issues relating to bilateral economic cooperation and trade.

On balance, South Africa's economic relations with the mainland raises concerns about Pretoria's industrial strategy. With few core industries gaining from the economic opportunities present in the Chinese market, consideration must be given to those industries where South African competition is threatened. South Africa also needs to understand how its economic relations with China will impact on its presence in the immediate region and the wider continent. In addition, a more pertinent issue that must be evaluated is whether China's economic boom is sustainable. Finally, the trade deficit that exists between South Africa and China needs urgent attention. Meanwhile, although both governments have become allies in various trade groupings (for example, the G20), challenging the dominance of the established economies in the WTO trade negotiations, China's own economic fluidity and market barriers, especially in the banking sector and price controls, raise concerns about China's trade liberalisation and how South Africa will deal with this.

These considerations notwithstanding, economic relations between South Africa and China are set to continue and intensify – but Pretoria needs to proceed cautiously if it wants the relationship to be pragmatic.

Migration[32]

South Africa boasts a large Chinese diaspora, estimated at between 200 000 and 300 000. The first wave of immigrants arrived during the Gold Rush of the 1800s; others were brought to Robben Island as prisoners. In the late 1970s and early 1980s, the second wave saw the arrival of people from Taiwan. And the third wave witnessed the emergence of the 'New Chinese' who have entered the country over the last ten to fifteen years. The trajectory of the new arrivals is closely aligned to two distinct phases: the first when South Africa was undergoing its transition and new economic opportunities were opening up, and the second, after diplomatic ties between Pretoria and Beijing were formalised.

So far much of the emphasis in Sino-South African relations has focused on the macroeconomic engagement. Yet the arrival of the 'New Chinese' signals that economic relations at the micro level have become more complex and sometimes tense. Not only have the 'New Chinese' become significant traders in the local market, with the sale of cheap goods, but they are also setting up trading posts in rural areas. On one level, this has expedited the entry of cheap Chinese goods into the market, while on the other level, it has also meant that local traders, especially in the informal market, cannot compete with the Chinese traders.

A more embedded tension that is now emerging in South Africa centres on the classification of South African Born Chinese (SABC). Under apartheid, the Chinese community was classified either as 'coloured' or 'alien'. In terms of this racial segregation, today, Chinese South Africans, especially those who are fourth and fifth generations of the first SABC group, are fighting for equal opportunities in terms of employment equity and BEE. Essentially their argument is that because they were also discriminated against under apartheid's racial classification policy, the definition of and benefits assigned to who is 'black' should also extend to this section of the Chinese community.[33] This is a poignant issue as it demonstrates expressions of post-apartheid identity amongst the SABC and the impact this has on their economic mobility. This has certain similar overlaps with the Indian community who also find themselves in a similar socio-economic context.

CONCLUSION: BALANCING A STRATEGIC PARTNERSHIP?

At the beginning of this chapter, two questions were posed concerning the nature of the relationship between Pretoria and Beijing: How should it be conceptualised, and what makes this relationship a strategic partnership? The answer to both questions lies in the way each interprets the strategic partnership and to what extent it represents a set of mutual interests. While the simple response is to confine Sino-South African engagement to that of expediency, it is worth interrogating whether this strategic partnership is a balanced one.

To engage in a strategic partnership means that both partners must be able to influence each other's behaviour. A strategic partnership also means that leverage underscores the relationship and that neither partner becomes more powerful than the other. Finally, to be a strategic partner entails a strategic plan, which informs this engagement. Therefore, in line with the latter and in exploring the aforementioned questions, several issues come to the fore, which warrant further insight into the nature of South Africa's strategic partnership with China.

First, it would appear that China and South Africa have very different approaches and interpretations about their relationship. For the Chinese, it is an integrated relationship that aligns itself concretely to the goals and objectives of the White Paper on China's Africa Policy and is expressed through the institutional vehicle of FOCAC. Setting the agenda through such policy instruments means that Beijing has a structured view of how this engagement should be harnessed. Politically, economically and socially, China has calibrated its strategic partnership with South Africa based on the synergies of what is seen as like-mindedness on global issues, Africa's development and normative value expressions on a multilateral international system.

Whereas the South African government also aligns its engagement with China based on its foreign-policy ideals of South-South cooperation, peace, stability and development in Africa and more broadly multilateralism, it seems that there is no single instrument that governs this engagement. Nor is it clear from the policy-makers what constitutes a 'strategic partnership'. Consider Deputy-Minister Aziz Pahad's statement on President Hu's visit to South Africa in 2007: 'It is very important to declare that our relations should be strategic . . . it means many things.'[34]

It would seem that the value and cohesiveness of the strategic partnership remains embedded in the normative agenda of like-mindedness on South-South cooperation and multilateralism. While this may hold attractiveness for mutual benefits, at a more substantive level, it is unclear whether South Africa will move toward supporting the

China position in international institutions where it may run contrary to South Africa's engagement with traditional partners in the North.

Second, Africa has become a new frontier for both Pretoria and Beijing politically and economically. With Chinese exports and imports looming large in African markets, this poses some critical political and economic concerns for the Mbeki administration. China's deepening engagement with African states indicates that Beijing is seen as more of a trusted ally than South Africa. This does not bode well for Pretoria's African Renaissance project or in terms of developing an African consensus on the China engagement with respect to FOCAC and NEPAD.

It also complicates issues surrounding the transparency and accountability of governments in Africa and puts at risk the work of institutions such as the African Peer Review Mechanism (APRM).

Third, in so far as South African corporates may be threatened by the footprint of Chinese firms into the African market, they have also become susceptible to China's economic largesse. The 20 per cent stake by the Industrial and Commercial Bank of China (ICBC) in Standard Bank reflects this new trend in China's corporate activity in Africa. The deal, which is considered to be one of the biggest investment stakes in an African bank at US$5.5 billion, enables China's commercial interests in Africa to be further augmented through the equity and portfolio stocks of Standard Bank. The deal also signifies that Chinese companies are recognising that South African corporates provide an invaluable competitive advantage in African markets. So, instead of competing with them, it is easier to harness such skills and experience through joint ventures, mergers and acquisitions, rather than through greenfield investments. This will be facilitated through the US$1 billion equity fund that has been set up between Standard Bank and ICBC, which will be used for investing in mining projects and other sectors.

As this new trajectory takes root, other sectors where South African capital has made significant inroads will also catch the eye of Chinese investors. These include the telecommunications sector, leisure and hospitality, retail and electricity. There were rumours in the market that China Mobile was preparing to make an offer to buy into telecommunications company MTN. Not only would this legitimise and deepen Chinese corporate activity across the continent, but it would also enable Chinese firms to deal with other challenges such as human resources, which seem to be a key strength of South African corporates.

Fourth, as South Africa moves closer towards institutionalising a development aid policy, assessments will be made about how this will dovetail with China's development assistance to the continent. At present, China's foreign aid is interpreted to be more pragmatic and fruitful in assisting African countries with their developmental needs. As South Africa moves into this sphere, this will indeed raise significant issues about whether this will be seen as complementary to China's role as a donor in Africa, or if it is about greater leverage within Africa vis-à-vis China. At present, China's development assistance is viewed as entrenching Beijing's commercial interests in African markets. This is seen by some within the South African diplomatic community as unfavourably prejudicing South African corporates from benefiting from increased market access that could be had if the South African state garnered a donor leverage relationship on the continent. This begs the question of why South Africa is contemplating such a policy and, whether this is being pushed by traditional development partners as a way to have a strategic ally on the continent that can act as a lever for their own development policies.

Fifth, South Africa's industrial policy is being challenged by China's manufacturing competitiveness. The clothing and textile industry became the first casualty of China's competitiveness. According to the local trade union movement, this resulted in almost 60 000 job losses and has seen small-medium enterprises close their doors. While the Department of Trade and Industry responded by imposing a voluntary import quota on certain clothing and textile items coming from China, this did not do much in protecting local producers. In fact, as mentioned earlier, local retailers substituted Chinese imports with imports from Vietnam and Bangladesh, which does not rule out the possibility that Chinese companies operating in these countries could still be exporting their cheap textiles to South Africa through third markets.

As much as Pretoria has initiated a reorientation of its industrial policy to develop a more competitive global export base, the structural problems embedded in the economy, especially the skills shortage, have been a setback to its macroeconomic strategy. To this end, China has announced a US$31.3 million development package for technical training under the Skills, Education and Training Authorities (SETAs) programme. In so far as the Chinese have used this platform to channel this money to harness the skills and vocational training of entrepreneurs and workers in the textile industry, the response from the South African side, especially the Department of Labour, has been poor. As a result, the Office of the Deputy-President has engaged in the process and is disbursing the money through the Accelerated Shared Growth Initiative for South Africa (ASGISA) and JIPSA. Interestingly, none of the money is being spent on the development of the textile industry as originally intended. Instead, it is being used for technical training in agriculture, tourism, defence and foreign affairs. What this illustrates is that while China may extend assistance to improve South Africa's industrial capacity, this is something that China may not always do in the future, especially if the process is frustrated by bureaucratic inertia. Moreover, as much as the voluntary textile export restraint was deemed as a gesture of political goodwill, Pretoria cannot expect that Beijing will continue to do so in the future, especially when it is seen as contrary to the WTO protocols and China's own industrial strategy. Therefore, in terms of the strategic partnership, the indirect effects on South Africa's industrial policy places pressure on Pretoria to develop a coherent strategy that is not undermined by Beijing's industrial strength.

On balance, the strategic South Africa-China partnership is determined by the direct and indirect effects this has for both sides in terms of their global, regional and domestic ambitions. To this end, it represents both an opportunity and a threat to South Africa. If defined from the realist perspective of international relations, China's behaviour is anything but anomalous. Realist theorists conceptualise the behaviour of states in the international system as based on national interests and survival of the fittest within a hostile environment. In light of these assumptions, China conducts its current international relations according to its self-interest and pursues its foreign policy with aggression and on its own terms. Yet liberal theorists would counter that China's foreign-policy behaviour undermines the foundations of the international system, namely cooperation, democracy, transparency and human rights.

The argument here is that in the case of Sino-South African relations, the realist interpretation of China's behaviour holds true. Beijing has aligned its national interests to its economic sustainability and political ambitions, underpinned by the shift away from ideology to pragmatism. The fact that Beijing is able to infuse the rhetoric of its historical anti-imperialist support to forge closer ties with the developing world, especially in Africa, has created favourable conditions for entrenching strategic partnerships. Sometimes this historical rhetoric can be used as a means to an end (see the other case study chapters in this volume) or in other instances conjure up feelings of like-mindedness on global issues and the sharing of a similar past (take, for example, the view that China has never enslaved or colonised Africa, but shares in the continent's imperialist humility because China also suffered the indignity of external domination).

Whereas the post-apartheid government would similarly argue that the formalising of its diplomatic ties with the PRC was dictated by South Africa's national interests, ten years later, the benefits flowing from these considerations – and whether the relationship can be construed as a strategic partnership – are still debatable. Economic relations remain in China's favour, while Pretoria is uncertain how China will react on issues relating to security in the UN. Moreover, China is becoming an important economic and political force in Africa, which may unsettle Pretoria's Africa policy. And even within the dynamic of the South, China remains the dominant pole with much more influence than South Africa.

As it stands, this strategic partnership appears to be pragmatically defined from the Chinese side, while it is reactive from the South Africa side, following international consensus that China must be engaged. It also appears that balancing a strategic partnership with China has to take into consideration that the engagement must involve all actors in society. Currently, it is only the political and economic elites in South Africa for whom the relationship is strategic. For the rest of ordinary South Africans, including significant sectors of society, such as unions, South Africa's relationship with China is anything but strategic or mutual. For them, the relationship masks more of the hidden threats than the mutual opportunities and makes South Africa the subordinate partner in the engagement. What this means is that the post-apartheid government must be more confident and clear about what it means to be strategic. While it makes infinite sense for South African corporates to penetrate the Chinese market, if they want to have a global presence, it is even more imperative and logical that the South African government understands that its relations with China are fundamentally about the idea of 'business of business is business' within the confines of realpolitik. A strategic partnership should mean more than just normative agendas and like-mindedness.

NOTES

1. See 'South Africa's Relations with the People's Republic of China: Mutual Benefits or Hidden Opportunities?', in S. Buhlungu et al. (eds.), *The State of the Nation 2005–2006* (Cape Town: HSRC Press, 2005).
2. *Taipei Times*, 28 December 2004.
3. G. le Pere, K. Lambrechts and A. van Nieuwkerk, 'The Burden of the Future: South Africa's Foreign Policy Challenges in the New Millennium', *Global Dialogue* 4(3), 1999: 3–8.
4. G. Mills, 'The Case for Exclusive Recognition', in *South Africa and The Two China's Dilemma* (Johannesburg: SAIIA/IGD, 1995), p. 85.
5. R. Suttner, 'Dilemmas of South African Foreign Policy: The Question of China', in *South Africa and the Two China's Dilemma*.
6. It was reported that the ANC received R33 million from Taiwan for its electoral campaign in 1994, but Taipei denied this and instead argued that the money was earmarked for assisting returning ANC soldiers (Mills 'The Case for Exclusive Recognition'). *The Star*, 25 February 1995, reported that following the democratic elections in 1994, the Taiwanese authorities embarked on a massive sponsorship drive of all

expenses-paid trips for South Africa's new parliamentarians (248 members including key cabinet ministers, such as Joe Modise and Jeff Radebe, as well as controversial personalities, such as Winnie Mandela and Peter Mokaba) and members of the media and academics to visit Taipei, hoping to lobby support for the maintenance of relations.

7. Mills notes that the announced Taiwanese investment comprised the following: the Taiwan Railway Administration awarded a contract of R420 million to Union Wagon and Carriage of South Africa, a joint computer venture with Acer; that the Taiwan Feed Industry Association would purchase 300 000 tonnes of maize before April 1995 worth R122.5 million, while the Taiwan Power Company would also increase the purchase of coal by 0.5 million tonnes and R140 million would be donated to vocational training under the RDP. The loans to Eskom, MacSteel and the Development Bank of Southern Africa were valued at R105 million, R70 million and US$15.5 million respectively (see Mills 'The Case for Exclusive Recognition').
8. *The Sowetan*, 2 August 1993.
9. *Weekly Mail*, 3 December 1993.
10. I. Taylor, 'The Ambiguous Commitment: The People's Republic of China and the Anti-Apartheid Struggle in South Africa', *Journal of Contemporary African Studies* 18(1), 2000: 91–106.
11. See http://www.dfa.gov.za/docs/2004/chin0621.htm.
12. See 'Hi-Sense to Increase TV Production in South Africa', *People's Daily Online*, 22 January 2007. http://www. english.peopledaily.com.cn/200701/22/eng20070122_343604.html.
13. See http://www.sinoprima.co.za/DNA.htm.
14. See http://www.engineeringnews.co.za/eng/sector/energy/?show=64356.
15. Interview in Johannesburg, 28 June 2007, by C. Burke.
16. See 'Crime Deters Chinese Investment', *Business Report*, 4 November 2007.
17. Interview in Johannesburg, 30 June 2007, by C. Burke.
18. Interview in Pretoria, 20 July 2007, by C. Burke.
19. See http://www.miningweekly.co.za/eng/features/sasol/?show=58298.
20. See http://www1.cei.gov.cn/ce/doc/cenf/200407012185.htm.
21. See http://www.southafrica.info/doing_business/sa_trade/exporting/sasol-260907.htm.
22. *Business Day*, 14 December 2004.
23. See http://www.naspers.co.za/English/inter.asp.
24. *Financial Mail*, 18 February 2005.
25. *Engineering News*, 21–27 January 2005.
26. *Engineering News*, 21–27 January 2005.
27. L. Reddy, 'A China–SACU FTA: What's in it for South Africa?' *South African Foreign Policy Monitor*, August/September 2004.
28. Interview in Pretoria, 20 July 2007, by C. Burke.
29. *Business Day*, 28 February 2005.
30. *Business Day*, 28 February 2005.
31. *Engineering News*, 5–7 November 2004.
32. See J. Wilhelm, 'The Chinese Communities in South Africa', in Buhlungu et al., *State of the Nation*, pp. 350–68.
33. See D. Accone, 'Recognition of Apartheid Travails behind Chinese Race-Rights Case', *Sunday Times*, 27 January 2008.
34. See 'Hu's Visit Set to Boost China-South Africa Strategic Partnership', 4 February 2007, http://www.csc.mofcom.gov.cn/csweb/sacc/info/Article.jsp?a_no=60485andcol_no=615.

11

A Tale of Two Giants

Nigeria and China

Alaba Ogunsanwo

INTRODUCTION

Formal diplomatic relations between the People's Republic of China (PRC) and the Federal Republic of Nigeria were established in February 1971. Before that, informal relations had existed for years, with the ambassadors of both countries to Egypt signing a statement pledging their support and collaboration with the anti-colonial struggles of liberation movements.[1]

Following the establishment of diplomatic ties, a six-man delegation led by the Nigerian Commissioner for Economic Reconstruction and Development, Adebayo Adedeji, visited Beijing in August 1972, where an agreement on economic and technical cooperation, including one on trade, was signed between the respective countries. The trade agreement was hardly significant as it had no impact on the largely unregulated imports of Chinese goods that had been entering Nigeria for years and were to become impossible to control in the years ahead. Nevertheless, both agreements were described as providing a solid foundation for economic and technical cooperation between the two countries.[2]

The economic cooperation agreement was unique as it was open-ended. In theory, this meant there was no limit to the number of projects that Nigeria could request the Chinese to implement in the country. There was relatively little demand for Chinese resources in Nigeria compared with other African states.

This was the position that the Chinese had worked for in vain since 1960. The Nigerian engagement had differed from Beijing's relations with other African states, where technical and financial assistance usually began to flow almost immediately after forging formal relations. For one thing, China was now dealing with a confident Nigeria whose new-found oil wealth would soon catapult the country to the ranks of powerful regional actors.[3] Also, China had only recently emerged from the setbacks of the Cultural Revolution and was not in a position to undertake the type of assistance programme that would have had a noticeable impact on Nigeria.

Between 1972 and 1974, Nigerian exports to China totalled US$14 million, whereas imports from China totalled US$249 million. During this period, five Nigerian delegations visited China, including the September 1974 delegation headed by Nigeria's Head of State, General Yakubu Gowon. These visits were politically significant since they sought to further concretise the 1972 economic and technical agreements on bilateral cooperation. In 1975, after a change of government in Nigeria, a group of officials and scholars spent time in China studying its organisational system, with a view to seeing whether China's experiences could be applied to the reorientation and mobilisation efforts in Nigeria. Given the complexities of the prevailing socio-economic and political power configurations in Nigeria, this proved to be a futile exercise. Other delegations also made visits to China. A government technical cooperation delegation led by the Commissioner for Transport, Colonel Mohammed Magoro, held discussions with Chinese railway officials, with a view to acquiring Chinese assistance in developing and modernising Nigeria's railway system.[4] However, these discussions did not result in any firm commitments from China, and the Nigerian government contracted Indian Railways with the initial task of making the management of Nigerian Railways more efficient. The complete modernisation of Nigeria's 3 200 km railway system was obviously too much for China to undertake in 1979, after completing the Tanzania-Zambia (TAZARA) Railway (see Chapter 9). In October 1972, a Nigerian oil delegation also visited China to study its petrochemical installations.[5]

In 1975 and 1976, Nigerian imports from China totalled US$69.86 million and US$140.87 million respectively, while Nigeria's exports to China for these combined years amounted to US$8.85 million. In 1977, imports stood at US$146 million, while exports to China were US$11.8 million. This disparity in China-Nigeria trade was greater than that of any other African country. The Nigerian government was particularly concerned about the adverse trade balance in view of declining foreign reserves in 1978. This led to a visit by Chinese Vice-Premier, Geng Biao, in October of the same year. In April 1979, a Nigerian delegation led by the Chief of Staff, Supreme Headquarters, General Shehu Yar'Adua (the brother of President Umaru Yar'Adua), and including the Commissioner for Foreign Affairs, General Henry Adefope, arrived in Beijing to begin discussions with Chinese officials on matters of mutual interest. Apart from international issues, Nigeria's preoccupation was with the problem of narrowing the trade deficit and the ineffective use of the economic and technical cooperation agreement signed between the two countries in 1972. Chinese agricultural experts were already working on a paddy rice scheme in Lagos state that entailed showing farmers new techniques in rice-growing, as well as sinking boreholes for irrigation purposes in the northern part of the country, but these were considered inadequate. After negotiations with Vice-Premier Geng Biao and other Chinese officials, the two countries agreed to cooperate in the fields of agriculture, industry and trade. Beijing agreed to buy palm kernels, cocoa, cashew nuts and cotton as an initial step towards correcting the trade imbalance.

In the area of agriculture, China agreed to reinforce its borehole drilling activities in Nigeria in order to boost farming irrigation. Nigerian-designed farming tools would also be manufactured in China.[6] In the absence of an annual trade agreement, however, the trade imbalance continued. The Chinese could not have been particularly satisfied with this arrangement since it did not identify any substantial or meaningful project that they could work on or highlight as their contribution to Nigeria's development. Virtually all the important Western and Soviet bloc states were engaged in some form of project activity in Nigeria. Even the Nigerian-designed farming tools manufactured in China would still have to be imported by Nigeria, and would therefore show up in the trade figures as Chinese exports to Nigeria. Perhaps, with hindsight, building such a factory in Nigeria would have been a better contribution to reversing the trade deficit. There were Nigerian requests for Chinese medical personnel to work in Nigerian hospitals, especially in areas outside the big cities where noticeable shortages existed. This demand was not difficult for China to meet. During this period, some 300 Chinese personnel were working in Nigeria, while fewer than ten Nigerian students were studying in China.

Contextualising the Nigerian-Chinese engagement

Nigeria-China relations must be seen within the larger context of developments in Africa that affected both countries. The April 1974 revolution in Portugal produced some positive changes for Africa, as well as challenges for Africa's leaders. Of all the Portuguese colonies, Angola presented the greatest challenge. Nigeria supported and recognised the government of the Popular Movement for the Liberation of Angola (MPLA) in 1975 and urged other African states to do so. This was at a time when apartheid South African troops had secretly entered Angola and penetrated several hundred kilometres towards Luanda at the invitation of Jonas Savimbi, leader of the National Union for the Total Independence of Angola (UNITA).[7]

The Chinese position in Angola was very different and caused consternation in Nigeria, as well as among other African countries from Tanzania to Guinea, Algeria and Congo-Brazzaville. That China chose to react to the conflict in Angola from a Sino-Soviet rivalry perspective and condemned the intervention of the Cuban internationalist forces in Angola in driving out the apartheid troop invasion as a mercenary operation, was considered unacceptable by African governments. This contradicted Beijing's earlier position of anti-colonialism, and was robustly challenged by Lagos during the second Nigeria-China Dialogue in Beijing in July 1979.[8]

Beijing felt compelled to withdraw one of the professors taking part in the 1979 bilateral discussion in order to reduce the tensions.[9] Officially, however, the vigorous exchanges did not adversely affect bilateral China-Nigeria relations. This was because the achievement or attainment of each country's foreign policy objectives could not be affected adversely by the action or deliberate inaction of the other.

China continued to pursue its own Africa policy, getting closer to those states with which it had developed strong historical ties on a multidimensional level. By some coincidence, at the time of the China-Nigeria Dialogue in Beijing in 1979, Nigeria's Head of State, General Olusegun Obasanjo, was also engaged in pressuring the British government of Margaret Thatcher to initiate the Lancaster House talks and agreement on independence for Zimbabwe the following year. The direct economic pressure applied to British companies in Nigeria helped to persuade London to agree to the need for genuine independence in Zimbabwe: a goal that Beijing also strongly supported.[10]

The economic imperatives

As noted elsewhere in this volume, China had taken a quantum leap at the end of the 1970s when, under the leadership of Deng Xiaoping, it chose to open its doors to selected and specified areas or zones of the country for experimentation with a different system of resource utilisation, ownership and management. Both China and Nigeria then could be said to have chosen paths that would make cooperation easier. Yet it was also clear that they would need to compete for the limited globally investible funds, which would only be advanced where the environment was conducive to business. For Nigeria, a situation had evolved in which the Nigerian state controlled the 'commanding heights of the economy' and thus made important decisions affecting productive activities. Many government enterprises had seen billions of dollars, without producing the desired results. They had become bottomless pits, gobbling up resources with virtually nothing to show for it. Even the monumental iron and steel project at Ajaokuta, intended to produce flat sheets and other categories of steel product with the assistance of the former Soviet Union, was not exempt from the long litany of failed government projects in Nigeria.[11] Enterprises that would have thrived under private-sector management and ownership in the country automatically began to make losses once under state control. Joint ventures with foreign partners, such as motor vehicle assembly plants, made losses, whereas in other countries, such as Brazil and South Africa, such ventures were successful and integral parts of their industrialisation processes. The Nigerian state has been highly parasitic and characterised by the appropriation of public resources for private use. This is one of the major reasons why state-owned and state-run enterprises have often failed to contribute profits to the public treasury. Moreover, the deliberate weakened nature of the state has meant that state institutions have not been able to protect security of life and property. This is perhaps why Nigeria's Minister of Foreign Affairs, Ojo Maduekwe, asserted in Lagos in July 2007 that Nigeria has no state and no market.[12]

But the level and depth of China-Nigeria relations will be more meaningful if we examine the figures in the tables below.

Table 11.1 Total value of Nigeria's exports and imports, 1980–2005 (US$ millions).

Year	Exports	Imports	Balance
1980	25 934	16 643	9 291
1990	19 671	5 627	14 044
1995	13 371	8 222	5 149
1999	13 227	8 588	4 639
2000	21 174	8 721	12 453
2001	17 688	11 586	6 102
2002	18 573	12 442	6 131
2003	24 047	14 873	9 174
2004	31 148	14 164	16 984
2005	42 277	15 200	27 077

Source: Adapted from *UNCTAD Handbook of Statistics* 2005 and *UN Monthly Bulletin of Statistics* 2007

Table 11.2 Crude oil exports as percentage of total exports, 1996–2005.

Year	Percentage
1996	95.3
1997	94.7
1998	96.9
1999	99.0
2000	99.6
2001	99.6
2002	92.2
2003	96.4
2004	87.1
2005	94.4

Source: *Nigeria Foreign Trade Summary, January–December 2005*. Abuja: National Bureau of Statistics

Table 11.3 Nigeria's imports from PRC, 1995–2006.

Year	US$ millions
1995	152.74
1996	170.85
1997	316.46
1998	357.37
1999	396.00
2000	563.88
2001	917.15
2002	1 047.09
2003	1 787.49
2004	1 719.27
2005	2 305.28
2006	2 855.67

Source: World Trade Atlas (http://www.tralac.org/scripts/content.php?id=6073)

Table 11.4 Nigeria's exports to PRC, 1995–2006.

Year	US$ million
1995	59.71
1996	6.82
1997	10.63
1998	27.46
1999	182.49
2000	292.93
2001	227.44
2002	121.31
2003	71.68
2004	462.58
2005	527.06
2006	277.75

Source: World Trade Atlas (http://www.tralac.org/scripts/content.php?id=6073)

The first clear message from the tables above is that for Nigeria-China relations to become advantageous to Nigeria, more than just the willingness of China to help turn things around will be required.

It is not only Nigeria's trade relationship with China that is heavily weighted on imports. The European Union (EU)-Nigeria relationship, in which Nigeria – as a member of the African, Caribbean and Pacific (ACP) countries – has had a preferential trading agreement since the 1970s, has resulted in the total volume of Nigeria's exports being an infinitesimal proportion of the country's total trade with the EU market. In addition, the export of manufactured items to the EU is miniscule. This is a result of the monocultural structure of the Nigerian economy – an economy that depends on the export of crude oil and gas. This situation prevails despite efforts by successive administrations to diversify the economy. Nigeria's economy is often described as a 'cargo economy', with ships laden with containers docking at Nigeria's ports and returning almost empty to their places of origin, as Nigeria does not have much to export. The same has been true with regards to Nigeria's trade with North America, Europe, Asia and South Africa. The reasons for this are glaring: the basic infrastructure required for manufacturing endeavours in Nigeria is grossly inadequate. Public power supply to industry remains erratic at best, with manufacturers having to generate their own electricity, provide water and, in some cases, build access roads. Competitiveness is the first casualty in such a situation. Nigeria's railways and major road arteries also remain moribund, with consequences that even government functionaries complain about.

Can China help to turn this situation around?

Nigeria wishes to become a major economic actor regionally and globally by the year 2020. For this reason, Olusegun Obasanjo, Nigeria's president from 1999–2007, publicly invited foreign investors, including China, to participate in the Nigerian economy, promising to create a business-friendly environment.[13] An annual inflow of at least US$10 billion was expected when Obasanjo assumed office in May 1999. Efforts were made to ensure that China participated in these endeavours to promote foreign direct investment (FDI). The eventual transformation of the Nigerian economy, which is the main objective of this exercise, is assumed to be compatible with China's national interests. In the past fifteen years, China has been able to attract FDI of not less than US$40 billion annually. These investments have, however, been monitored by Beijing. In addition, the opening of important American and European markets, as well as the Association of Southeast Asian Nations (ASEAN) and Japanese markets, to Chinese manufactured products has ensured export-driven growth in the Chinese economy (see Chapters 16 and 17), which has made it the fourth largest economy in the world. China's positive trade surplus was estimated at US$250 billion in 2007. The country needs raw materials to feed its rapidly expanding manufacturing industry and large markets abroad for its manufactured products. To the extent that Nigeria's aspirations are compatible with China's interests, success can be achieved through mutual cooperation.

Nigeria wishes to move away from being just an exporter of crude oil to becoming an exporter of petroleum products: a development that could turn the country's fortunes around. Licenses were approved for no less than twenty companies to establish refineries in Nigeria. President Obasanjo, who was directly in charge of the petroleum portfolio for eight years (declining to appoint a petroleum minister), ensured that highly lucrative oil blocks were allocated to a Chinese state company in the expectation that Beijing would utilise that opportunity to take over the government-owned Kaduna oil refinery.[14] While the media reported in October 2006 that the refinery had been sold to the Chinese, the reality was somewhat different. The Chinese company did not make the oil block offer concretely operational, meaning that the refinery was not purchased by China. In fact the Chinese bid was set deliberately low.[15]

The Chinese are now heavily represented in the Nigerian economy, and are fully aware that an oil refinery needs to be located in the country's export processing zone. The Nigerian environment is not yet prepared to allow a free market to operate in the petroleum sector. This was one of the reasons why Foreign Minister, Ojo Maduekwe, insisted in his statement at the Nigerian Institute of International Affairs (NIIA) in July 2007 that Nigeria does not have a market.

China requires huge quantities of oil and is looking for this resource everywhere, including Angola, Sudan, Nigeria, Gabon and elsewhere in Africa.[16] However, Beijing cannot actively encourage crude-oil-exporting countries such as Nigeria to convert to the export of petroleum products.

High expectations of China's participation in Nigeria's economic transformation predated the Obasanjo presidency in 1999. Indeed, it was the pariah government of late autocrat General Sani Abacha that, in 1995, commenced the steps that drew China closer to Nigeria. The impact of sanctions imposed by some Western countries on Nigeria at the time led Abuja to 'Look East' as Robert Mugabe had done in Zimbabwe (see Chapter 7). As the trade figures indicate in Table 11.3, Nigeria's imports from China increased considerably in 1997 and kept rising. China did not join the West in attacking the Nigerian government following the execution in 1995 of Ken Saro-Wiwa and his eight Ogoni environmental and human rights' activists in the Niger Delta. This was seen as an entirely internal affair in which China did not wish to interfere. In December 1995, the Nigerian Federal Ministry of Transport signed an agreement with the China Civil Engineering Construction Corporation for the rehabilitation of Nigeria's railways at a cost of US$529 million, which included the supply of coaches.[17] This was reportedly followed in May 1997 by agreements on oil cooperation, bilateral cooperation in the steel industry, a protocol on cooperation in an electric power project and reciprocal promotion and protection of investments.[18]

It was clear at the time that Nigeria was not in a position to invest in China and, therefore, the promotion and protection of the investments protocol was designed to attract Chinese investments into Nigeria. China has done so successfully: more than 100 Chinese companies now operate in Nigeria in various fields, from construction, to agriculture to water and oil. Signing a loan agreement of US$2 billion with China for the railway was questioned by those who felt that, with some US$47 billion in foreign reserves, Nigeria had no reason to borrow more funds. The Obasanjo administration was apprehensive about the whole railway project collapsing, and ensured that China held the purse strings of the project to enhance the chances of more efficient delivery, rather than entrusting the disbursement of funds to Nigerian government functionaries.

One area where effective cooperation has taken place between Nigeria and China is in the telecommunications sector. The efforts of the Obasanjo administration to extend telephones to the country's rural areas through the connection of Nigeria's 774 local governments to a network led to the signing of a loan agreement of US$200 million at a concessionary rate from three Chinese companies, Alcatel Shangai Bell,

Huawei and Zhongxing Communications (ZTE). The agreement was guaranteed by the Chinese government with the Nigerian Ministry of Communications representing the Nigerian side in the deal.[19] By August 2007, some unexpected problems in the area of technology and management had stalled the operational services of the project.

Beijing was involved in Nigeria's telecommunications sector even earlier. In December 2004, the National Space Research and Development Agency in Abuja signed a contract with the Great Wall Industry Corporation of China for the building, delivery and launching of a Nigerian communications satellite, NigComSat-1. This was to be based on the Donagfanghong-4 Satellite platform. NigComSat-1 carries transmitters for 28 wavebands and was designed to ensure that the country meets the demand for telecommunications, broadcasting and broadband multimedia services.[20] The Chinese provided a soft loan for the project, which was completed on schedule, and NigComSat-1 is now in orbit, having been launched into space before Obasanjo's departure as president. At a cost of US$200 million, this was one project that was not abandoned.[21]

Not a bed of roses . . .

The increased Chinese presence in Nigeria has met with resistance in some quarters. There are accusations of Chinese companies dumping cheap goods, produced through cheap labour in China, on the Nigerian market, thus displacing infant industries in Nigeria. As highlighted earlier, Nigerian enterprises have had to operate under difficult conditions due to a lack of a basic and supportive infrastructure, making their products uncompetitive, even in Nigeria. The collapse of the textile industry has been blamed on the influx of cheaply produced alternatives from abroad, including China. However, there is arguably little that Beijing can do about this as it is not responsible for the trade liberalisation regime, which Nigeria's membership of the World Trade Organisation (WTO) compels it to adhere to.

The complaints of the Standards Organisation of Nigeria are similar to those of the European Commission regarding some substandard Chinese products entering the market. Nigeria's National Agency for Food and Drug Administration and Control (NAFDAC) has traced some toxic products and expired drugs to China and India. Several companies from these two countries have been publicly named as being responsible for manufacturing these drugs for the Nigerian market. This is a difficult situation to resolve since, in many instances, such products are brought in by Nigerian businessmen. The executive head of NAFDAC, Dora Akunyili, has been fighting an unrelenting battle against these unscrupulous Nigerians, and has received both national and international commendation for her work. The regulatory body in Beijing has not been rigorous in ensuring that what leaves the country as Chinese exports conforms to World Health Organisation (WHO) standards.

In August 2007, Akunyili suggested to a visiting Pakistan delegation that Nigeria would welcome the establishment of drug-producing factories in the country by enterprises from abroad including China, India and Pakistan. This would enable the Nigerian regulatory agencies to monitor the production of drugs. Whether the Chinese will take up this offer remains to be seen.

In the same year, NAFDAC announced a crackdown on all foreign-manufactured toothpaste, following the discovery of a harmful agent in a Chinese-made brand. An anti-freeze agent, diethylene glycol (DEG), was discovered in Chinese-made Colgate. DEG reportedly can cause abdominal pains, nausea, vomiting and damage to the kidneys and liver. Nigerian authorities announced that no foreign-manufactured toothpaste is registered in Nigeria and should therefore be avoided, as its safety could not be guaranteed.

A case of collusion and large-scale bribe-taking was established against the head of the Chinese regulatory agency responsible for food and drugs standards and safety in 2007. He was found guilty and publicly executed.[22] This harsh penalty by itself is not an effective solution to the problem. While Chinese production/manufacturing capacity has caught up with the First World, the inspection capacity of its regulatory agencies is still Third World. As a result, the quality of goods produced in China suffers, as corners are cut by those who wish to accelerate the export-driven production goals of the Chinese state.

Another area of public concern about China in Nigeria is the participation of Chinese men and women in the retail trade or petty commercial activities. The mushrooming of what are called 'illegal Chinatowns' – where goods are sold without passing through Nigerian customs service checkpoints – has received increasing attention from state and federal agencies, which point out that the development is not covered by any protocol between the two countries. As with so many issues in Nigeria, however, public attention has not been sustained, and although it disappears from the pages of newspapers, the problem continues to fester.

The need for China not to overplay its hand

At the international level, Nigeria-China relations often get subsumed in the politics of international fora in which both become involved. The regional positions of the

Organisation of African Unity (OAU) – now the African Union (AU) – or sub-regional issues, as in the Economic Community of West African States (ECOWAS), do not necessarily make provision for the interests of non-members. Neither China nor Nigeria can, for example, shape the decision of the AU or ASEAN on issues of direct interest to Abuja and Beijing. When Nigeria's position on Africa accepting a watered-down permanent seat without a veto on the UN Security Council was rejected by AU members by a vote of 47 to 5 in Addis Ababa in 2005, there was little that China – one of five veto-wielding members of the UN Security Council – would have been able to do to assist Nigeria,[23] despite its support for two permanent African seats on the Security Council. In the same manner, when Rwanda's candidate defeated Nigeria's in the contest for the president of the African Development Bank (ADB), Beijing could not help Abuja. When, in 2004, African states rejected Nigeria's offer to host the administrative headquarters and appoint officials to manage the Regional Africa Satellite System (RASCOM), China could not reverse the African states' decision. Perhaps this is why China agreed to help finance, build and launch the NigComSat-1. Beijing's public support for Nigeria's bid to become a permanent member of the UN Security Council is not at the expense of the other two key African states that were competing for the position: South Africa and Egypt. In reality, it does not lie within the powers or capability of China to deliver such an outcome. China has, however, promised to help achieve the objectives of the New Partnership for Africa's Development (NEPAD), originally the pet project of President Thabo Mbeki of South Africa that was latched onto by Nigeria's President Obasanjo.

In the area of defence, Western countries had always provided Nigeria's military purchases and personnel training for its armed forces, except during the period of the civil war between 1967 and 1970 (when Beijing had reportedly supported the secessionist republic of Biafra to counter Soviet backing of Lagos). There is no indication that this is about to change fundamentally, notwithstanding Nigeria's purchase of fifteen f-7NI multi-role combat trainer aircrafts from China in 2003 and of coastguard or patrol boats for use by the Nigerian Navy in the Niger Delta in 2006.[24] Since 1960, more than 275 000 Nigerian personnel have participated in peacekeeping operations throughout the world under the auspices of the UN, the OAU, ECOWAS and the AU. The country has gained tremendous experience in this field and this is not an area of rivalry between Abuja and Beijing. Indeed, since a major component of Nigeria's current foreign policy is conflict management and resolution in Africa, to ensure that the continent's resources are devoted to peaceful development and not to war, China's willingness to participate in this area is a welcome development for Nigeria. This, of course, is quite different from China's supply of weapons and ammunition to several African states such as Zimbabwe, Ethiopia and Eritrea on a commercial basis, which arguably China as a sovereign state has a right to do.[25] There are genuine fears that such actions may embolden autocratic governments in places like Zimbabwe and Sudan, but each case must be assessed on its merits, and China is not the only major power selling arms to African autocrats (see Chapter 13).

What does the future hold?

What leverage will countries such as Nigeria have on China in the future? From the trade figures highlighted in the tables earlier, not much should be expected in this regard. Between 1993 and 1998, under the regime of General Sani Abacha, and when Nigeria's internal problems led to the imposition of sanctions by some countries, Nigeria supplied one-fifth of the crude oil imported to America's east coast. Consequently, the only sanctions that could have hurt the Nigerian government at the time – oil – were not imposed by the United States.[26] Indeed, not only was there no boycott of Nigeria's crude oil, but FDI in this sector continued.

The highest proportion of total Chinese imports that Nigeria provided was in 2000, with 0.1301 per cent: a negligible figure. There is no doubt that Chinese imports of Nigeria's crude oil will increase exponentially in the near future, but this will be at a time when the export of liquefied natural gas from Nigeria is expected to surpass the current revenue generated by crude oil exports. In addition, China is diversifying the sources of its oil imports and is most unlikely to be in a situation in which Nigeria's oil will constitute a significant proportion of its energy needs.

With foreign reserves of over a US$1.5 trillion, China is now being courted by all and sundry. A China that can now afford to commit, if it chooses to do so, billions of dollars to projects in Nigeria in the energy, railway and power sectors, puts Beijing in a strong position in which it no longer needs to plead with Abuja to assist Nigeria's development, as was the case in 1961. This offer was scorned at the time by Nigeria's Finance Minister, Festus Okotie Eboh. Nigeria-China relations are bound to develop further, hopefully ensuring mutual benefits, but such gains largely depend on how Nigeria leverages its own interests.

The new Nigerian President, Umaru Yar'Adua, while welcoming a Chinese delegation to Abuja in August 2007, suggested that the delegation should return specifically with proposals for assisting Nigeria in tackling its electricity-generation problem. He noted that all of China's provinces have constant electricity and it should be possible for Nigeria to learn from Beijing's experience and expertise in this area.[27]

The immediate concern of the Chinese delegation was the export-processing zone at Olokota in Ogun state where investment in this sector is planned. Yar'Adua reciprocated this visit when he travelled to Beijing in February and March 2008, when both countries agreed to pursue a 'strategic partnership' and establish a forum for their bilateral economic cooperation.

This leads us to the Forum on China-Africa Cooperation (FOCAC), which held three meetings between 2000 and 2006 (see Chapter 2). While participating in FOCAC will enable officials to gain multilateral experience, direct bilateral relations between China and Nigeria would hold greater promise for Nigeria. Such engagements must be followed by concrete measures.

A close examination of the two Nigeria-China agreements signed in August 2001 in Beijing and in February 2006 in Abuja clearly shows that FOCAC cannot be a substitute for bilateral agreements between the two countries. The framework agreement on petroleum industry cooperation of 2001 was to have been valid for four years. While it lasted, there was no record that a Chinese company was one of those awarded any of the contracts for the Turn Around Maintenance (TAM) of any of Nigeria's refineries, as would have been expected under article A(4) of the agreement.

The 1997 bilateral agreement between Nigeria and China was to have been valid for a period of ten years but was substituted in less than four years with another agreement, which dropped the word 'reciprocal' as it became clear that Nigerian enterprises had not taken advantage of China's open-door policy in the same way that Western transnational corporations (TNCs) had done. The 2001 agreement explicitly sought to attract Chinese enterprises to Nigeria with their investments of capital, technology and know-how. If the West could facilitate the process of China embarking on a road to becoming a significant economic power by 2025, why has the long presence of the West in Nigeria not produced the same result? Does China hold the key to Nigeria's development? This remains a critical question. One senses, however, that Nigeria holds the key to its own development. As late as August 2007, the Nigerian government could not state categorically the exact volume of crude oil loaded and actually transported out of the country each day. This information comes from the oil companies themselves.

In terms of the Nigeria-China agreement, Chinese enterprises operating in Nigeria do so on a purely commercial basis. Any strategic partnership between China and Nigeria cannot be based on history, ideological solidarity, or sentiment, but on concrete national interests.

NOTES

1. Xinhua News Agency, 10 February 1971.
2. *Daily Times*, 30 August 1972.
3. Nigeria declined the US offer to help with reconstruction after the civil war. The government was confident enough to do that.
4. Xinhua News Agency, 14 July 1976.
5. Xinhua News Agency, 10 October 1976.
6. Xinhua News Agency, 3 May 1979.
7. The South African military penetration into Angola was vehemently denied by the Western media until it became impossible to hide it.
8. The author was a member of the Nigeria-China dialogue in Beijing in July 1979. Earlier in January of the same year, he had also been part of the delegation that had discussions in Luanda in Angola with Defence Minister Lucio Lara, Prime Minister Lopo do Nasimen and President Agostinho Neto. See also A. Ogunsanwo, *The Nigeria Military and Foreign Policy, 1975–1979* (Princeton, NJ: Centre of International Studies, Princeton University, 1980).
9. This hapless Chinese professor was unfortunately one of those 'sent down' to a rural area for four years during the Cultural Revolution and the trauma took its toll on him.
10. The Nigerian government nationalised British Petroleum in Nigeria and refused to consider the bids of British companies for lucrative projects in Nigeria.
11. The former Soviet Union had been involved in the project for more than 28 years and spent billions of dollars, without any concrete results.
12. This engagement at the Nigerian Institute of International Affairs (NIIA) on 30 July 2007 was Maduekwe's first public engagement as Minister of Foreign Affairs. His remarks were a lamentation at the weakness of the Nigerian state and the lack of markets. He promised to emphasise citizen diplomacy in the new dispensation, but this has yet to be spelt out.
13. Immediately after his election as president in February 1999, but before his inauguration in May, Obasanjo undertook a tour of 30 countries, which included the major economic giants soliciting for investments in a new Nigeria. The author received him in Brussels as Nigeria's Ambassador to the EU, Belgium and Luxembourg.
14. China National Petroleum Corporation was reportedly allotted two oil blocks by President Obasanjo to encourage the company's strong participation in the downstream of Nigeria's oil sector.
15. For the story on the reversal of policy on the Kaduna and Port Harcout refineries by the new president, see *Business Day*, 6 August 2007.
16. After the US, China is currently the second largest consumer of oil. Domestic sources are inadequate.
17. See B. Bukarambe, 'Nigeria-China Relations: The Unacknowledged Sino-Dynamics', in U.J. Ogwu (ed.), *New Horizons for Nigeria in World Affairs* (Abuja: NIIA, 2005).
18. See the useful work by former Nigerian Ambassador to China, V.N. Chibundu, *Nigeria–China Foreign Relations 1960–1999* (Ibadan: Spectrum Books, 2000).
19. See A. Ukodie, 'Politics of NigComSat-1 and the Chinese Invasion', *Sunday Independent*, 5 August 2007.
20. Ukodie's article in Note 19 was a follow-up to an earlier one on 2 August 2007 in the *Daily Independent* in Nigeria, where the question of this government-owned company awaiting privatisation was raised. The real issue is not whether it was built and launched for Nigeria by China, but whether it should compete unfairly with private companies in the same field.

21. The launch in China was attended by Nigerian officials who saw it as evidence of successful Nigeria-China cooperation, despite the original cost of US$100 million having doubled by completion.
22. Another tragedy occurred when a toy-manufacturing company manager, whose products were recalled in millions from the North American market in August 2007, committed suicide as a sign of accepting responsibility for the company's loss and the consequent dent on the Chinese image of quality and standards.
23. It is because of this tendency to gang up against Nigeria that the Forum on China-Africa Cooperation (FOCAC), as promising as it sounds, offers little to Nigeria, at least not as a replacement for bilateralism.
24. Arms sales to any country may conceivably be interpreted to be an interference in the internal affairs of that country. What is of greater concern is a promise to stand by each other at the UN Human Rights Council in Geneva when issues of violation come up for discussion. Nigeria should be more concerned with respecting the human rights of its people at home, thus making it unnecessary for attacks to be directed at the country at the Human Rights Council. Fortunately, there is now a government in power that respects the rule of law and cares for the human rights of the people. See also W.O. Alli, 'China-Africa Relations and the Increasing Competition for Access to Africa's Natural Resources', paper presented at the International Conference on the New Scramble for Africa, State House, Abuja, April 2007, p. 10.
25. Mao Zedong's contention that China would never become a merchant of death, like the big powers, by selling weapons to small countries was abandoned long ago, as his altruism gave way to the reality of international politics and state interests.
26. President Clinton instead appointed a special envoy, Ambassador Howard Jeter, to be his point-man with the Nigerian head of state, Abacha. In this capacity, Jeter met Abacha more than fourteen times, discussing the problem in Liberia and working harmoniously with the Nigerian government.
27. President Umaru Yar'Adua's invitation to the Chinese delegation to return to Nigeria with a proposal to assist in electricity generation could only confirm the fact that he was not satisfied with the briefing he received on the state of Nigeria's power-generation sector. The previous administration had in the months before its exit from office awarded contracts committing the country to spending some US$8 billion on electricity projects.

12

French Puppet, Chinese Strings

Sino-Gabonese Relations

Douglas Yates

INTRODUCTION: THE DISCOVERY OF GABON

Diplomatic relations between China and Gabon were officially established in 1974. But it took 30 years for the diplomatic relations to translate into tangible economic results. While the president of Gabon has visited Beijing eleven times[1] – meeting every generation of leaders since the formation of the People's Republic of China (PRC) – the truly emblematic event of Sino-Gabonese relations was the first official visit by a Chinese head of state to Libreville in October 2004.

During that historic trip, President Hu Jintao and his Gabonese host, President Omar Bongo, signed an oil-exploration-and-production agreement: a case study of the famous 'pork platter' diplomacy, mixing business and politics, for which China has become so famous. During Hu's state visit, Chen Tonghai, chairperson of China Petroleum and Chemical Corporation (Sinopec), led a major business delegation to the country and reached 'an extensive mutual understanding' with respect to cooperation in the field of energy resources through 'friendly' negotiations with Richard Onouviet, Gabon's Minister of Mines.

On the night of 2 February 2004, Presidents Hu and Bongo appeared at a signing ceremony, during which Chen Tonghai and Onouviet signed a memorandum of understanding (MOU) for a sales contract between Total Gabon and the subsidiaries of Sinopec and China International United Petroleum and Chemicals Co. Ltd (Unipec) involving 1 000 000 tonnes of crude oil per year. China was already the third largest buyer of Gabonese crude oil, after the United States and France. In addition, more than 60 per cent of the lumber production was exported to Asia, principally to China.

Hu also provided a cash grant of US$2 million and an interest-free US$6 million loan for Gabon's development.[2]

In addition to the crude oil purchases, on the same day, Sinopec signed a technical evaluation agreement with the oil ministry for three onshore oil fields, one of which is located some 200 km south-east of Gabon's economic hub, Port Gentil, which lies south of the capital on the Atlantic coast. The other two are around 100 km north-east of Port Gentil. This agreement was aimed at 'facilitating the investment Sinopec would have to make under a production-sharing contract because', explained Onouviet, 'prospecting for oil on land in Gabon is very difficult and costly because we are a heavily forested country.' Small deposits of oil were already in production in the zones housing the three blocks and, said Onouviet, 'We hope that Sinopec will discover a large deposit that is lying dormant under Gabonese soil.'[3]

Onouviet's hopeful words reflect a new thinking about both China and its businesses. The rise of China as an industrial and exporting power over the past few years has been remarkable. The success of Chinese oil enterprises in the scramble for African oil has resulted in China's entry into almost all of the continent's petroleum exporters: Angola (1983), Sudan (1995), Congo-Brazzaville (2000), Libya (2001), Algeria (2002), Nigeria (2002), Mauritania (2003) and Gabon (2004).[4] But, as this chapter shows, they have equally penetrated into non-oil minerals sectors.

The Chinese presence in Gabon is but the latest act in a dramatic performance that began at the first Forum on China-Africa Cooperation (FOCAC) in 2000, when the Chinese Communist Party invited 44 African countries – including Gabon – to Beijing to promote trade and build strong commercial ties. In a spectacle of economic diplomacy, the Chinese sold China as a developing country that wanted to share the secrets of its economic success with its poor southern partners. This emphasis on South-South cooperation is seen as a key element in efforts to oppose unilateral global dominance.[5]

While in Gabon, President Hu raised the issue of China-Africa solidarity, suggesting that a common history of 'struggle against colonialism' remains a central tenet of Chinese thinking with regard to relations with Africa. This reminder was welcomed in Africa as a central feature of Sino-African interaction and served to corroborate the historical link between Africa and China.[6]

As has been well documented in Chapter 2 and elsewhere, the most spectacular demonstration of China's renewed commitment to Africa occurred in November 2006, when 40 African leaders – including President Bongo – gathered in Beijing for a special China-Africa summit.

President Bongo, and his half-Chinese Foreign Minister, Jean Ping,[7] attended the summit, eagerly cultivating their new friendship with the cash-rich communists. It is hard to overstate the importance of Chinese cooperation to the economy of Gabon. With high per capita income figures (due to a small population and big oil) Gabon has been trying to get some debt relief from the West for decades without success. So the promise of billions of dollars of loans from China in 2004, with no strings attached, was not without interest to President Bongo. Facing a post-petroleum era of falling production and dwindling oil reserves, Bongo has been trying to attract foreign investors to accept his risky production-sharing contracts. So the arrival of Chinese seismic crews and drilling rigs in 2005 did not leave him indifferent. With large deposits of manganese and iron for sale, Gabon has also been trying to attract international mining houses to develop its reserves, also without success due to low prices on world markets. So the deal for major Chinese corporate investments in those sectors in 2006, including the construction of new railway lines, was the first really exciting move in decades towards exploiting these non-oil mineral resources. Gabon needs infrastructure, such as roads and buildings, which the Chinese are efficient at providing. Chinese construction of new palaces for the National Assembly in 2004 and the Senate in 2006 were perhaps not necessary, but were prestige projects certainly appreciated by the regime officials who occupied them.

Before going into the details of the major Chinese 'development' projects, it is important to look at the historical/political context that preconditioned them. For business is never done in a vacuum, and the sudden entry of China into a country that has long been described as a 'neo-colonial enclave of enduring French interest',[8] where French oil companies, French foresters, and French mining concerns exploited the natural resources of their former colony, deserves at least a moment's digression.

FRENCH PUPPET, CHINESE STRINGS

Omar Bongo Ondimba, the 72-year-old president who has ruled Gabon since 1967, easily secured a new seven-year mandate in November 2005, after the death of Togo's Gnassingbé Eyadéma in January of that year, and thus inherited the mantle of *le doyen d'Afrique*, a nickname given to the continent's longest-serving head of state. A canny political survivalist, Bongo has cultivated close ties with key foreign leaders, helping to add to his mystique and stature at home and convince the average Gabonese voter that no one else is fit to be president. 'After all, what other head of state anywhere in the world can claim to have been personally received by Mao Zedong, Zhou Enlai,

Deng Xiaoping, and Jiang Zhemin?'[9] He has hinted that this could be his last term in office. But as the country's political stability largely depends on his patronage networks, warned one Economist Intelligence Unit reporter: 'The greatest risk to stability would probably be his sudden departure from the political scene.'[10] The story of Bongo is emblematic of the story of Gabon, a country granted independence in 1960 but deeply enmeshed in a complicated dependency relationship with France.

Some consider Bongo a French puppet. Agents of Charles de Gaulle such as Jacques Foccart certainly pulled the strings that raised him to power. 'Albert Bernard' Bongo was born in 1935 during the colonial era at the village of Lewai (now Bongoville) in the district of Lekoni in the Haut-Ogooué region of south-eastern Gabon. The youngest of nine children whose father abandoned them when he was only eight years old, he was raised by an uncle. Coming from one of the smallest ethnic groups in Gabon (the Batéké), from a tiny village in one of the most remote and least-developed regions of the colony – so remote, in fact, that it was not officially part of Gabon until 1946 – he was sent to primary school in Brazzaville, where he later attended a vocational high school, and was appointed as a clerk in the colonial postal service.[11] In 1958 he joined the French army and became a second lieutenant stationed successively in Brazzaville, Bangui and N'djamena (Fort Lamy).[12] The French army proved instrumental in his rise from obscurity.

In 1960, when France granted independence to the colonies, African soldiers such as Bongo found themselves unemployed. Often they were told to return to their country of origin and enlist in their new national armies. But military service had given Bongo some influential friends in the French secret services, especially the shadowy réseau Foccart, which operated throughout the former empire to preserve French interests, economic and political. So when Bongo left the French army with the rank of Lieutenant, he immediately found work in Gabon's Ministry of Foreign Affairs, where he quickly made a reputation for himself as a discrete African collaborator who could be trusted. Agents in Libreville working in the réseau convinced their boss, Foccart, to appoint the Napoleon-sized junior officer as cabinet director in the presidential palace of Léon Mba. In this way, wrote one investigative journalist, Bongo 'rapidly made himself familiar with all the secrets of Gabon'.[13]

In those days, Gabon was a sleepy timber enclave, largely run by the French foresters. The leading producer of tropical hardwoods in Africa, timber made up 80 per cent of the country's exports at independence. Yet the French had done little to modernise the economy. There weren't any industries, nor any important plantations, roads or hospitals (except for the famous hospital at Lambaréné run by Albert Schweitzer). Even the forestry industry was far from being industrialised. Large trees were felled near the river; then simply floated downstream to the port, where they were shipped off raw and unprocessed. Mahogany, ebony and walnut were exploited in large quantities by French firms during the 1920s, the most important species being okoumé, a type of mahogany used in the production of plywood. During the first years of independence, the French foresters lobbied for a willing pro-French collaborator who would serve their interests. The man they opted for was the Fang politician Léon Mba, mayor of Libreville. With their backing, his party won the first legislative elections in 1957, he became Prime Minister in 1958 and then President of Gabon in 1960.[14] It was into his cabinet that the young Bongo was implanted by the French.

At this time, the Gabonese economy underwent a major metamorphosis from a timber to a mining enclave. The early 1960s saw the first commercial petroleum production, and the first significant exports of uranium and manganese, which resulted in a shift of power from the foresters to the petroleum and mining corporations. At the same time, there were profound changes within the Gabonese government. Only three years after independence, the political institutions were in crisis, with Mba pushing for strong authoritarian leadership. He changed the Constitution to a presidential system. When opposition parties protested, he used repressive measures against them, which, in turn, provoked an attempted coup in February 1964. It was in response to this that the French first intervened with their pre-positioned military forces on standby at Libreville.[15] The 1964 French military intervention restored Mba to office, allowed him to establish a one-party regime and, most important of all, enabled him to transfer his power intact to his/their handpicked successor: Albert Bernard Bongo.

Bongo's rise to power, and his lengthy 40-year term in office, is the result of his life-long collaboration with the French. When President Mba became ill with cancer, he flew to Paris for treatment, and Foccart paid frequent visits to his deathbed to pressure the ailing old man to change his country's Constitution once more, this time to create a post of vice-president of the Republic.[16] He then pressured Mba to appoint Bongo as vice-president, and as his running mate in the March 1967 presidential elections. With Foccart's organisational and financial assistance, the still unknown Bongo was thus able to launch a nationwide campaign, thereby legitimising his selection as Mba's running mate, and his succession to the presidency upon the old man's death on 28 November 1967.

Bongo remained loyal to the men who brought him to power. He personally admired Charles de Gaulle, and openly declared his gratitude to the French for their assistance in the development of his country. He cultivated strong personal ties with all subsequent presidents of France and worked closely with Foccart and his network of agents and mercenaries, the Franco-Gabonese elite who exploited the natural resources of Gabon for their personal enrichment, all of this at the expense of the country and its population. Exaggerating French influence is difficult. French remains not only the official language of Gabon, but also the spoken language of the majority of the population, who read French newspapers, listen to French radio, watch French television, study French law, literature and history in their schools, send their children to France for higher education, and have adopted French habits and tastes, including the importation of almost all of their food from France. In addition to its cultural imperialism, France has been the principal aid donor, lender and trading partner. French businesses have dominated the industrial, commercial and financial sectors. France runs the Gabonese currency (the CFA franc) and determines Gabonese monetary policy. French companies dominate the petroleum (Elf/Total), uranium (Comuf), manganese (Eramet/Comilog), and forestry (Rougier) sectors, while French troops protect the Bongo regime.[17]

But, from the beginning of his presidency Bongo undertook a gradual re-orientation in foreign policy, which involved the abandonment of the isolationism established by his predecessor and a search for worldwide support in order to escape underdevelopment. In 1973 Bongo enunciated the main lines of this new orientation under the slogans 'Gabon First' and 'realism'. He expressed a wish to establish relations with all nations that would respect Gabon's sovereignty and its role as a free arbiter and that would cooperate in its development.

As part of the new orientation, between 1968 and 1973, he established commercial and/or diplomatic relations with other non-French Western states (Switzerland, Italy, the United Kingdom, the Netherlands, Canada, Japan), eastern European states (Bulgaria, Czechoslovakia, Romania, Yugoslavia, the Soviet Union), and Arab-speaking states (Mauritania, Morocco, Egypt, Libya, Algeria, Sudan). From all three groups, he hoped for profitable commercial exchanges plus aid and assistance for development. In the case of Arab nations, he was propelled in their direction by the general movement of black African countries after the 1973 Arab-Israeli war. Bongo converted to Islam and changed his name to 'El Hadj Omar' Bongo. He acquired additional contacts and common interests with Arab oil producers when his country became a member of the Organisation of Petroleum Exporting Countries (OPEC).

In the case of communist nations, he had feared that diplomatic relations would bring the dangers of subversion through liaisons with local Marxists, but in 1972 Bongo spoke of an 'open door' for Gabonese products towards the East. He established relations with the PRC on 20 April 1974, and subsequently broke off diplomatic relations with Taiwan, though it continued to buy Gabon's oil and timber nevertheless.

OLD ALLOYS, NEW ALLIES

The decline of oil production has raised serious doubts about the future well-being of the country. Without entirely losing hope of a new oil discovery, the government has opted for a policy of diversification of its economy. This new policy targets the non-oil mining sector. After various exploration and cartographic studies, run in cooperation with the French, the Gabonese mining ministry announced that there was evidence of some 900 different mineral deposits in the country. Of these, only manganese and gold were currently being exploited. Manganese production has recently been driven by high international prices arising from strong Chinese demand. The exploitation of this metal – an essential component in steel production – began in 1962 around Moanda in the Haut-Ogooué province. It was carried out under the auspices of the French-owned Compagnie Minière de l'Ogooué (COMILOG). The company was established in 1953, when France changed its policy of reserving its overseas territories for French investors and sought foreign partners to promote more rapid development. US Steel originally owned 49 per cent of the company and French interests owned the rest. In 1974, Bongo acquired a share for the Gabonese state. In 1999, the French group, Eramet, purchased the interests of US Steel and other European investors, which gave it 57 per cent ownership. By 2003, Eramet held 61 per cent of the stock, while the Gabonese state retained 27 per cent, and private Gabonese investors 3 per cent.

Gabon's manganese reserves, which are estimated at more than 330 million tonnes, contain an average content of 50 per cent manganese, which permits the production of the purest natural manganese dioxide in the world. The world's fourth largest producer of manganese from the 1960s to the 1990s, Gabon exported more than one-third of all the output of the non-communist world. But stagnant market conditions in the steel market during the late 1980s caused COMILOG to downsize and make changes to reduce extraction costs and improve the quality of the ore. By 2003, total company production had fallen to 2 million tonnes, compared to 2.5 million tonnes in 1989.

But now, with prices rising, total receipts from this smaller manganese production have actually increased in absolute value. Between 2001 and 2004, manganese prices increased by 80 per cent and averaged US$199 per ton in 2005.[18] Gabon became the second most important exporter of manganese in the world, and Richard Onouviet expressed the hope that it would become the number-one producer, after the China National Machinery and Equipment Import-Export Corporation (CMEC) signed a series of agreements with Brazilian Companhia Vale do Rio Doce (CVRD), the world's largest iron-ore producer and third largest manganese producer, behind COMILOG, in April 2005.

The Brazilians began a pilot project in May 2005, above an estimated 175 million-tonne manganese reserve. When the Chinese arrived, they promised to create more jobs. In a communiqué dated 8 June 2005, the mining minister noted:

> The priority in the matter of hiring will be reserved for Gabonese, in conformity with the engagement made by President Omar Bongo Ondimba to create thousands of jobs for Gabonese nationals. The construction projects for the mine and other infrastructures will generate 26 850 jobs for Gabonese nationals. The Chinese are predisposed for their part to join the Gabonese authorities in their effort to win the battle against unemployment and poverty.[19]

According to Onouviet, the cost of these works, including the construction of 200 km of railway line from Belinga to Booué, the deep-water port at Santa Clara, and the hydroelectric dam at Mayibout is estimated at US$600 million.

With such enormous financial stakes, the Brazilians and the Chinese soon disputed who would run the operations. So, quickly, each side decided to present its own separate bid. This dispute split the Gabonese government between the partisans of Brazil, led by Richard Onouviet, Minister of Mines, and those of the Chinese, led by the Foreign Minister, Jean Ping (who became chair of the African Union Commission in January 2008). The Chinese state offered a financial guarantee and undertook to buy all of the production from Belinga. At the same time, the project piloted by CMEC foresaw the construction of a new railway line between Belinga and the coast at Santa Clara, while that of the Brazilians foresaw only a branch between the mine and the already existing Transgabonais railway line. The 'pork platter' approach triumphed, and China won the duel.

While awaiting the completion of an environmental impact report, work has not yet begun on the railway or mines. However, thanks to increased Chinese demand, COMILOG reported that its production of manganese had increased by 8 per cent to 3.2 million tonnes in 2006 and that it would reach a maximum capacity of 3.5 million tonnes in the last quarter of 2007.[20] In February 2007, the Chinese company Huazhou

Industrial and Commercial Mining Company (CICMH) began the development of a US$35 million manganese mine in the Bembélé Mountains, at a site 36 km from the town of Ndjole, near the Transgabonais railroad. The mine is estimated to contain 30 million tones, and is forecast to produce one million tonnes a year.

THE AGE OF IRON

The existence of iron deposits in Gabon, particularly in the south-west, far north and north-east, has been recognised for centuries. The discovery and spread of ironworking had evolved before the arrival of European explorers, and the people who lived in these areas made iron tools and weapons. But it was not until the colonial era that prospecting revealed important deposits in three different provinces. The Belinga deposits, in the Mekambo region in the north-east, are considered to be one of the last great unexploited iron ore reserves in the world. They have a very high ore quality of 65 per cent iron, and are estimated at one billion tonnes. Exploitation was originally assigned in the 1950s to a consortium in which the Bethlehem Steel Company of the United States had a 50 per cent share and French and German companies most of the rest. In 1974, the Gabonese state acquired 60 per cent of the Société des Mines de Fer de Mékambo (SOMIFER). It was expected to start production as soon as it could extend the Transgabonais railway, but by the time the railway had reached Booué in 1983, funding for construction was lacking and world market conditions for iron were unpromising, a situation that persisted for more than two decades.

The story of the extension of the Transgabonais railway to these iron reserves is important in order to get a sense of the past and future potential of Sino-Gabonese relations. Between 1974 and 1986, Bongo undertook the construction of a 648 km railway between Owendo on the Estuary to Franceville on the upper Ogooué, a *chemin de fer* (literally, 'way of iron') that sought to reach the forest and mineral riches of the interior, where the rivers are not navigable for long stretches or where road-building and maintenance are not viable or would be more expensive. Facilities to handle the timber were completed at the port of Owendo in 1979 and for the manganese in 1988.

However, plans for constructing a section of the railway from Booué, 240 km north-east to the iron ore of Belinga had to be postponed, most of all, because of weak demand for iron on world markets. The Belinga iron ore reserves had been considered too expensive to operate because of the large distances through difficult terrain that needed to be covered for the product to reach the coast. Limited use of the Transgabonais railway, high maintenance costs, overstaffing and unpaid debts owed by the government, meanwhile, had produced annual deficits of US$20 to US$30 million. Still, in the late 1980s, Gabon discussed with China the possibility of constructing the third stage of the Transgabonais railway from Booué to Belinga. Although the plan fell through, the idea continued to linger in the filing cabinets of Libreville, waiting for its moment to arise – the Chinese, after all, know how to build railways.

Increased global demand for steel has now made the development of iron and construction of facilities financially viable. On 8 September 2004, the PRC contracted to develop the iron deposits at Belinga, and proposed to construct a railway extension from Booué to Belinga, a deep-water port at Santa Clara on the northern coast to ship out the iron, and a railway extension from Ntoum in the Estuary to Santa Clara. In addition, the Chinese promised to install a hydroelectric facility at Poubara on the Ogooué and another on the Ivindo to create the power needed at Belinga to extract 20 million tonnes of ore per year.

Other foreign firms tried to participate. In April 2005, four international mining companies signed an agreement to create a consortium to exploit Belinga. The four companies were the Brazilian mining giant CVRD, the French mining giant Eramet's local subsidiary COMILOG, CMEC and another Chinese company, Sinosteel. But this partnership soon turned to bickering over who would get what, and by the end of the year, the Chinese and the Brazilians were engaged in a rude battle for control. The French were pushed out because they could not raise the capital required. 'Iron ore brings in giant mining companies with giants investments,' explained the COMILOG president-general director, 'that are not really within our reach.'[21] He also denounced the hard lobbying on the part of Chinese authorities, which Libreville was unable to resist. Even a personal visit by the Brazilian head of state, Lula da Silva, didn't sway the Gabonese government from the ambitious Chinese plan.

Richard Onouviet, the Minister of Mines, explained that 'there were political pressures from both sides, and at the highest levels!' But in the end the Chinese proposition made him feel safer:

> This dossier was estimated at more than US$3 billion in investments. The Chinese offer was based on public capital through Exim Bank and guaranteed by the authorities in Peking. They also assured us the complete consumption of all future iron production, with an understanding that starting in 2010 the steel market risked turning around. The Brazilians only had private capital at their disposal. Besides, they had 16 billion tons of iron reserves at their site in

> Carajas, which in the eventuality of a drop in prices risked leading to a slowdown in production.[22]

Thereafter, Onouviet granted the 100 per cent Chinese, state-owned Wanbau Mining Company Ltd authorisation to prospect for iron in the Nyanga province. The accord was signed in Libreville on 16 December 2006 with Sui Ping, president of China North Industries Corporation (NORINCO), the parent company of Wanbau, following a mission undertaken in September of that year in China by the Gabonese General Director of Mines and Geology. Arriving in Libreville on 14 December, the delegation went to the Nyanga province and explored the iron deposit site of Milingui-Tchibanga, then visited the construction site at Mayumba, where the deep-water port was to be located to excavate the minerals. According to Onouviet, this enterprise was a candidate after Sui Ping had followed the Gabonese mining code and created a Gabonese affiliate for the Chinese parent company. Another protocol agreement was signed between the Gabonese state and the Wanbau group for the exploitation of the iron deposits of Tchibanga and for the construction of necessary infrastructure, including a 90 km railway line between Milingui-Tchibanga and Mayumba, and a hydroelectric dam on the Nyanga. According to the first studies undertaken in the 1950s, the deposit holds an estimated 500 million tonnes of ore with 37.5 per cent iron content. Concerning the financing of the project, Sui Ping indicated that Beijing had funds available for loans to African states, proposing that 'Gabon could benefit from this envelope'.[23]

A massive ceremony was held on 7 September 2006 for all of the iron mining projects, at which President Bongo gave a speech in which he ordered that all of the projects be started simultaneously – the mines, the railway lines, the ports, the hydroelectric dams. 'It's the operation of the century,' he pronounced, 'the biggest operation since the Transgabonais':

> It would be appropriate to provide the Gabonese people with a little history. For a long time there has been a desire to construct the Booué-Belinga railway, and the will to make Belinga our number-two city. Personally, I am very attached to the idea. We have looked for partners left, right and centre, but we never found any. But finally, thanks to our diplomatic relations, we found two countries, China and Brazil. Of the two projects, we chose the Chinese. Believe me, it wasn't easy. But the choice has been made, taking into account our excellent relations with the Chinese. China has done a lot for our country: National Assembly, Senate, George Rawiri City which is also the City of

Information, bridges, art works, roads, in short, that has contributed to our policy of cooperation with China. We have just achieved a grand operation. People have written and said many things about it. We think that it's simple. But you must know that the Belinga iron project didn't just happen yesterday. It was the BRGM who discovered it, a French enterprise. And among those who worked on it, there were Americans, like US Steel. All of those were companies who did business in our country and who tried to realize this project, but didn't manage to do so. They left . . . But it is these countries that are asking the question, what it is that China has in particular with Gabon? For me and for the Gabonese, it's simply a very important operation. And I believe that it's the operation of the century.[24]

For the Minister of Foreign Affairs, Jean Ping, there is nothing disquieting about the Chinese presence. 'The importance of Chinese influence in Africa is exaggerated. China is looking for raw materials throughout the whole world, and the largest reserves are found in Africa. So it's natural that they are coming here. Our premier client and investor remains Europe, and in particular, France.'[25]

It was announced in 2006 that the Belinga project will get underway in early 2008 and reach completion by 2011.[26] For the moment, the journey from Makokou to Belinga is either a muddy drive through hills on a dirt road or a more leisurely motor canoe trip up the Ivindo River, past villages where pygmies eke out a meagre living by hunting and fishing.

Infrastructure work was expected to begin in 2006, but was put off several times, due to complicated 'regulation procedures'. These included creating a shady joint-venture company called Compagnie Minière de Bélinga (COMIBEL) to manage and oversee the project's operation. In this new consortium, Chinese CMEC remained majority shareholder with 85 per cent, while the Bongo government took 15 per cent. Environmental activists working in Gabon demanded to see the 2006 contract, which was signed in total opacity. They accused the Bongo regime of exonerating the Chinese consortium from paying any taxes, and they ridiculed the president as being 'Mr Fifteen Percent'.[27]

Bongo suggested that his critics were slandering him, but as one activist replied, 'Is it a crime of lèse-majesté to want to understand what might justify the blank check signed to the Chinese in the Belinga project?'[28]

To respond to mounting criticism, Bongo held a cabinet meeting on 11 October 2007 and gave a speech providing the particulars of the contract: since the Chinese were providing his government with the capital necessary to construct the mine, railroad, hydroelectric dam, and mineral port (all of which the Gabonese state would acquire in 25 years, once its debt was reimbursed), the contract stipulated that no taxes would be collected until then. Bongo also rejected criticisms that the project threatened to disrupt the ecological systems of Gabon's newly created national parks: 'Should all of the many indices of gold, diamonds, barytine, iron, mangenese, uranium, and so on, be left underground for eternity, just so we can assure the well-being of future generations? No! Because the primary mission of any head of state is to pursue his country's development.'[29]

Now that Bongo's shady financial arrangements have been negotiated (always a headache for any foreign investor in Gabon) perhaps the Chinese can actually begin to do some work. They hope to complete the project in three years, just in time for the next presidential (re-)elections.[30]

The environmentalists, however, accused the Chinese of having already started work on a hydroelectric dam near a national park, even though the necessary environmental impact assessments had not been conducted.[31] Onouviet explained that preliminary work has been undertaken at the mining site, but that work on the associate infrastructure would only start in 2008. He also explained that the choice of Kongué, a waterfall near Ivindo National Park, for the hydroelectric dam, was based on it being closest to the mine, and less costly for technical reasons.[32] But he did not deny the absence of an environmental impact report.

The production of oil operated exclusively by Total-Gabon represented around 37 per cent of total national crude oil production in 2005, but when one includes what it produces in partnership with Shell-Gabon, then the French super-major produces almost all the oil.[33] In 2006, the last year for which revised figures have been published, Total produced an average of 87 000 barrels a day (36.7 per cent of total). Despite all the sensational press, the Chinese are not producing any oil whatsoever. For the time being, they are only purchasing it.

Only one Sinopec crew has been exploring for oil in Gabon, with an onshore exploration permit that it acquired in the newly created national wildlife park at Loango. And this became a scandal. Four years after Bongo reserved a tenth of his country's territory as natural reserves, including Loango along the southern coastline, Chinese seismic crews began using dynamite, clear-cutting roads, chopping down trees, spilling pollutants into the waters, and generally committing environmental mayhem at this onshore oil exploration permit. The Wildlife Conservation Society, an American non-governmental organisation (NGO) that had been instrumental in lobbying for the wildlife reserve, reported these infractions to the government, but nothing was done until Gabon's creditors formally complained to the Minister of Forestry, Emile Doumba, and threatened to withdraw US$10 million in forest conservation aid.

'What Sinopec did cannot be tolerated,' claimed Doumba. 'If they find a major oil reserve under a park, we are not going to draw an X over it, that's clear. But I think that we have to make sure to privilege the long-term development of ecotourism, of which the potential is considerable for Gabon.' After several lengthy discussions, the national parks council finally ordered the suspension of the Sinopec operations, and its crews to remove their equipment from the park in the autumn of 2006. According to the ecologists, the lesson learned was: 'If we let Sinopec do what it wants in Loango, we risk numerous catastrophes in Belinga. We don't have the intention of preventing Gabon from exploiting its minerals, but it must show a good example in the application of its own environmental laws.'[34]

CONCLUSION

Despite the longstanding domination of France, despite its military, cultural, political and economic influence, despite the loyalty of Omar Bongo, its role in his rise to power, its protection of his presidency from popular protests and opponents, despite its major oil, mining and forestry companies, France is slowly losing control, and the Chinese have penetrated Gabon.

The question that is now on everybody's minds is whether China will replace France? The answer to this question depends on what kinds of relations one believes really matter. If one examines only trade statistics, then it is entirely plausible that Gabonese raw materials could be sucked into the vortex of Chinese consumption. But if one considers how few Gabonese will ever learn Chinese, go to China, study there, write books in Mandarin, adopt Chinese lifestyles, settle there, and so on, then the sublime role of French cultural imperialism should become apparent. Patterns that have taken centuries to form will not disappear overnight. Jean Ping has stated that China will never replace France, but realistically, his promises mean nothing.

In the larger scheme of things, Gabon is located in the Gulf of Guinea, geographically closer to Europe and America than to China. It plays a small but important role in Western security for central Africa, as the site of a French military base, and possibly a future American one. Only the conscious abandonment of the country by the French or the Americans would open the door to greater Chinese strategic influence. That being unlikely, in the present configuration, one should expect to find Chinese activities in Gabon developing under the aegis of Western domination, or at best, under a depoliticised globalisation. But one has no reason to predict that China will establish a relationship anything like the neo-colonialism of France, at least not in Gabon.

NOTES

1. Bongo visited China in 1974, 1975, 1977, 1978, 1983, 1987, 1991, 2004, 2005 and 2006.
2. F. Lafargue, '*Etâts-Unis, Inde, Chine: Rivalités Pétrolières en Afrique*', *Afrique Contemporaine* 48, 2005.
3. L. Wuyi, 'China's Thirst for Overseas Oil and Gas Resources', *China Oil and Gas* 1, 2004: 19.
4. D.A. Yates, 'Chinese Oil Interests in Africa', in G. le Pere (ed.), *China in Africa: Mercantilist Predator, or Partner in Development?* (Johannesburg: Institute for Global Dialogue/South African Institute of International Affairs, 2007).
5. 'In this context, South–South cooperation is defined as the promotion of economic interaction among developing nations at the bilateral, regional and global level to achieve the goal of collective self-reliance.' See G. Shelton, 'China and Africa: Advancing South–South Cooperation'. Paper presented at FES/Institute for Global Dialogue Conference (Johannesburg, 15–22 October 2005).
6. 'Bongo Signs Accords on Aid, Cooperation, Oil Exploration and Interest-Free Loan', *Business Day*, http://www.bday.co.za.
7. Ping has a Chinese father who settled in Gabon during the 1930s. He was promoted to the rank of Deputy-Prime Minister in January 2007.
8. J. Ghazvinian, *Untapped: The Scramble for Africa's Oil* (Orlando, FL: Harcourt, 2007), pp. 278–79.
9. M.C. Reed, 'Gabon: A Neo-Colonial Enclave of Enduring French Interests', *Journal of Modern African Studies* 25, 1987: 283–320.
10. Ghazvinian, *Untapped*, p. 109.
11. Economist Intelligence Unit, 'Gabon', *Business Africa*, 1–15 June 2006, p. 8.
12. D. Gardinier and D. Yates, *Historical Dictionary of Gabon*, 3rd ed. ([AQ: Place of publication?]: Scarecrow Press, 2007) pp. 38–39.
13. O. Bongo, *El Hadj Omar Bongo: Par lui-même* (Libreville: Editions Multipress, 1983), p. 9.
14. P. Péan, *Affaires Africaines* (Paris: Fayard, 1983), p. 46.
15. B. Weinstein, *Gabon: Nation-Building on the Ogooué* (Cambridge, MA: MIT Press, 1966).
16. C. Darlington and A. Darlington, *African Betrayal* (New York: David McKay, 1968).
17. The office of vice-president does not exist in French Fifth-Republic-style governments.
18. D.A. Yates, *The Rentier State in Africa: Oil-Rent Dependency and Neo-Colonialism in the Republic of Gabon* (Trenton/Asmara: Africa World Press, 1996).
19. D.A. Yates, 'Gabon', in A. Mehler, H. Melber and K. van Walraven (eds.), *Africa Yearbook: Politics, Economy and Society South of the Sahara in 2005* (Leiden: Brill, 2006), p. 244.
20. *Gabon Selection* 576, 16 June 2006: 5.
21. Economist Intelligence Unit, 'Country Report, Gabon' (3 August 2007).
22. V. Lescot, '*Le Scandale Géologique d'Afrique Central est Encore Vierge*', *Marchés Tropicaux et Méditerranéens*, 21 July 2006: 42.

23. Lescot, '*Le Scandale Géologique d'Afrique Central*'.
24. *Gabon Selection* 566, 6 January 2006: 3.
25. *Gabon Selection* 581, 22 September 2006: 4.
26. V. Lescot, '*Priorité aux Relations Sud/Sud et Sud/Est*', *Marchés Tropicaux et Méditerranéens*, 21 July 2006: 13.
27. 'Gabon Iron Mine to Hit the Rails', *Business in Africa*, 18 June 2007.
28. The comparison to American oil middle-man Calouste Gulbekian derives from Bongo's habit of acquiring shares in all the major corporations created during his tenure in office. Whenever a firm wanted to get licensed in Gabon, it had to make 'contributions' to the president's personal bank accounts. For a discussion of how this worked, see Péan, *Affaires Africaines*, pp. 102–05.
29. '*Projet "fer" de Belinga: Seule Une Formule BOT était Envisageable*', *Marchés Africains* 1 570, 17 October 2007: 10.
30. '*Le projet "fer" de Belinga ne Remet Nullement en Cause la Politique Initiée en Matière d'Environment*', *Marchés Africains* 1 569, 3 October 2007: 7.
31. L. Corkin, 'China's Engagement in Africa: Preliminary Scoping of African Case Studies: Angola, Ethiopia, Gabon, Uganda, South Africa, Zambia'. Report prepared for the Rockefeller Foundation and the Centre for Chinese Studies at the University of Stellenbosch (September 2007), p. 91.
32. Economist Intelligence Unit, 'Country Report, Gabon' (1 November 2007).
33. Economist Intelligence Unit, 'Country Report, Gabon' (1 November 2007).
34. '*La Production de Brut du Gabon s'est Maintenue aux Environs de 97 millions B en 2005*', *Gabon Selection*, 17 July 2006: 5.
35. Agence France Press, 28 September 2006.

PART 3

Comparative Great Power Rivalries

13

An Axis of Evil?

China, the United States and France in Africa

Adekeye Adebajo

INTRODUCTION

In this post-11-September 'age of terror', one of the most infamous and inelegant political phrases that has been coined was United States President, George W. Bush's depiction of Iran, Iraq and North Korea as forming an 'axis of evil'. This chapter seeks to examine whether a similar caricature can be applied to the roles of the three main external powers in post-Cold-War Africa: China, the United States and France. An historical approach is adopted and some of the political, military and economic roles that all three countries have played and are currently playing on the continent are assessed. Carrying the Bushism further, these actors can also be depicted as three cowboys in a spaghetti Western of 'the Good, the Bad and the Ugly', with France arrogating to itself the *mission civilisatrice* of spreading 'enlightenment' and culture to barbarous natives; with Western 'Orientalists' hypocritically seeking to convince us about how bad and evil rapacious Chinese 'mercantilists' are for Africa; and with 'ugly' Americans continuing to rampage through Africa in search of markets to conquer and 'mad mullahs' to vanquish. This chapter seeks to shatter the 'Orientalist' myth that often describes China's role as that of a 'yellow peril' seeking to monopolise markets, coddle caudillos and condone human rights' abuses on the continent; while Western powers such as the United States and France are portrayed in contrast almost as knights in shining armour, seeking to assist Africa's economic recovery, spread democracy and contribute to conflict-management efforts. By focusing comparatively on the historical and contemporary role of the United States and France in Africa, these ahistorical distortions are hopefully dispelled. China's own historical and contemporary role is likewise assessed without unrealistically romanticising or unfairly condemning it.

CHINA AND AFRICA: THE GREAT LEAP FORWARD

In examining China's role in Africa, it is important to place this relationship in an historical context of Afro-Asian cooperation during the age of decolonisation from the 1950s, before analysing Beijing's more contemporary role in the post-Cold-War era. Most, but not all members of the Non-Aligned Movement (NAM) are part of the Group of 77 (G77) of the now 130 developing countries that have historically been aligned to China. The G77 was set up in June 1964 in the context of the first UN Conference on Trade and Development (UNCTAD), and continues to dominate the UN General Assembly's agenda. The Africa Group at the UN was created in 1958 and soon, along with Asian allies, made its presence felt on decolonisation and anti-apartheid issues, eventually ostracising South Africa at the UN and maintaining pressure for the liberation of Zimbabwe/Rhodesia and Namibia/South-West Africa. NAM states led the expansion of the UN Security Council and the Economic and Social Council (ECOSOC) by the mid-1970s.[1]

During this period, the Convention on the Elimination of Racial Discrimination was agreed upon, a committee on decolonisation was established and the special committee against apartheid was created. As a result, the pressure of a determined southern majority, including 26 African states, and led by Tanzania's formidable permanent representative at the UN, Salim Ahmed Salim, the People's Republic of China (PRC) took its permanent seat on the UN Security Council in 1971 in the face of strong opposition from Washington. Solid African backing also helped China to secure the 2008 Olympic Games.

China's relations with Africa have thus historically been grounded in a shared history of political and economic dominance by Western colonial powers. Following his victory in 1949, Chinese leader, Mao Zedong, was determined to spread his revolution abroad against 'anti-imperialist' forces. Legendary Chinese Premier, Zhou Enlai, had famously noted that 'revolutionary prospects' were 'excellent' in Africa. Consequently, on historic trips across the continent in 1963–64, Zhou consistently stressed the shared history of colonial oppression. Beijing proved that this was not mere rhetoric by providing essential support and military training to liberation movements across the continent. It also channelled economic assistance to agriculture and light industries, contributing US$2.5 billion to 36 African countries between the mid-1950s and mid-1970s. Algeria, Egypt, Somalia, Tanzania and the then Zaire – now the Democratic Republic of Congo (DRC) – received the lion's share of Chinese assistance (see Chapter 2).

Between 1961 and 2006, 2 000 students from 48 African countries studied in China, while 15 000 Chinese technical experts were sent to Africa to grow rice and build factories, roads, bridges and airports. Some of these projects were, however, criticised for not transferring technology to recipients and for not using sufficient local content. Despite such criticisms, the Chinese assistance included some grand projects such as the 2 000 km, US$484 million Tanzania-Zambia (TAZARA) Railway, completed in 1975. This was an impressive feat of engineering that took five years and more than 50 000 labourers to finish. Beijing had provided long-term, interest-free loans to complete the project after the World Bank, Washington, London and Ottawa had turned down requests from Lusaka and Dar es Salaam to fund the project (see Chapter 9).[2] Under Deng Xiaoping's open-door policy from 1978, the PRC de-emphasised the 'export' of its revolution abroad and focused on a strategy of promoting trade and investment to strengthen its economy, adopting a policy of 'socialism with Chinese characteristics': a move towards a capitalist-market economy.

China's economy has grown at an unprecedented 9 per cent for the last two decades and its gross domestic product (GDP) has tripled. The country has the world's largest population at 1.3 billion people; it has lifted more people (400 million) out of poverty than any other nation in history and, by some estimates, China is on course to overtake the United States as the world's largest economy by 2025. As a corollary, China's growing political, economic and security ties in Africa since the end of the Cold War have attracted much attention as one of the most important developments in the geo-strategy of this age. Beijing's 'peaceful rise' to Great Power status has been nothing short of breathtaking, and Africa must now devise strategies to engage the world's next superpower. China, unlike the West, is investing heavily in the infrastructure sectors – roads, railways, electricity – that Africa needs for its industrial take-off. Beijing has helped to revive Zambia's copper mines and exported timber from Mozambique. It has also invested in the oil sectors of countries such as Nigeria, Angola, Sudan, Equatorial Guinea, Gabon and Chad, ruffling Western feathers as American and French companies are also operating in most of these countries. By 2006, China was importing about a third of its energy from Africa.[3]

Such developments have caused some concerns from China's Western competitors who have often failed to note that India, Malaysia and North and South Korea have also joined the quest for Africa's energy and other resources. As United States' Congressman, Christopher Smith, ahistorically and hypocritically noted in July 2005: 'China is playing an increasingly influential role on the continent of Africa, and there is concern that the Chinese intend to aid and abet African dictators, gain a stranglehold on precious African natural resources, and undo much of the progress that has been made on democracy and governance in the last 15 years in African nations.'[4] But the view from Africa has often been quite different from this hysteria. As Garth le Pere aptly puts it: 'The imperative of coherent policy responses towards China by Africans must . . . not fall prey to lazy caricature and crude stereotyping lest we fall into a trap of moral relativitism where the West is held to one set of standards and China to another' (see Chapter 2). Former Nigerian finance minister, Ngozi Okonjo-Iweala, was equally blunt in noting: 'China should be left alone to forge its unique partnership with African countries, and the West must simply learn to compete.'[5] Meanwhile, in policy terms, Beijing has increasingly stressed political non-interference and a need for countries to find their own paths, rather than adopting a Chinese model.

High-level visits to Africa by the Chinese leadership and to Beijing by African leaders have confirmed the strong bonds between China and Africa. The former Chinese president, Jiang Zhemin, visited Africa in 1996; following that, President Hu Jintao visited the continent five times between 1999 and 2007, while over 30 African leaders have visited China since 1997. Beijing held the first Forum on China-Africa Cooperation (FOCAC) in October 2000 with 44 African governments. At the summit, Western aid conditionalities were criticised, and Beijing soon announced the annulment of US$1.2 billion of African debt to 31 African countries. A second FOCAC summit was held in Addis Ababa, Ethiopia, in December 2003. By 2004, Africa's exports to China had reached US$11.4 billion; Sino-African trade had grown from US$2 billion in 1999 to US$55.5 billion in 2006. Beijing offered the continent US$5 billion in loans and credit in the same year and had become the third largest foreign investor on the continent (at an estimated US$6.6 billion) behind the United States and Europe, having set up over 1 000 enterprises in Africa. In November 2006, 43 African leaders trekked to Beijing for a third FOCAC summit where China promised to double aid to the continent, train 15 000 Africans, and provide 4 000 scholarships. More than 400 Chinese lecturers have been sent to Africa, while 15 000 of its medical experts were dispatched to 42 African countries.

Though China's trade with Africa is only 2 per cent of its total global trade, its direct investment in Africa represents 16 per cent of its total global investment. What is significant about these growing ties is the diversity of Beijing's trade with Africa, ranging from oil in Nigeria, Angola, Sudan and Congo-Brazzaville (an impressive 28 per cent of China's oil imports came from Africa in 2006); to tourism, construction, wholesale, retail, energy, transport, communications and health across the continent; to education in Sierra Leone, Seychelles, Ethiopia and Senegal; to manufacturing in

Morocco and Zimbabwe; to fisheries in Gabon and Namibia; to building stadia in Mali, Djibouti and the Central African Republic; and to agriculture in Zambia and Tanzania.

But some of Beijing's actions in Africa have not been without controversy: China became a large investor (40 per cent of the largest oil venture) and importer of oil from the Sudanese government of Omar al-Bashir, which has been accused of widespread human rights violations in Darfur. Oil was also imported from the equally controversial government of Equatorial Guinea, and arms sold to Ethiopia and Eritrea during their bloody civil war between 1998 and 2000.[6] Beijing's insistence on a policy of 'non-interference' and close ties with autocratic and/or corrupt regimes have been criticised, as has its use of an estimated 80 000 Chinese labourers in its projects in Africa.[7] By the end of 2004, Chinese textile exports to South Africa had grown from 40 per cent to 80 per cent, forcing an estimated 75 000 people out of jobs and, in neighbouring Lesotho, 10 000 jobs were lost and ten clothing factories shut as a result of competition from cheaper Chinese imports. Nigeria's textile industries in Kano and Kaduna were said to have been similarly negatively affected.[8]

A critical area of interest to Africa in which China is currently playing a supportive role is peacekeeping through the UN. After debacles in Somalia and Rwanda in 1993 and 1994 respectively, Western peacekeepers largely abandoned the continent for several years (see more below). By May 2007, China had deployed 1 800 peacekeepers to UN missions in Sudan, the DRC, Liberia, Côte d'Ivoire, Ethiopia/Eritrea and Western Sahara. Though this is not a large number out of 80 000 UN peacekeepers deployed globally, the symbolic value of these troops is greatly appreciated in many African quarters, particularly when contrasted with the more selective and often self-interested Western peacekeeping engagements on the continent. But China's large arms sales to countries such as Zimbabwe, Ethiopia and Sudan continue to cause some discomfort on the continent.

In August 2007, the powerful fifteen-member UN Security Council decided to deploy 26 000 'Blue Helmets' to Sudan's volatile Darfur province by the end of 2007. The UN/African Union (AU) hybrid operation in Darfur (UNAMID) was mandated to bolster the struggling 7 000-strong AU mission in Darfur which had been deployed by 2004. Diplomatic pressure exerted by China – one of five veto-wielding permanent members of the UN Security Council along with the United States, Russia, Britain, and France – appears to have been instrumental in twisting the arm of Sudanese leader Omar al-Bashir. Beijing thus reversed its traditional policy of 'non-intervention' in Africa to convince Khartoum – in which China has invested US$4 billion and from which it buys more oil than any other country – to accept a UN force, apparently under threat of a boycott of China's showpiece US$40 billion Olympic Games in 2008: Beijing's 'coming-out' party as a superpower (see Chapter 4).[9] In another sign of Beijing's growing assertiveness, China pushed for UN Security Council action in Somalia in 2007. Despite concerns about China's self-interested role in Africa, however, Beijing is clear about what its interests are in its relations with Africa. It is likewise incumbent on African governments to devise a coherent, collective approach to defining their own interests, using China's presence on the continent to reduce their dependence on and increase their leverage with Western powers, such as the United States and France.

THE UNITED STATES AND AFRICA: IN SEARCH OF ENEMIES[10]

After the Second World War ended in 1945, the United States at first portrayed itself as an anti-colonial power, urging decolonisation in Africa and Asia. This notion was, of course, absurd to Latin Americans and Caribbeans who had suffered decades of 'Yankee imperialism' in places such as Cuba, Haiti, Nicaragua and the Philippines, and which had all been militarily occupied by the United States in an age of 'gunboat diplomacy'. A third of Mexico's territory had also been swallowed up in the 1840s by a rampaging American colossus. Pax Americana had been imposed on its neighbours with vague justifications of 'manifest destiny' and a God-given right to conquer the lands of lesser 'barbarians'. The genocide against America's indigenous inhabitants and the enslavement and disenfranchisement of its black population were further chinks in Uncle Sam's anti-imperialist armour.

With the onset of the Cold War by the 1950s, Washington changed its anti-colonial tune in Africa and talked instead of a global struggle for 'containment' and 'anti-communism'. The United States no longer urged its European allies – Britain, France, Portugal and Spain – to surrender their African possessions, but instead came to regard the ubiquitous presence of the French gendarme in Africa as a useful way of keeping the Soviet bear out of large parts of the continent. Washington also provided military assistance to its North Atlantic Treaty Organisation (NATO) ally, Portugal, which helped it maintain its colonial presence in Angola, Mozambique and Guinea-Bissau, and delayed the independence of these countries until a military coup in Lisbon in 1974.

The Cold War's 'axis of evil' involved the two superpowers – the United States and the Soviet Union – and France. All three powers turned Africa into a strategic play-ground to conduct their ideological games, resulting in the deaths of millions of Africans. The continent was flooded with billions of dollars of weapons provided to local proxies in countries such as Angola, Ethiopia, Liberia, Mozambique and Somalia. During the Cold War, Washington's policies in Africa frequently ignored principles as basic as democracy and development and focused parochially on containing the 'red peril' through protecting and providing military and financial assistance to often brutal and undemocratic clients, such as Liberia's Samuel Doe, Zaire's Mobutu Sese Seko, and Somalia's Siad Barre, in exchange for political support and military bases.[11]

The Clinton administration, 1993–2000

After the end of the Cold War in the early 1990s, Washington announced that its Cold-War-era obsession with 'containment' was to be replaced by what President Bill Clinton's National Security Adviser, Anthony Lake, described as a policy of 'enlargement', which envisaged the United States seeking to enlarge democracies worldwide, rather than keeping tyrants in power. Though Washington abandoned its former African clients on whom it had lavished billions of dollars in arms and aid during the Cold War, Clinton's democratisation record in Africa was abysmal. Policy often resembled the Cold-War era, as strategic rationales were found to justify a failure to support multi-party democracy in various African countries.[12] Despite the efforts of courageous African civil society activists and democrats to replace autocratic regimes in countries such as Benin, Mali, Niger, Zambia, Sierra Leone and Nigeria, 'enlargement' of democracies was soon replaced by American support for a cantankerous warlord's gallery that Clinton, during a diplomatic safari to Africa in 1998, arrogantly dubbed Africa's 'new leaders': Uganda's Yoweri Museveni, Ethiopia's Meles Zenawi, Eritrea's Isais Afwerki and Rwanda's Paul Kagame. None of these leaders could be accurately described at the time as operating anything like a genuine multi-party system, and most of them were thinly disguised autocrats. No sooner had Clinton anointed them as Africa's model rulers than these leaders went to war against each other: Ethiopia and Eritrea fought a bloody border war between 1998 and 2000, while Uganda and Rwanda, after invading the DRC in a bid to topple the regime of Laurent Kabila in 1998, soon fell out over strategy and the spoils of war in the mineral-rich country and turned their guns on each other, killing scores of Congolese civilians in clashes in Kisangani. A large part of United States support for these regimes was in fact based on its need to maintain an anti-Sudan coalition. All four countries, for example, received US$30 million in American military assistance in 1996.

An important concern of Washington's post-Cold-War policy towards Africa is that a 'green menace' (green is the colour of Islam) may be replacing the 'red peril' of the Cold War, particularly after the bombings of American embassies in Kenya and

Tanzania in 1998 and, more significantly, the terrorist attacks on New York and Washington, DC of 11 September 2001. The Clinton administration had bombed what it erroneously described as a chemical factory in Sudan in 1998 in response to the East African embassy bombings. (Al-Qaida leader, Osama bin Laden, had in fact operated out of Sudan between 1991 and 1996 before United States pressure led the Khartoum government to expel him to Afghanistan.) The administration of George Bush Sr had earlier turned a blind eye to the annulment by military brass hats in Algeria of democratic elections in 1991 that Islamist parties were poised to win. Continued terrorist attacks in Algeria have killed more than 100 000 people since 1991. Washington also consistently refused to pressure the historically repressive regime in Morocco – the so-called 'moderate' gatekeeper of the Mediterranean – to curb domestic human rights abuses and to accept a UN referendum in Western Sahara, a territory unlawfully annexed and occupied by Moroccan military force since 1975.[13]

Undoubtedly, the worst failures of United States policy towards Africa in recent times were Clinton's actions in Somalia and Rwanda. In a secret, botched mission to hunt down Somali warlord, Mohammed Farah Aideed, which was planned entirely by the Pentagon without the UN's knowledge, 18 American soldiers and about 1 000 Somalis were killed in October 1993. In order to deflect the strong domestic backlash and to prevent the Republican Party from making political capital from these events, Clinton inaccurately blamed the military fiasco on the UN and withdrew his troops from the Horn of Africa, effectively crippling the mission without achieving peace in Somalia.[14]

Six months after the Somali debacle, the Clinton administration led efforts in the UN Security Council to force the withdrawal of most of a 2 500-strong UN peacekeeping mission (which had no American soldiers) from Rwanda. As the Canadian UN Force Commander, Roméo Dallaire, has often noted, the UN peacekeepers could probably have prevented the worst excesses of the Rwandan genocide if their mandate had been strengthened to enforce peace.[15] Washington, however, blocked any effective UN response to the killing of 800 000 people. It is important to note that the United States was not being asked to provide peacekeepers in Rwanda, but merely to mandate the UN to take action to save helpless victims of genocide. But with congressional mid-term elections approaching in the United States, cynical political calculations took precedence over an international moral and legal obligation to prevent genocide. Clinton's officials were ordered not to describe the massacres as 'genocide' in a bid to escape pressure for the UN Security Council to mandate a military intervention to stop the massacres.

Following the debacles in Somalia and Rwanda, Washington devised an African Crisis Response Initiative (ACRI) in 1996 – later renamed the African Contingency Operations Training Assistance (ACOTA) – ostensibly as a way of strengthening the capacity of African armies to intervene in humanitarian crises.[16] In reality, the idea was that Africans would do *most* of the dying, while the United States would do some of the spending to avoid being drawn into politically risky interventions in an area of low strategic interest. The US$20 million annual cost of the programme is grossly inadequate, and this programme has mostly conducted training of armies in countries such as Ethiopia, Uganda, Ghana, Mali and Senegal, without addressing the much more urgent logistical needs of African armies. ACRI/ACOTA supported key American allies bilaterally, rather than the multilateral efforts of African organisations, such as the African Union, the Economic Community of West African States (ECOWAS), the Southern African Development Community (SADC) and the Inter-governmental Authority on Development (IGAD), which are all striving to strengthen their own capacity to manage regional conflicts.

In the area of development, 85 per cent of American trade and investment in Africa was concentrated during the Clinton era, as it still largely is today, in four mostly oil-rich countries: Nigeria, Angola, Gabon and South Africa. The fact that US$2 billion of American aid annually went to the autocratic regime of Egypt (Israel received over US$3 billion), while 48 sub-Saharan African states, comprising some of the poorest countries in the world, had to share less than US$1 billion of American aid annually is the clearest sign that political and strategic considerations, rather than poverty and democratic considerations, continued to drive Washington's policy towards the continent.

The US Congress passed the African Growth and Opportunity Act (AGOA) in May 2000, granting more generous access to African goods in selected sectors of the American market. The controversial Act called for African countries to fight corruption, respect intellectual property, and remove barriers to US trade and investment. (Some 37 African countries were deemed eligible for the programme by 2007.) AGOA yielded some dividends for Africa. In the first seven months of 2002, African apparel exports to the United States exceeded US$100 million, while an estimated 200 000 new jobs were created in Africa between 2000 and 2002 as a result of increased exports from AGOA.[17] But, despite this progress, AGOA's critics have argued that the Act allows market access to a limited number of African goods in selected sectors of the American market in exchange for low tariffs and free access for US investors to a wide range of African industries.[18] Most of the benefits of AGOA were also from oil imports to the

US, which grew by 53 per cent in 2005, while non-oil African exports fell by 16 per cent. Significantly, AGOA does not envisage opening up America's wasteful and heavily subsidised agricultural sector – at a cost of US$108.7 billion in 2005 – in which Africa has a comparative advantage, with about 70 per cent of its population working in this vital sector.[19]

The Bush administration, 2001–08

Under the administration of George W. Bush between 2001 and 2008, Washington's foreign policy has been widely perceived to be arrogant and unilateral. In what most of the world regarded as the illegal invasion of Iraq in March 2003, the United States was widely seen as having behaved like a rogue elephant, simply throwing its weight around and treating allies and enemies like grass that can simply be trampled under its rampaging feet. Bush's invasion of Iraq – undertaken without the authorisation of the UN Security Council – was seen to have undermined the authority of the UN, an organisation historically viewed with great reverence by African states as the best guarantor of their security and sovereignty.

Bush's post-11-September actions in fact followed an ignominious tradition of a schizophrenic 'hyperpower' that seems to be endlessly in search of enemies. Uncle Sam has historically exhibited a crusading zeal in pursuing historical causes that he deems vital to his national security. During the Second World War, the United States fought the twin evils of Nazism and Fascism; during the Cold War, it battled the 'evil' communist empire; and in the post-Cold-War era, Pax Americana's new ideological crusade appears to be the war it has declared against terrorism and an 'axis of evil'. In this new age, communist infidels appear to have been replaced by mad mullahs and 'rogue regimes' as America's new ideological bogeymen.

Drawing on a sanctimonious, muscular, born-again Christianity, Bush's arrogant and deeply insulting insistence – in the days following 11 September – that the whole world decide whether it was with America or with the terrorists came right out of an atavistic Old Testament world where doctrines such as 'an eye for an eye' reigned supreme. In this absolutist 'new world order' there was no more room for nuance or subtlety. One could not at the same time condemn terrorism and caution America not to kill innocent civilians in Afghanistan and Iraq in a vainglorious attempt to 'impose' democracy around the world through the barrel of a gun. Bush's frequent depiction of America as 'liberators' was also repugnant in its hypocrisy and historical inaccuracy – at least as viewed by Africans, Asians, Caribbeans, Latin Americans and Middle Easterners who have suffered and continue, in some cases, to suffer from the brutality of American-backed tyrants.

Prominent Africans added their voices to the widespread criticisms of American unilateralism under the Bush administration. Former South African president, Nelson Mandela, launched a scathing attack before the United States invasion of Iraq in 2003: 'What I am condemning is that one power, with a president who has no foresight, who cannot think properly, is now willing to plunge the world into a holocaust. Why does the United States behave so arrogantly? . . . Who are they now to pretend that they are the policeman of the world?'[20]

Nigerian Nobel laureate, Wole Soyinka, also noted in March 2003: 'The present occupant of the White House in the United States of America is one of the most dangerous fanatics ever to bestride the destiny of the world.'[21] African leaders were almost unanimous in expressing opposition to an American military invasion of Iraq. Nigeria's president at the time, Olusegun Obasanjo, Senegal's Abdoulaye Wade and South Africa's Thabo Mbeki, signed a letter to President Bush in March 2003, opposing any action on Iraq without UN authorisation. (Though Wade, in typically erratic fashion, later distanced himself from this joint letter!)[22] The United States suspended military assistance to Nigeria shortly after the publication of the letter in the Nigerian press. Though American officials claimed that the suspension was due to earlier massacres of civilians by the Nigerian army, the timing of the United States action was widely viewed with suspicion. Algeria, Morocco, Burkina Faso and Kenya also publicly opposed the war. There were anti-war demonstrations from the Cape to Cairo. Ethiopia and Eritrea, with autocratic regimes that have clamped down harshly on internal dissent, were among the handful of African countries that publicly identified themselves as belonging to Washington's 'Coalition of the Willing'.[23]

The profound concerns in Africa about Bush's 'War on Terrorism' is that new justifications will be found – as occurred under the Clinton administration – to back autocratic allies who support the United States in its declared hunt for terrorists, rather than supporting democratic allies and principles. The establishment, in 2002, of a United States military base and a Joint Task Force Horn of Africa Command in Djibouti, with about 1 500 soldiers, with the goal of tracking terrorists in the region, may yet come to mirror Washington's support of autocratic governments in Kenya, Somalia and Sudan during the Cold War. The support of these three countries was justified at the time by the need to protect strategic sealanes used for transporting oil from the Middle East. In 2003, a US$100 million United States-East Africa Counter-terrorism Initiative (EACTI) was launched to provide training and equipment to states in the region, particularly Kenya and Ethiopia. In the same year, Djiboutian leader, Ismael Omar Guelleh, was invited on a state visit to the White House, where Bush promised to reopen the United States Agency for International Development (USAID) office in Djibouti, and pledged US$8 million in American education grants.[24] The United States also strengthened security ties with Eritrea, while Washington continued to maintain strong ties with Ethiopia, with the aim of benefiting from the intelligence network of the pre-eminent military power on the Horn of Africa. Bush's meeting in the White House with the leaders of Ethiopia and Kenya in December 2002 further reinforced Washington's emerging anti-terrorism alliance in East Africa.

Another American counter-terrorist Pan-Sahel Initiative (PSI) worked with autocratic regimes in Mauritania and Chad. The United States European Command further collaborated with Senegal, Gabon, Mali, Ghana, Uganda, Namibia and South Africa to upgrade ports and airfields and signed access agreements allowing the United States to deploy rapidly to counter terrorists in Africa. In 2005, a US$500 million five-year Trans-Sahara Counter-Terrorism Initiative (TSCTI) was launched to build the capacities of African states such as Algeria, Chad, Ghana, Mali, Morocco, Niger, Nigeria, Mauritania and Tunisia to patrol borders and intercept terrorist groups.[25]

American fears of Africa becoming a sanctuary for terrorists had been heightened by terrorist attacks on an Israeli airliner and Israeli tourists in a hotel in Mombasa, Kenya in November 2002. Reports also noted that American Central Intelligence Agency (CIA) agents were collaborating with Somali warlords in pursuit of terrorist suspects inside Somalia.[26] Some African regimes appeared to be taking advantage of these fears to crack down on domestic dissent. In a striking replay of Washington's response to the attacks of 11 September, Morocco, with its autocratic political system and draconian press laws,[27] rushed anti-terrorism legislation through its rubber-stamp Parliament, allowing capital punishment against terror suspects. This followed the deadly suicide attacks in Casablanca in May 2003.[28] Such attacks have continued. The CIA has also reportedly used Moroccan territory to question suspected terrorists, conducting interrogations that have often disregarded due process.[29] Other countries, such as Tanzania, have drawn up anti-terrorism legislation that civil libertarians have criticised as giving the government too much power to clamp down on genuine domestic dissent.

These concerns were further confirmed by autocratic Liberian leader Charles Taylor's decision to castigate his domestic opponents as 'terrorists' and his holding of dissidents as 'unlawful combatants'. (Taylor was arrested from a three-year Nigerian exile in 2006 and was put on trial for war crimes following United States pressure for his arrest, after the former warlord-president was implicated in unsubstantiated reports by *Washington Post* journalist, Douglas Farah, of Sierra Leonean rebels selling US$30 to 50 million worth of diamonds to al-Qaida the month before the 11 September attacks on America.) Eritrea's government has accused its exiled Alliance of Eritrean National Forces (AENF) opponents of having links to al-Qaida, while the government in Ethiopia has branded its opponents in Oromo areas as being involved in 'international terrorism'. Mauritania's autocratic leader, Ould Mohamed Taya, who was deposed in July 2005, had also branded his opposition as 'Islamic extremists'.

During the presidential campaign in 2000, Bush had reiterated his lack of interest in Africa and subsequently spoke about Africa as if it was a country, rather than a continent. As he noted in June 2001: 'Africa is a nation that suffers from incredible disease.'[30] That his administration includes as Vice-President, Dick Cheney, who, as a congressman in 1986, voted against Nelson Mandela's release from prison, branding the African National Congress (ANC) a 'terrorist' organisation is also a good indication of the US attitude towards Africa. To further underline the point, it is also worth noting that Walter Kansteinner III, the first US Assistant Secretary of State for African Affairs under the George W. Bush administration, had opposed sanctions against apartheid South Africa in the 1980s, and as late as 1990, considered Mandela's ANC to be unrepresentative of the aspirations of the majority of South Africans.

Even more disappointing was the fact that African-American Secretary of State, Colin Powell, failed to attend, as scheduled, the UN's World Conference against Racism in Durban, South Africa, in September 2001. Concerns about criticisms of Israel's harsh occupation of Palestine apparently led to Powell's last-minute withdrawal from the conference. This was the clearest sign, if any were needed, of how powerful the Jewish-American lobby is in stark contrast to the powerlessness of the African-American lobby. In a global conference to discuss slavery, reparations, and racism – the issues closest to the hearts of many African-Americans – Uncle Sam could not muster the political will to send a representative to a conference in Africa. Powell's support for Washington's misguided policy of 'constructive engagement' with apartheid South Africa[31] – crafted by Chester Crocker, the prejudiced and patronising Assistant Secretary of State for African Affairs under President Ronald Reagan in the 1980s – was a further blot on his record. The former General endangered his historical legacy by presenting flimsy and unconvincing evidence to the UN Security Council in February 2003, asserting the existence of weapons of mass destruction (WMD) and links between Iraq and al-Qaida. Powell subsequently told confidants that he did not entirely believe the case he was arguing at the UN.[32]

In June 2001, Andrew Natsios, head of USAID until January 2006, argued that AIDS drugs would be useless in Africa since Africans 'don't know what Western time is. You have to take these (AIDS) drugs a certain number of hours each day, or they don't work. Many people in Africa have never seen a clock or a watch their entire lives. And if you say, one o'clock in the afternoon, they do not know what you are talking about. They know morning, they know noon, they know evening, they know the darkness at night.'[33] This statement perfectly demonstrates the stereotypical prejudices that still pervade the highest levels of policy-making in America.

By 2006, the US Congress had cut funds for Bush's Millennium Challenge Account (MCA), launched in 2002, to assist African states. The rhetorical commitment of the administration to democratic governance was not matched by funds to promote the principle in Africa. The programme was slow to disburse funds (only US$1.75 billion by 2006 instead of the US$5billion target); and only Madagascar, Cape Verde and Benin had signed a 'compact' to receive assistance.[34] Like AGOA, the MCA laid down strict, but nebulous criteria for African governments to receive funding, such as 'encouraging economic freedom', 'investing in people' and 'ruling justly'. These conditions were less than transparent, as regimes such as Burkina Faso and The Gambia qualified for funding. Though Washington provided Africa with US$4 billion of 'aid' in 2005, as much as US$1.2 billion of this figure (25 per cent) was emergency food aid, mostly bought from US producers, shipped by American vessels, and distributed by US non-governmental organsiations (NGOs). Only US$517 million of these funds went directly to development assistance.[35]

The one area, however, that the Bush administration can be given some credit for is its substantive contributions to the global battle against AIDS, announced in January 2003.[36] The President's Emergency Plan for Aids Relief (PEPFAR) involves a five-year commitment of US$9 billion between 2004 and 2008 to fifteen of the most heavily affected countries, including twelve in Africa: Botswana, Côte d'Ivoire, Ethiopia, Kenya, Mozambique, Namibia, Nigeria, Rwanda, South Africa, Tanzania, Uganda and Zambia. However, questions have been raised as to why heavily affected countries such as Malawi and Lesotho were not included in the programme.[37] However, the Bush administration does deserve credit for providing resources in this vital area, far exceeding the spending of the Clinton administration, which talked a good game, but delivered little to Africa.

Profound concerns have further been expressed by many Africans that the current obsession of the Bush administration with the 'War on Terrorism' will divert American assistance to the continent from economic development and democratisation to terrorism-related security issues. Many African analysts have called on Washington to address the root causes of terrorism – such as poverty, injustice and social inequalities – rather than simply launching military strikes against an elusive enemy.[38] Anti-terrorism, like anti-communism during the Cold War, should not become the new condition for receiving future American assistance, with Uncle Sam rewarding states that are seen to be fighting terrorism and punishing those whose efforts are perceived to be lacklustre. The 1 000-strong Ugandan contingent deployed in Somalia under an AU flag in 2007, alongside Ethiopian troops that are propping up a weak interim government, represented, to many in Africa, a misguided mission that is utterly unable to stem the reckless bloodbath in Mogadishu, and is more of an auxiliary of Pax Americana's erratic 'War on Terrorism' than a mission to promote sustainable peace on the Horn of Africa. As Ali Mazrui has noted: 'I am saddened by it, as an admirer of the Ethiopian people, that they allowed themselves to be more or less bought by the Americans, to be their mercenaries in Somalia.'[39]

Equally disturbing to many Africans is the United States' decision in February 2007 to establish a new (United States) Africa Command (AFRICOM) on the continent by September 2008. This plan, championed strongly by Donald Rumsfeld – the disgraced former US defence secretary and architect of the Iraq debacle – is ostensibly meant to strengthen United States military cooperation with Africa. The details are still vague, but it seems that the Pentagon wants to consolidate three commands covering Africa into one in order to be able to intervene more effectively on the continent to fight terrorism, stem conflicts and provide humanitarian assistance. This approach could further increase America's prioritising of militaristic anti-terrorist approaches to engaging Africa. Although Africans are being assured by American planners that AFRICOM will not mean that Washington will establish a large military footprint on the continent and could deploy troops from bases elsewhere, Africa would be wise to be wary of such a close embrace with Uncle Sam and the dangers that such intimacy could bring for its own long-term security. Ethiopia has been touted as the location of AFRICOM, and it would be ironic if the seat of African diplomacy were to be overshadowed by a self-appointed American policeman offering to patrol the continent in search of enemies.[40]

FRANCE AND AFRICA: *FOLIE DE GRANDEUR*[41]

For nearly four decades, France's relations with its former African colonies have smacked of a paternalistic neo-colonialism.[42] Brazzaville had been the seat of General Charles de Gaulle's government-in-exile during the Second World War, and military victories in Africa had helped restore some French honour. As former French President, François Mitterrand, remarked in 1957: 'Without Africa, France will no longer have a history in the twenty-first century.'[43] An intricate network of political, military, economic and cultural ties have been used to promote what French leaders since De Gaulle have regarded as a *politique de grandeur*. France has attempted to use Africa to raise its status from a middle-ranking to a great power. With the end of the Cold War, the idea of an exclusive French sphere of influence in Africa has been increasingly challenged, leading to policy reversals in Rwanda and Zaire (now the DRC) that left France's Africa policy in disarray.

France's policy in sub-Saharan Africa has historically been one of *folie de grandeur*: a chronic delusion of greatness. Humiliated by Hitler's blitzkrieg, Dien Bien Phu and Algeria, post-war France was a nation in deep psychological trauma. The Suez debacle of 1956 was a further blow to the already fragile national psyche. Britain drew the lesson from Suez that the world had changed from the 'gunboat diplomacy' of the old world to the superpower diplomacy of the nuclear age. France, however, attempted to cling to the illusion of remaining a great power by creating its own sphere of influence in Africa.[44] France lost an empire, but found a new role as an African power. In the process, as Ali Mazrui put it: 'De Gaulle succeeded in creating the impression that France in imperial decline was, at the same time, France in international ascendancy. French-speaking Africans continued to follow with awe.'[45]

La gloire de notre père et l'enfant terrible

Charles de Gaulle created the 'imperial presidency' of the Fifth Republic and attempted to re-establish France's grandeur through its African colonies. This was a form of diplomacy that entailed an emphasis on style over substance, as De Gaulle withdrew from NATO's military command in 1966, established an independent nuclear *force de frappé*, and railed against American economic imperialism in Europe. In reality, the economic recovery and military security of France still depended largely on the United States.

France's quest for grandeur and glory demanded that in the 1950s, African leaders such as Léopold Senghor, Félix Houphouet-Boigny, Modibo Keita and Sékou Touré were carted off to the Assemblée Nationale in Paris where they served as *députés*. De Gaulle encouraged a paternalistic relationship, with some African leaders referring to him as 'Papa': they were his children, and as inexperienced infants they had to do as they were told. Under French rule, in countries such as Algeria – which was claimed as a French *département* despite the geographical absurdity of such a notion – Arabic was not allowed to be taught in schools, and students had to learn in French. France's relations with Africa were entrusted to one man in the Elysée Palace's shady Cellule Africaine (African Unit): Jacques Foccart. This *éminence grise* was a master of the *secret du roi*, establishing his infamous *réseaux africains*: clandestine networks of spooks and soldiers, murderers and mercenaries, and priests and policemen.

In a 1958 referendum, De Gaulle offered his African colonies a choice between a *Communauté française*, in which France would still retain control over their foreign and defence policy, or independence, in which France would sever all financial and economic ties. Only *l'enfant terrible,* Guinea's Sékou Touré, urged his people to vote '*oui*' to independence. Despite a 96 per cent vote in favour of independence, De Gaulle's riposte was that of a ruthless and vindictive father: all economic aid was stopped, Guinea was expelled from the franc zone, and telephones, archives and civil service files were all carted back to France. *Liberté, égalité* and *fraternité* were never principles to be applied to Africans. This was a clear lesson to other *enfants terribles*: there were enormous costs in disobeying *Père* de Gaulle. Though all francophone African countries were eventually granted nominal independence by 1963, all signed neo-colonial cooperation agreements: economic and military pacts that gave France continued influence over their sovereign affairs.

Gendarme de l'Afrique

There are three pillars to French policy in Africa: military, financial and politico-cultural. By adroitly creating an intricate network of dependency around these areas, Paris was able to retain influence over its former African colonies. This was the patron-client system that came to be known as *Françafrique*.[46] The most sensitive areas of sovereignty (defence, foreign and monetary policies) were circumscribed by post-independence agreements with all of France's former possessions.[47] Paris also maintained military bases in Djibouti, the Central African Republic, Côte d'Ivoire, Gabon and Senegal.

Since 1960, the French gendarme has acted like a 'pyromaniac fireman', intervening more than 30 times in Cameroon, the Central African Republic, Chad, Congo-Brazzaville, Côte d'Ivoire, Djibouti, Gabon, Mauritania, Niger, Rwanda, Senegal, Togo and Zaire (DRC). As former Foreign Minister, Louis de Guiringaud, arrogantly put it: 'Africa is the only continent . . . where [France] can still with 300 men, change the course of history.'[48] In the most extraordinary incident, Paris flew David Dacko to the Central African Republic in 1979 to replace tyrannical leader, Jean-Bédél Bokassa. Bokassa had squandered a third of his country's national income on staging a Napoleonic coronation, crowning himself Emperor Bokassa I in 1977. His killing of school children and the revelation of a gift of diamonds to President Giscard d'Estaing finally proved too embarrassing for France. Giscard thus toppled a hunting companion he had once described as France's best friend in Africa. The French argument that its military agreements in Africa ensured political stability was clearly bogus: between 1963 and

1966 there were thirteen coup attempts in francophone Africa. French intervention often kept despotic dinosaurs such as Zaire's Mobutu Sese Seko, Togo's Gnassingbé Eyadéma and Gabon's Omar Bongo in power long after their sell-by dates.

La chasse gardée

The franc zone saw thirteen francophone African states tying their CFA (Communauté Française Africaine) franc to the French franc, with Paris effectively controlling the zone's central banks and the French treasury holding all their foreign reserves. *Pour faire le* CFA, 80 000 French expatriates flooded into Africa. French industrial giants such as CFAO, SCOA, Elf-Aquitaine and Bouyges continued to monopolise markets they had cornered in colonial days. France's cooperation agreements gave it priority access to Africa's strategic minerals: Gabon and Niger provided Paris with 100 per cent of its uranium, Guinea 90 per cent of its bauxite, and Cameroon, Congo-Brazzaville and Gabon 70 per cent of its oil.[49] In return, France channelled 80 per cent of its foreign aid to francophone Africa, although some of this was tied to compulsory purchases of French products at inflated prices.

For a while, the franc zone created a stable, convertible currency that helped economic growth and attracted investment. But devaluations in Ghana and Nigeria led to smuggling and uncompetitive industries in the franc zone. The overvalued CFA franc also resulted in capital flight and distressed banks. An important aspect of French policy was to keep Nigeria and other trespassers out of its *pré carré* (backyard) or *chasse gardée* (private hunting-ground). De Gaulle therefore sent arms to Biafran secessionists during Nigeria's civil war between 1967 and 1970, while President Georges Pompidou encouraged francophone states to create their own economic community to counter Nigeria's strength in ECOWAS, which was established in 1975 to promote economic integration.

La francophonie

Presidents Georges Pompidou, Valéry Giscard d'Estaing, François Mitterand and Jacques Chirac all continued De Gaulle's activist Africa policy. France created a Ministry of Cooperation in 1961 to conduct its Africa policy. The Quai d'Orsay (foreign ministry) was simply bypassed, allowing the Elysée to continue its peculiar form of personalised diplomacy with African autocrats. Pompidou extended French influence to the former Belgian colonies of Burundi, Rwanda and Zaire, and established a biannual Franco-African summit in 1973. Mitterand created a wider *francophonie* involving Canada, Vietnam and the Levant in 1986 and set up a Ministère de la *francophonie.* In 1996, France spent over US$1 billion on promoting its language and culture abroad. Since 1969, Paris has sponsored a film festival in Burkina Faso, which has contributed positively to the development of African cinema.

At international fora such as the UN and the Organisation of African Unity (OAU), 22 francophone African states often supported France, even on issues such as decolonisation, French arms sales to apartheid South Africa and French nuclear testing in the Algerian Sahara. In Gabon, the French ambassador frequently attended cabinet meetings, while Gabonese officials submitted annual reports of imports from non-francophone countries for French approval.[50] French officers continued to serve in the Senegalese army and Côte d'Ivoire's civil service until the 1970s. French *coopérants* provided technical assistance to African ministries, sometimes overruling ministers and acting as powers behind the throne. *La francophonie*, though, is a somewhat hollow concept in Africa. Despite the aping of French culture by a few culturally assimilated elites, over 70 per cent of so-called francophone Africans do not, in fact, speak French. The often quoted statistic that the DRC is the world's second largest francophone country is a misguided illusion: most Congolese are illiterate farmers who are more concerned with basic survival than haute couture. France's preposterous *mission civilisatrice* was largely used to enslave the vast majority of its colonial subjects, while a tiny elite played at being black Frenchmen, carrying baguettes under their armpits in cities such as Abidjan, Ouagadougou and Libreville.

La fin d'une époque

By 1990, pro-democracy demonstrations in Benin, Côte d'Ivoire, Gabon and Niger had forced many francophone states to adopt various forms of multi-party democracy. At the Franco-African summit in the town of La Baule in 1990, Mitterand announced a policy shift that was subsequently dubbed Paristroika: it sought to link continued aid to democratic reforms. But the French applied democracy inconsistently, sanctioning sham elections in Burkina Faso, Chad, Côte d'Ivoire, Cameroon, Gabon, Niger and Togo between 1992 and 1996, and resuming aid to fraudulent, undemocratic regimes.

Having periodically rigged elections in its African possessions during colonial times, it has been easy for France to condone undemocratic behaviour in Africa. Former President Chirac described democracy as a 'luxury' for Africa, demonstrating a paternalism that is all too typical of the French political class, many of whose members – including Chirac himself – have themselves often been embroiled in sleaze and scandals. Countries such as Côte d'Ivoire and Gabon funded the political campaign of Gaullist parties, which returned the favour on assuming parliamentary power in 1993.

Mitterand's son, Jean-Christophe – nicknamed '*Papa-m'a-dit*' (Daddy told me) – ran Africa policy from the Elysée in a Foccartiste manner, establishing close personal relations with African autocrats. However, the deaths of Ivorian leader Félix Houphouet-Boigny in 1993 and Jacques Foccart in 1997 symbolised a definite *fin d'une époque* in Franco-African relations. Both figures were the most symbiotic of the personalised relationship between France and Africa: Houphouet was the unrivalled doyen and sage of francophone African diplomacy and the most respected interlocutor between France and Africa; Foccart was, for over two decades, the most influential French official in African affairs.

In the post-Cold-War era, modernisers eventually appeared within the French political establishment who favoured *l'ouverture*: a policy of ending the 'special relationship' with francophone Africa and focusing more on Eastern Europe and Asia. President Mitterand's Minister of Cooperation, Jean Pierre Cot, and his Defence Minister, Pierre Joxe, unsuccessfully pushed for such change. On entering the Hôtel Matignon in 1993, patrician Premier, Edouard Balladur, enunciated the famous 'Balladur Doctrine' – sometimes also referred to as the 'Abidjan Doctrine' – of with-holding future French assistance to African states until they had signed up to the strict dictates of the World Bank and the International Monetary Fund (IMF). Paris thus signalled an end to *la fin du mois*: payment of civil-service salaries in francophone Africa by the French Treasury. President Chirac's Premier, Alain Juppé, was also an advocate of change, but had to contend with traditionalists such as Chirac himself and the Cooperation Minister, Jacques Godfrain. The 50 per cent devaluation of the CFA franc in January 1994 dealt a devastating blow to the Franco-African relationship. In the words of Kaye Whiteman: 'There is a sense of something having been lost or broken, never to be repaired . . .'[51] For four decades, the CFA had been tied to the French franc at an exchange rate of 1:50. Not surprisingly, African leaders regarded the fait accompli as treacherous and, as some noted at the time, it was as if an umbilical cord had been broken. France's commitment to the *franc fort* and efforts to reduce its own budget deficit to qualify for the European Monetary Union (EMU) in 1999 were more pressing priorities. France thus shifted its African burden to Bretton Woods institutions it had earlier castigated as being neo-imperialist American creatures.

Events in Africa's Great Lakes region further revealed France's weakening grip on its former colonies. Having armed and given military support to the Hutu-dominated regime of Juvénal Habyrimana in Rwanda in its struggle against the Uganda-based, Tutsi-dominated Rwandan Patriotic Front (RPF), France's clients lost power to the RPF by June 1994.[52] The new Rwandan regime – seen as part of an 'Anglo-Saxon' plot due to its close ties to Uganda in what has been dubbed France's 'Fashoda syndrome'

– was excluded from the Franco-African summit in Biarritz in 1994. Paris also tried to prevent European Union (EU) funds going to Rwanda; its Opération Turquoise of July 1994 allowed Hutu génocidaires who had massacred 800 000 mainly Tutsi civilians to escape into eastern Zaire, and human right groups implicated France in continued military assistance (including providing training, supplying arms and engaging in diplomatic contacts) to its former genocidal Hutu allies.[53] Events in the DRC in 1997 would also see France wrong-footed in its support for a sinking Mobutu Sese Seko. (France now seeks increasingly to intervene in African countries such as the DRC and Chad under the multilateral cover of the EU). In May 1996, an angry mob burnt down the French cultural centre in the Central African Republic. In the same country in January 1997, a bloody French reprisal in revenge for the killing of two French officers left 100 civilians and 50 mutinous African soldiers dead.[54] This followed a pattern established in colonial times: in Madagascar in 1947, French soldiers had massacred an estimated 86 000 Madagascans after a raid by independence fighters on a French military base. Proving further that old habits die hard, in October 1997, Paris helped Denis Sassou-Nguesso use military means to topple the elected government of Pascal Lissouba in Congo-Brazzaville.[55]

France's problems in Africa were glaringly evident by now. Among the most influential critics of its Africa policy was Jean-François Bayart, a respected adviser to the French government, who noted in 1996: 'Drugged by easy money and substitutes for imperial ideology, France has not realised that its sub-Saharan diplomacy has ossified and is no longer responding to either the changes on the continent or the new demands of the international system.'[56] Bayart called for a *regroupement* in which Paris reviewed its relations with African countries, maintaining a strong presence in some parts of Africa and withdrawing from less strategic areas. He also counselled France to find political accommodation with Nigeria in order to enhance cooperation in West Africa and to leave regional leadership to local actors, while itself maintaining a lower profile.[57]

There were other interesting developments in Franco-African relations during this period. Under the socialist government of Lionel Jospin between 1997 and 2002, Foreign Minister Hubert Védrine and Cooperation Minister Charles Josselin were identified as reformers of French policy in Africa. The budget of Rue Monsieur (the Ministry of Cooperation) was slashed from 8.3 billion French francs in 1992 to 6.7 billion in 1997, and the ministry has since been absorbed into the Quai d'Orsay. Meanwhile, the French military presence in Africa was reduced from 8 000 to about 5 600, leading to the closure of two military bases in the Central African Republic in April 1998. But, as long as France retains its historical quest for grandeur, as long as

African despots continue to deliver votes in diplomatic fora and to fund French political campaigns, as long as French businesses continue to profit from cosy and sometimes corrupt African relationships, and as long as French national pride remains tied to an image of cultural superiority, France is unlikely to disengage totally from its African sphere of influence.

David contre Goliath?

The sterile debate in the late 1990s about a Franco-American rivalry in Africa was often an irrelevant red herring. It is clear that America still views Africa through a tainted Somali prism. Its botched 1993 intervention in the Horn of Africa ensured that Washington's policy was transformed into one that largely avoided politically risky entanglements in an area where it viewed its interests to be few. The United States' reluctance to intervene in Rwanda and Zaire in the 1990s was in stark contrast to French willingness to get involved in both countries. As earlier noted, Washington's policy was based on improving Africa's capacity to handle its own conflicts; protecting investments in strategic countries; and, after the 11 September attacks, waging a 'War on Terrorism', largely centred on the Horn of Africa.

The Franco-American duel had its roots in American actions, which were misconstrued by paranoid French policy-makers as trespassing in its *chasse gardée*, and which included:

- Washington's calls for democratic reform in francophone Africa;
- Assistant Secretary of State for African Affairs Herman Cohen's call for a devaluation of the CFA franc in 1992;
- American oil company Occidental Petroleum Corporation's entry into Congo-Brazzaville's oil market in 1993;
- the holding of Africa/African-American summits in the francophone capitals of Abidjan, Dakar and Libreville;
- the aggressive promotion of trade and investment in the *francophonie* by Clinton's late African-American Commerce Secretary Ron Brown; and
- Clinton's Secretary of State Warren Christopher's proposal for an African Crisis Response Force on a visit to Africa in October 1996, when he warned: 'The time is past when outside powers could consider whole groups of countries as their own private domain.'[58]

By 1998, French Foreign Minister, Hubert Védrine, had coined the famous *hyper-puissance* (hyperpower) phrase to describe the United States as 'incapable of implementing a viable Africa strategy . . . the giant Gulliver finding himself hamstrung by hundreds of ropes tied by six-inch Lilliputians'.[59]

Although France has the sixth largest economy in the world (after the United States, Japan, Germany, China and Britain), this is about the size of the economy of California, America's 'golden state'. Paris can in no way claim to be either an economic or a political superpower. It is struggling desperately to retain its seat at the top table of global diplomacy by grand posturing in Africa, the Middle East and the Gulf. France is, however, clearly not a great power.

Adieu, l'Afrique?

Domestic problems, such as high unemployment, racial tensions and increasing social malaise, as well as the diplomatic need to balance the strength of a newly reunified Germany, are increasingly forcing France to focus more attention closer to home. The country can no longer afford its extravagant Africa policy merely for the sake of a nebulous and elusive grandeur. A new generation of leaders is also emerging in francophone Africa with less sentimental attachment to the former metropole. Benin's Nicéphoré Soglo, Côte d'Ivoire's Alassane Ouattara, Rwanda's Paul Kagame and Senegalese Foreign Minister, Cheikh Tidiane Gadio, are American-trained political and military technocrats who are less enamoured with the myths of French grandeur. Francophone scholars such as V.Y. Mudimbe, Georges Nzongola-Ntalaja and Achille Mbembe are American-trained intellectuals who are well established in the *anglophonie*. Washington has also trained peacekeepers from francophone Benin, Mali and Senegal. Francophone states such as the DRC, Rwanda and Gabon have sought economic and political ties outside the French sphere of influence.[60]

As France's xenophobic and draconian immigration laws are brutally applied to African citizens, leaders such as Mali's former president and former chair of the AU Commission, Alpha Konaré, openly criticised the excesses of the 'mother country'. By 1990, nearly five million Muslims lived in France. During the 1991 Gulf War, French Muslims were openly suspected of being 'fifth columnists'. Populist politicians such as Interior Minister Charles Pasqua fanned the flames of populist xenophobia by suggestions in the late 1980s of stripping children born in France to immigrant parents of their citizenship. Muslim girls wearing foulards soon started being expelled from public schools. The infamous Debré law in 1997 was a throwback to the Nazi era: citizens were asked to report anyone harbouring foreigners to the authorities, as asylum rights were being effectively rescinded. Despite complaints that foreigners were stealing jobs from French citizens, in the late 1990s, while national unemployment stood at

12 per cent, it was 30 per cent among North African youths and 50 per cent among black Africans in France. The environment was ripe for Jean-Marie Le Pen, a fascist, right-wing populist and former parachutist to spread fear and xenophobia. In the event, Le Pen won 15 per cent of presidential votes in 1995, which he increased to 17 per cent seven years later, making it into a second-round run-off with President Chirac. That nearly one in five French voters were prepared to vote for an openly racist politician was itself a disturbing sign of the Gallic loss of a national moral compass.[61]

The changing relationship between France and Africa was further evidenced in Côte d'Ivoire, a country embroiled in civil war since 2002, in which 4 600 French troops are deployed alongside a UN peacekeeping force. In one of his typically arrogant moments during a visit to Senegal in February 2005, President Chirac complained that the peace process in Côte d'Ivoire was too slow because the South Africans did not understand 'the soul and psychology of West Africans'. Regional actors, not least South African President Thabo Mbeki, were taken aback by the arrogance and insensitivity of this statement, which underlined the continuing paternalism with which many French politicians still regard their former colonies. In November 2004, after government soldiers in search of rebels killed nine French soldiers in the northern city of Bouaké, French troops destroyed the entire Ivorian air force of nine planes, resulting in violent demonstrations against French interests and a mass evacuation of 10 000 mostly French citizens from Côte d'Ivoire. Jittery French troops killed about 50 government-backed demonstrators outside Abidjan's Hôtel Ivoire. The distrust between the former colonial master and many Ivorians – fanned by a government that feared that Paris was bent on its removal – soon reached new heights. Ivorian leader Laurent Gbagbo's supporters accused France of trying to 'recolonise' the country by using 'agents' such as Burkina Faso. While Gbagbo talked of leaving the French-dominated CFA franc currency zone, his hard-line Speaker of Parliament, Mamadou Coulibaly, called for a complete break with the former colonial power.[62]

The election of President Nicolas Sarkozy in 2007 saw the rise to power in France of a former right-wing interior minister, who had increased police harassment of immigrants. In 2005, Sarkozy had infamously dismissed alienated and marginalised rioting Maghrebi and black African youth in Paris's hopeless, impoverished *banlieues* as *racaille* (scum) who needed to be cleaned up with a water-hose. This was after French police had allegedly accidentally electrocuted two immigrant youths that they had been chasing. Sarkozy had also earlier supported the United States invasion of Iraq.[63] This acerbic, deeply prejudiced politician did not waste time in revealing his true colours on the global stage. During a speech in Dakar, Sarkozy noted: 'One cannot blame everything on colonisation – the corruption, the dictators, the genocide, that is not colonisation.' He went on to note that France might have made 'mistakes', but believed in its 'civilising mission . . . and did not exploit anybody'. The French president then echoed American official Andrew Natsios' earlier sentiment in noting: 'Africans have never really entered history. They have never really launched themselves into the future. In a world where nature controls everything, man has remained immobile in the middle of an unshakable order where everything is determined. There is no room either for human endeavour, nor for the idea of progress.'

This speech was widely condemned in West Africa, by AU Commission chair at the time, Alpha Konaré, and in some French intellectual circles. Mbeki, who had earlier been insulted by Chirac, sent Sarkozy a bizarre letter published in *Le Monde*, praising parts of the same speech and noting: 'What you have said in Dakar, Mr President, has indicated to me that we are fortunate to count you as a citizen of Africa, as a partner in the long struggle for a true African renaissance in the context of a European renaisasance . . .' Achille Mbembe's eloquent riposte perhaps best captures the surprise of many in Africa: 'That two years before he exits power, Mbeki would tie his impeccable pan-Africanist credentials to Sarkozy is but the latest paradox in the political journey of a man who has thrived on contradictions.'[64] A few days later, Sarkozy returned the favour to Mbeki by calling for the Group of Eight (G8) industrialised countries to be expanded to a G13 with South Africa as the only African country in this proposed new club! Sarkozy subsequently made a state visit to South Africa in March 2008.

Paris continued to back autocrats Didier Ratsiraka until 2002 and Gnassingbé Eyadéma until his death in 2005, again due partly to fears of their 'Anglo-Saxon'-influenced opponents: Marc Ravalomanana and Gilchrist Olympio. This paranoid attitude again underlined the continuing curse of the 'Fashoda syndrome'. France also provided military support to prop up the autocratic regimes of Chad's Idriss Deby and the Central African Republic's François Bozizé as late as 2006,[65] and saved Deby's regime from falling again in 2008. But these actions may well represent the last gasps of a dying gendarme. This century will surely see the end of five decades of an often sordid and pernicious relationship between France and Africa. Paris will most likely retain interests in wealthier countries such as Cameroon, Congo-Brazzaville and Gabon, and is already trading more profitably with South Africa, Nigeria and Algeria, and involving non-francophone countries in its diplomatic summits and military training programmes. When France does decide to bid a final farewell to Africa, all those with a genuine concern for the future of the continent will heave a huge sigh of relief. In the post-Cold-War era, French intervention has become a costly anachronism and a relic of a bygone age of neo-colonial delusion. A fitting epitaph on the tombstone of the extinct gendarme could read: '*C'est magnifique, mais ce n'est pas la grandeur*' (It's magnificent but it's not greatness).

CONCLUDING REFLECTIONS

This chapter has assessed comparatively the roles of China, the US and France in Africa. Unlike Paris and Washington, Beijing was a member of the global South and acted with the Group of 77 developing countries at the UN, often portraying itself – even now – as an anti-colonial power and a poor, developing country. China benefited from Third World support to gain its seat at the UN in 1971 and to deflect criticisms of its policies on the UN Human Rights Commission (now the Human Rights Council) and other bodies. In the current age, Beijing still employs the rhetoric of anti-colonialism and non-interference in its dealings with Africa, but the country is in fact becoming a more status quo power and less revisionist Third World ally wanting to overturn an unjust international system dominated by Western great powers. As China grows richer and becomes tied ever deeper into a web of Western investments, trade and global institutions, the country relies increasingly on the West to maintain its staggering growth rates. China – already one of five veto-wielding permanent members of the UN Security Council – was admitted into the World Trade Organisation (WTO) in 2001. For all the talk about Africa and China, the West still remains far more important politically and economically to China than Africa. Beijing also seeks the West's acceptance far more than it does Africa's. China's sensitivity to Western criticisms over human rights issues in Tibet before its hosting of the 2008 Olympics clearly demonstrated this fact. Beijing's larger interests are likely to continue to coincide more with the West's than Africa's, though Chinese economic rivalry is also likely to continue with the United States, France and other countries in the quest for Africa's resources. Like American firms, French companies have lost contracts to the Chinese in places such as Angola and Gabon (see Chapters 6 and 12). This will be a complex relationship of cooperation and competition.

China has started to play a more assertive role in the UN Security Council, as evidenced by its taking the lead on UN action in Sudan and Somalia in 2007, and its deployment of peacekeepers to six UN missions in Africa. The one advantage that Beijing has over its Western rivals is that most African leaders do not perceive it to be a neo-imperial power.[66] This is indicated by the strong admiration expressed by most of the 43 African leaders that made the trip to the FOCAC summit in Beijing in 2006. Many African leaders seem to view China – in contrast to countries such as the United States and France – as representing an opportunity to increase their leverage towards the West. The fact that Beijing is prepared to invest in the much-needed infrastructure that Africa badly needs for its industrial take-off, and that China's purchase of Africa's raw materials has helped to increase global prices, has been widely seen as positive on the continent.

But it should also be noted that many African countries are still politically, economically and culturally tied more closely to the West than with China. Anglo-Saxon and French culture are far more pervasive in Africa than Chinese influence, though Bruce Lee's and other Kung Fu movies have been a staple diet on the continent for decades. Africans still travel much more to the West than to China, and most Africans seeking education abroad still prefer the West to China. American, French and British universities and military institutions are thus still more likely to educate future African leaders than Chinese ones. Washington and Paris also still have much larger, often long-standing military and trade ties on the continent than Beijing. One should, therefore, not exaggerate China's ability to dislodge Western interests from Africa in the short term. While China's trade with Africa was US$50.5 million in 2006, US trade with the continent was US$71.1 billion.[67] It must also be noted that, though Washington has been critical of China's role in Sudan and Angola, there are increasingly contacts and cooperation between American and Chinese officials on Africa – through a China-US dialogue – which appear to have been helpful in efforts to deploy a UN/AU peacekeeping force to Darfur in 2007.

The fear about US policy towards Africa remains that its 'anti-communist' support for autocratic regimes during the Cold War could be replaced by an 'anti-terrorist' support for similar regimes in the post-Cold-War era. As with China, African leaders must be strategic about seeking to support more positive aspects of US policy, such as the funding of HIV/AIDS programmes, while seeking to improve initiatives such as AGOA (trade) and ACOTA (military cooperation) through pro-Africa lobbies in the US Congress and American NGOs. Pressure must also be put on Washington to use its clout in institutions like the WTO, the World Bank and the IMF – where it plays a dominant role – to ensure fairer trade for Africa and an annulment of the continent's external debt. The United States must be urged to support democratisation, economic development and integration efforts in Africa more effectively.

France appears to be loosening its old neo-colonial ties with Africa, not only because the anachronistic system of *Françafrique* has been discredited by embarrassing policy failures in Rwanda and the DRC, but also because it has become financially difficult for Paris to maintain extensive military bases and financial support for its 22 former colonies on its own. France has thus sought increasingly to share this burden with its allies through three key means. First, Paris has engaged key countries like South Africa and Nigeria, which it would previously have lumped into an 'Afro-Saxon'[68] camp. Second, Paris has encouraged its former colonies to sign up to structural adjustment programmes with Bretton Woods institutions it had previously dismissed as instruments of Anglo-Saxon control. The third approach has been to multilateralise French initiatives by using the EU and the UN to lend cover to largely unilateral geo-strategic interventions in the DRC, Chad and Côte d'Ivoire. There remain elements of change and continuity in France's Africa policy. Nicolas Sarkozy's rise to power has, however, failed to convince Africans that the French leopard is capable of changing its spots.

It is not only China's post-Cold-War relations with Western powers in Africa that could trigger controversy. Beijing's ties with key African actors could also ruffle feathers. South Africa's President Thabo Mbeki warned in December 2006 that Africa risked entering into a 'colonial relationship' with China, if the continent continued to export raw materials to the country, while importing Chinese manufactured goods. But another danger is that both South Africa and China could come to be regarded as the new 'economic imperialists' in Africa. Tensions have been reported in the DRC where China provided a US$5 billion loan for infrastructure projects in 2007 in one of South Africa's most strategically important countries (see Chapter 5). In the same year, the Industrial and Commercial Bank of China (ICBC) announced the purchase of 20 per cent of the shares of South Africa's Standard Bank – which operates across Africa – at the cost of R36.7 billion (approximately US$252 billion). This represents the largest foreign direct investment in South Africa's history. Such trends could establish a future partnership between China and South Africa for the economic dominance of the continent. However, as with Western actors in Africa like the United States and France, both rivalry and cooperation are the more likely outcome of this growing relationship.

In conclusion, China, the United States and France are all involved in the epic game of great power rivalry for which Africa is again – as in the era of the Cold War – providing a backdrop and a grand stage (see Chapter 14). All three powers are pursuing economic, military and political strategies to augment their own interests, and it is important to underline that they broadly (perhaps with the exception of France) seem to know what they want from Africa and how to pursue it as part of an overall global strategy. African leaders, however, do not seem to know what they collectively want from these three powers, and how to use their new-found leverage with China's increasing presence on the continent in order to pursue their own goals to produce more mutually beneficial relationships. Africa must act strategically to define its own interests and negotiate more skilfully and firmly to ensure that these three powers continue to provide infrastructure projects in ways that promote regional integration; that the United States and France remove agricultural subsidies that hurt African farmers; that the three powers contribute to peacemaking efforts in Africa in less self-interested ways; that Africans, and not citizens of these countries, lead projects on the continent; that infant industries on the continent not be destroyed and that investments be made in ways that allow Africa to grow; and that regimes abusing human rights and rattling sabres not be provided with arms and political support. Only then will a potential 'axis of evil' be transformed into an 'axis of virtue'.

NOTES

1. See S. Morphet, 'Multilateralism and the Non-Aligned Movement: What is the Global South Doing and where is it Going?' Review essay, *Global Governance* 10, 2004: 517–37.
2. The author is indebted for the information in this paragraph to G. le Pere and G. Shelton, *China, Africa and South Africa: South–South Cooperation in a Global Era* (Johannesburg: Institute for Global Dialogue, 2007), pp. 41–63.
3. See the informative article by S. Naidu and M. Davies, 'China Fuels its Future with Africa's Riches', *South African Journal of International Affairs* 13(2), 2006: 69–83.
4. Quoted in Naidu and Davies, 'China Fuels its Future', 69.
5. N. Okonjo-Iweala, 'Viewpoint: China Becomes Africa's Suitor', BBC News, 24 October 2006. http://www.news.bbc.co.uk/1/hi/business/607938.stm.
6. See I. Taylor, 'The "All-Weather" Friend? Sino-African Interaction in the Twenty-First Century', in I. Taylor and P. Williams (eds.), *Africa in International Politics: External Involvement on the Continent* (London and New York: Routledge, 2004), pp. 83–101. See also G. le Pere, *China through the Third Eye: South African Perspectives* (Johannesburg: Institute for Global Dialogue, 2004).
7. See C. Alden, *China in Africa* (London and Cape Town: Zed and David Philip, 2007); G. le Pere (ed.), *China in Africa: Mercantilist Predator or Partner in Development?* (Johannesburg: Institute for Global Dialogue and SAIIA, 2006); G. Mills and A. Trejos, 'China and Africa – Can it be Win-Win?', *Business Day*, 22 February 2007; D. Thompson, 'China's Emerging Interests in Africa: Opportunities and Challenges for Africa and the United States', *African Renaissance* 2(4), 2005: 20–29; A. Versi, 'China and Africa: A Meeting of Minds – and Needs', *African Business* 322, 2006: 16–21; N. Ford, 'Economic War for Africa's Loyalties Begins', *African Business* 322, 2006: 16–21.
8. Council on Foreign Relations, 'More Than Humanitarianism: A Strategic US Approach toward Africa', Independent Task Force Report 56, 2006: 49.
9. See R. Dowden, 'China's Healing Power', *Time* 170(6), 2007; J. Miles, 'China's Coming-out Party', *The Economist* 'The World in 2007', 2007: 46.

10. This section builds on A. Adebajo, 'Africa and America in an Age of Terror', in R. Kadende-Kaiser and P.J. Kaiser (eds.), *Phases of Conflict in Africa* (Toronto: De Sitter Publications, 2005), pp. 26–42.
11. See S. Booker, 'US Foreign Policy and National Interests in Africa', *South African Journal of International Affairs* 8(1), 2001: 1–14; M. Clough, *Free at Last? US Policy toward Africa and the End of the Cold War* (New York: Council on Foreign Relations Press, 1992); J. Herbst, *US Economic Policy toward Africa* (New York: Council on Foreign Relations Press, 1992); P. Schraeder, 'Removing the Shackles? US Foreign Policy toward Africa after the End of the Cold War', in E. Keller and D. Rothchild (eds.), *Africa in the New International Order: Rethinking State Sovereignty and Regional Security* (Boulder, CO and London: Lynne Rienner, 1996).
12. On Clinton's Africa policy, see J.E. Frazer, 'The United States', in M. Baregu and C. Landsberg (eds.), *From Cape to Congo: Southern Africa's Evolving Security Challenges* (Boulder, CO and London: Lynne Rienner, 2003), pp. 275–99; G.M. Khadiagala, 'The United States and Africa: Beyond the Clinton Administration', *SAIS Review* 21(1), 2001: 259–73; C. Landsberg, 'The United States and Africa: Malign Neglect', in D.M. Malone and Y.F. Khong (eds.), *Unilateralism and US Foreign Policy: International Perspectives* (Boulder, CO and London: Lynne Rienner, 2003); M. Ottaway, *Africa's New Leaders: Democracy or State Reconstruction?* (Washington, DC: Carnegie Endowment for International Peace, 1999); J. Stremlau, 'Ending Africa's Wars', *Foreign Affairs*, July 2000: 117–32.
13. See A. Adebajo, 'Selling out the Sahara: The Tragic Tale of the UN Referendum', occasional paper series, Cornell University Institute for African Development, Spring 2002; W. Durch, 'The United Nations Mission for the Referendum in Western Sahara', in W. Durch (ed.), *The Evolution of UN Peacekeeping: Case Studies and Comparative Analysis* (New York: St Martin's Press, 1993), pp. 406–34; F. Ziai, 'Keeping it Secret: The United Nations Operation in Western Sahara', *Human Rights Watch Middle East* 7(7), 1995.
14. See H. Adam, 'Somalia: A Terrible Beauty Being Born?', in I.W. Zartman (ed.), *Collapsed States: The Disintegration and Restoration of Legitimate Authority* (Boulder, CO and London: Lynne Rienner, 1995) pp. 69–78; B. Boutros-Ghali, *Unvanquished: A US-UN Saga* (London: I.B. Tauris, 1999); W. Clarke and J. Herbst (eds.), *Learning from Somalia: The Lessons of Armed Humanitarian Intervention* (Boulder, CO and Oxford: Westview Press, 1997); J.L. Hirsch and R.B. Oakley, *Somalia and Operation Restore Hope: Reflections on Peacemaking and Peacekeeping* (Washington, DC: United States Institute of Peace, 1995); T. Lyons and A.I. Samatar, *Somalia: State Collapse, Multilateral Intervention, and Strategies for Political Reconstruction* (Washington, DC: The Brookings Institution, 1995); M. Sahnoun, *Somalia: The Missed Opportunities* (Washington, DC: United States Institute of Peace, 1994).
15. See R. Dallaire, *Shake Hands with the Devil: The Failure of Humanity in Rwanda* (London: Arrow Books, 2004).
16. See H.G. Campbell, 'The US Security Doctrine and the Africa Crisis Response Initiative', Africa Institute of South Africa, occasional paper 62, December 2000; J. Frazer, 'The Africa Crisis Response Initiative: Self-Interested Humanitarianism', *Brown Journal of World Affairs* 4(2), 1997: 103–18; E. Hutchful, 'Peacekeeping under Conditions of Resource Stringency', in J. Cilliers and G. Mills (eds.), *From Peacekeeping to Complex Emergencies: Peace Support Missions in Africa* (Johannesburg and Pretoria: SAIIA and the Institute for Security Studies, 1999), pp. 113–17; P. Omach, 'The African Crisis Response Initiative: Domestic Politics and Convergence of National Interests', *African Affairs* 99(394), 2000: 73–95.
17. A. Versi, 'At Last, a Win-Win Formula for African Business', *African Business* 285, 2003: 12–15.
18. See, for example, R. Robinson, *The Debt: What America Owes to Blacks* (New York and London: Plume, 2000), pp. 182–87.

19. R.W. Copson, *The United States in Africa* (London and Cape Town: Zed and David Philip, 2007), pp. 34–36.
20. Quoted in *The New York Times*, 1 February 2003, p. A11.
21. Quoted in *The Guardian* (Lagos), 23 March 2003, p. 58.
22. 'Nigeria to US: Don't Intimidate us on Iraq', *The Guardian* (Lagos), 22 March 2003, pp. 1–2.
23. 'African Leaders Condemn War', *The Guardian* (Lagos), 22 March 2003, pp. 1–2.
24. Economist Intelligence Unit, 'Country Report, Djibouti', March 2003, p. 41.
25. See Council on Foreign Relations, 'More Than Humanitarianism'.
26. D. Butler, '5-Year Hunt Fails to Net Qaeda Suspect in Africa', *The New York Times*, 14 June 2003, pp. A1 and A6.
27. See Economist Intelligence Unit, 'Country Report, Morocco', February 2003, p. 15.
28. See A. Jamai, 'Morocco's Choice: Openness or Terror', *The New York Times*, 31 May 2003, p. A25.
29. E. Sciolino, 'At a Traumatic Moment, Morocco's King is Mute', *The New York Times*, 27 May 2003, p. A3.
30. Quoted in F. Bruni, 'Deep US-Europe Split Casts Long Shadow on Bush Tour', *The New York Times*, 15 June 2001, p. A6.
31. E. Cose, 'The American Dream in Living Color', *Newsweek* CXXXVII(10), 5 March 2001, p. 15.
32. B. Keller, 'The Boys Who Cried Wolfowitz', *The New York Times*, 14 June 2003, p. A15.
33. Quoted in B. Herbert, 'Refusing to Save Africans', *The New York Times*, 11 June 2001, p. A17.
34. Copson, *The United States in Africa*, p. 28.
35. See Copson, *The United States in Africa*, pp. 17–41.
36. See Council on Foreign Relations, 'More Than Humanitarianism'.
37. Copson, *The United States in Africa*, pp. 42–65.
38. See, for example, M. Baregu, 'Terrorism and Counter-Terrorism: Dialogue or Confrontation?', in A. Adebajo and H. Scanlon (eds.), *A Dialogue of the Deaf: Essays on Africa and the United Nations* (Johannesburg: Jacana, 2006), pp. 261–74.
39. A. Mazrui, 'A Danger of Mushrooming Religious Enthusiasms', interview by Patrick Smith, *The Africa Report* 6, 2007: 44.
40. See M. Ruiters, 'AFRICOM Bodes Ill for Africa', *Global Dialogue* 12(1), 2007: 4–5 and 38; T. Whelan, 'Why AFRICOM?' *Global Dialogue* 12(2), 2007: 31–36.
41. This section builds on A. Adebajo, '*Folie de Grandeur*', *The World Today* 53(6), 1997: 147–50.
42. See J. Chipman, *French Power in Africa* (Oxford: Basil Blackwell, 1989); P. Gifford and W.R. Lewis (eds.), *The Transfer of Power in Africa: Decolonization 1940–1960* (New Haven: Yale University Press, 1982).
43. Quoted in C.M. Andrew, 'France: Adjustment to Change', in H. Bull (ed.), *The Expansion of International Society* (Oxford: Clarendon Press, 1984), p. 337.
44. For a review of France's Africa policy, see Chipman, *French Power in Africa*.
45. A. Mazrui, *Africa's International Relations* (Boulder, CO: Westview Press, 1977), p. 55.
46. See J.-F. Médard, 'Crisis, Change and Continuity: Nigeria/France Relations', in A. Adebajo and R. Mustapha (eds.), *Gulliver's Troubles: Nigeria's Foreign Policy after the Cold War* (Pietermaritzburg: University of KwaZulu-Natal Press, 2008).
47. See, for example, G. Martin, 'Continuity and Change in Franco-African Relations', *Journal of Modern African Studies*, March 1995.
48. Quoted in Chipman, *French Power in Africa*, p. 134.
49. Martin, 'Continuity and Change in Franco-African Relations': 9–10.

50. See D. Yates, *The Rentier State in Africa: Oil-Rent Dependency and Neo-Colonialism in the Republic of Gabon* (Trenton and Asmara: Africa World Press, 1996).
51. K. Whiteman, 'The Party's Over', *Africa Report*, March/April 1994: 14.
52. For two recent detailed studies on French complicity in Rwanda's genocide, see D. Kroslak, *The Role of France in the Rwandan Genocide* (London: Hurst and Company, 2007); A. Wallis, *Silent Accomplice: The Untold Story of France's Role in Rwandan Genocide* (London and New York: I.B. Tauris, 2006).
53. See H.K. Anyidoho, *Guns over Kigali* (Accra: Woeli Publishing Services, 1999); T. Laegreid, 'UN Peacekeeping in Rwanda', in H. Adelman and A. Suhrke (eds.), *The Path of a Genocide: The Rwanda Crisis from Uganda to Zaire* (New Brunswick and London: Transaction Publishers, 1999), pp. 231–51; L. Melvern, *A People Betrayed: The Role of the West in Rwanda's Genocide* (London: Zed Books, 2000); G. Prunier, *The Rwandan Crisis: History of a Genocide* (New York: Columbia University Press, 1995); A. Suhrke, 'UN Peacekeeping in Rwanda', in G. Sorbo and P. Vale (eds.), *Out of Conflict: From War to Peace in Africa* (Uppsala: Nordiska Afrikainstitutet, 1997), pp. 97–113.
54. See F. Soudain, '*La Cooperation dans le Sang*', *Jeune Afrique*, 8–14 January 1997: 7.
55. See G. Martin, 'France's African Policy in Transition: Disengagement and Redeployment', in C. Alden and G. Martin (eds.), *France and South Africa: Towards a New Engagement with Africa* (Pretoria: Protea Book House, 2003), p. 105.
56. J.-F. Bayart, 'Endgame South of the Sahara? France's African Policy', in C. Alden and J.-P. Daloz (eds.), *Paris, Pretoria and the African Continent* (New York: St Martin's Press, 1996), p. 27.
57. Alden and Daloz, *Paris, Pretoria and the African Continent*, pp. 33–40.
58. Quoted in *The Economist*, 19 October 1996, p. 56.
59. Quoted in P.J. Schraeder, 'Belgium, France, and the United States', in G.M. Khadiagala (ed.), *Security Dynamics in Africa's Great Lakes Region* (Boulder, CO and London: Lynne Rienner, 2006), p. 168; see also the excellent chapter by K. Whiteman and D. Yates, 'France, Britain and the United States', in A. Adebajo and I. Rashid (eds.), *West Africa's Security Challenges: Building Peace in a Troubled Region* (Boulder, CO and London: Lynne Rienner, 2004), pp. 349–79.
60. See A. Kirk-Greene and D. Bach (eds.), *State and Society in Francophone Africa since Independence* (London: Macmillan Press, 1995); R. Lavergne (ed.), *Regional Integration and Cooperation in West Africa* (Trenton and Asmara: Africa World Press, 1997); K. Whiteman, 'Confused Voices', *West Africa* 4 170, 1997: 1 643–644.
61. N. Atkin, *The Fifth French Republic* (Hampshire and New York: Palgrave Macmillan, 2005), pp. 163–72.
62. See A. Adebajo, 'Pretoria, Paris, and the Crisis in Côte d'Ivoire', *Global Dialogue* 11(2), 2006: 20–22, 36; A.R. Lamin, 'The Conflict in Côte d'Ivoire: South Africa's Diplomacy and Prospects for Peace'. Occasional Paper 49, Institute for Global Dialogue, Johannesburg, 2005; K. Whiteman, 'Côte d'Ivoire: The Three Deaths of Houphouet-Boigny', in African Centre for Development and Strategic Studies, *African Conflict, Peace and Governance Monitor* (Ibadan: Dokun Publishing House, 2005), pp. 43–59.
63. A. Parker, 'Sarkozy's Balancing Act', *The Weekender*, 28–29 April 2007, p. 7.
64. All quotes in this section are from A. Mbembe, '*Sacré Bleu!* Mbeki and Sarkozy?' *Mail and Guardian*, 24–30 August 2007, p. 24.
65. 'Central Africa: On the Brink', *Africa Confidential* 48(1), 12 January 2007: 6.
66. See, for example, 'The New Colonialists', *The Economist*, 15–21 March 2008, p. 13.
67. Alden, *China in Africa*, p. 104.
68. This expression is borrowed from A. Mazrui.

14

Western Hegemony, Asian Ascendancy and the New Scramble for Africa

Adam Habib

INTRODUCTION

A new scramble for Africa is underway. After decades of neglect, the continent and its riches are once again being sought by the outside world. This is most graphically demonstrated in the data on foreign investment to the continent. The United Nations Conference on Trade and Development's (UNCTAD) *World Investment Report 2006* indicates that foreign direct investment (FDI) in Africa increased from lows of US$2 to US$3 billion per annum in the early 1990s to US$31 billion in 2005. This represented a 78 per cent increase on 2004 figures and all indications are that the figures have risen for 2006 and 2007.[1]

These figures also demonstrate that all of the world's major economic actors have a presence on the continent. The Europeans still remain Africa's leading trading partners, with 32 per cent of Africa's exports (see Chapter 15). They are closely followed by the United States, which receives 29 per cent, while the Asians come in at a close third with 27 per cent.[2] But these figures do not give us the whole picture. Asia's trade with Africa has risen exponentially from the late 1990s, easily outstripping that of other regions. Its exports to Africa have risen by an annual 18 per cent. African imports have almost doubled from 14 per cent in 2000, and have tripled since 1990. But perhaps the most telling statistic for what the future holds is the fact that Europe received 50 per cent less of Africa's exports than it did in 2000.[3] As a result, Asia looks set to become the dominant economic presence in Africa in the years to come.

Is this Asian presence likely to change the pattern of Africa's relations with the outside world? This is, of course, not the first scramble for Africa's resources. The last two centuries have witnessed two scrambles on the continent. The first, managed by the Europeans, carved up the continent and led to the formal establishment of colonialism.[4] The second, which occurred immediately after decolonisation and the establishment of newly independent African states, occurred between the United States and the Soviet Union, and culminated largely in neo-colonial relations, proxy wars, political instability and economic decline.[5] As with earlier scrambles, the third involves both foreign states and their multinational corporations playing in the game. Unlike the earlier ones, however, the third scramble is distinguished by the involvement of two developing nations from the Asian continent: China and India. Is Asia's potential economic dominance, then, likely to repeat these exploitative and oppressive relations of the past, or is it to herald a new dawn?

In reflecting on this issue, this chapter analyses Asia's growing footprint in Africa by investigating China and India's growing economic and political presence on the continent. However, proceeding from the methodological recognition that countries' engagement and impact cannot simply be read from the noble intentions cited in their leaders' speeches and their policy pronouncements, but are also conditioned by the actions of their competitors, the chapter investigates the intentions, behaviour and impact of not only China and India, but also of the United States. All these countries, as well as those in Europe, are conditioned by what the others do, their successes and failures, and most importantly, their influence among political elites on the African continent.

The European Union (EU) has not been dealt with in this chapter, partly because it is the subject of Chapter 15. However, the author's contention is that the future national footprints with the most lasting legacy in Africa are likely to be those of the United States, China and India. This is borne out not only by the economic data demonstrating the declining influence of the EU, but also by the fact that even in the second African scramble, Europe was a junior political partner to the United States (see Chapter 13).[6] In the current context, Europe is becoming increasingly marginalised from significant political decision-making on Africa's future, in particular because of the United States' greater assertiveness in Africa prompted by its 'War on Terrorism' and its desire to reduce its dependence on Middle Eastern oil.

This chapter continues with an investigation into the growing political and economic footprint of the United States, China and India in Africa since the turn of the century. It then critically reflects on how different scholars have interpreted this development for the economic development of and democratic consolidation on the continent. Finally, the chapter considers what African countries themselves can do to ensure that the new scramble for the continent's riches is managed to the advantage of Africa's inhabitants.

IMPERIAL AND SOUTHERN RIVALRIES FOR AFRICA'S AFFECTION AND RESOURCES

The collapse of the Berlin Wall and the end of the Cold War prompted the evaporation of external interest in Africa. 'Benign neglect' perhaps best describes the outside world's relations with Africa in the 1990s. There were, of course, some exceptions. South Africa's democratic transition between 1990 and 1994 did inspire some interest, as did that of Nigeria after 1998. But the Rwandan genocide of 1994 perhaps best typifies the outside world's relations with the rest of the continent: in the midst of one of the world's worst episodes of genocide since the Second World War, the United States, Europe and the United Nations (UN) merely looked on, mouthing platitudes of concern every now and then.[7]

The lack of will is also apparent in the data reflecting the flows of FDI to the continent and its economic performance. Until at least the turn of the millennium, FDI flows remained below and within range of worker remittances to the continent.[8] As a result, economic performance was either negative or stagnant for much of the 1980s and 1990s. An economic turnaround emerged only after 2000. By 2006, the growth rate of the continent touched 5.7 per cent, up from 5.3 per cent and 5.2 per cent in 2005 and 2004 respectively.[9] This was a consequence of the rising price of primary commodities and the increased levels of investment that this and macro-economic stability prompted. Between 2000 and 2004, Africa's average investment rate of gross domestic product (GDP) was 20.7 per cent, while that of sub-Saharan Africa was 18.1 per cent, up from 9.6 per cent of GDP a decade earlier.[10]

The United States figured prominently in this renewed interest in the continent. Driven initially by the Clinton administration (1993–2000) and subsequently by that of George W. Bush (2001–08), the revival in Africa was inspired by a variety of concerns. The final years of the Clinton presidency witnessed an increased engagement with Africa, largely driven by the United States' increased appetite for oil and universal guilt at having abstained from doing anything about the Rwandan genocide. After 2001, the concerns shifted. Now, driven by its need to diversify its sources of energy away from the Middle East and constrained by the Chavez factor in Latin America,[11] the United States has begun to cast a longing eye at Africa's sources of oil. Moreover, concerned about Africa becoming a haven and a breeding ground for terrorists, it has recast the gaze of its 'War on Terrorism' on parts of the continent.[12]

This mix of concerns, then, has led to political and economic innovations in engagements with Africa. On the economic front, the African Growth and Opportunity Act (AGOA) was passed in May 2000, and subsequently extended in 2007; it gave African countries preferential duty-free treatment for certain articles if particular conditionalities were met, including among other things, market reforms of their economies, and compliance with United States national security and foreign policy goals.[13] In addition, United States investment in and trade with Africa began to pick up from 2000: in 2001, it was US$10.2 billion, less than 1 per cent of the US$1 381.7 billion direct investment of the country abroad;[14] trade between the United States and sub-Saharan Africa increased by 33.3 per cent in 2003 to US$32.1 billion, up from US$24.1 billion in 2002. This period witnessed a 39 per cent increase in African imports to the United States, from US$18.2 billion in 2002 to US$25.5 billion in 2003.[15]

But most of this investment was concentrated in the energy sector and in a small band of countries: Angola, Botswana, Gabon, Equatorial Guinea, Nigeria and South Africa figured prominently in this investment drive. The United States International Trade Commission data demonstrate that this pattern of investment and trade has not changed. Between 2004 and 2006, these were the only countries that registered significant increases in their exports to the United States. This prompted Stephen Hayes, president of the US Corporate Council on Africa, to complain that American interests, with the exception of energy, are lagging behind those of China, India and Europe.[16] But these patterns of trade and investment are likely to continue, given that the United States' dependence on African oil is projected to rise from its current 12 to 25 per cent by 2015.

There have also been significant political innovations prompted both by this increased United States investment and its 'War on Terrorism'. In 2002, the United States established a military base in Djibouti, East Africa, and it is considering the establishment of another in West Africa. In order to protect its interests and stabilise and contain the continent from the perspective of its 'War on Terrorism', the United States has identified four anchor states in sub-Saharan Africa with which to partner –Ethiopia, Kenya, Nigeria and South Africa – all of which are strategically placed on the continent and have relatively significant economic and/or military capacities in their own right.[17]

But perhaps the political innovation that has raised the most eyebrows is the decision to establish a new US military command, (United States) Africa Command (AFRICOM), to take direct responsibility for United States interests in Africa. Officially the purpose of a unified command and the abandonment of the division of Africa among many commands – European, Central and Pacific – is to coordinate security and humanitarian interventions (HIs) in order to 'prevent problems from becoming crises, and crises from becoming catastrophes'.[18] In order to facilitate this, the command is to be staffed with both civilian and military personnel and a senior diplomat is to be part of the chain of command and one of the two deputies reporting directly to the Commander of AFRICOM. But most African commentators and much of the continent's political elite are sceptical of these noble intentions, believing that it is part of a broader imperial agenda to develop a rapid response capacity for protecting the United States' interests on the continent.[19] Many fear that it will further militarise external engagements with Africa and re-establish the continent as a battlefield for foreign powers. After all, this would be consistent with the past behaviour of the United States, especially in the Cold-War era (see Chapter 13).

The United States, however, is not the only actor in the play. China has also begun to play the field in Africa. Again a mix of motives is at play. New sources of energy are obviously a major motivating factor. Fifty per cent of China's oil requirements will be imported in the near future, and 25 per cent would be sourced in Africa.[20] The country also requires other raw materials – timber, copper, non-ferrous materials and iron ore – if its robust economic performance is to be maintained. The Chinese also view Africa as an ideal market for their low-cost manufactured products.

But there are also political motives. Much is made of the historical linkages between Africa and China that go back to the fourteenth century, and the compatibility of their colonial experiences and the solidarity that this generates (see Chapter 2). Liu Guijin, currently China's special envoy on African Affairs and former ambassador to South Africa, was quick to remind critics that '. . . when Zheng He, the great Chinese navigator led his fleets to the east coast of Africa in the 15th century, China was by far the biggest world power at that time, enjoying the largest population and one-third of the world's GDP. But China didn't colonise an inch of African land or trade a single African slave as did the European colonists 100 years later.'[21] Another Chinese official is quick to retort to Western critics:

> With every major Western power now enjoying strong economic ties with China, I do not think that all of them are happy about every policy of China. And, while making loud noises about some policies of China, none of them is pursuing a policy of disengaging China or stopping doing business with China. Not accidently, those who singled China out for blame actually did not enjoy a glorious history in Africa. It is not difficult to see that there might be a double standard here.[22]

There is, of course, some truth in this. But care must be taken not to overplay this solidarity card. China correctly recognises that a unipolar world dominated by the United States is not in its own long-term interests. It has thus partnered African countries and others to contain the United States and facilitate the development of a multilateral system, both of which are compatible with the continent's long-term development and political interests. Coincidence of interests, rather than solidarity, is the crucial political impetus for the alliance between African nations and China.

The institutional manifestation this has taken is the Forum on China-Africa Cooperation (FOCAC). Formally established in 2000, FOCAC represents a mechanism that brings together Chinese and African political elites for consultations on ways to strengthen China-Africa trade and investment links and to develop common positions on the transformation of the global political and economic order. In addition, China makes much of what it perceives to be its principled approach to constructing international alliances. Unlike the United States and other Western countries, China recognises the sovereignty of its partners and does not demand conditions for aid, engagement, investment and trade. This mix of institutional and political innovations represents an alternative approach to international and transnational engagement that has, to date, prevailed with Africa and the developing world.

This alternative approach has enabled China to make significant political and economic inroads into the continent. It has formal political relations with 49 of the 54 African countries and close partnerships with almost all of the important ones. Moreover, FOCAC has facilitated a significant increase in two-way trade. China currently has some 800 businesses in 49 African countries, and the amount of total trade reached US$73.6 billion in 2007, up from US$56 billion in 2006, and US$40 billion and US$29 billion in 2005 and 2004 respectively.[23] These figures are astounding when one considers that they represent more than a quadrupling of total trade in the seven years since the turn of the millennium.

China's competitor from the developing world is, of course, India. India's motivation in the African scramble is perhaps best described by Navdeep Suri, India's consul-general in Johannesburg:

> Africa emerges as an important market for our goods and services, a vital element in our quest for energy security, a significant source of minerals and other natural resources for our burgeoning economy and a potentially attractive destination for our farmers . . . It is in India's enlightened self-interest to become a strong and reliable partner in Africa's quest for economic development . . .

> In doing so, we do bear in mind that from the political perspective, Africa, with its 54 seats in the United Nations General Assembly and three in the (unreformed) Security Council, will always matter – whether in terms of our aspirations for a permanent seat on UNSC [UN Security Council] or the more recent candidature of Mr Shashi Tharoor for Secretary General of the United Nations.[24]

Given that it has entered 'the Great Game' late, and as a result has much ground to cover, India has decided to interact with the continent in its areas of need and strength. Need, of course, speaks to energy, and India's dependence on oil imports is expected to grow by 91.6 per cent by 2020. The country spent US$38.8 billion on importing crude oil in 2005–06, up from US$25.9 billion a year earlier.[25] To satisfy the growing energy needs, the government, through its energy parastatals, ONGC Videsh Ltd, has begun to pursue foreign oil and natural gas exploration projects aggressively. As a result, India has a significant presence in the energy sectors of Egypt, Côte d'Ivoire, Nigeria and Sudan, and has narrowly lost out to China in acquiring an energy concession in Angola.[26]

How has China succeeded in getting a significant foothold in these countries in such a short period of time? It has done this by playing to its strengths and offering development assistance in a range of areas. Indian companies are currently involved in renovating oil fields and building petroleum pipeline projects in Sudan, establishing oil refineries, power plants and steel mills in Nigeria, and launching information technology projects that will electronically connect the continent, so as to facilitate e-commerce, e-governance and more generic healthcare, education and research initiatives.[27] India has also been party to the establishment of the Cyber Towers IT Park in Mauritius, the Ghana-India Kofi Annan Centre for Excellence in IT in Accra, and in a range of agricultural support initiatives, in Chad, Mali and Senegal.[28] In addition to its own direct developmental initiatives such as seconding farmers to cultivate land in East African nations, the Indian government is involved supportively through its Export-Import Bank of India (Exim Bank) in extending credit facilities for these projects.

But the credit from the Exim Bank is not only deployed for developmental initiatives approved by the government. It is also used to support Indian conglomerates to expand their presence on the continent, particularly in the heavily indebted poor countries (HIPCs) which do not have a viable and competitive banking sector. As a result, Indian companies are now involved in African industries, such as automobile manufacture, banking, information technology, textile manufacture, pharmaceuticals and steel. Tata vehicles are on the roads in Senegal and South Africa, being challenged in South Africa by another competitor, Mahendra. The Tata group is also involved in the telecommunications sector in South Africa. Other Indian companies have chemical ventures in North and East Africa, and mining prospects in southern and West Africa.[29] Overall bilateral trade between Africa and India has risen from US$967 million in 1991 to US$4.2 billion in 2001 and US$9.14 billion in 2005.[30] And, all assessments are that it is likely to rise further given that the Indian economy is expected to grow by 7 to 8 per cent per annum for the next decade.

The Indian government has shifted up a political gear by hosting its first India-Africa summit in New Delhi in April 2008. Obviously, much of the speculation about the summit centred on India's competition with China, and whether the former was emulating the latter in its engagements with the African continent. But the central message emanating from the Indian government at the summit was that it does business differently. Stressing a 'partnership of equals' and a win-win scenario in Indian-Africa relations, much was made of New Delhi's commitment to assist Africa in enhancing its human capacities with regard to the beneficiation of minerals. The Africanisation of the diamond industry, it was claimed, was not a threat, but an opportunity for India.[31] Similarly, India's relations with Angola were highlighted at the summit, especially India's commitment to take a stake in the Lobito refinery, establish a petrochemicals research and training facility and build a gas-fired power station. On the continental level, India announced a doubling of its credit facilities to Africa to US$5.4 billion, a US$500 million aid package and tariff cuts that would benefit 34 out of Africa's 53 countries.[32]

Nevertheless, it would be worthwhile to note that despite all of this, India is very much the junior competitor in the new scramble for Africa's resources. And this is likely to remain the case for the foreseeable future for a number of reasons. First, economic data from 2006 demonstrate that India's US$904.2 billion GDP is only a third of China's US$2.7 trillion. Similarly, India's US$181.4 billion imports and US$124.6 billion exports are about a quarter, and just under one-ninth of China's imports and exports respectively. Second, China's growth rate, even in the last three years, has been marginally ahead of India's, and in all likelihood, this will remain the case for the next decade. Finally, with more than US$1.3 trillion in reserves and a more centralised political and socio-economic system,[33] Beijing is in a much better position than New Delhi to organise and manage a strategic investment roll-out on the continent. The net effect of all this will be that despite India's strategic alliance with South Africa in the international forum of the India-Brazil-South Africa (IBSA) Forum and the optimism of Navdeep Suri that there is respect for the Indian model on the continent,[34] China seems to have the edge, at least for the foreseeable future.

Thus, while there are multiple foreign footprints becoming evident on the continent, it is two of them – the United States and China – that could leave the most lasting legacy. And, as things currently stand, this legacy is unlikely to be positive.

INTERPRETING THE NEW AFRICAN SCRAMBLE

The new African scramble has provoked a plethora of voices on both its significance and its consequences, and the appropriate responses to it. Most of the voices emanate from business, government and academia and the debate that has emerged reflects three distinct interpretations.

First, there is a myriad of voices who advocate Africa throwing its lot with the United States and the Western camp. Emanating mainly from African businessmen and some opposition politicians in South Africa, and warning of the autocratic nature of the Chinese regime, its relations with unsavoury leaders on the continent, and the capacity for corruption to flower to the detriment of the continent's citizens, they argue that partnerships with the United States are likely to have the most positive democratic and developmental effects on the continent.[35] But very few scholars – especially African ones – would have the temerity to advance this argument. Most recognise that the role of the United States and European nations has not been a noble one. And, other than a few journalistic endeavours of the mainstream press and consultancy reports commissioned largely by the United States Congress and government,[36] only few analysts such as Jeffrey Herbst and Greg Mills have ventured to advance a pro-Western agenda in this debate. Even then, they advocate a pragmatic engagement with China driven by the United States and by policies inspired by structural adjustment, rather than simple involvement with the superpower.[37] It would be worth stating that Herbst and Mills seriously misread the Chinese success story. After all, China's success emanates not simply from freeing the market, but also from manipulating the market for its own developmental ends.[38] If there is a lesson to be learnt by Africa, it is not only about creating favourable conditions for FDI in Africa; it is also about the value of pragmatism and of knowing how to develop and use leverage to condition the behaviour of foreign governments and investors, so that they are compatible with poverty alleviation and development.

A second voice to be heard is from a set of scholars, located mainly on the left of the ideological centre, who view China's engagement with Africa as no different from that of the United States. These scholars, such as Margaret Lee and Ian Taylor, cannot be accused, as Le Pere and Shelton assert, of having their discourse '. . . skewed by the neo-liberal prism and a lack of knowledge concerning African opinion and African conditions'.[39] Rather, their fear that China's engagement in Africa is a form of imperialism or neo-colonialism is founded on some sense of reality. Taylor, in his analysis of China's search for oil in Africa, demonstrates the dangerous practices it engenders on the continent.[40] Similarly, Lee's careful description of European, American and Chinese diplomacy, investment and business practices in Africa concludes that they are all merely different expressions of imperialism.[41]

Yet, despite there being a measure of truth in their analyses, care must be taken not to paint the Chinese and United States' experience, with the same brush. After all, there are significant differences. The United States operates its aid and trade diplomacy on an explicit 'conditionalities' foundation, whereas the Chinese adopt a much more pragmatic approach. Such pragmatism may be informed by opportunism at times, but it has given much relief to a debt-laden and poverty-stricken developing world, which has had structural adjustment policies imposed on it for far too long.[42] China's engagement, then, has the potential of enabling the subversion of some of the imperial agendas that are at play on the African continent.

Yet this should not lead us to be blind to the problems of Chinese expansion. The Chinese approach, which is founded on two principles – bilateral engagements organised through political elites and ignoring the domestic record of governments as a matter for the internal affairs of states – could have adverse consequences for democracy and development, if only because so many of the regimes they engage are authoritarian and unresponsive to the concerns and interests of the African citizenry. Ultimately, it would be prudent for advocates of African development to recognise that all countries involved in Africa are here to advance their own national interests, and any harbouring of contrary illusions can only result in future disappointment.

Unfortunately, this realisation is not widespread among progressive academics and intellectuals. While many progressive African advocates of development see through the propaganda of the United States and the EU in this regard, a number are too easily beguiled by the Chinese promise of an alternative path to development. The most dramatic example of this is Garth le Pere and Garth Shelton's *China, Africa and South Africa*, which provides one of the more sophisticated defences of Chinese engagement in Africa. Le Pere and Shelton, concerned with the China bashing, which they perceive as largely the product 'of western-inspired hypocrisy, disingenuousness and arrogance',[43] insist that the Middle Kingdom's engagement with Africa holds the potential for a more equitable and citizen-responsive development of the continent. They make this case by arguing that not only has there been a tenfold increase in Chinese-African trade to US$56 billion between 1999 and 2006, but China has also been willing to provide economic assistance (US$5.7 billion by 2006) without imposing political conditions, and has an extensive social and educational involvement in the continent.[44] Le Pere and Shelton, of course, acknowledge that there is some merit in the charge that China is too willing to deal with authoritarian governments and look the other way when citizens' rights are trampled, and that it could do more about mitigating the environmental and social consequences of its investments,[45] but they insist that this could be easily achieved with a more transparent and managed engagement with Africa.[46]

This attempt to correct the overly paranoid analyses of China must be welcomed. But care must be taken not to replace paranoid analyses with romanticised ones, and there are echoes of the latter in Le Pere and Shelton's contributions. This is evident at three levels. First, on the methodological front, it is useful to note that the case for China's involvement in Africa cannot be made simply on the basis of what is stipulated in official documents. All official documents, and especially foreign policy ones crafted in diplomatic gatherings, are drenched with lofty phrases and promises, little of which gets to be implemented. Therefore, the case to be made – if there is one – has to be premised on the actual practice and behaviour of China. It is worthwhile to note that, as in the case of Washington-Moscow relations in the Cold-War era, the interventions by foreign powers in Africa are as much determined by their competitors' actions as by their own interests. In this regard, Chinese behaviour is greatly conditioned by the nature and character of United States' involvement in the continent.

Second, Le Pere and Shelton and others have trumpeted China's approach to providing aid and loans without demanding political conditionality, suggesting that not only is there an implicit equality between giver and receiver in the relationship, but it also has better developmental consequences for the continent.[47] This argument is attractive, especially since much of the conditionality demanded by Western powers and international financial agencies in structural adjustment programmes over the last two decades has primarily advantaged multinational corporations and domestic political elites.[48] Conditionality is thus widely perceived as an instrument that enables the family silver to be sold off and Africa's future to be mortgaged to the West. Yet, while there is much truth in this assessment, it needs to be realised that conditionality can have both positive and negative consequences, depending on the specific parties, the nature of their relationship and the stipulated preconditions for the aid. Obviously, if the target of the conditions is an authoritarian government and the purpose is to protect citizens from arbitrary action and repression, then such conditionality can have positive outcomes. China's respect of 'sovereignty' in these cases, and its refusal to consider domestic variables in its aid engagements, could have adverse consequences for some of the continent's citizens.[49]

Finally, the recommendations advanced by Le Pere and Shelton, which are located mainly at the level of managerial processes, really do not go far enough in creating the conditions for a more equitable Sino-African relationship. The problem is that Le Pere and Shelton, while recognising that ultimately Chinese engagement in Africa is driven by national interest, argue that the skewed benefits in favour of Beijing are largely the result of a lack of administrative capacity on the African side. But is the lack of administrative capacity not just one symptom of a broader unequal distribution of power between China and African countries? If the goal is to construct a more mutually beneficial relationship, this unequal distribution of power between the parties has to be addressed. Moreover, although it is true that China has successfully implemented an alternative development path,[50] which may have more developmental possibilities for the African continent, it is important to note that the promise will be realised only if Africans do not become compliant with Chinese agendas, but are able to play off the competitors for Africa's resources with a view to maximising the benefits for the continent. In Taylor's graphic description, Africa needs to transform the 'mineral curse' into a vector for socio-economic development.[51] This requires a strategic engagement and a set of actions designed specifically to enhance the leverage of African countries in their relations with China.

Such a transformation in the distribution of power is also necessary for averting what is perhaps the greatest danger looming in this new scramble for Africa's resources: the emergence of proxy wars and the establishment of client states. The last time such a scramble took place, which was during the period of the Cold War, the consequences were devastating for the African continent. Both foreign powers – the United States and Soviet Union in that case – established client regimes, funded rebel armies and engaged in proxy wars.[52] The result was a continent wracked by civil wars, displacements of citizens and cross-border refugee flows.[53]

There are some who would dismiss this potential threat to Africa as a doomsday scenario. Yet these same individuals would be hard pressed to explain current developments in Sudan and Somalia without reference to the destructive roles of the United States and China. In the Sudan, we have an autocratic regime supported by China, with rebel insurgents both in the south and in Darfur being provided with aid, political and military support and international legitimacy by the United States and its allies. Similarly, the Ethiopian invasion of Somalia was encouraged and supported by the United States in particular.[54] The intention: to stabilise the Horn and strengthen the United States' interests in the region. Sudan and Somalia, then, represent the first proxy wars of the new scramble for Africa.

How to avoid these scenarios should be the overriding concern of Africa's political and economic elite. The elite have as much to lose from the spread of political instability as do Africa's poor and marginalised. But no one has more to lose than the economic and political elite of Africa's richest and most industrialised country. The African continent is the one arena where South Africa has continuously generated a trade surplus.[55] It is also the continent that absorbs a significant proportion of South Africa's industrial output. This is in part why South Africa's political elite has spent so much energy and time in resolving Africa's conflicts and stabilising the continent. The new scramble for Africa's resources, however, threatens this future. Given this, and the fact that its own prosperity is tied to the continent's stability, South Africa has perhaps the greatest incentive to ensure that the scramble is managed to the benefit of Africa.

WHAT IS TO BE DONE?

What can be done to avoid both Chinese and United States' dominance in their engagements with Africa, and the more general threat of proxy wars and political instability occasioned by the race for Africa's resources? It needs to be kept in mind that development is a product of both national initiatives and a facilitative global environment. Both these features were present in the development of Western Europe and Southeast Asia. The primary feature in the national equation is the presence of elites who desire, are organised for and focused on comprehensive collective national development. The necessary feature in the global environment is the presence of at least one country that is conditioned to provide aid for development and organise the global economic environment, or at least a part of it, so that international trade is structured in favour of the developing nation.

Aid is absolutely necessary. The development of Western Europe would have been unimaginable without the role of the Marshall Plan. Similarly, the Asian 'tigers' – Indonesia, Singapore, Taiwan and South Korea – were major beneficiaries of United

States aid. UNCTAD's *Economic Development in Africa* estimates that US$500 million per year was given to Japan by the United States between 1950 and 1970. South Korea received economic and military investment that amounted to US$13 billion between 1946 and 1978, whereas Taiwan received US$5.6 billion during that same period.[56] But trade was as crucial as aid. The United States provided preferential access to its markets for both Western Europe and its Asian allies. Moreover, it did not demand reciprocal access, enabling these societies to develop their competitive capacities before they integrated into the global economy. This restructuring of international trade by the United States in favour of its allies was crucial to the development of Western Europe and Southeast Asia in the post-Second-World-War period.

But why did both the United States and national elites act in ways that were systemically beneficial? This is often not highlighted in the debate and literature on development. Most of the literature has a policy bent and is mainly descriptive, detailing the particular policies that generated the positive socio-economic outcomes in these development states.[57] Others tend to a have a more institutional focus, emphasising the embedded but relatively autonomous character of the state, which speaks to the structural linkages and social interactions between political and economic elites.[58] But a description of policies, institutions and networks cannot explain why elite coalitions adopt national development agendas. Neither can such a description explain why international political elites would allow these development states to implement a series of policies that discriminate against foreign capital.

Yet some explanation for this is evident in the development literature itself. Chalmers Johnson, for instance, explicitly accounts for the rise of the Japanese economic model by arguing that it was essentially a product of the Cold War and the competitive relations between the United States and the Soviet political elites.[59] Other more recent accounts speak of systemic vulnerability generated by specific political, security and financial conditions,[60] and yet others highlight the role of social mobilisation and extra-institutional popular action in prompting these elite coalitions in the direction of broader developmental outcomes (see Chapter 16).[61]

These accounts demonstrate that appropriate development policies are not simply the product of good political leaders or clever technocrats.[62] Rather, they emerge within particular political circumstances that are distinguished by a dispersal of power. At the international level, competition between equally powerful states is good for development because it conditions international political elites to act in ways that favour developing nations. At the national level, the experience of West European nations, including Norway, and Asian countries such as Malaysia, suggests that a robust civil society, including powerful trade unions, is important for conditioning local political elites to adopt policies and behave in ways that facilitate poverty alleviation and national development.

But, as was indicated earlier, the competitive international environment during the Cold War did not benefit Africa. How, then, can its elites avoid repeating this experience? How can they ensure that they are able, like the Asians and Europeans, to use the competitive international environment to facilitate their own development? Two preconditions would be required for this outcome in this era. First, African political elites must develop the political will to pursue a comprehensive development agenda that benefits their citizens. And, as the European and Malaysian experiences indicate, such a political will can emerge when the political elite are kept in check by a plural political system and/or an independent robust national civil society.[63] Where this does not exist, as in Gabon (see Chapter 12), Ethiopia and Sudan (see Chapter 4), these political elites easily become proxies for foreign powers and interests. Substantive democratisation, then, facilitates the accountability of elites to their citizens, thereby enabling such elites to develop the political will to pursue a comprehensive developmental agenda.

Second, African political elites would have to be much more cohesive at the continental level if they are to be able to use the competitive international environment to their collective advantage. Such cohesion could emerge from initiatives towards a continental unity. What form would this take? Some would argue for a pan-African solution in the form of a United States of Africa. While such a development would be positive, it is for all practical purposes unfeasible in the short to medium term. But a continental charter of rights governing investments and engagements on the continent need not be. Such a charter, which would have to be negotiated in the African Union (AU), could supersede bilateral agreements and force all external, and perhaps even continental, powers to accord to a specific set of business and diplomatic practices. Of course, the administrative weaknesses and the capacity constraints of the AU may hinder compliance. But if such a charter were to be agreed to by the AU, it could be subsequently ratified in the UN, thereby extending and strengthening its institutionalisation, and enhancing the reach of its compliance.

Is this possible? It has been argued that democratisation, political stability and development would benefit significantly from one or two regional powers – South Africa and perhaps Nigeria – pursuing a hegemonic agenda. Such a hegemonic agenda need not be militaristic. It need only involve advancing, managing and underwriting the costs of a political and socio-economic vision that prioritises substantive democracy, elite cohesiveness at a continental level and African development.[64] Why should South Africa pursue and underwrite such an agenda? This is because it stands to benefit most from it. As indicated earlier, Africa is the only arena in which South African corporates have a competitive edge, and it is the only region with which the country runs a trade surplus. Given this, should South Africa's foreign policy not be directed at focusing African minds in a realistic attempt to develop a collective African response to the developing continental threat emanating from the contemporary African scramble (see Chapter 10)?

CONCLUSION

In sum then, the new African scramble has provoked a myriad of voices, almost all of which assert that Africa could benefit significantly if only it were to throw in its lot with one or other foreign power. The analysis here, however, contests this conclusion. Rather, it suggests that there are great dangers inherent in this new African scramble. It demonstrates that all of the countries in the scramble are driven largely by national interest, and that their behaviour is conditioned far more by competition with each other than by the noble sentiments enshrined in their policy documents and press releases. The consequence is that this scramble is likely to repeat the results of its predecessor: neo-colonial relations, proxy wars, and, ultimately, political instability and economic devastation.

The only way this outcome is going to be avoided is if African elites themselves take charge of their own destiny. This would require these elites, like the Asians of a quarter of a century ago (see Chapter 17), to be willing to play the foreign powers against each other to obtain the best terms for their own comprehensive development. Of course, they must be conditioned to want such comprehensive development in the first place, and they would need the institutional capacity to manage the foreign relations to achieve this. Both of these preconditions would require a united political elite on the continent, which is only possible, of course, if one or other regional power – South Africa and/or Nigeria – were to lead this agenda. Only then could the continent begin to establish the foundation of South African President Thabo Mbeki's mythical dream, the African century, which has long been the mantra of generation after generation of African leaders.

NOTES

1. UNCTAD, World Investment Report 2006 – *FDI from Developing and Transitional Economies: Implications for Development* (New York and Geneva: United Nations, 2006), pp. xvii, 40, 41.
2. I. Umunna, 'Africa Goes East', *Africa Today*, 14–15 December 2006.
3. Umunna, 'Africa Goes East', 15.
4. B. Freund, *The Making of Contemporary Africa* (London: MacMillan, 1984).
5. G. Arrighi, 'The African Crisis: World Systemic and Regional Aspects', *New Left Review* 15, 2002; M.C. Lee, 'The 21st Century Scramble for Africa', *Journal of Contemporary African Studies* 24(3), 2006.
6. The exception, of course, may be France, which played and continues to play an important and sometimes destructive political role in its ex-colonies.
7. It should be remembered that the genocide occurred under the watch of Kofi Annan and Bill Clinton and is a blot on their public-service careers.
8. UNCTAD, *Economic Development in Africa – Reclaiming Policy Space: Domestic Resource Mobilization and Development States* (New York and Geneva: United Nations, 2007), pp. 26–27.
9. UNCTAD, *Economic Development in Africa*, p. 2.
10. UNCTAD, *Economic Development* in Africa, p. 3.
11. As the leader of the largest oil producer in Latin America and having been a victim of repeated attempts by the United States to effect regime change in Venezuela, Chavez has become a hostile critic and a thorn in the ambitions of the Bush regime in the region.
12. In recent years, the United States has repeatedly warned that the explosive mix of political instability, porous borders and adverse socio-economic conditions has made Africa an ideal recruiting ground and a haven for terrorists. See T. Whelan, 'Why AFRICOM? An American Perspective'. Situation report, Institute for Security Studies, Pretoria, 2007.
13. I. Ferguson and L. Sek, 'US Trade Investment Relationship with Sub-Saharan Africa: The African Growth and Opportunity Act and Beyond'. Report commissioned by the US Congress, March 2003.
14. Ferguson and Sek, 'US Trade Investment Relationship'.
15. US International Trade Commission, 'US Trade Investment with Sub-Saharan Africa', December 2004, p. 1.
16. US International Trade Commission, 'US Trade Investment with Sub-Saharan Africa'.
17. White House, 'The National Security Strategy of the United States of America' (Washington, DC: September 2002), p. 11.
18. Whelan 'Why AFRICOM?', p. 7.
19. This is the view of the South African foreign-policy officials, which is why the country has been so reticent in supporting the initiative.
20. G. le Pere and G. Shelton, *China, Africa and South Africa: South-South Cooperation in a Global Era* (Midrand: Institute for Global Dialogue, 2007), p. 121.
21. Quoted in Umunna, 'Africa Goes East', p. 18.
22. Quoted in Umunna, 'Africa Goes East', p. 19.
23. Le Pere and Shelton, *China, Africa and South Africa*, pp. 149–50, 156–57.
24. N. Suri, 'India and Africa: A Contemporary Perspective', in A. Sinha and M. Mohta (eds.), *India's Foreign Policy: Challenges and Opportunities* (New Delhi: FSI, 2006), p. 512.
25. A. Biswas, 'India's Engagement in Africa: Scope and Significance'. Paper delivered to the CODESRIA-HSRC Workshop on South Africa in Africa, Gold Reef City, Johannesburg, 10 October 2007, p. 5.

26. China swung the deal in its favour by offering aid to the tune of US$2 billion, compared to the US$200 million offered by India. See Biswas, 'India's Engagement in Africa', p. 9.
27. For trade data between India and African countries, see the Federation of Indian Chambers of Commerce and Industry (FICCI), *Destination Africa: India's Vision* (New Delhi: FICCI, 2005). See also Umunna, 'Africa Goes East', p. 20; Biswas, 'India's Engagement in Africa'.
28. Suri, 'India and Africa', p. 516.
29. Exim Bank, 'Research Brief: Southern African Countries: A Study of India's Trade and Investment Potential', 2004, p. 3; Exim Bank, 'Research Brief: Select West African Countries – A Study of India's Trade and Investment Potential', 2006, p. 21.
30. Biswas, 'India's Engagement in Africa', p. 10.
31. See N. Dawes, 'India's African Inroads', *Mail & Guardian*, 11–17 April 2008, p. 12.
32. See E. Roche, 'India Loosens Purse Strings', *Mail & Guardian Online*, 8 April 2008.
33. See https://apkmail.uj.ac.za/exchange/ahabib/Drafts/?Cmdew#_ftn1.
34. Quoted in S. Baldauf, 'India Steps up Trade Ties with Africa', *The Christian Science Monitor*, 3 November 2006. http://www.csmonitor.com/2006/1103/p04s01-wosc.html.
35. The most vocal and significant exponent of this view is the Democratic Alliance in South Africa, which reflects it, implicitly and explicitly, in the resolutions that it tables in the national legislature.
36. E.J. Wilson, 'China's Influence in Africa: Implications for US Policy'. Testimony before the Subcommittee on Africa, United States House of Representatives, Washington, DC, 28 July 2005.
37. J. Herbst and G. Mills, 'Africa in 2020: Three Scenarios for the Future'. Brenthurst Discussion Paper 2, 2006.
38. Can one truly imagine the economic success of China without the won having been artificially pegged against the dollar?
39. Le Pere and Shelton, *China, Africa and South Africa*, p. 135.
40. I. Taylor, 'China's Oil Diplomacy in Africa', *International Affairs* 82(5), 2006; see also D.M. Tull, 'China's Engagement in Africa: Scope, Significance and Consequences', *Journal of Modern African Studies* 44(3), 2006.
41. Lee, 'The 21st Century Scramble for Africa'.
42. Arrighi, 'The African Crisis'; T. Mkandawire, 'Thinking about the Development State in Africa', *Cambridge Journal of Economics* 25(3), 2001; A.O. Olukoshi, 'The Elusive Prince of Denmark: Structural Adjustment and the Crisis of Governance in Africa', in T. Mkandawire and C. Soludo (eds.), *African Voices on Structural Adjustment* (Dakar: CODESRIA, 2003).
43. G. le Pere, 'Prospects for a Coherent Policy Response: Engaging China'. Paper delivered to Africa Day, hosted by the Centre for Chinese Studies, 1 June 2007.
44. Le Pere and Shelton, *China, Africa and South Africa*, pp. 135–38, 145–59; Le Pere, 'Prospects for a Coherent Policy Response'.
45. Le Pere and Shelton, *China, Africa and South Africa*, pp. 122–23.
46. Le Pere, 'Prospects for a Coherent Policy Response'; Le Pere and Shelton, *China, Africa and South Africa*, pp. 209–15.
47. Le Pere and Shelton, *China, Africa and South Africa*, pp. 136–37.
48. Arrighi, 'The African Crisis'; UNCTAD, *Economic Development in Africa*, p. 82.
49. Take the example of the victims of Darfur or even Zimbabwe.
50. Le Pere and Shelton, *China, Africa and South Africa*, pp. 182–208.
51. I. Taylor, 'China's Foreign Policy towards Africa in the 1990s', *Journal of Modern African Studies* 36(3), 1998: 445.

52. Note the Reagan administration's funding of UNITA and RENAMO, rebel armies in Angola and Mozambique respectively. Of course, this funding was in part facilitated by the apartheid government, which benefited from the broader political instability on the continent.
53. Lee, 'The 21st Century Scramble for Africa', 304.
54. S. Lone, 'In Somalia, A Reckless US Proxy War', *International Herald Tribune*, 26 December 2006; B. Slavin, 'US Support Key to Ethiopia's Invasion', *USA Today*, 1 August 2007.
55. J. Daniel, V. Naidoo and S. Naidu, 'The South Africans Have Arrived: Post-Apartheid Corporate Expansion into Africa', in J. Daniel, A. Habib and R. Southall (eds.), *State of the Nation: South Africa 2003–2004* (Cape Town: HSRC Press, 2003).
56. Arrighi, 'The African Crisis', pp. 30–31; UNCTAD, *Economic Development in Africa*, pp. 80–81.
57. D.W. Nabudere, 'The Development State, Democracy and the Global Society in Africa'. Paper presented to the Conference on Investment Choices for Education in Africa, Faculty of Education, University of Witwatersrand, 20 September 2006; R. Southall, 'Introduction: Can South Africa be a Developmental State?', in S. Buhlungu et al. (eds.), *State of the Nation: South Africa 2005–2006* (Cape Town: HSRC Press, 2006).
58. P. Evans, *Embedded Autonomy: States and Industrial Transformation* (Princeton, NJ: Princeton University Press, 1995).
59. R. Wade, *Governing the Market: Economic Theory and the Role of Government in East Asian Industrialization* (Princeton, NJ: Princeton University Press, 1999).
60. R. Doner, K. Ritchie and D. Slater, 'Systemic Vulnerability and the Origins of Development States: Northeast and Southeast Asia in Comparative Perspective', *International Organization* 59(2), 1995: 327–61.
61. K.F. Chin and K.S. Jomo, 'Financial Sector Rents in Malaysia', in M. Khan and K.S. Jomo (eds.), *Rents, Rent Seeking and Economic Development: Theory and Evidence in Asia* (Cambridge: Cambridge University Press, 2000); B. Freund, 'State, Capital and the Emergence of a New Power Elite in South Africa: Black Economic Empowerment at National and Local Levels'. Paper presented to the Harold Wolpe Memorial Trust 10th Anniversary Colloquium, Cape Town, 22–23 September 2006.
62. This is the implicit assumption of much of the policy-oriented literature on development in Africa and elsewhere.
63. A. Habib, 'State-Civil Society Relations in Post-Apartheid South Africa', *Social Research* 72(3), 2005.
64. A. Habib and N. Selinyane, 'Constraining the Unconstrained: Civil Society and South Africa's Hegemonic Obligations in Africa', in W. Carlsnaes and P. Nel (eds.), *In Full Flight: South African Foreign Policy after Apartheid* (Midrand: Institute for Global Dialogue, 2006). For a counter-view, see M. Schoeman, 'South Africa as an Emerging Middle Power: 1994–2003', in Daniel, Habib and Southall (eds.), *State of the Nation 2003–2004* and G. le Pere, 'South Africa: An Emerging Power', *Global Dialogue* 3(1), 1998.

15

The European Union and China in Africa

Daniel Bach

INTRODUCTION

Until 2007, the European Commission (EC) did not comment publicly on China's increasing engagement with Africa through trade, aid and investment, as well as high-profile politico-diplomatic initiatives. By October 2005, a kind of business-as-usual approach prevailed in Brussels as the EC prepared the release of its new strategy for Euro-African relations. The communication that was eventually released acknowledged China's rising importance to Africa, through a tangential and low-key reference that carefully steered away from drawing any conclusion:

> China merits special attention given its economic weight and political influence . . . Despite radical domestic changes, the country has retained links with different African countries which are now attracted by China's trading potential. Especially for oil- and commodity-dependent countries, China represents a substantial and continued source of financial income, mostly outside the traditional development and governance frameworks.[1]

A few weeks later, the Council of the European Union (EU) adopted a statement that endorsed the strategy recommended by the EC in its communication.[2] This time, however, no reference was made to China, a silence that contrasted with the extensive policy debates that, within the EC, in the European parliament and among member-states, focused on China's emergence as a global actor.[3] Each in their own way, the EC and the Council of the EU seemed unable or unwilling to address the implications of China and India's rising interactions with Africa and increasing significance in the hierarchy of global governance.

Eighteen months later, in May 2007, the EC called for a rejuvenated EU-Africa strategic partnership, while noting that China's ability to 'rapidly emerge . . . as Africa's third most important trade partner' would mean that 'if the EU wants to remain a privileged partner and make the most of its relations with Africa, it must be willing to reinforce and in some areas reinvent the current relationship – institutionally, politically and culturally'.[4] A few weeks later, the EC also gathered in Brussels 180 policy-makers, senior officials, diplomats, academic and think-tank experts, civil society representatives and businessmen originating from China, Africa and Europe to discuss 'how the relations between the three actors can be brought into play to yield the best results for a win-win partnership around an African agenda'.[5] In his inaugural speech, Louis Michel, the EC Commissioner for Development and Humanitarian Aid, made a plea for the establishment of a triangular partnership, after stressing that 'we are competitors, but we are also partners and Africa must benefit from a reinforced relationship among ourselves and not suffer from it'.[6] Concrete steps initiated in Brussels and designed to translate the political dialogue into cooperation initiatives included suggestions of a visit by the European Commissioner for Development to China and the possible invitation of China to the Euro-African summit in Lisbon.

The identification of areas suited for an EU-China 'partnership' over Africa was yet to translate into tangible results by January 2008. As Michel announced his intention to visit Beijing in March, he was pressed by journalists to clarify what interest China would find in commiting itself to such a venture. The EU Commissioner answered that Beijing could secure 'through cooperation with Europe', a new 'credibility' to pursue its investment strategy. Michel added that he believed that African elites were increasingly aware of the rise of Chinese interest in Africa, and concluded that 'this will inevitably provoke reactions . . . Idyllic relations between Africa and China, are bound to end.'[7]

Prospects for a partnership with China were also being discussed at a time when protests aroused by the EU's Economic Partnership Agreements (EPAs) did not show any sign of weakening within Africa. By the beginning of 2008, President Abdoulaye Wade of Senegal, the leader of one of the two African countries where democratic governance has gone uninterrupted since independence, was still one of the chief critics of the EU templates. He deftly capitalised on the issue domestically, while hammering in international fora and media that the EU 'should practice what it preaches', with respect to the translation of financial pledges into effective commitment and the emulation of (China's) 'best' practices. Wade's widely circulated philippics targeted the 'West' in general and the EU in particular:

> China's approach to our needs is simply better adapted than the slow and sometimes patronising post-colonial approach of European investors, donor organisations and non-governmental organisations . . .
>
> With direct aid, credit lines and reasonable contracts, China has helped African nations to build infrastructure projects in record time . . .
>
> . . . I am a firm believer in good governance and the rule of law. But when bureaucracy and senseless red tape impede our ability to act . . . African leaders have an obligation to opt for swifter solutions. I achieved more in my one hour meeting with President Hu Jintao in an executive suite at my hotel in Berlin during the recent [2007] G8 meeting in Heiligendamm than I did during the entire, orchestrated meeting of world leaders at the summit . . .
>
> . . . For the price of one European vehicle, a Senegalese can purchase two Chinese cars . . . [W]estern complaints about China's slow pace in adopting democratic reform cannot obscure the fact that the Chinese are more competitive, less bureaucratic and more adept at business in Africa than their critics.
>
> . . . If Europe does not want to provide funding for African infrastructure – it pledged $15bn under the Cotonou Agreement eight years ago – the Chinese are ready to take up the task, more rapidly and at less cost. Not just Africa but the West itself has much to learn from China.[8]

Wade's criticism, relayed by those of non-governmental organisations (NGOs) and left-wing members of the European parliament, stigmatised the EU's extensive reliance on intrusive normative and regulatory frameworks for the conduct of its external relations with Africa. What was at stake was the effectiveness but also the legitimacy of regimes of inter-hemispheric governance that ever since the conclusion of the first Lomé Convention, have been branded as quintessential expressions of inter-regional 'partnership' and 'ownership'.

The following pages provide a cursory survey of evolving interactions characterised by a streamlining of EU-Africa relations consonant with the EU's increasing marginal economic engagement in Africa. The EU's adherence to norms, soft power and the 'politicisation' of its cooperation with the African, Caribbean and Pacific (ACP) countries sharpens the contrast with China's rising economic and diplomatic engagement and stated policy of non-interference in their domestic affairs. China's holistic and atypical approach combines aggressive capitalism with softened state-backed government-to-government deals and an ability to deliver substantial financial packages quickly.

Politically, emphasis is also laid on strict respect of state sovereignty and non-interference in other countries' domestic affairs.

The short-term implications of the emergence of distinctive regimes of interactions with Africa were symbolically highlighted by the contrast between the Forum on China-African Cooperation (FOCAC) summit, held in Beijing in November 2006, and the Euro-African summit that was organised in Lisbon a year later. Europeans, after reluctantly agreeing to the invitation of African states, had to face the public recriminations of a number of African leaders, who were pressured to sign reciprocal trade liberalisation – a key component to the EPAs – by 31 December 2007. The concluding section of this chapter discusses how the rise in revenues, status and global opportunities that characterised a number of African states provide an overarching framework that shapes Africa's international insertion, but also highlights the opportunities associated with competititon between old and new players in Africa

THE EU: SOFT POWER, NORMS AND REGULATORY FRAMEWORKS

The EU's strong African focus goes back to the Treaty of Rome that offered special treatment to the French and Belgian colonies from sub-Saharan Africa through the association status. The group that came to be known as the États Africains et Malgache Associés (EAMA) benefited from a non-discriminatory and reciprocal trade regime that went along with a commitment to allocate aid to investment and infrastructure development. The United Kingdom's membership of the European Common Market consolidated Europe's focus on sub-Saharan Africa after 1973. The conclusion of the negotiations of the Lomé Convention, signed in February 1975, resulted in the incorporation of the EAMA into the group of sub-Saharan ACP states that today includes all 48 sub-Saharan African states.

The Lomé Convention, negotiated in the aftermath of the oil embargo of September 1973, initially carried the ambition to offer a model for the reordering of North-South relations. In effect, the model rapidly became the symbol of unfulfilled promises and bifurcated expectations due to the failure of the Paris (1976) and Cancun (1981) conferences on a new North-South international order.[9] The Lomé Convention itself was dysfunctional in so far as it acted as a disincentive to the diversification of ACP exports. The ACPs were located at the apex of the EU pyramid of trade preferences, but African exports kept losing ground on the EU market as competition grew from Asia and Latin American developing economies.[10] Reforming relations with sub-Saharan

Africa nonetheless remained a taboo subject until the early 1990s.[11] Following the fall of communism in Europe, the EU's changing priorities and the conclusion of the Uruguay round of negotiations suddenly made the reappraisal of Lomé inevitable. Following the establishment of the new World Trade Organisation (WTO) dispute-settlement procedure, the ACP preferential banana regime was condemned as discriminatory. The decision prefigured a condemnation of the entire EU-ACP non-reciprocal trade regime on the grounds that WTO rules would not allow discrimination among developing countries beyond the category of least developed countries (LDCs).

On 23 June 2000, after half a decade of semi-official debates and a two-year renegotiation process, the EU and 77 ACP states signed the Cotonou Agreement that superseded the Lomé IV Convention. Cotonou purports to provide the roadmap towards a new and original inter-hemispheric 'partnership', based on subscription to common political norms, trade reciprocity and the conclusion of EPAs between the EU and six regional groupings formed by ACP states, four of which are in sub-Saharan Africa. The resulting template streamlines and dilutes into a broader approach the ad hoc treatment previously granted to the ACPs. Human rights, democratisation and the rule of law are defined in the Cotonou Agreement (article 9) as an 'essential element' that may result, in the case of 'particularly serious and flagrant violation' in aid and trade sanctions.[12] This identification of clear steps and procedures, while new to the ACPs, merely endorses the general practice of incorporating human rights and democracy clauses into the EC's European and international association agreements since 1992.

The other key aspect of Cotonou is the continuation of the WTO waiver, namely a special exemption to global trade rules, until 31 December 2007. Since this date, WTO compliance requires the progressive liberalisation of all trade over a twelve-year period, so as to reach full compliance by 2020. In Africa, as elsewhere in the world, LDC economies are entitled to claim the benefits of unreciprocated trade preferences under the EU's 'Everything but Arms' (EBA) offer.

Changing international regulatory frameworks has significantly contributed to reducing the value of EU trade concessions to sub-Saharan Africa. Since December 2004, the ACP's previous exemption from the requirements of the Multifibre Arrangements (MFA) is also undermined by the end of restrictions imposed by the EU on textile and clothing imports. More generally, adverse rulings by WTO arbitration panels have severely dented the preferential treatment that special EU protocols used to offer to ACP exports for sugar, bananas and beef.[13]

The streamlining of EU trade and development interactions with the ACPs is also evident in the reform of EC institutions. Since the transformation of Directorate General

(DG) VIII into DG Development in 1999, responsibility for the conduct of EU relations with the ACPs has been split among the DGs and agencies of the 'Relex' family (trade, politics, enlargement, humanitarian ECHO and Europaid). The adoption of a thematic perspective, along with the contraction of the portfolio covered by the DG Development, was interpreted as a 'clear signal of the Commission's intentions that trade with the ACP would be subordinate to the overall principles of EU external trade relations'.[14] Since then, EC recommendations towards 'the full integration of cooperation with ACP countries in the EU budget' and their support by a number of key EU donors also suggest that the days of ACP aid management through extra-budgetary contributions to the European Development Fund (EDF) are numbered.[15]

In 2003, six European member-states (France, Germany, the United Kingdom, Belgium, the Netherlands and Italy) of the EC accounted for precisely half (39 and 11 per cent) of total donor contributions to the continent. Sub-Saharan Africa and North Africa received 44.3 per cent and 9.5 per cent respectively of the EC's gross disbursements of bilateral Overseas Development Aid (ODA) in 2003–04. On average, the sixteen European member-states of the Development Assistance Committee (DAC) allocated 51.3 per cent of their total net disbursements to sub-Saharan Africa, against an average 42 per cent for all DAC contributors.[16] Ongoing normative and geo-political concerns contribute to the continuing focus of European aid on sub-Saharan Africa. In spite of the decline of post-colonial ties and the new EU members' unevenly shared sense of responsibility towards the continent, aid to Africa has remained a priority. Since 2000, eradicating poverty is formally described by the EU as the 'primary and overarching objective' of its development cooperation, in line with the Millennium Development Goals (MDGs).[17] As part of its endorsement of the objective of the MDGs, the EU has adopted a timetable for member-states to bring aid budgets to the level of 0.56 per cent of gross national income (GNI) by 2010 and 0.7 by 2015. At least half of this aid increase should be disbursed in Africa where 37 out of the 48 countries are least developing countries (LDCs), least landlocked developing countries (LLDCs), or both. Targeting LDCs and LLDCs specifically with regard to trade, debt or aid packages automatically demands the EU to prioritise sub-Saharan Africa. So does the broadening of EU external commitments beyond aid and development agendas in order to include conflict prevention, support to peacekeeping and humanitarian aid in emergency situations.

By the mid-2000s, South Africa constituted the only exception to a pattern of dereliction that permeated trade and investment flows between Europe and sub-Saharan Africa since the aftermath of the end of the Cold War in Europe. In 2004, South

Africa accounted for 42 per cent of EU trade with sub-Saharan Africa. European foreign direct investment (FDI) also crystallised in a country widely perceived by business circles as the only economy of continental and global significance. South Africa's specific status as an 'emerging' market economy accounts for its conclusion of an ad hoc trade agreement with the EU, as neither Brussels nor the WTO would agree to a non-reciprocal trade regime.

South Africa also benefited from a specific aid package that, unlike in the case of the other ACPs, is nested in the budget of the EU. The bilateral Trade, Development and Cooperation Agreement (TDCA) signed by the EU and South Africa in 1999 was a test case for the free trade templates that inspired Cotonou and a whole generation of free trade agreements (FTAs) with emerging economies. The twin-track approach pursued during the negotiations also retrospectively appears to have been the product of a unique EU readiness to combine a specific trade and development aid package with opportunities for political enhancement, through South Africa's ability to be a full member of ACP and EU-ACP political institutions.

The EC's specific support to the African Union's (AU's) new security architecture and its peacekeeping efforts represented in many ways an exception to a process otherwise characterised by the streamlining and downsizing of EU-Africa relations.[18] Immigration and asylum-related issues were perhaps the most emblematic illustration of such a trend. It was during the 1990s that migrants from West Africa and the Sahel started travelling north in increasingly large numbers with the hope of reaching the southern shores of Europe. By 2003, the flow of migrations across the Sahara into the countries of the Maghreb was estimated to have reached between 65 000 and 80 000 people a year.[19] Sub-Saharan Africans formed the bulk of the transnational migrants seeking opportunities for illicit crossovers from Morocco, Tunisia or Libya.[20] By mid-2006, stricter enforcement of migratory routes through the Maghreb countries prompted migrants to focus extensively on Mauritania and Senegal, from where they tried to reach the Spanish Canary archipelago.

Since then, logistic and financial support from EU member-states and Frontex, the EU's external border security agency, has kept increasing in order to bolster Spanish efforts to ensure air and maritime control of the West African coast off Senegal and The Gambia.[21] As the Lisbon summit was about to be held in December 2007, EU member-states acknowledged that despite restrictive immigration policies, large numbers of illegal migrants kept reaching Europe. It was also noted that Europe would require an extra 20 million, often highly skilled workers, by 2025. Debates were therefore shifting towards the adoption of common policies and EU legislation designed to enhance the mobility of highly skilled or seasonal labour across the Mediterranean, while countering the explosion of unskilled migrations through increased operational cooperation between member-states.[22]

CHINA'S MATTER-OF-FACT APPROACH: ENGAGEMENT WITHOUT INTERFERENCE

Chinese engagement in Africa has been on the rise since the 1990s, in sharp contrast with the streamlining of interaction between the EU and the continent over the same period. Since the third meeting of FOCAC was held in November 2006, the web of China's bilateral interactions and agreements has also acquired a pan-African reach. The successful gathering of 48 African states, proudly presented by the Chinese as the largest diplomatic summit ever held in Bejing, was accompanied by the announcement of an ambitious politico-diplomatic blueprint. China's road map for cooperation over the 2006–09 period was presented by President Hu Jintao through eight key measures that pledge, inter alia, to double 2006 aid to Africa by 2009; provide US$3 billion of preferential loans and US$2 billion of preferential buyer's credits over the following three years; establish a US$5 billion China-Africa Development Fund to promote Chinese investment across the continent; build a conference centre for the AU in Addis Ababa; initiate a programme of debt cancellation for the African heavily indebted poor countries (HIPCs) and LDCs that maintain diplomatic relations with China; and cancel tariff barriers on an increased number of items exported by African LDCs.[23] The establishment of three to five trade and economic cooperation zones in Africa in the next three years also featured in the 'Action Plan 2007–09'. This formulation, together with Beijing's earmarking of 2006 as its own 'Africa year' and its stated ambition to conclude a 'new kind of strategic partnership' with Africa, helped to entrench Western impressions of an attempt by China to provide a counterpoint to initiatives such as the G8 action plan, the Paris declaration on aid effectiveness or the EU-AU strategic partnership.[24] Last but not least, the uncritical monitoring of the conference by the Chinese media also contributed to building an idyllic image of FOCAC and its stated ambitions.

In 2005, China accounted for 20 per cent of sub-Saharan African exports of raw materials and 15 per cent of fuels. Figures are well known and only need to be cursorily recalled. Trade between China and sub-Saharan Africa totalled more than US$50 billion in 2006 – mostly oil imports from Angola and Sudan, timber from Central Africa and copper from Zambia. As observed by Sindzingre, while this has been the source of a substantial increase in revenues for these countries, 'China's demand for natural resources maintains sub-Saharan Africa in its century-long export structure and may even increase its dependence on primary products'.[25]

China's emerging trade, aid and investment, like the EU's older and more seasoned track record, point to strands of interaction and transaction that beyond their idiosyncratic features, postulate the deepening of their insertion into the global world economy. In the case of China, this represents a follow-up to the country's readiness to implement a string of domestic reforms that have opened the economy to international trade and investment. Prospects for joint EU-China initiatives are bound to consolidate within the next few years, not least through synergies resulting from business ventures crafted within the EU, North America, Japan or China. The treatment of China by EU firms as a global economic frontier (and vice versa) also contributes to the ringfence perceptions of strategic competiton in Africa. The outcome will be the development of cross-investments, merger and acquisitions policies conducted by European and Chinese Transnational Corporations (TNCs) with and within Africa. This pattern may in turn generate incentive to insert interactions between China and Africa into a changing global landscape, marked by the fast-increasing socialisation of China into international norms and regimes, a trend bolstered by Chinese aspirations to global legitimacy and status.[26]

Depictions of China as a strategic competitor of the West due to its growing interest in sub-Saharan Africa's oil and natural gas resources have been more commonly voiced in North America than in Europe. This may be a result of the fact that despite China's increasing dependency on oil from Africa (30 per cent of the country's imports), its National Oil Corporations (NOCs) are still minor actors – an estimated 3 per cent of the combined commercial value of all the investments in African oil in 2006.[27] Unlike in the United States, where throughout the Bush administration, ratification of the Kyoto Protocol was fiercely rejected, the European approaches to oil dependency are encased into an overall commitment to reduce fossile energy consumption. In 2004, 37 per cent of the EU-25's total energy consumption depended on imports that essentially originated from Norway (16 per cent), Russia (27 per cent) and the Middle East (19 per cent). North Africa represented 12 per cent of EU oil imports – an incentive to the re-juvenation and deepening of EU relations with North Africa – while sub-Saharan Africa, Central Asia and South America supplied a mere 5 per cent.[28] European dependency on natural gas, which accounted for one-quarter of EU energy consumption in 2004, was expected to increase sharply within the next few years. EU domestic production covered 46 per cent of European needs in 2004 and import scenarios were pointing to an increased geo-political reliance of the EU-25 on its immediate neighbourhood – in 2005, 25 per cent of EU supplies originated from Russia, 15 per cent from Norway and14 per cent from Libya, Algeria, Nigeria and the Middle East.[29]

The only sub-Saharan African state expected to become an increasingly significant energy supplier for Europe is Nigeria due to its expanding production of Liquified Natural Gas (LNG).[30] So far, China's NOCs have shown limited activity in such a sector, unlike Russia's state-owned Gazprom, the world's biggest natural gas producer. Since Gazprom also happens to be the largest supplier of natural gas to the EU, its moves towards massive investment into the LNG industries of Nigeria and Equatorial Guinea raised particular concern among European governments when such plans were announced in January 2008.[31]

One of the short-term effects of China's fast-rising engagement in Africa is the re-introduction of a geo-strategic dimension into the continent's international relations. Strategic significance was not at stake when European and G8 aid pledges were made at Gleneagles. As the Africa plan was being launched, much of its adoption was premised on moral and caritative grounds. As a result, noted subsequently by the authors of the US bi-partisan report on Africa, '2005 was the year of Africa but we missed the point . . . that Africa is becoming more central to the United States and to the rest of the world in ways that transcend humanitarian interests.'[32]

China's government-to-government relations or de facto interactions with African states and societies challenge and undermine the (post)-Washington Consensus and the 'social, human rights and governance standards' that feed the development blueprints of Western donors and the IFIs.[33] Africa, due to its inclusion of a large group of LDCs (36 out of 53 states) with pervasive problems of state failure, along with much sought after natural resources and dependence on the EU for over half of ODA, offers an ideal turf for the surge and expression of contending norms and policy orientations towards governance and what development should be about. Perhaps for the first time since the 1960s and the heydays of Soviet influence in developing countries, 'an alternative view to what development is [about] and how to achieve it' is gradually becoming apparent.[34]

When faced with criticism of its development templates, the EU could easily respond by pointing to its active contribution to the spread of peace and prosperity within Europe, through a process of enlargement from 6 to 27 countries that has meant turning into developed economies countries previously labelled as developing. There is little doubt, however, that the EU's unique emphasis on structural reforms, adhesion to common norms, and the deepening of democracy is yet to succeed in the context of inter-hemispheric agreements that do not carry any prospects for adhesion.

In Africa, as in other parts of the world, the EU also suffers from a severe credibility gap due to its weak ability to craft and enforce policy orientations, despite its soft power and global pre-eminence as a donor and a trade bloc. The EU's peculiar institutional architecture, a mixture of inter-governmentalism with quasi-federalism and a sprinkle of consociationalism, contributes in its own way to the EU's disempowerment. Civil society, lobbying at national and regional levels, contributes to and shapes policy outputs that often achieve consensus at the expense of operational implementation. To African regimes permeated by neo-patrimonial governance, the resulting policy orientations appear far less coherent, more apt to be challenged and much less attractive than China's readiness to take short cuts on rules and procedures. Equally attractive for African leaders are the opportunities generated by China's disregard for the constraints propogated by international regimes and codes of conduct such as the Organisation for Economic Cooperation and Development's (OECD) Guidelines for Multinational Companies, the Extractive Industries Transparency Initiative (EITI) or the nascent African Forest Law Enforcement and Governance Process (AFLEG).

Discontent voiced publicly during the December 2007 Lisbon summit may be interpreted as an episode in the history of EU-Africa interactions. The conference may also be viewed as a symbolic, but no less significant, manifestation of a changing landscape due to the rise of alternative players and opportunities. The representatives of the 27 European member-states were then made aware that European policy templates in the field of trade (dismantlement of tariff protection on ACP imports) and governance (attendance of Mugabe) may have to be adjusted. More generally, it was the EU, OECD or WTO templates, with their blueprints focused on trade liberalisation and human rights that were stigmatised.[35]

The EU decision to abide, despite the strong opposition of Britain's Prime Minister Gordon Brown – who eventually boycotted the summit – to African demands that Mugabe should be invited did formally bring an end to a seven-year-old crisis. Indeed, since the adjournment *sine die* of the April 2003 Lisbon summit meeting over the issue of the invitation of the Zimbabwean president, EU-Africa dialogue had been confined to meetings between ministerial troikas. The EU's change of mind was clearly linked to the concern that the success of FOCAC should not be left unmatched. The attendance of 80 states and their adoption of an ambitious Africa-EU joint strategy for 2007–10 was, in this sense, a frank success.[36] The Lisbon summit also reflected on the ability of Europeans and Africans to discuss the substance of their relationship, a sharp contrast with China's hub-and-spoke, hand-down approach during a FOCAC summit where the African continent showed its incapacity to craft any collective response.

The Lisbon summit also stressed the need for Europeans to take into account the new margins of manoeuvre gained by African states within the international system, not least due to the lure of the 'Beijing waiver', namely China's pledge to adhere to a strict respect for the sovereignty of governments. The Lisbon summit could only be held because of the decision of the EU to take stock of new limitations to its emphasis on norms, democratisation and the 'politicisation' of agendas since the mid-term review of the Lomé IV Convention. In the process, the conference also confirmed an overall reduction of the sensitivity of African regimes to international pressure, as the ACPs' opposition to the dismantling of the tariff barriers benefiting from the 'Lomé/WTO waiver' was publicly and forcefully voiced.

CONCLUSION

A few years ago, a longstanding analyst of commodity markets concluded his survey of Africa with the remark that 'primary goods will not save Africa and, most paradoxically, we should perhaps celebrate Africa's decline in this field. With the end of the "cargo cult" from which African elites have suffered, Africa may discover, a few decades after Asia, that its true wealth resides in the men and women that inhabit it.'[37] Today, Africa, with the exception of South Africa, remains weakly integrated into the global economy, but commodity prices and investment in energy projects are fuelling economic growth and investment. The old debate on 'growth without development' that was launched by Samir Amin's study of Côte d'Ivoire seems more topical than ever.[38] Unlike what was anticipated by the Egyptian economist, the emergence of alternative templates does not stem from socialism, but from the contribution of China and other emerging economies to the global expansion and even – in the case of the sub-prime crisis in the United States – consolidation of capitalism. The promotion of international regulatory regimes, no longer associated with the tenets of socialism, has become the hallmark of industrialised countries from the North, especially the EU. For the ruling elites of Africa's commodity-exporting countries, new resources mean unprecedented opportunities for the restructuring of their economies, but this is occurring at a time when external and short-term inducements to do so have never been weaker.

Controversies over the contours, substance and trade-liberalisation agendas of the EPA groupings offer a good example of such a conundrum. The EPA controversy, like the Singapore issues during the Doha round, are a powerful reminder of the nevralgic importance of the resources associated with the control of public politics and bureaucratic processes. Prospects for trade liberalisation challenge boundaries that combine 'porosity' with strong monetary, fiscal, tariff or normative disparities. This contributes, as I have emphasised elsewhere, to survival, but also enrichment strategies that fuel the dissociation between regionalism as a project and regionalisation as a process.[39] Within Africa, the member-states of the Regional Economic Communities (RECs) have spent several decades postponing the implementation of their stated plans towards the formation of a customs union, thus conveying a tangible expression of the opportunities associated with border-management under (neo)-patrimonial rule. It is less surprising that trade liberalisation within an EU-Africa context would trigger much more open reactions of hostility.[40] The capacity of trans-border networks to permeate the territory and the institutions of African states also contributes to shaping the continent's insertion within the global economy.

There is, however, an even greater paradox with respect to the postponements observed in the effective implementation of trade liberalisation agendas within Africa's RECs or – in the case of the eleven countries not eligible to the EBA initiative and its offer of non-reciprocal trade liberalisation – the EPAs. While reducing pressure for domestic economic reforms, the preservation of tariff barriers enhances the attractiveness of the imports of more cheaply manufactured products originating from China and other emerging economies. The EU and WTO are bearing the brunt of accusations against the destructive effects of 'trade-not-aid' policy orientations, yet it is trade and investment from the Asian drivers that has been undermining Africa's domestic industries (as discussed in other chapters here).

Assumptions that fair transactions will promote pro-poor growth and sustainable development within African states often underestimate the constraints associated with the issue of fair revenue transcription. How increased resources drawn from trade, investment, aid or debt relief trickle down within societies hinges on the nature of their governance and policy orientations. In the energy- and mineral-exporting countries, the rejuvenation or decline of the 'paradox of plenty' syndrome will act as a litmus test. For a number of governments, the current thirst for Africa's commodities means new resources. It should also mean fresh commitment to undertake domestic economic reforms, promote societal change and address the implications of heavy structural dependence on the revenues of non-renewable resources. Unless these questions are substantively addressed, the intensity of global demand for the continent's resources may turn out to be little more than a hyped reincarnation of the African commodity curse.

NOTES

1. European Commission (EC), 'Communication from the Commission to the Council, the European Parliament and the European Economic and Social Committee' (Brussels: EC, 12 October 2005). http://europa.eu.int/eurlex/lex/LexUriServ/site/en/com/2005/om2005_0489en01.pdf.
2. Council of the European Union (EU), 'The EU and Africa: Towards a Strategic Partnership', Brussels, 19 December 2005. http://ec.europa.eu/development/ICenter/Pdf/the_eu_and_africa_towards_a_strategic_partnership_european_council_15_16_12_2005.pdf.
3. A. Huliaras and K. Magliveras, 'In Search of a Policy: European Union and US Reactions to the Growing Chinese Presence in Africa', *European Foreign Affairs Review* 13, 2008 (forthcoming).
4. Commission of the European Community, 'Communication from the European Commission to the European Parliament: From Cairo to Lisbon, the EU-Africa Strategic Partnership', Brussels, 27 June 2007, p. 3. http://ec.europa.eu/development/ICenter/Pdf/2007/Communication-EU-Africa-communication_357_EN.pdf.
5. U. Wissenbach, 'Partners in Competition? The EU, Africa and China'. Conference summary, Brussels, 28 June 2007, p. 1. http://ec.europa.eu/development/ICenter/Pdf/2007/partners_in_competition_Africa-china_summary-of-proceedings.pdf.
6. L. Michel, '*UE-Chine-Afrique: D'une Relation de Concurrence à un Partenariat Triangulaire pour le Développement de l'Afrique*', Brussels, 28 June 2007. http://europa.eu/rapid/pressReleasesAction.do?reference=SPEECH/07/442andformat=HTMLandaged=0andl.
7. '*Bruxelles Veut Proposer un "Partenariat" avec la Chine en Afrique*', Agence France Press, 9 January 2008; '*Partenariat UE-Chine en Afrique: Réaliste?*', *Le Soir* (Brussels), 10 January 2008, p. 18.
8. A. Wade, 'Time for the West to Practise What it Preaches', *Financial Times*, 23 January 2008.
9. K. Arts and A.K. Dickson (eds.), *EU Development Cooperation: From Model to Symbol* (Manchester and New York: Manchester University Press and Palgrave, 2004).
10. A.K. Dickinson, 'The Unimportance of Trade Preferences', in Arts and Dickson (eds.), *EU Development Cooperation*, pp. 42–59.
11. D. Bach, '*Un Ancrage à la Dérive: La Convention de Lomé*', *Revue Tiers Monde* 136, October–December 1993: 749–59.
12. See text of the Cotonou Agreement at http://www.europa.eu.int.
13. ACP trade privileges involved the combination of duty-free access for fixed quantities with purchases at heavily subsidised European market prices. See *Financial Times*, 28 October 2005, p. 6 and *Le Monde*, 26 October 2005, p. 2.
14. J. Ravenhill, 'Back to the Nest? Europe's Relations with the African, Caribbean and Pacific Group of Countries', University of California, Berkeley Institute of European Studies Working Paper 9, December 2002, p. 14.
15. EC, 'Communication from the Commission to the Council and the European Parliament towards the Full Integration of Co-operation with ACP countries in the EU Budget', COM/2003/0590 final, 8 October 2003. http://europa.eu.int/eur-lex/lex/LexUriServ/site/en/com/2003/com2003_0590en01.pdf.
16. Development Assistance Committee (DAC), *Development Co-operation Review, European Community* (Paris: Organisation for Economic Cooperation and Development (OECD), 2002), p. 220.
17. EU, 'The European Consensus on Development', 20 December 2005, p. 3.
18. See D. Bach, 'The AU and the EU?', in J. Akokpari, A. Ndinga-Muvumba and T. Murithi (eds.), *The African Union and its Institutions* (Johannesburg: Jacana, 2008), pp. 355–70.

19. In 2002–03, the number of sub-Saharan Africans in irregular situations was estimated to range between 6 000 and 15 000 in Morocco, around 2 000 in Tunisia and between 50 000 and 150 000 in Algeria. Around 1.5 million Africans from the south of the Sahara were believed to be from Libya, see M. Lahlou, '*Le Maghreb: Les Migrations des Africains du Sud du Sahara*'. Colloquium, '*Entre Protection des Droits et Mondialisation*', Casablanca: 13–15 June 2003, mimeo, p. 17. http://www.generiques.org/migrations_marocaines/interventions/Lahlou_article.pdf.
20. H. Boubakri, 'Transit Migrations between Tunisia, Libya and Sub-Saharan Africa'. Study based on Greater Tunis (Strasbourg: Council of Europe, MG-RCONF, 2004), mimeo, pp. 2–3; M. Alioua, '*La Migration Transnationale des Africains Subsahariens au Maghreb: l'Exemple de l'Etape Marocaine*', *Maghreb-Machrek*, 185, 2005: 37–38.
21. *Le Monde*, 25 June 2006, p. 6.
22. EC, 'Towards a Common European Immigration Policy', September 2007, at http://ec.europa.eu/justice_home/fsj/immigration/fsj_immigration_intro_en.htm. In 2007, it was estimated that 85 per cent of the unskilled immigrants from Africa and Asia went to the EU, against only 5 per cent to the United States, and that 55 per cent of the migrants into the United States were highly skilled, against a mere 5 per cent for Europe (*Financial Times*, 3 September 2007).
23. K. King, 'Aid within the Wider China-Africa Partnership: A View from the Beijing Summit'. Paper presented at the 'China-Africa Links' workshop, 11–12 November 2006, Hong Kong: The Hong Kong University of Science and Technology. http://www.cctr.ust.hk/china-africa/.
24. K. Hofmann et al., 'Contrasting Perceptions: Chinese, African and European Perspectives on the China-Africa Summit', *Internationale Politik und Gesellschaft* 2, 2007: 75. http://www.fes.de/ipg/inhalt_d/pdf/07_Hofmann_US.pdf.
25. A. Sindzingre, 'Trade Structure as a Constraint to Multilateral and Regional Arrangements in Sub-Saharan Africa: The WTO and the African Union', GARNET second annual meeting, 18–19 September, 2007, p. 10.
26. In December 2007, China symbolically shifted from its past status as a beneficiary to that of contributor to the International Development Agency (IDA) of the World Bank. Characteristically, this contribution to what resulted in an unprecedented increase of IDA funding for the 2008–11 period (US$41.6 billion) was also interpreted as a reassertion of the World Bank's global legitimacy by the 45 contributors (*Le Monde*, 27 December 2007, p. 11).
27. E. Downs, 'The Fact and Fiction of Sino-African Energy Relations', *China Security* 3(3), Summer 2007: 44.
28. EC, 'A European Strategy for Sustainable, Competitive and Secure Energy', annex to the Green Paper, staff working document, SEC 317/2, p. 19 (Brussels, 2006). http://www.ec.europa.eu/energy/green-paper-energy/doc/2006_03_08_gp_working_document_en.pdf.
29. EC, 'A European Strategy', p. 24.
30. *The Petroleum Economist*, May 2007, p. 15; *Oil and Gas Journal*, 9 July 2007, pp. 60–62.
31. D. Mahtani and M. Green, 'Gazprom Nigeria Move Bodes Ill for the West', *Financial Times*, 6 January 2008. Already in 2006, European concern at the possibility of a coordination of the investment and pricing policies of major gas-exporting countries was triggered by the signature of a memorandum of understanding on cooperation in upstream activities between Gazprom and Algeria's Sonatrach.
32. Council on Foreign Relations (CFR), *More than Humanitarianism: A Strategic Approach to US Interest in Africa* (Washington, DC: CFR, 2006), p. 5. For a denunciation of Europe's moralising representations of Africa, see L. Michel, '*Europe-Afrique: L'Indispensable Partenariat*', European Policy Centre, speech 07/782 (Brussels, 30 November 2007).

33. D. Messner, 'The European Union: Protagonist in a Multilateral World Order or Peripheral Power in the Asia-Pacific Century?' *Internationale Politik und Gesellschaft* 1, 2007: 25. http://www.fes.de/ipg/arc_07_d/01_07_d/pdf/03_A_Messner_GB.pdf. See also J. Humphrey and D. Messner, 'China and India as Emerging Global Governance Actors: Challenges for Developing and Developed Countries', *IDS Bulletin* 37(1), January 2006: 107–14.
34. Humphrey and Messner, 'China and India as Emerging Global Governance Actors', 109.
35. As violence spread in Kenya in the aftermath of the December 2007 elections, China's *People's Daily*, the Communist Party's newspaper, observed that 'Western-style democratic theory simply isn't suited to African conditions, but rather carries with it the root of disaster.' (Associated Press, 14 January 2008)
36. See http://www.ec.europa.eu/development/icenter/repository/EAS2007_joint_strategy_en.pdf#zoom=100.
37. P. Chalmin, '*L'Afrique et la Malédiction des Matières Premières*', *Marchés Tropicaux et Méditerranéens* 9 May 2003: 1 001.
38. S. Amin, *Le Développement du Capitalisme en Côte d'Ivoire* (Paris: Editions de Minuit, 1967).
39. D. Bach (ed.), *Regionalisation in Africa: Integration and Disintegration* (London: James Currey, 1999).
40. D. Bach, 'New Regionalism as an Alias: Regionalisation through Trans-State Networks', in J.A. Grant and F. Söderbaum (eds.), *New Regionalism in Africa* (Aldershot: Ashgate, 2003), pp. 21–30.

16

The Ideological, Political and Economic Imperatives in China and Japan's Relations with Africa

Kweku Ampiah

INTRODUCTION

It is popularly believed in diplomatic and business circles in Japan that former Japanese Prime Minister Junichiro Koizumi's trip to Africa in March 2006 was in direct response to Chinese President Hu Jintao's tour of the continent in February of that year. If this is even remotely true, then Koizumi's trip could be seen as a reaction to concerns in Tokyo that 'a familiar rival, China, seems to be gaining the upper hand in Africa',[1] not least because 'China seems to be outdoing Japan in forging closer economic relations – and increasing influence – with Africa'.[2] As if to confirm Japan's concerns, the country's Chief Cabinet Secretary, Yasuhisa Shiozaki, has welcomed China's support for the development of Africa, but in the same breath invoked the need for the application of international standards and transparency in China's international economic assistance.[3] Yasuhisa Shiozaki's comment was a riposte to the establishment of the China-Africa Development Fund (CADF) in June 2007, and the censure in his words was, rather transparently, a parody of the West's anxieties about China's expanding relations with Africa, as were Japanese Prime Minister Shinzo Abe's comments (earlier) about China's failure to live up to international standards of democracy, with regard to the crisis in Darfur.[4] Suffice to say, these recent developments in Sino-Japanese interests in Africa testify to how the region has become the focus of attention for China, and perhaps also point to the differences in how the two East-Asian countries relate to and deal with issues about sub-Saharan Africa. Such differences may be attributable to the experiences, thoughts and sensibilities of the policy-makers of these two East-Asian countries who are so close (geographically), and yet so far apart in the way they perceive and respond to world events.

The principles of the rationality of the foreign policy behaviour of the state can be located, as Michel Foucault would argue, primarily 'in that which constitutes the specific reality of the state'.[5] Invariably, this determines and guides the national interests of the state. The specific reality of the state would also include, however idiosyncratic the state might be, the responsibility of working with and within the prevailing discourses of international politics; after all, 'practices don't exist without a certain regime of rationality'.[6] The 'regime of rationality is historically rooted; and . . . it works as a structure of knowledge, allowing, at any particular time, certain events and patterns of agency . . . and rendering unthinkable, unsayable, and undoable others . . .'[7] As Steven Levine's analysis of Chinese foreign policy attests, the application of the professional approach to foreign relations by the specialists in China's foreign affairs system 'was based in part on the mastery of empirical knowledge and reflected a degree of cosmopolitanism that had been acquired through experience as well as specialised education and in-service training'.[8] This, as Suisheng Zhao also argues earlier in Chapter 3, implies structural constraints and therefore, to some extent, a submission to the hegemonic discourse. Thus, however striking the differences between Japan and China's relations with Africa might be, they will also, invariably, include moments and points of convergence in the attitudes and outcomes of their initiatives towards the region, if only because they both operate within the forms of rationality that have inscribed themselves in the system and practices of international relations.

This chapter investigates the policies of the People's Republic of China (PRC) and Japan towards sub-Saharan Africa by, first, engaging the principles of the rationality determining their respective attitudes towards the region. By also relating the determinants of their foreign policy behaviour to their modern history, the chapter attempts to map out the trajectory of China and Japan's engagements with sub-Saharan Africa during and after the Cold-War era. It shows that China's relations with Africa have experienced a profound transformation since the 1990s, notably as a result of its recent economic initiatives in the region. Japan's engagements with the region have also changed since the same period, but only slightly. At the same time, certain decisive patterns of behaviour in the way the two countries relate to Africa endure. Underlying the respective attitudes of these countries towards Africa are two contrasting patterns of behaviour: while China, perhaps in respect of the principle of state sovereignty (based on the Five Principles of Peaceful Coexistence),[9] seems determined to manage its relations with the African countries through the bilateral arrangements it has with them without recourse to an external power, Japan is content with instrumentalising its foreign policy objectives with regard to Africa through working with dominant powers. We shall, for now, concentrate on the principles of the rationality of the foreign policies of China and Japan and how these might have impacted on their relations with Africa. The first and most important point for consideration in our analysis would be how the foreign policies of these two Asian giants have been influenced and shaped by the cadences of the Cold War, as well as the changes brought about by the post-Cold-War era.

As Foucault reminds us, history is the descriptive analysis and theory of political transformations.[10] Consequently, it is through history that we can properly understand the given forces that transformed China from a fractured semi-colonial entity into a consummate communist state, and Japan from a colonial power into a neutered ally of the United States after the Second World War. The creation of the PRC under the leadership of the Chinese Communist Party (CCP) in 1949, on the one hand, and the establishment of the United States-Japan alliance in 1951 following Japan's defeat in the Pacific war in 1945, on the other hand, set the tone for our analysis of how these two Asian countries initiated and managed their relations with Africa after the war. The other historical factor that brings yet another measure of profundity to our study is the issue and process of the decolonisation of Africa, and how these two countries respectively responded to it. It is worth stating that the different responses of China and Japan to this most momentous event in the history of the region also derived from the fact that Japan had been a colonial power, while China was a victim of imperial ruthlessness.

THE COLD-WAR ERA

The transformation of China into a communist state occurred just two years before Japan was confirmed as an ally of the United States in 1951, thereby locking Beijing and Tokyo in yet another conflict, although this time it was essentially ideological and an aspect of the Cold War. It was within this context that both China and Japan attended the Asian-African (Bandung) Conference of 1955. Not surprisingly, Japan's leaders agonised about participating in a conference organised by Asian countries that had been victims of Japanese imperialist and aggressive foreign policies. The leadership of the PRC, on the other hand, was delighted that China had been invited to join the newly independent states of Asia and Africa in celebration of their independence, in condemnation of colonialism and imperialism, and in their attempts to redefine the existing structure of international politics. For its part, China hoped to transmute the occasion into a searching drama of historical revelations and crises – essentially to take advantage of the event to expose the United States' attempts to 'undermine the hard won sovereignty of the PRC'; and to radicalise the Afro-Asian states' collective intolerance of imperialism. Most importantly, the PRC saw the conference as an opportunity for China to forge coalitions with the Asian and African countries, 'for even though the Chinese people had [finally] stood up, they could not remain standing alone or unaided': they had to find allies.[11] Overall, the Chinese leadership was determined to avail itself of the opportunities that the conference might offer to lead the moral crusade against the West, and as a corollary, to take a leadership role in the struggle of the (poor) South against the (rich) North.[12] In essence, China was eager to serve as the defiant head of a 'household' of politically invigorated Third World countries.[13]

Beijing's contribution to the conference was indicative of a country that was stirred by a defiant knowledge of its self-worth, inspired in the main by its glorious period of vitality after the Pacific war and its own domestic war. With the huge reserves of optimism and faith in the ingenuity of Marxist-Leninism and Maoist thought, China initiated a vigorous foreign policy that was driven more by political values, as 'ideology provided a general framework within which CCP leaders could analyse foreign relations'.[14]

Ever determined to establish a strident voice in international politics, China hurled itself, seemingly blithely, into confrontation with the 'imperialist powers', and subsequently with the revisionists of the Soviet Union. At the same time, it was possible for China to recalibrate to circumstances, and it did so effectively by fine-tuning its *Weltanschauung* 'into a set of abstract principles and behavioural norms' that were used flexibly in its relations with other countries. The Five Principles of Peaceful Coexistence, as part of its informal ideology, was one of the pliable tools for Chinese foreign policy, argues Steven Levine.[15] Thus, at the Bandung Conference, Zhou Enlai tried to stitch together the anxieties of the African and Asian countries about Western imperialism and China's ideological contests with the United States. At the same time, China was whipping up support among the Third World against the United States' 'intrusion' into its 'domestic' affairs – a reference to the conflict between the PRC and the Taiwanese separatists. By constantly invoking the Five Principles of Peaceful Coexistence as a guideline for China's relations with the Third World, and intuiting the needs and aspirations of the poor peoples of the world even before those needs were formulated, by the mid-1950s Beijing had become a credible leader within the Afro-Asian community of states.

Conversely, Japan was surviving on a coarse parody of independence, as a result of the United States' encroachments on its foreign policy. Unlike China's, Japan's foreign policy was, in general, inarticulate, in part because it was predicated on self-doubt, repentance and contrition. Thus, Japan ventured rather reticently onto the world stage, and in relation to Africa, Tokyo chose to operate reclusively behind the hegemonic powers, in particular the United Kingdom and the United States. Yet, desperate for a more independent foreign policy and determined to improve relations with its neighbours, Japan accepted the invitation to attend the Bandung Conference. Interestingly, for the less conservative administration of Prime Minister Hatoyama Ichiro, which seemed to have been affected by the neutralist vogue of the period, Japan saw in the conference an opportunity for it to underline a more independent foreign policy position vis-à-vis Japan's chief ally, the United States, and attempt to reintegrate itself fully into the Asian community.[16]

If Beijing was motivated by primeval political ambitions, Tokyo's primary aim was to build its economy on an epic scale, and through that to establish and amplify a role for Japan in international affairs. The importance of Southeast Asia to these calculations was enormous, precisely because the region contained some of the strategic natural resources that Japan needed to build its economy.[17] In that sense, the conference was also a means for striking business deals with the countries in the region. Attendance at the conference was also viewed among Japanese policy-makers as potentially capable of kick-starting Japan's leadership role in the region. Even so, Japan was somewhat divorced from the political imperatives of the conference, and as a result Japanese policy-makers warned against giving succour to the conference's anti-colonialist agenda since this 'could [negatively] affect our relations with the colonial powers'.[18] Despite the government's efforts to reclaim an independent foreign policy, 'above all else [Tokyo had] to reach a proper understanding with the US about participating in the Conference', since the State Department was nervous about the event, in view of China's role in it. Relevant to this is our point concerning Japanese modes of instrumentalising foreign policy objectives through working with dominant powers, a modern rendition of a traditional diplomacy – *nagai mono ni wa makarero*.[19] Even at the height of the decolonisation process and despite the Bandung Conference's emphasis on ending colonialism in all its manifestations, Japan, in its eagerness to rekindle its economic relations with Africa in the early 1960s, chose to join forces with the United Kingdom in what was known as 'the Anglo-Japanese Collaboration about Africa'.[20] In that sense, Japan failed its commitment to the spirit of Bandung.

CHINA'S INITIATIVES TOWARDS AFRICA

China, meanwhile, approached the African states directly, and certainly not through the medium of a former colonial power, thus confirming its ideological stance and determination to forge independent relations with the newly liberated and sovereign states of Africa. Previous chapters in this volume have confirmed the extent of China's commitment to the decolonisation of Africa, not to mention programmes for the region's economic development, although the prominent aspects of its initiatives in this regard were confined to a few countries.

The economic assistance to the selected African countries from the 1960s were naturally conceived to build up Beijing's popularity in the region, at the same time as they were designed to make the African countries less dependent on China's main adversaries, the United States and the Soviet Union. Thus, while in theory the broad formula of its assistance to the African states rested on the principle of the sovereignty of the recipient state, and non-alignment of the African states, in reality Beijing 'attempted to induce the African states to accept fully [its] world view and major policy objectives'.[21] Consequently, we have to regard Chinese aid during this period as a political tactic, a 'technique possessing [its] own specificity in the more general field of exercising power',[22] as Foucault might put it. As one might expect, however, no African country took China's advice to reject Western aid and other forms of economic assistance from Eastern Europe seriously, not least because the African states meant to diversify their external relations as much as possible, with the view to gaining, even if through an act of dalliance, from as many donors as possible.[23] Consequently, during his first visit to China in 1965, President Julius Nyerere of Tanzania made it abundantly clear to his hosts that Tanzania insisted on maintaining its independence in international affairs: 'We offer the hand of friendship to China as to America, Russia, Britain and others . . . The fears of others will not affect Tanzania's friendship with China any more than our friendship with other countries will be affected by what their opponents say of them.' [24]

All the same, the African governments failed on the principle of sovereignty and non-interference in one particular respect: most of them allowed Beijing to influence them on the issue of its One-China policy.[25]

Throughout most of the second half of the twentieth century, China managed to render its national interests and those of the African countries more identifiable by highlighting their common anti-colonial and anti-imperialist heritage in its foreign policy and Cold-War agenda.[26] Hence we could argue that within the context of the aims and objectives of the spirit of Bandung, Chinese foreign policy towards Africa was consistently *inclusive*.

JAPANESE ENGAGEMENTS WITH AFRICA: THE DYNAMICS OF A SPLIT BEHAVIOUR

While China was enchanted with the political gains it accrued from the Sino-African solidarity, Japan was enthralled, if vaguely, by the continent in quite a different sense: the perceived mercantilist opportunities that lay waiting in the region to be 'harvested'. Japan's attempts to 'collaborate' with the United Kingdom with regard to Africa were alluded to earlier; they were aimed, essentially at gaining access to the markets and natural resources in the region. Indeed, by the mid-1960s, Japan had accumulated huge trade surpluses vis-à-vis some of Africa's major markets, notably Nigeria, Kenya and Ghana.[27] The enormous balance-of-payments differential between Japan and the two West African countries led to some intense and acrimonious negotiations between Tokyo and the governments in Lagos and Accra, as a result of which a few Japanese manufacturing firms were established in Nigeria (in particular) in the 1960s and 1970s, to circumvent the imposition of sanctions on Japanese exports to the country. However, such investments did not last beyond the 1980s.[28] From then on, Japanese policy-makers systematically and perennially spoke of the huge geographical distance between Japan and Africa as a fundamental reason for the lack of more constructive economic relations between Tokyo and the African states. Incidentally, however, roughly the same geographical distance has not deterred China from expanding its economic initiatives into Africa in recent times.

Evidently in pursuance of certain strategic raw materials, Tokyo systematically expanded trade and economic relations with South Africa throughout the 1970s and 1980s, even as the global anti-apartheid campaigns were at their peak. The contribution of Japanese companies to the Sishen-Saldanha Bay Development Project in the early 1970s confirmed the extent of the economic relations between Tokyo and Pretoria.[29] Exasperated by Japan's behaviour, at a press conference to commemorate the tenth anniversary of the Organisation of African Unity (OAU) in May 1973, the Ethiopian ambassador to Tokyo, representing the African diplomats, warned Tokyo against supporting the apartheid regime: 'We expect Japan as an Asian nation to give its political support to the struggle against the [minority] regimes . . .', he pontificated. In a rather belligerent tone, he announced: 'All the other Asian countries . . . have supported us and I warn you that Japan will be isolated from the Afro-Asian group unless it joins us now.'[30] The threat strategy did not work: Tokyo became South Africa's largest trade partner in both 1981 and 1983, and in the latter year, the magnitude of the trade between the two countries stood at US$3.325 billion, which was larger than Japan's trade with France (at US$3.312 billion) in the same year.[31] As such, Japan stood out among the Afro-Asian bloc of countries at the UN General Assembly by consistently abstaining, during the 1970s and 1980s, from voting on sensitive anti-apartheid resolutions, evidently because it wanted to protect its economic interests in South Africa. After all, Tokyo depended on Pretoria for strategic resources, such as iron ore, chromium, platinum and uranium. In that sense, Japan's responses to the South African problem were heavily dictated by the hegemonic stance orchestrated by the United States and the other Western countries, which insisted on a diplomatic approach to sorting out the problem in South Africa, a policy that invariably kept the apartheid regime very much alive.

While operating a policy of almost total abstinence in regard to the political situation in Africa, Japan at the same time tried to alleviate the self-inflicted diplomatic predicament engendered by its economic ties with South Africa by cultivating, through its aid policies, good relations with the leading front-line African states.[32] When, in 1987, to its dismay, it emerged again as South Africa's leading trade partner (a fact that this time blasted Tokyo's love affair with Pretoria into the open), it was hounded by the international media for giving succour to the apartheid regime. This unhinged the (intuitive rather than cerebral) attempts by Japan's post-war policy-makers to separate economics from politics (*seikei bunri*, an orthodoxy that was grafted onto post-war Japanese foreign policy) in their country's relations with Africa, making the policy intractable. If anything, it succeeded only in confirming that Japan was operating a dual diplomacy towards Africa: supporting the minority white regimes of southern Africa, on the one hand, and mollifying the OAU member-states, on the other hand. Effectively, this confirmed how divorced Japan was from the political and moral imperatives of the Bandung Conference, indicating, in essence, that within the constructs of the ideals of the Afro-Asian community of states, Japan was pursuing what might well be referred to as a unilateralist foreign policy.

THE POST-COLD-WAR ERA

As the Cold War ended and the political climate in Africa took on what purported to be a new lease of life, the attitudes of both China and Japan towards the region also started to change, although it might be appropriate to suggest that the changes in China's attitude to the region were equally, if not more, attributable to transformations within China itself. The end of the Maoist era and the opening up of the country from the 1980s, not to mention the changes in the formula for its economic development, had already initiated a revision and readjustment of China's relations with Africa well before the transformations brought about by the end of the Cold War.

Japan's revised attitude towards Africa: The Tokyo International Conference on African Development

The changes in the political landscape of Africa (in part as a result of the closure that was brought to the issue of minority rule in southern Africa) forced Japan to reconfigure its relations with African countries in terms that suggested that it was prepared to take African issues more seriously than it had done in the past. Previously, economic interests predicated Japan's relations with Africa, while it systematically de-emphasised the political implications of its economic engagements with the region. Concerns for Africa's economic development were equally lacking in Japan's relations with the region, even as it ceremoniously gave aid to selected African states. The Tokyo International Conference on African Development (TICAD), which the Japanese government launched in 1993, however, testifies to a shift in Japan's attitude towards Africa. The change in attitude is, symbolically at least, demonstrated by the visit of two incumbent Japanese prime ministers, Yoshiro Mori (in 2001) and Koizumi (in 2006), to the region, whereas no Japanese prime minister in office had visited Africa before 2001.

Consequently, with TICAD – defined as a forum for international consultations about the socio-economic problems of Africa – Japan stepped on stage and into visibility, as it were, and affirmed its interest in African issues.[33] Yet Japan still seems to be applying the old formula of working not so much with the African states (despite the rhetoric) as with the major powers and multilateral institutions, the 'development partners'. The indications are that Tokyo cannot seem to deviate from the prevailing development paradigm, even though it funds every aspect of the TICAD process. Basically, TICAD defines, in a form of corpus of knowledge and rules, a way of governance, accounting and production that conforms to the manifestos, prescriptions and forecasts of the hegemonic development discourse, in the parlance of the neo-liberal formula for development. Yet, to further paraphrase Foucault, the trend proposes, in the form of a regimen, a 'voluntary' and rational structure of conduct seemingly in support of the concept of African ownership of its own development initiatives.[34] The idea of ownership, as stipulated in paragraph 5 of the Tokyo Declaration of African Development in TICAD I of 1993, affirms that 'political, economic and social reforms must be initiated and carried out by African countries themselves, based on their visions, values and individual socio-economic background'. The Tokyo Agenda for Action of TICAD II of 1998 further affirms, in paragraph 9, that 'the 1995 Cairo Agenda for Action . . . defines the economic and social development priorities for Africa as determined by Africa itself . . .' and proceeds to confirm that 'ownership is derived when development priorities, as set by Africa, are pursued'. The Draft Yokohama Declaration of TICAD IV of May 2008 further stresses 'the importance for Africa exercising full "ownership" as the "developmental state" of its own development agenda . . .'[35]

In theory, then, Tokyo urges African self-reliance, which is not unlike China's position on Africa's development. At the same time, the Japanese concept of 'African ownership' seems to contrast with China's policy of 'non-intervention', not least because, unlike China, Japan is seemingly content with inviting all the 'development partners' to participate in the conceived development of Africa. Thus, as with previous TICAD declarations, we find in the above-mentioned Yokohama Declaration a statement to the effect that 'while acknowledging that Africans are the agents for the development of the African continent', there is also recognition of 'the need for Africa's many development partners to work together with individual countries . . . to actively strive for greater synergy and effective coordination between and among existing and future initiatives in support of African development'. In their proposals for TICAD IV, however, the members of the African Diplomatic Corps in Tokyo assert that the 'the process and the entire manner in which it operates requires revamping so as to more fully reflect the "partnership" ideals on which it rests'.[36]

Certainly, the role of the 'partners' in the development process itself is a laudable idea (in principle) but African policy-makers seem to have a problem with the concept of 'partnership' and indeed with its operationalisation. They insist that 'Africa must become a true partner in the process – fully consulted and fully engaged at all stages and in all relevant aspects'; and they note that 'this is the essence of the partnership we seek'. Seemingly frustrated, they express their dissatisfaction about the fact that '. . . notwithstanding our frequent expressions of concern, it is an unfortunate fact that the African Diplomatic Corps in Tokyo has hitherto been largely "absent" in terms of the preparation of the substance of TICAD – and in the monitoring and evaluation of the overall process'. This, in essence, calls into question the whole concept of African ownership with regard to the TICAD process. In effect, the concept of partnership as enshrined in the TICAD process is yet to be fully implemented. As the diplomats put it, 'the . . . process has yet to adequately reflect its own fundamental principle of genuine "ownership and partnership" '.[37]

Not surprisingly, therefore, after admitting that 'when TICAD was launched, in 1993, it was a unique Forum, and alone in its focus on African developmental issues', the Zimbabwean Ambassador to Tokyo, Stuart H. Comberbach, expressed some concerns about the process.[38] He stated that TICAD, in contrast to other Asia-based, Africa-focused fora, 'has been far more discreet in style and more modest in terms of its measurable impact – specifically with regard to its trade and investment promotion initiatives'. His point was that TICAD is devoid of an action-oriented approach: 'an approach which focuses heavily on concrete outcomes – and most specifically in the promotion and facilitation of trade and investment flows with Africa'. Indeed, although the overriding goals of TICAD II were economic growth and poverty reduction, as we contemplate the almost fifteen-year role of TICAD in the dynamics of Africa's political economy, we cannot help but agree with Ambassador Comberbach that it has essentially played the role of what he called a 'developmental software' – with primary concentration of effort in the field of social development: the environment, gender, democracy, poverty reduction, education, health and nutrition, etc.

While accepting that 'it is difficult . . . to make an accurate or detailed evaluation of the TICAD process and its effectiveness . . . on the ground . . . in terms of producing or facilitating progress towards sustainable African development . . .', the African ambassadors in Tokyo confirm Comberbach's views. They note, for example, that 'measured against the broader yardstick of the Millennium Development Goals, it is not clear that the TICAD process has met Africa's expectations – in terms of making a significant impact in driving or progressing sustainable development on the continent'.[39] Another of their indictments against the process is that 'TICAD's limited effectiveness on the ground reflects, in part, Japan's own approach to the continent – strong in terms of social development, but limited in the sector of economic development'. Consequently, Japan's paradigm of economic development in Africa seems to have been shaped (since the 1990s) more by a certain 'theology' (which the Japanese government itself may not believe in, given Japan's own history of state-centred, trade- and investment-oriented economic development) that masquerades as economics. In the process, TICAD has paid far less attention to economic development and trade and investment flows between Japan and Africa remain insignificant. Africa's share of Japan's total imports has not changed significantly in the last fifteen years: in 1990, 2000 and 2005, the region's share was 1.8 per cent, 1.0 per cent and 1.4 per cent respectively.[40] In 2004 and 2005, sub-Saharan Africa's share of the Japanese market was US$8.3 billion and US$9.4 billion in value, and 5.9 and 5.3 in percentage terms, respectively (see Table 16.1).[41] As demonstrated in Figure 16.1, Japan's overall trade with Africa totalled US$16 billion in 2005, and was approximately 2 per cent of Japan's international trade.[42] Regarding investments, Tokyo seems to be serving the role of an observer to the significant inflows of foreign direct investment (FDI) into Africa from the other Asian countries.[43]

In 2000, Africa accounted for 0.1 per cent of total outward FDI from Japan.[44] Between 2002 and 2004, Japanese FDI in sub-Saharan Africa amounted to just US$415 million, which is roughly 0.4 per cent of Japan's total FDI of US$108.5 billion during the period. Japanese investments in Africa were still below 1 per cent of the total figure in 2004,[45] and 85 per cent of the investment in Africa was concentrated in two countries: Liberia and South Africa, with the former accounting for virtually 50 per cent of all current Japanese investments in the region. It is also important to note that the Japanese investments in Liberia are mainly concerned with Japanese ships using the Liberian flag of convenience and are, therefore, simply a matter of legal convenience, rather than development promotion and wealth creation. Effectively, Japan's economic engagement with Africa even since TICAD has been and remains putatively uneventful.

So far, the only discernible and predictable long-term goal in Japan's relations with Africa seems to be TICAD and more of the same, suggesting that Japanese policy-makers are perhaps more interested in the idea of TICAD than in what it was actually designed to achieve.

Africa within the context of China's economic boom

If Japan, through TICAD, resurrected the debate about Africa's socio-economic malaise in the 1990s, China's recent economic initiatives in the region have rekindled questions about the persistent economic marginalisation of Africa. As discussed by Garth le Pere in Chapter 2 earlier, it has also generated profound interest among Africans and African policy-makers about the benefits that the 'strategic partnership' between China and Africa could bring to the region. Apparently, China 'hopes to stimulate African economies and thereby increase the demand for Chinese products'.[46] In other words, Africa is important as a market for China's burgeoning manufacturing economy, in the same way, perhaps, as Southeast Asia was to Japan from the 1960s to the 1980s. In addition (as Japan did with Southeast Asia), China is also importing large quantities of raw materials from several countries in Africa, with its growing dependence on a number of these countries for oil being currently the most prominent aspect of its commercial interactions with the continent. As the indicators show, oil alone represented 71 per cent of the region's exports to China in 2006,[47] followed by metal-ferrous ore, which accounted for 13 per cent. This is boosting Chinese FDI into Africa, particularly to the sources of these raw materials, such as Angola, Sudan, Nigeria and Gabon.

Between 1979 and 2002, almost 10 per cent of Chinese FDI went to Africa, and 'in 2004 they [came to] more than $900 million of the total $15 billion in FDI received by Africa'. Chinese official sources have also noted that in the first ten months of 2005 'Chinese companies invested a total of $175 million in African countries, primarily on oil exploration projects and infrastructure'.[48] China's FDI stock in Africa had reached US$1.6 billion by 2005, in contrast to Japan, with Chinese companies present in 48 African countries,[49] although Africa still accounts for only 3 per cent of China's outward FDI. For sub-Saharan Africa, the figure was US$976.9 million for the same year. It is pertinent to note that a huge share of these investments (more than US$700 million), was made in 2004 and 2005, and that this does not take into account the US$2.7 billion investment commitment made by the Chinese state-controlled energy company, China National Offshore Oil Cooperation (CNOOC) Ltd, to a 45 per cent stake in a Nigerian oil field in 2006.[50] Although the bulk of China's FDI in the region is, like Japan's, concentrated in a small number of countries, it is, unlike those of its neighbour,

Table 16.1 Sub-Saharan Africa's principal trading partners (US$ billions and market share).

	2004	% share	2005	% share
Imports				
China	9.9	6.9	13.4	7.7
Germany	10.7	7.4	11.7	6.7
France	9.8	6.8	10.8	6.2
United States	8.5	5.9	10.3	5.9
United Kingdom	7.4	5.1	8.1	4.7
Japan	5.7	4.0	6.3	3.6
Italy	4.0	2.8	4.8	2.8
Spain	2.0	1.4	2.4	1.4
Total EU	47.7	33.0	54.3	31.3
Exports				
United States	37.8	27.1	52.4	29.6
China	14.5	10.4	19.3	10.9
United Kingdom	11.3	8.1	12.6	7.1
Japan	8.3	5.9	9.4	5.3
Spain	7.0	5.0	9.1	5.2
France	7.0	5.0	8.6	4.8
Germany	6.3	4.5	7.1	4.0
Italy	5.4	3.9	6.3	3.6
Total EU	50.6	36.2	61.0	34.4

Source: Derived from IMF *Direction of Trade Statistics Yearbook*, 2006

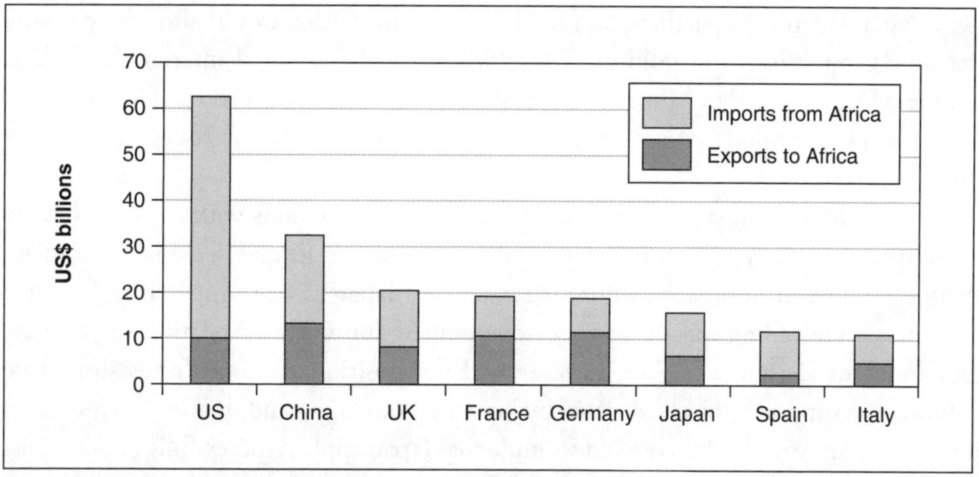

Figure 16.1 Africa's principal trading partners, 2005.

at least oriented towards economic development. Whether these would be supported, augmented and stimulated in the medium and long term to contribute to sustainable economic growth in Africa certainly remains to be seen.

Meanwhile, as noted previously in other chapters, there is widespread media and international criticism of China's engagement with Africa. A constant refrain against China in this regard is that it is undermining the agency of good governance in Africa; and its economic assistance to the African states is not transparent enough, as was intimated by Japan's Chief Cabinet Secretary, Yasuhisa Shiozaki. Masato Kitera, the Director-General for African Affairs (Ministry of Foreign Affairs, Japan), was also recently quoted as saying that China bankrolls rogue states in Africa 'and doesn't cooperate with other donor counties'.[51] There is also no doubt that China's economic assistance to Africa is choreographed to achieve certain foreign-policy objectives, like, for example, the attempt to influence African states against Japan's bid for a permanent seat at the UN Security Council.[52] Through the Forum on China-Africa Cooperation (FOCAC) China has also been reinforcing African support for its One-China policy.[53] It is also worth recalling, however, that Tokyo has been criticised for using TICAD to consolidate certain national interests, including its bid for a permanent seat at the UN Security Council.[54] There is, therefore, concern that since Chinese foreign policy is now essentially propelled by pragmatism, Beijing will exploit Africa's natural resources in pursuance of its national objective of rising up and retrieving its past glory.[55] As with Japan regarding apartheid South Africa, it seems China would also conveniently separate economics from politics, if that will serve the national interest. Indeed, as Chinese Deputy Foreign Minister, Zhou Wenzhong, argued in defence of his country's strong economic bonds with Sudan: 'Business is business . . . We try to separate politics from business.'[56]

Interestingly, China's idea of mutual benefit in its relations with Africa is having an impact in policy circles in Japan, with some policy leaders seeking to emulate Beijing's 'win-win' approach as a useful strategy for Japan as well. Apparently, Japanese 'businesses are calling for a private sector-oriented approach [in relation to Japanese development assistance]'. They have argued the position that 'aid funds should be allocated to support projects initiated by Japanese companies and thus lead to increased investment in Africa'. This is an old formula that Japan applied successfully in Southeast Asia throughout the 1970s and 1980s. Most importantly, it is an idea that has been perennially raised by African leaders in the context of Japan's relations with the region. The operative phrase that African governments have consistently invoked in their negotiations with the donors and particularly Japan is 'trade not aid.' As Kitera concedes, 'Industrialization is the main interest of African leaders'. Apparently, the idea of the private-sector-oriented approach to aid with regard to Africa is seemingly gathering support within the government, which 'hopes to use aid to prod Japanese companies to invest more in Africa'.[57] If this is so, then it is conceivably because the Japanese government and business community are keen to contest China's expansion into Africa. In that context, it is noteworthy that Tokyo has invited Beijing to participate in TICAD IV, but whether China will accept the invitation remains to be seen. Incidentally, however, Japan's official development assistance is in decline again: Japan slipped into fifth place among the aid donors,[58] as its official development assistance plunged by 30 per cent from 2006, leaving officials of the (Japanese) Ministry of Foreign Affairs at a loss, in terms of finding the appropriate responses to counteract China's expanding 'resource diplomacy' in Africa. One of the main agenda items at the forthcoming TICAD IV will be how to accelerate and ensure sustainable growth through infrastructure development, investment and trade. How Japan's policy-makers respond to these issues is what really matters.

CONCLUSION

While in the Cold-War era, China was contesting for diplomatic space and influence in Africa with the major powers, Japanese foreign policy towards Africa was exercised from an aloof distance and not through active participation in the affairs of the region.

This was, in part, because of Japan's attitude of instrumentalising foreign-policy objectives through working with dominant powers. At the same time, and as dictated by the specific reality of the state – the pursuance of economic growth – Tokyo established strong economic ties with South Africa against the stipulations of the Afro-Asian community.

The transformations in international politics engendered by the end of the Cold War have ensured a new rationality in Japan's perception of the African situation, leading to an inherent change in its attitude towards sub-Saharan Africa. The outcome of this is TICAD, which has broadened the range of Tokyo's engagement with the region. The TICAD process has 'certainly contributed towards raising and maintaining awareness of the myriad challenges facing Africa and in helping to bring Africa and Asia closer'.[59] Paradoxically, however, through TICAD, Tokyo has reconfirmed its attitude of dealing with African issues via the dominant powers – the development partners in this case. Although the discourse of TICAD extols and promises African ownership of its own development initiatives, the indications are that this has so far proved to be empty rhetoric. The partnership between Tokyo and African states has not moved beyond the relationship between the aid donor and the aid recipient. In effect, Tokyo's relations with the region are, essentially, predicated on 'aid' instead of trade and investment. Beijing, on the other hand, although equally propelled by a principle of rationality that is premised on economic gains and prestige, is progressively transforming its economic assistance to African states into viable commercial entities. As such, its policy statements emphasise mutual (economic) benefits, in contrast to the one-way aid operations that were characteristic of Sino-African relations during the Maoist era. Thus, while China's new initiatives towards the region are seemingly empowering the African states economically, TICAD remains a promising 'developmental software' and modest in its achievements.

Another engaging difference between Beijing and Tokyo in their respective relations with African countries is that Tokyo has taken to giving instructions to the African states, among other things, about 'good governance', 'human rights', 'accountability' and 'transparency', and thereby instituted conditions on its economic assistance to the region.[60] Conversely, China has refrained from the didactic approach in its relations with Africa, sticking to its proverbial policy of non-intervention in the affairs of sovereign states. In relation to Sudan and Zimbabwe, for example, Beijing has ignored the international criticism of these countries' human rights' records, and side-stepped demands for sanctions against them. In this particular respect, China and Japan seem to have traded places: as with Japan regarding apartheid South Africa, China has attempted to de-emphasise the political implications of its economic relations with Sudan, for example, and is purporting to separate economics from politics. The similarity in attitude between China and Japan in this regard – even if in different eras – is striking, and it goes to show that nation-states operate essentially within the constraints of national interests. It is, therefore, tempting to suggest that China's glorified policy of non-interference is merely rhetorical, self-serving and intrinsically flawed. After all, its relations with African countries are highly correlated with the sacred One-China policy, which invariably interferes with the sovereignty of the African states. In addition, China has recently sent special envoys to countries where it has substantial economic interests but feels that these interests could be endangered by local political problems.

Overall, the indications are that China is providing African economies with a much-needed momentum, something African policy-makers hoped TICAD would do when it was conceived in the early 1990s. Meanwhile, Japan's relations with the region remain in an incipient state and the TICAD process is seemingly in danger of becoming like the other multilateral initiatives for African development that end up in a cul-de-sac. Incidentally, China's growing popularity among African states is partly linked to this. The emphasis on trade and investment in China's relations with Africa, not to mention its political initiatives towards the region, have bolstered what purports to be a South-South initiative; Japan's relations with the region, conversely, are more a replication of a North-South engagement.

Evidently frustrated, African representatives in Tokyo have remarked that TICAD 'is no longer alone in terms of Asia-based fora focused on Africa'. In the same breath they also mention the 'action-oriented approach and the aggressive, highly-visible character of some of the other initiatives to have emerged over the past few year . . .' and warn that 'the TICAD process is at risk of being overshadowed – specifically in terms of delivery and effectiveness on the ground'.[61] 'If TICAD is to retain its relevance', the African ambassadors further warned, the process must refocus on the twin concepts of ownership and partnership, 'and must seek not only reinvigoration but . . . also . . . some form of coordination between and amongst the now multiple regional and international initiatives'.[62] The assumption is that this would 'ensure effective utilization of funding, tangible progress towards sustainable development and the acceleration of Africa's integration into the global economy'. Ultimately, however, the political and economic realities of China and Japan's engagements with African states will be determined and confirmed by the impact they have on Africa's developmental efforts. In this sense, the test will not be the rhetoric but the reality, and the outcome of these engagements will underline the principles of the rationality undergirding the ambitions of each of the parties, including those of African states, of course.

NOTES

1. 'China Outstripping Japan in Diplomatic Race to Woo Africa', *The Asahi Shimbun*, 5 March 2005. http://www.asahi.com/english-asahi/TKY200605030114.html.
2. H. Masaki, 'Japan Takes on China in Africa', *Asia Times*, 15 August 2006. http://www.uofaweb.ualberta.ca/chinainstitute/nav03.cfm?nav03=49151andnav02=43782andnav01=43092.
3. 'Japan Welcomes China's Aid, but Calls for Transparency', *Japan Today*, 28 June 2007. http://www.japantoday.com/jp/news/410683.
4. Agence France Presse (AFP), 'Japan's PM Faults China over Darfur', 13 June 2007.
5. M. Foucault, 'Governmentality', in G. Burchell, C. Gordon and P. Miller (eds.), *The Foucault Effect: Studies in Governmentality* (London: Harvester Wheatsheaf, 1991), p. 97; S.I. Levine, 'Perceptions and Ideology in Chinese Foreign Policy', in T.W. Robinson and D. Shambaugh (eds.), *Chinese Foreign Policy: Theory and Practice* (Oxford: Clarendon Press, 1994), pp. 30–33.
6. M. Foucault, 'Questions of Method', in Burchell, Gordon and Miller (eds.), *The Foucault Effect*, p. 79.
7. B. Rossi, 'Revisiting Foucauldian Approaches: Power Dynamics in Development Projects', *The Journal of Development Studies* 40(6), 2004: 2.
8. Levine, 'Perceptions and Ideology', pp. 39–40.
9. Mutual respect for each other's territorial integrity and sovereignty; mutual non-aggression; mutual non-interference in each other's internal affairs; equality and mutual benefit; and peaceful coexistence.
10. M. Foucault, 'Politics and the Study of Discourse', in Burchell, Gordon and Miller (eds.), *The Foucault Effect*, p. 59.
11. Quoted in W.C. Kirby, 'Traditions of Centrality, Authority, and Management in Modern China's Foreign Relations', in Robinson and Shambaugh, *Chinese Foreign Policy*, p. 13; Levine, 'Perceptions and Ideology', p. 38.
12. Levine, 'Perceptions and Ideology', p. 44.
13. Kirby, 'Traditions of Centrality', p. 13; Levine, 'Perceptions and Ideology', p. 44.
14. Levine, 'Perceptions and Ideology', p. 36.
15. Levine, 'Perceptions and Ideology', p. 39.
16. K. Ampiah, *The Political and Moral Imperatives of the Bandung Conference of 1955: The Reactions of the US, UK and Japan* (London: Global Oriental, 2007).
17. '*Ajia-Afurika kaigi sanka ni taisuru ronchô no ken*', from 'Okamoto to Shigemitsu', 18 January 1955, Gaimusho gaikôkiroku bunsho (Ministry of Foreign Affairs Archives, Tokyo, B0049).
18. M. Taizo, *Bandon kaigi to nihon no ajia fukki: Amerika to ajia no hazama de* (Tokyo: Soshisha 2001), p. 82.
19. J. Welfield, *An Empire in Eclipse: Japan in the Post-War American Alliance System* (London: Athlone Press, 1988).
20. 'Meeting on Anglo-Japanese Co-operation in Africa', *Agenda*, 9 April 1962, FO 371/164971 (PRO).
21. 'Meeting on Anglo-Japanese Co-operation in Africa', p. 468.
22. M. Foucault, *Discipline and Punishment: The Birth of the Prison* (London: Penguin Books, 1991) p. 23.
23. A. Ogunsanwo, *China's Policy in Africa, 1958–1971* (Cambridge: Cambridge University Press, 1974) p. 260.
24. Quoted in A. Hutchison, *China's African Revolution* (London: Hutchinson, 1975), p. 256.
25. Hutchison, *China's African Revolution*, p. 851.
26. Y. Sun, 'Militant Diplomacy: The Taiwan Strait Crises and Sino-American Relations, 1954–1958', in K.C. Statler and A.L. Johns (eds.), *The Eisenhower Administration, the Third World, and the Globalization of the Cold War* (Lanham: Rowman and Littlefield, 2006), pp. 134–35.

27. P. Kilby, *Industrialization in an Open Economy: Nigeria, 1945–1966* (Cambridge: Cambridge University Press, 1969), p. 112.
28. K. Ampiah, 'Japanese Investment in Nigeria: Ignoring the Resource Potential', in K. Ampiah, *The Dynamics of Japan's Relations with Africa: South Africa, Tanzania and Nigeria* (London: Routledge, 1997).
29. J. Morikawa, *Japan and Africa: Big Business and Diplomacy* (London: Hurst and Company, 1997), pp. 120–25.
30. G. Morrison, 'Japan Year in Africa, 1973–1974', in C. Legum et al. (eds.), *Africa Contemporary Record: Annual Survey and Documents* (London: Rex Collins, 1974) p. A104.
31. J. Morikawa, 'Japan and Africa after the Cold War', *African and Asian Studies* 4(4), 2005: 500.
32. K. Ampiah, 'Japanese Aid to Tanzania: A Study of the Political Marketing of Japan in Africa', *African Affairs* 95(378), 1996.
33. TICAD has been convened three times: in 1993, 1998 and 2003, and a fourth one (to be held in 2008) is on the way. See K. Ampiah, 'Japan and the Development of Africa: A Preliminary Evaluation of the Tokyo International Conference on African Development', *African Affairs* 104(414), 2005; S. Horiuchi, 'TICAD after Ten Years: A Preliminary Assessment and Proposals for the Future', *African and Asian Studies* 4(4), 2004; Morikawa, 'Japan and Africa'.
34. M. Foucault, *The Care of the Self: The History of Sexuality, 3* (London: Penguin, 1990), p. 100.
35. TICAD IV, 'Draft Yokohama Declaration: Towards a Vibrant Africa' (Confidential), 18 March, 2008, p. 1.
36. African Diplomatic Corps, Tokyo, 'Executive Summary: Proposals for the Fourth Tokyo International Conference on African Development, TICAD IV', Tokyo, March 2007, p. 5.
37. African Diplomatic Corps, Tokyo, 'Executive Summary', p. 4.
38. Presentation by Ambassador S.H. Comberbach to the ADC/UNU Africa Day Symposium, United Nations University, Tokyo, 25 May 2007.
39. African Diplomatic Corps, Tokyo, 'Executive Summary', p. 7.
40. United Nations, *UNCTAD Handbook of Statistics, 2006–2007* (Geneva: UNCTAD, 2007), p. 66.
41. US Department of Commerce, 'US-African Trade Profile', March 2007, p. 5.
42. African Diplomatic Corps, Tokyo, 'Executive Summary', p. 7.
43. Presentation by Ambassador S.H. Comberbach to the ADC/UNU Africa Day Symposium, p. 2.
44. C. Dupasquier and P.N. Osakwe, 'Foreign Direct Investment in Africa: Performance, Challenges and Responsibilities', *African Trade Policy* 21 (Economic Commission for Africa, September 2006): 8–9.
45. O. Watanabe, chairperson and CEO, JETRO, 'Development through Markets in Africa: New Development of Public-Private Partnership', Africa Symposium welcome address, 1 September 2006; African Diplomatic Corps, Tokyo, 'Executive Summary', p. 13.
46. G. le Pere, 'China and Africa: Advancing South–South Cooperation', in G. le Pere (ed.), *China in Africa: Mercantilist Predator, or Partner in Development?* (Midrand: Institute of Global Dialogue and SAIIA, 2007), p. 104.
47. This was 8.7 per cent of China's oil imports for 2006, compared to 36 per cent of the EU's and 33 per cent of the United States'.
48. E. Pan, 'China, Africa, Oil', Council on Foreign Relations (n.d.), http://www.cfr.org/publication/9557/.
49. UNDP, *Asian Foreign Direct Investment in Africa: Towards a New Era of Cooperation between Developing Countries* (New York: United Nations, 2007), pp. 52–53.
50. 'Nigeria Nears Deal to Prefer Beijing on Oil Drilling Rights', *Financial Times*, 27 April 2006, p. 10.
51. 'ODA Fall Poses Africa Policy Dilemma: China Filling the Vacuum', *The Japan Times*, 4 April 2008, p. 3.

52. 'China Outstripping Japan'; 'China to Promote Talks with Japan to Resolve UN Reform Conflict', 15 October 2005. http://findarticles.com/p/articles/mi_m0WDQ/is_2005_Oct_17/ai_n15700070.
53. 'Beijing Summit Adopts Declaration, Highlighting China-Africa Strategic Partnership', Beijing Summit and Third Ministerial Conference of the Forum on China-Africa Cooperation, November 2006, http://english.focacsummit.org/2006-11/05/content_5166.htm.
54. R. Drifte, *Japan's Quest for a Permanent Security Council Seat: A Matter of Pride or Justice?* (Basingstoke: Macmillan, 2000), pp. 145–54.
55. S. Zhoa, 'China's Geo-Strategic Thrust: Partners of Engagement', in Le Pere (ed.), *China in Africa*, p. 38.
56. Quoted in H.W. French, 'China in Africa: All Trade, with No Political Baggage', *The New York Times*, 8 August 2004, http://www.nytimes.com/2004/08/08/international/asia/08china.html?ex=1249704000anden=30ac3abb13a189a6andei=5090andpartner=rssuserland.
57. 'ODA Fall Poses Africa Policy Dilemma', p. 3.
58. ODA Fall Poses Africa Policy Dilemma', p. 5.
59. African Diplomatic Corps, Tokyo, 'Executive Summary', p. 4.
60. Japan's ODA White Paper, 2003, http://www.mofa.go.jp/policy/oda/white/2003/part3_3_2.html; Masaki, 'Japan Takes on China'.
61. African Diplomatic Corps, Tokyo, 'Executive Summary', p. 5.
62. African Diplomatic Corps, Tokyo, 'Executive Summary', p. 4.

17

China and Southeast Asia

Some Lessons for Africa?

Amitav Acharya

INTRODUCTION

What are the lessons and implications of China's relations with Southeast Asia for Africa? To be sure, one might be sceptical about such a comparison, given the differences between the two regions in geographical, ethnic and political terms. Moreover, neither Africa nor Southeast Asia is a singular entity. Hence, any talk of a regional response to China must be qualified. But there are some lessons that can be derived from the way Southeast Asia (used here interchangeably with the members of the Association of Southeast Asian Nations [ASEAN] – comprising Indonesia, Malaysia, Singapore, Brunei, Vietnam, Myanmar, Thailand, Laos, the Philippines and Cambodia) has faced and responded to the rise of China in the past two decades. First, the economic and military sources of China's influence in Southeast Asia are explored. Then the strategies pursued by Southeast Asian states to cope with growing Chinese power are examined. In the concluding section, some observations about Africa's engagement with China from a Southeast Asian perspective are made. The main argument of the chapter is that regionalism and a multilateral approach constitute an important and, perhaps indispensable, element of the response of weaker states to a rising power with the potential for regional hegemony. ASEAN's response to China's rise has been mixed, consisting of elements of balancing, bandwagoning and binding, but it is the last element that accounts mostly for the reduced suspicions and tensions in their overall relationship.

SOURCES OF CHINESE POWER IN SOUTHEAST ASIA

As China's power grows, its ability to influence Southeast Asian affairs also increases. In terms of size, economic resources and military strength, China dwarfs Southeast Asia. By the early 2000s, China's gross domestic product (GDP) and defence expenditures were already more than double that of all the ASEAN members combined. Economic differentials between China and ASEAN have grown, as China's economy has continued to soar, and many Southeast Asian economies remained mired in the lingering effects of the 1997 economic crisis. A particularly significant trend has been the differential rates of foreign direct investment (FDI) that both entities attract. In 1990, according to UN Conference on Trade and Development (UNCTAD) estimates, ASEAN received 52.6 per cent of total FDI to Asia, whereas China received 14.4 per cent. In 2001, in a dramatic reversal of the trend, these figures stood at 14.7 and 55.5 per cent respectively.

The level of China-ASEAN trade increased from US$8 billion in 1991 to more than US$40 billion in 2001. The past decade had seen a rapid increase in Chinese manufactured exports to ASEAN, from 47 per cent of total exports in 1980 to 90 per cent in 2000.[1] Such was the trend that it provoked fears about Southeast Asia becoming a market for cheap Chinese manufactured goods, as its own industries were hollowed out as a result of the rush of foreign multinationals to China in search of cheap labour and a larger market.

Optimists have argued that in an era of global production networks and economic regionalisation, the traditional notion of an economic sphere of influence does not hold true. The shift in Beijing's export structure is a result of foreign enterprises using China as an assembly platform for components of finished products. Supachai Panitchpakdi, former World Trade Organisation (WTO) director-general and current UNCTAD head, believes that ASEAN and China's trade structures are diversified enough that Beijing's demands for imports will be 'tremendous' and will include both raw materials and manufactured products from Southeast Asia.[2] Yet the economies of the Chinese and Southeast Asian countries are competitive, rather than complementary: ASEAN competes head on with China in their target markets in developing countries. As economic modernisation in China progresses, competition with ASEAN economies will intensify and may even result in some crowding-out effects on the ASEAN economies' exports in the markets of developed countries. As is already occurring, the ASEAN economies are facing competitive pressure from China, which is fast becoming a manufacturing threat to many Asian countries. This may still be a far cry from

ASEAN becoming a backyard for Chinese raw material imports and manufactured exports, and hence a natural candidate for a Chinese sphere of influence. What it might entail, however, is that China will have increasing regional economic clout over ASEAN, including an ability to offer incentives and punishments. Beijing will also be able to develop a strong economic influence in the less economically developed ASEAN members: Laos, Myanmar and Cambodia. Selective Chinese trade concessions and economic aid could persuade these countries to support Chinese foreign policy and strategic objectives.[3]

In the military sphere too, China-ASEAN disparities have grown. While within Southeast Asia the talk of a Chinese threat has diminished in the face of creative diplomacy by Beijing, long-term concerns about Chinese power projection capabilities remain. The main target of China's military build-up, as a July 2002 Pentagon (US defence) report noted, is to 'diversify its options for use of force against potential targets such as Taiwan and to complicate United States intervention in a Taiwan Strait conflict'.[4] But as the report also notes, forces being developed against Taiwan can be used against other Asian states, such as the Philippines.

China's overall capacity to project power deep into Southeast Asia is currently limited. Its projection forces would allow it to pursue a 'limited harassment' of ASEAN by sea and air.[5] Beijing may be able to seize most islands in the disputed areas in the South China Sea, but holding on to them is another matter. Its power projection is constrained by a number of factors: a limited range of force projection assets and long-range strike capabilities, and a lack of combat experience and training. China and ASEAN have undertaken important moves to reduce military tensions. The most dramatic example of this was the November 2002 signing of a 'declaration' on a code of conduct in the South China Sea at the ASEAN summit in Cambodia. The most significant words of the declaration concern an undertaking by the parties 'to exercise self-restraint in the conduct of activities that would complicate or escalate disputes and affect peace and stability including, among others, refraining from action of inhabiting on the [currently] uninhabited islands, reefs, shoals, cays, and other features and to handle their differences in a constructive manner'. The declaration does not include a specific commitment to freezing the erection of new structures in the disputed area, a commitment sought by the Philippines but refused by China. A demand by Vietnam that the proposed code should apply to the Paracel Islands (claimed by Hanoi but now occupied by Beijing) was resisted by China, although the problem was overcome through the acceptance of a Philippine initiative, which suggested dropping any reference to the geographic boundaries of the declaration, thereby allowing Hanoi to claim coverage of the entire South China Sea. Moreover, the declaration is not a legally binding code of conduct. Arriving at such a code is stated as a long-term goal of the parties. Malaysia intervened to push through this interim measure, even though the Philippines had insisted on a more binding framework. But these shortcomings do not deny the declaration's significance. It does represent a confirmation of China's gradual move towards a posture of dealing with ASEAN multilaterally on a subject that it had previously insisted on resolving on a bilateral basis. The declaration also reflects the fact that China sees a military confrontation over the Spratly Islands in the South China Sea as being detrimental to its interests. China's satisfaction with the agreement may also have to do with the exclusion of Taiwan as a party to the declaration. This could be seen as an endorsement by ASEAN of its One-China policy, which insists on Taiwan as part of the mainland.

Sceptics also argue that China's restraint in the Spratly matter is a tactical move at a time when Beijing is preoccupied with the Taiwan issue. The South China Sea dispute has receded to the background amidst other, more pressing challenges to regional order, such as terrorism, and non-traditional dangers such as severe acute respiratory syndrome (SARS). Resolving the question will release China's energy for attention to its territorial claims against Southeast Asian states. Shen Dingli, a well-known Chinese expert on strategic affairs, fuelled such speculation when he warned: 'Once the Taiwan front is closed, we may turn to the South China Sea.'[6] According to a senior People's Liberation Army (PLA) official interviewed by the author, three factors influenced China's efforts to reduce tensions in the South China Sea:

- a desire to maintain good relations with ASEAN;
- a focus on other priorities of the government, such as the Taiwan issue; and
- preventing intervention by 'third parties' – meaning the United States – taking advantage of the conflict.

The PLA is unhappy with the decision by the top political leadership to make concessions that freeze Chinese territorial expansion. The current Chinese position is that it will not be the first to use force in the South China Sea, and will react only if provoked. But in a situation of conflict, deciding the aggressor and the victim could be highly problematic.

Strategic influence and power projection can be undertaken by means other than direct application of military force, especially through the acquisition of facilities and the development of close security ties with weaker states. For example, analysts have pointed to China's building of dams in the upper reaches of the Mekong River, which would give it an ability to control the flow of water to other riparian states, such as Laos, Cambodia and Vietnam. Another aspect of Beijing's influence-seeking in Southeast Asia is the China-Myanmar security relationship: the Chinese strategic presence in Myanmar covers a wide variety of activities, ranging from the sale of military equipment, arms-production facilities and training programmes to the stationing of Chinese military personnel to train and operate sophisticated electronic communication and surveillance equipment. Some of the more sensitive activities reported in the media concern the establishment of Chinese military facilities for the purposes of communication and logistics, including support from Chinese air and naval (submarine) deployments. Even when not independently verifiable, reports of Beijing's military presence in Myanmar have influenced the strategic perspectives of Southeast Asian states towards Myanmar, explaining, in part, ASEAN's opposition to sanctions by the West and its pursuit of a policy of 'constructive engagement'. Moreover, the desire to reduce Myanmar's strategic and economic dependence on China explained ASEAN's decisions to admit Myanmar as a full member in 1997.

REGIONAL RESPONSES TO CHINA'S RISE

In responding to Chinese power, Southeast Asian states have, to varying degrees, employed three main strategies: balancing, bandwagoning and binding. While international relations' scholars view these strategies as mutually exclusive, they appear to feature concurrently in ASEAN's response to the rise of China. None is pursued exclusively, and each strategy seems to act as a check on the fuller pursuit of the other(s).

Balancing is seen in Southeast Asian states' strategic ties with the United States, Japan and India. Singapore's former prime minister, Goh Chok Tong, on being asked by the author at a public forum to comment on how Singapore and ASEAN would deal with a militarily powerful, economically prosperous, but geo-politically assertive China, replied that a regional 'balance' would be important in countering such a development. '[W]e need to have a US presence over here. We need to have a strong ASEAN, we need Japan to be present in the region. We need Europeans to be here.'[7]

ASEAN countries, such as the Philippines, Singapore and Thailand, have considerably enhanced their security cooperation with the United States. Manila and Bangkok now enjoy major non-North Atlantic Treaty Organisation (NATO) ally status with Washington. While ostensibly geared to countering the threat of terrorism and separatism in Mindanao (the second largest and easternmost island in the Philippines), Manila also seeks to rebuild its defence links with the United States with a view to responding to Chinese military provocations in the Spratly Islands. Singapore has recently signed security cooperation agreements with both the United States and India. Malaysia has cooperated with the United States on defence by quietly developing extensive security links with Washington. In coping with the most pressing security challenge facing the region – terrorism – ASEAN remains dependent on Washington's help. By contrast, Beijing's role in Southeast Asia's 'War on Terrorism' has been rather marginal.

ASEAN has also maintained its close ties with Japan, as Tokyo has grown increasingly sensitive to Beijing's influence in Southeast Asia. During the past few years, Japan has taken diplomatic measures (such as the new Japan-ASEAN dialogue on security, acceding to ASEAN's Treaty of Amity of Cooperation [TAC], and a Japan-ASEAN summit) and economic measures (closer economic cooperation) to counter it. To be sure, Japanese diplomacy in the region has been reactive and lags behind proactive Chinese efforts. Japan did not sign the TAC until a year after China. Its planned economic links with ASEAN fall far short of Beijing's comprehensive free-trade initiative. Japan, however, remains the largest provider of development aid to Southeast Asia, far outstripping China. But China's aid has been more selective and 'strategic'. Japan faces problems in competing effectively with China in Southeast Asia because of its military limitations, the historical baggage linked to its wartime role in Southeast Asia and its relative economic decline. But Japan will work with India and the United States to maintain a countervailing posture in Southeast Asia directed at China's rise.

It is also noteworthy that China's growing ties with ASEAN have been accompanied by closer ASEAN-India cooperation.[8] ASEAN gave New Delhi the status of full dialogue partner, invited it to join the Asia Regional Forum (ARF), and has hosted it at an annual summit, partly out of recognition of India's potential role in balancing China in the region.[9] India's profile and presence in Southeast Asia is growing, whereas its military presence and role in the region is still limited. And India's clout in the region is contingent upon the state of its economy, which remains uncertain. An Indian role in Southeast Asia is also limited by regional sensitivities, based on past experience, about diplomatic arrogance and heavy-handedness. But this may be changing. New Delhi is developing a naval presence in the region, has undertaken joint naval patrols to safeguard shipping in the Straits of Malacca, and is offering increased aid to Myanmar, partly to counter Chinese influence. Like China, it is also negotiating a free trade agreement (FTA) with ASEAN, although its future is less certain than the China-ASEAN FTA. The lure of the Indian economy in Southeast Asia is growing and trade has increased by a significant margin.

There is growing talk among academic analysts about Southeast Asian states bandwagoning with China. This may have already happened in the case of Myanmar and, perhaps, Cambodia. But the talk of such bandwagoning by the region as a whole has grown in keeping with China's 'charm diplomacy' in the region in the past few years. There is also increasing talk in the region of Chinese 'soft power'. Some analysts in China and Southeast Asia have raised the possibility of a return to the old tributary system and Southeast Asia's historical acceptance of a 'hierarchical' interstate order with China at its core.

But this scenario is unlikely. Despite their desire to cultivate Beijing, and their weaker economic and strategic position, the core ASEAN countries are unlikely to bandwagon collectively with China. Except in the case of Myanmar, there is no military alignment – a key indicator of bandwagoning – between China and any of the original members of ASEAN. Defence relations between China and ASEAN members remain rudimentary and are aimed at confidence-building, rather than operational issues. Security relations with Vietnam have improved since the two countries reached border agreements: a land border agreement in 1999, an agreement on the delimitation of the Tonkin Gulf and an agreement on Fishery Cooperation on 25 December 2000.[10] Vietnam and China are also not in a bandwagoning relationship. Recent joint statements involving China and Singapore, and China and the Philippines have included modest proposals for defence exchanges.[11] The main ASEAN members are yet to develop defence links with Beijing involving arms transfers, joint exercises or operational planning. This is explained partly by domestic politics (in Malaysia and Indonesia) and close security ties with the United States (for Singapore, the Philippines and Thailand). At the same time, it would be a mistake to assume that ASEAN countries have completely eschewed a balancing posture towards China. While the arms build-up in Southeast Asia is by no means solely geared to countering China, the possibility of Beijing developing an expansionist security approach is an important factor for Malaysia, Singapore and, especially, the Philippines.[12] The kind of convergence of threat perception between China and the major ASEAN members that led to Thailand's buying some Chinese weapons is unlikely to be replicated in the post-Cold-War period. It is highly unlikely that the rhetorical opposition of some ASEAN members, such as Malaysia, to United States hegemony – a concern it ostensibly shares with China – would translate into military alignment with China.

A return to a tributary system, such as the relationship in China-Southeast Asia relations is implausible under the sovereign state system, which China both accepts and defends. The classical tributary system or what is also called the 'Chinese World

Order', features a single great power, China. Although Sino-ASEAN relations seem unequal at present, ASEAN is not without bargaining clout in its dealings – especially its collective dealings – with China. To sustain its economic growth, Beijing needs Southeast Asian resources and markets, as well as a stable regional environment, which ASEAN can help to provide. China also requires Southeast Asia's acquiescence and cooperation to realise its leadership ambitions in Asia and the world. Its relationship with ASEAN is a test case of Beijing's credibility as an engaged and constructive world power. While China remains wary of ASEAN's pressure on the South China Sea dispute and the pro-United States defence orientation of many ASEAN members, there are also reasons for Beijing to view Southeast Asia as a relatively safe and benign area within which to cultivate positive and mutually beneficial relationships. Beijing is also mindful that an adverse relationship with Southeast Asia could move many of its member states towards closer alignment with China's competitors, such as Japan and the United States. This offers an opportunity to Southeast Asian states, provided they can stay united and purposeful, to extract strategic restraint from China and develop cooperative security strategies.

Against this backdrop, it seems unlikely that China can build a regional sphere of influence by excluding Washington and other extra-regional powers from Southeast Asian affairs. Such a Chinese sphere of influence, or a Chinese Monroe Doctrine (which excludes other external actors from the region as the United States did with regard to the Americas with the Monroe Doctrine in 1863) over Southeast Asia, is unlikely to develop as an automatic by-product of the rise of Chinese economic and military power. While there is little likelihood of a neo-Confucian Chinese World Order developing spontaneously because of the cultural-historic tendency of East Asia to bandwagon with China, in an era of transnational production, intra-firm trade and high capital mobility (which means capital can flee China as easily as it came, should there be a major political and security crisis involving China, such as war in the Taiwan Straits), a Chinese economic *dependencia* in Southeast Asia is unlikely as a natural outgrowth of Sino-ASEAN competition.

Aside from balancing and bandwagoning, Southeast Asian states have actively pursued a binding strategy towards China. A key element of this scenario is the continuation of engagement with Beijing through regional institutions. ASEAN's approach seeks to ensure that China is enmeshed in a system of regional order in which the costs of any use of force in dealing with problems with its neighbours will be outweighed by the benefits. The key element of this approach is the ARF.[13]

Indeed, China has maintained some important reservations about the development of regional institutions in Asia. It continues to oppose the institutional development of the ARF out of a fear that this could compromise the norms of sovereignty and non-interference. It has successfully blocked the extension of the ARF's role into preventive diplomacy in intra-state conflicts. China views the ARF primarily as a forum for consultations, confidence-building and dialogue, rather than mediation and problem-solving in regional conflicts. Instead of viewing ASEAN as the neutral anchor of multilateral security, China views ASEAN as a pole in an increasingly multipolar world and region. Notwithstanding its new security concept, which is ostensibly geared to the promotion of common security and multilateralism, there remains in China's world view a strong realist element in which power-balancing occupies an important place.

The ASEAN members have generally accommodated Chinese reservations about the ARF, out of concern that a Chinese withdrawal from the ARF would render the forum irrelevant. While not an adequate guarantee of the peaceful management of regional order, multilateralism, at least in its normative dimensions, has made significant inroads into Chinese thinking and behaviour. The ARF enables a continuous process of dialogue with China. Beijing itself has come to value multilateralism; early Chinese misgivings about the forum – that it would enable ASEAN countries to gang up against China or that it could be exploited by the United States to isolate and apply pressure on China – have given way to a growing appreciation of multilateralism as a valuable outlet for communicating Chinese security perceptions and approaches. Over the years, Chinese involvement in Asian multilateral security dialogues has increased.

In the economic sphere, too, ASEAN and China have pursued a mutually binding approach. The China-ASEAN free-trade area is billed as the largest free-trade zone in the world, covering as it does a total population of 1.7 billion people and a combined GDP of about US$2 trillion. The China-ASEAN FTA aims at reducing and eliminating tariffs by 2010 for China and the ASEAN-6 (Brunei Darussalam, Indonesia, Malaysia, Philippines, Singapore and Thailand), and by 2015 for Cambodia, Laos, Myanmar and Vietnam also. According to some estimates, the China-ASEAN FTA could bolster ASEAN's and China's GDP by 0.9 per cent and 0.3 per cent respectively. It would also increase ASEAN's exports to China by 48 per cent and China's exports to ASEAN by 55 per cent.[14] The ASEAN states, faced with continuing economic downturn and a growing terrorist menace, see a free-trade area as a means of avoiding further economic marginalisation. An FTA with China, with its large domestic market, will create more trade and investment opportunities for ASEAN member-states. The China-ASEAN free-trade area sets a model for similar concessions for ASEAN from future free-trade areas with Japan, Korea and India. It would make ASEAN more attractive as an FDI destination. Yet, Beijing has excluded two of Southeast Asia's major exports – rice and palm oil – from the 'early harvest' of tariff reductions and the products covered in the 'early harvest' scheme amount to less than 2.1 per cent of total China-ASEAN trade.

For China, while ASEAN's market of 500 million people and rich natural resources are important considerations behind its drive for an FTA with ASEAN, trade liberalisation also offers potential political benefits. China can exploit this to replace Japan as the primary driving force for economic growth and integration in the region. Indeed, China's likely political gains from its proposed free-trade area with ASEAN might have prompted Japan to propose its own trade initiative in the region. China's interest in an FTA with ASEAN is also challenging to the United States, and puts paid to any remaining hope of Washington promoting free trade through the Asia-Pacific Economic Cooperation (APEC).

If China is to turn away from this multilateral framework and view and use regional institutions as an instrument of leverage, these institutions will certainly unravel. This will set the stage for a more classic and unregulated balance of power geo-politics in the region in which China will be balanced by the United States and its allies, while losing legitimacy as a constructive regional actor. China's active interest in the development of the ASEAN Plus Three (APT) framework (comprising the ten ASEAN members and Japan, China and South Korea) as well as the East Asian Summit (ASEAN Plus Six, including India, Australia and New Zealand) is being seen by some as a way of encouraging the development of regional groups that exclude the United States. But the APT is unlikely to develop into an instrument of a Chinese Monroe Doctrine. Not only would Japan oppose such a development, but the ASEAN countries are likely to benefit from competitive wooing by China and Japan through the APT framework.

LESSONS FOR AFRICA

There are important differences between Southeast Asia and Africa when it comes to responding to the growth of Chinese power. Africa does not have a large ethnic Chinese minority – a majority in the case of Singapore – which has in the past served as one of the determinants of Chinese policy towards Southeast Asia. And while China provided ideological and material support to African regimes and movements in the past, this was nothing compared to its active support for communist insurgencies in Southeast Asia in the 1960s and early 1970s. Geographic proximity is a major factor in Sino-Southeast Asian relations; the sheer size of its next-door neighbour induces a natural fear of China's power and influence in Southeast Asia.

These differences make it difficult to apply lessons from Southeast Asia's response to the rise of China to Africa's own dealings with Beijing. But there are some parallels and lessons for Africa. Like the Southeast Asian states, African nations are developing countries rich in natural resources that China needs for its comprehensive modernisation. Like Southeast Asia, Africa also has a deep and growing sense of regionalism in both the economic and security arenas. Both Southeast Asia and Africa seek, as far as possible, to keep their regions free from outside interference and big-power rivalry, even if the declaratory posture is not always matched by reality.

Southeast Asia has learnt to live with Chinese power for several reasons. One is that Chinese power projection capabilities are still limited, even for a region virtually at its doorstep. Second, the pursuit of a mixed strategy, comprising elements of balancing, bandwagoning and binding, has been useful. Such a strategy may well be needed to cope with growing Chinese influence in Africa. Neither balancing nor bandwagoning, which realists regard as the only natural responses of states to any rising power, near or distant, will be effective by itself and may carry negative consequences for African stability. The most important lesson for Africa from Southeast Asia's response to the rise of China could be the use of collective bargaining and institutional binding. During its formative years in the late 1960s and early 1970s, ASEAN collectively bargained with Japan and other industrialised nations to secure higher prices for its natural commodities such as rubber. This was not adversarial bargaining, or cartelism in the form of the Organisation of Petroleum Exporting Countries (OPEC), but an act of collective positive persuasion by a group of resource-rich developing nations with legitimate aspirations for rapid economic development. And it was largely successful.

In the 1990s, Southeast Asian states brushed aside Chinese insistence on dealing with them on a strictly bilateral basis on matters of economics and security. They insisted on dealing with China multilaterally. The collective pressure bore fruit in the mid-1990s, as China agreed to talk to ASEAN collectively about regional disputes, such as the Spratly Islands conflict in the South China Sea. China also came up with the proposal for a free-trade area with ASEAN. In return, ASEAN rejected any United States move towards a strategy of containment of China and discouraged talk of a 'China threat'. This gave China a central place at the table in the region's nascent multilateral institutions, such as ARF, APT and the East Asia Summit. In short, ASEAN engaged China without courting its dominance. The degree of mutual reassurance resulting from this institutional-binding approach was striking.

The main lesson here is that Africa will suffer if it deals with China – including its demand for its resources – exclusively through bilateral channels, as a house divided against itself, with individual African nations competing among themselves for Chinese economic aid or political backing. Africa has a rich diplomatic tradition of seeking security multilaterally, of managing regional conflicts and of mitigating great power intervention. There is a strong case for a multilateral dialogue between China and the African Union (AU) and China and Africa's myriad subregional groupings. The revived Asia-Africa forum could also be a platform for such a dialogue.

NOTES

1. J. Wong and S. Chan, 'China's Rapidly Changing Export Structure', National University of Singapore, EAI, Background Brief 85, 9 April 2001.
2. Quoted in M. Richardson, 'China Seen by ASEAN as a Market: Hopes for Cash Ease Fears of Rising Giant', *International Herald Tribune*, 26 April 2002.
3. M. Vatikiotis, 'A Too Friendly Embrace', *Far Eastern Economic Review*, 17 June 2004: 20–22.
4. 'Pentagon Warns of China Threat', CNN, 17 July 2002, http://www.cnn.com/2002/WORLD/asiapcf/east/07/13/china.taiwan/.
5. 'Pentagon Warns of China Threat'.
6. Quoted in C.S. Smith, 'China Reshaping Military to Toughen its Muscle in the Region', *The New York Times*, 16 October 2002; see also S.P. Seth, 'US Not Likely to Forfeit Role in Asia', http://publish.gio.gov.tw/FCJ/past/02110862.html.
7. 'S'pore a Friend of the US, not a Client State', *The Straits Times*, 28 November 2002.
8. To quote G.C. Tong: 'We welcome India's participation in ASEAN for two reasons. One is strategic. We do want another big country to be actively engaged with ASEAN. Otherwise, ASEAN would be, in a sense, overwhelmed by the Northeast Asian countries – China, Japan. So, if we have another wing in terms of constructive engagement, and that is India, it will make for a more stable ASEAN.' (London: BBC, *East Asia Today*, 5 November 2002; source: Foreign Broadcast Monitor, Ministry of Information and the Arts, Singapore, 6 November 2002, pp. 7–8.)
9. S. Chatterjee, 'India, ASEAN Agree to Create Free Trade Area', *Indian Express*, 9 January 2003. http://www.expressindia.com/fullstory.php?newsid=16537.
10. 'Sino-Vietnam Border Treaties Equal to Both Countries', *People's Daily*, 25 January 2002. http://english.peopledaily.com.cn/200201/24/eng20020124_89291.shtml.
11. C.A. Thayer, 'China Consolidates its Long-Term Bilateral Relations with Southeast Asia', *Comparative Connections*, 2nd quarter 2000.
12. For further details, see M.C. Anthony, 'US-Philippines Relations Post-September 11: Security Dilemmas of a Front-Line State in the War on Terrorism', *IDSS Commentaries*, October 2002.
13. A. Acharya, 'ASEAN and Conditional Engagement', in J. Shinn (ed.), *Weaving the Net: Conditional Engagement with China* (New York: Council on Foreign Relations, 1996), pp. 220–48.
14. F. Wu, P.T. Siaw, Y.H. Sia and P.K. Keong, 'Foreign Direct Investment to China and Southeast Asia: Has ASEAN been Losing out?' *Economic Survey of Singapore* (Third Quarter 2002).

PART 4

Conclusion

18

The Sino-African Relationship

Towards an Evolving Partnership?

Kweku Ampiah and Sanusha Naidu

Writing in the eighteenth century, British political economist, Adam Smith, observed that 'China seems to have been long stationary' in terms of economic development.[1] Smith summarily attributed China's arrested development to what he perceived to be the isolationist tendencies of the Qing Dynasty which, according to European observers, had a profound lack of interest in international trade. 'A country which neglects or despises foreign commerce, and which admits the vessels of foreign nations into one or two of its ports only, cannot transact the same quantity of business which it might do with different laws and institutions,'[2] pontificated Smith. At the time he wrote this, Smith was postulating his ideas concerning the 'natural order' through which 'the enlightened selfishness of all men adds up to the maximum good of society'.[3] As has been well documented and popularised, the British economist perceived the extraordinary operations of a '"divine hand" which guides each man in pursuing his own gain to contribute to the social welfare'. The popular (and now over-rehearsed) abstraction of this concept is that 'the best programme is to leave the economic process severely alone'.[4] On the basis of this postulate in Smith's magnum opus, *The Wealth of Nations*, which was first published in 1776, amidst the extolling of the virtues of international trade, he proclaimed the economic orthodoxy of laissez-faire: the unregulated practice in trade and industry by private entrepreneurs, a practice which Alexander Carlyle, an associate of Smith who also glorified the paradoxes of unintended consequences, referred to as 'anarchy plus a constable'.[5] More than 170 years after Smith's publication, Mao Zedong and his comrades would dismiss capitalism as patently flawed in all its practices and manifestations, and declare economic liberalism an outrage to the good of society. Empowered and propelled by nationalism, but primarily inspired by Marxist-Leninist doctrines, the Chinese Communist Party (CCP) would fight off capitalism, that saw its opponents, the Kuomintang, flee from the mainland. Mao then instituted a regime of communist rule to counter anything and everything suggestive of the operations of the 'divine hand'.

The post-Mao reforms in China have certainly brought yet another new dimension to China's modern political economy, one which suggests that the new leaders of China have willingly traded the political and economic obscurantism of the communist system for Smith's prescriptions for economic growth. Unlike the Qing Dynasty and China under Mao Zedong, Deng Xiaoping adopted a systematic, yet pragmatic, programme of economic reforms in the late 1970s and early 1980s, which opened the country up to extensive international trade, but without subscribing to the supposed ideals of the 'divine hand'. Commonly referred to as 'socialism with Chinese characteristics', there is no denying the fact that the recent developments in China's economy may well correspond to Carlyle's idea of 'anarchy plus a constable', not least because the Chinese leadership strictly police the country's newly found interest in the operations of the market.

In the meantime, Chinese President, Hu Jintao, and his team are beginning to discover that the 'invisible hand of the market' is harder to contain than originally intended, despite state efforts to regulate corporate activity through the 'Going Out' strategy. Erica Downs illustrates this issue in the context of the overseas expansion of China's National Oil Corporations (NOCs). She notes that although the Chinese Ministry of Foreign Affairs (MFA) 'has a broad mandate to support Chinese firms abroad, Chinese diplomats have complained that they do not learn about overseas investments made by NOCs until after the fact'.[6] She points to the failed bid by China National Offshore Oil Corporation (CNOOC) for the US company, UNOCAL, as an example of this disconnection between the MFA and NOCs.

Yet through state guidance, China has emerged in the twenty-first century as the ultimate success story – a rags-to-riches phenomenon, and a laudable case of economic growth based on what might rightly be referred to as 'self-help'. The exponential growth of the Chinese economy since the formula for the country's economic development was reinvented in 1978 has been remarkable: China has averaged 9.4 per cent annual GDP growth, one of the highest in the world, with the result that perhaps the 'enlightened selfishness' of China's state-orchestrated market capitalism is creating better economic chances for the maximum good of China's 1.2 billion citizens. The expansion of the Chinese economy has necessitated an integrationist initiative on the part of Beijing to include Africa in its economic development by identifying the region as a source for strategic natural resources, such as oil, and as a market for its manufactured products, as discussed previously in this volume. The question that remains to be asked for our purposes is whether the growing economic interdependence between China and Africa will benefit the African continent, or whether the engagement will turn African states into victims of a Chinese mercantilist attitude. Is China aiding Africa along the path of industrial development through the Smithian sense of 'enlightened selfishness', or is it directing the continent towards further economic paralysis? Put more bluntly – as Devon Curtis has asked in Chapter 5: is China a partner or predator? South African President, Thabo Mbeki, has already warned African leaders not to allow a 'colonial relationship' to develop with China.

It would be fair to suggest that the relationship between Africa and China is currently enjoying something of a honeymoon. So far, for most African countries, China remains a cuddly mascot, not least because economic relations between Africa and China are booming. Moreover, Beijing's initiatives towards Africa are interpreted as an alternative to the Washington Consensus, with its strict prescriptions for neo-liberal economic policies. It should be noted, however, that while Beijing has projected itself as sympathetic to Africa's economic and political problems and concerns and correspondingly demonstrated a generosity that questions the perceived nonchalant attitude of Western countries to many African issues, China does not in any way advocate or prescribe a Beijing Consensus to Africa's development framework. One important point worth emphasising is that China interprets its political and economic engagement with African countries as creating a set of enabling conditions for them to find their own development path. This, no doubt, has instilled confidence in many capital cities in Africa. For example, as discussed by Lucy Corkin in Chapter 6, Angola confidently dismissed the transparency requirements imposed on it by the International Monetary Fund (IMF) as a condition for a loan agreement since China offered a US$2 billion soft loan. While the Angolan case study provides an interesting example, it also raises questions about whether African leaders perceive their relations with China as a way of circumventing the dogmatic engagement of the West or as a way of retreating from the principles of democratic transparency and accountability to their citizens.

Nevertheless, China's increasing political footprint in Africa has led to new impulses for the international financial institutions (IFIs) on the continent. These institutions have, for more than two decades, influenced the domestic politics of most African states. As such, according to Mark Leonard, 'today IMF officials struggle to be listened to even by the poorest countries of Africa'.[7] Not surprisingly, African policy-makers see China as a model for what could be achieved in the region.

President Hu Jintao's announcement in 2007 that China would build special economic zones (SEZs) in Africa, starting with one in Zambia's Copper Belt region of Chambishi, in addition to four others, has strengthened African expectations of what they can gain from China, compared to the West. A second SEZ is planned for Mauritius to provide China with 'a trading hub that will give forty Chinese businesses preferential access to the twenty-member states of the Common Market of East and Southern Africa [COMESA] that stretches from Libya to Zimbabwe, as well as access to the Indian Ocean and South Asian markets'.[8] The Chambishi SEZ will be designed to serve as a 'home to China's "metal hub" which should give China access to resources including copper, cobalt, diamonds and uranium'. The third economic zone, which might serve as a 'shipping zone', is expected to be established in the Tanzanian capital of Dar es Salaam, while a fourth is most likely to be located in Nigeria at one of its port cities. The location of the fifth zone is yet to be determined.[9] From an African perspective, these are suggestive of Smith's 'enlightened selfishness', which invests African policy-makers with some sense of optimism.

The fact that China has marched on successfully with its growth objectives without much concern for democratic governance seems also to give hope to African leaders who realise how far behind their countries are on the issue of democratic accountability. However, at the same time, African governments see no reason why that should make economic development impossible. At any rate, China's experience in this regard throws a challenge to the prevailing development discourse, which insists on a correlation between good governance and sustainable economic development. This also begs the following related questions: what is good governance, after all, and is there an inevitable correlation between democratic rule and economic growth and development? What exactly does good governance mean in the context of economic growth and sustainable development? These questions take into account the processes of economic development in East Asia since the 1950s, including those in Japan and Singapore. They also reflect the fact that capitalist development in Europe and America historically did not operate on the basis of democratic governance. But a caveat should be added here that China is not prescribing that democratic governance should be sacrificed in favour of economic development and modernisation. Instead, as indicated earlier, the argument is that Africa should pursue a development path that is relevant and suitable to its own political and economic circumstances. Moreover, the Chinese economic project was one that followed a functional theory in which the need to address the economic challenges was considered paramount, which would then create the ripened conditions for embarking on political freedom. Perhaps the key lesson for African governments to draw from the Chinese experiment is an inversion of Ghana's President Kwame Nkrumah's famous biblical dictum: 'Seek ye first Economic Freedom [in contrast to Nkrumah's political kingdom] and all else will follow.' The latter should be qualified by what Chinese officials and academics argue as being central to the achievement of democracy and governance, which is that democracy is only valid if people's socio-economic conditions are satisfied: a point that is central to the Chinese interpretation of the human rights' argument.

At any rate, the positive inclinations on the part of African policy-makers towards China are not merely determined by idealism. On the contrary, African policy-makers, as with all practitioners of international politics, are constantly assessing the developments and dynamics of world politics and are witnessing a gradual shift in the balance of power in favour of East Asia in general, and perhaps China in particular.[10] Japan currently has the world's second largest economy (after the United States), while China's economy currently ranks as the world's fourth largest. To that extent, African leaders are not oblivious to the fact that, for example, the IMF and the World Bank, 'the world's most powerful development agencies are struggling to enforce their priorities in the face of Chinese competition'.[11] In other words, African policy-makers seem to be following the trail of what may well be the relocation of the centre of capitalism to East Asia. At the very least, they see an emerging Beijing consensus that seems determined to challenge the Washington Consensus and they find this appealing. These African inclinations, it is worth noting, are also a result of the outcomes of Africa's historical relations with Europe and the United States.

Ultimately, African states see China as the leader of the developing world and a potential champion of issues of profound concern to developing nations. Thus, in the context of the reforms of the United Nations in 2005, for example, African states draw tremendous courage and hope from China's encouraging assurances that it also supports their moves for a reformed and more democratised UN Security Council, which could have two African permanent seats.

Most crucially, it is the boom that the engagement with China has brought to some African countries that has enhanced the popularity of Beijing on the continent. This 'boom is a potentially pivotal opportunity for African countries to move beyond their traditional reliance on single-commodity exports and move up from the bottom of the international production chain . . .', notes Harry Broadman, the Economic Adviser for the Africa Region at the World Bank.[12] Other forms of China's notable soft power further enhance the economic boom. For example, China's concessional loans to African countries reached US$800 million at the end of 2005 and covered 55 projects in 22 countries. In addition, through the 'China-Africa Policy' announced in 2006 by President Hu Jintao, Beijing has made a number of impressive promises, including the doubling of assistance to African countries by 2009. President Hu also announced the cancellation of the interest-free debt owed to China by as many as 33 African states.[13] He further promised to establish a US$5 billion fund to encourage Chinese investment in the region, not to mention the US$5 billion in concessional loans and credits allocated to African states.

China's charm offensive in Africa, as well noted by the chapters in this volume, has also included diplomatic initiatives towards African states that emphasise political solidarity against a common adversary: the West. As has been succinctly documented throughout this volume, China's ideological and diplomatic stance against Western imperialism in the Cold-War era has become part and parcel of the fabric of Beijing's engagements with Africa, as well as an instrument of its soft power in its dealings with African states. On the cultural level as well, there have been tremendous initiatives on the part of Beijing to endear itself towards African states. China awards about 1 500 scholarships annually to African students. There are also growing synergies between Chinese universities and their counterparts in Africa. In addition, Beijing has opened four Confucius institutes in sub-Saharan Africa to help promote the teaching of Chinese language and culture on the continent, evidently in an attempt to expose as many Africans as possible to Chinese values and ideas, both traditional and modern. While these laudable initiatives are symptomatic of Beijing's soft power vis-à-vis African states, they clearly suggest a relationship that is asymmetrical, despite lofty Chinese rhetoric and the presumptions of African people.

It is important to use the nature of the economic relationship between Africa and China as our point of reference. This relationship has several complications and problems, even though the differences in the economic endowments of the two entities make them complementary business partners: Africa has raw materials that China, with its vast wealth, can invest in. This, however, does not hide the potentially exploitative nature of the relationship between an industrialised economy and an economy that is based on natural resources and primary commodities. Effectively, taking our cue from Africa's modern history, the customer may well be different from the West, but the relationship could replicate the severely unbalanced economic relationship that exists between Africa and its traditional partners. Consequently, there is much international concern that China may well be another predator in Africa. This is partly because China's economic interests in Africa primarily determine its initiatives towards African states. Remarkably similar to the figures between the United

States and Africa, about 85 per cent of Africa's exports to China is derived from five oil-exporting countries: Angola, Equatorial Guinea, Nigeria, the Democratic Republic of Congo (DRC) and Sudan. Correspondingly, 50 per cent of China's investments are concentrated in a handful of countries, which have natural resources that Beijing needs. Conversely, 'value-added manufactured exports make up a mere 8 per cent of Africa's share of exports to China'.[14] Meanwhile, the exports of consumer goods from China to Africa undermine local producers in domestic sales and exports, sometimes displacing African workers, as evidenced in some of the country case studies in this volume.

We should also note that China's close affinity with African governments might not necessarily be in Africa's interest. Beijing's bankrolling of a state such as Sudan, which is constantly in the news for violating the human rights of its citizens, and others that defy requirements for good governance, should be condemned and exposed. In this sense, criticisms against China – irrespective of their source – should be encouraged, if only because they would hopefully force policy-makers in Beijing to deal with the political implications of China's economic relations with African states more proactively. Consequently, the role of African civil society in monitoring the China-Africa engagement should be encouraged, if only to compel African governments to become more transparent in their engagements with China, as well as expose the impact that Beijing's economic penetration has had at the micro-level, where local producers are faced with competition from petty Chinese traders. And although competition has the potential to generate efficiency, African governments, in conjunction with the African Union (AU) and relevant development partners, should also make Beijing aware of the problems that its exports to Africa are creating for host countries, as evidenced by, for example, the displacement of African producers in the textile sector as a result of a flood of textile goods from China.

On the whole, however, the onus is on African governments to ensure that the national interests of their countries are not subordinated to those of China in the economic agreements they reach with Beijing. The advice offered in this volume by Garth le Pere and Adam Habib (Chapters 2 and 14) is pertinent in this regard. In essence, for the partnership between China and African states to work more efficiently in the interests of all (a win-win equation, as Chinese officials say), the potential predator has to be properly monitored and the necessary checks and balances deployed. It is not good enough to hope that an 'enlightened selfishness' on the part of China, with its giant global ambitions, would necessarily prevent it from stripping Africa of its resources. At the same time, an 'enlightened selfishness' on the part of China may not necessarily add up to the maximum good of all the parties involved if, for example, African governments do not 'adopt policies that enhance African companies' international competitiveness, foster better governance, improve their countries' financial and labour markets, and attract investment infrastructure',[15] as has been perennially recommended. Ultimately, given the fact that African governments are not passive spectators to China's initiatives towards the region (on the contrary, they are active participants in the unfolding engagements), if Beijing turns out to be a predator in its relations with the continent, then surely, African leaders should share the blame? On this issue, African governments would do well to remember that, as Lord Palmerston, British prime minister and foreign minister in the Victorian age, noted: in the arena of international relations, 'nations have no permanent enemies and no permanent allies, only permanent interests'.

This discussion now leads us to return to the issues in Chapter 1 regarding the discourse on China in Africa. So far the debates in the discourse have tended to be reactive to China's engagement in Africa. On the one hand, it emphasises continuity with the previous 'scrambles' described by Margaret Lee[16] as a dimension of the latest phase of imperialism. On the other hand, China's role is viewed as a discontinuity in which Henning Melber sees Beijing's entry into Africa as introducing a critical difference with its 'charm offensive'.[17] Melber also goes on to note that the current African scramble ensued from the collapse of the Soviet Union, the end of the Cold War and the hegemonic dominance of the Unites States in a 'new world order'. For Melber, then, China's charm offensive in seeking access to African markets and resources creates a 'new stage of competing forces on the continent', which is perhaps aligned more closely than it is publicly asserted by Beijing, to challenging US hegemony.[18] But Melber also argues that 'in a matter of time, India, Brazil and Russia (as well as a number of other actors such as Malaysia and Mexico) are likely to add further pressure on the scramble for limited markets and resources'.[19]

Such interpretations of China's engagement in Africa have significant implications for our argument of the 'enlightened selfishness' on the part of China as it relates to African states. This is even more so as China's global rise as the next superpower becomes imminent. In this regard, we have argued that Africa's evolving partnership with China must consider the opportunities over the threats that entail maximum benefits for Africa at a domestic level. Equally important is for Africa to be mindful of how this goal is to be achieved at the global level where China is becoming more engaged in international regimes.

To this end, while we have advocated (and many of the chapters in this volume have leaned towards) an evolving partnership to be forged between Africa and China, we issue this with a warning that must take into consideration a few important issues.

China has embraced the neo-liberal character of the global capitalist system. In so doing, Beijing has become an important actor in the institutions that govern this system. Consider, for example, that Justin Yifu Lin, the senior vice-president for development economics at the World Bank, is Chinese, and that China is a member of the Paris Declaration for Aid Effectiveness. At a cursory level, inclusions into these institutions could be beneficial for Africa, as China could work from within in reforming the global economic architecture and increase Africa's integration into the global economy. Yet China also has its own strategic interests. Shalmali Guttal notes:

> China's relationship with the IFIs defies easy categories. On the one hand, China uses IFIs to leverage access to relatively cheap capital and technical support to meet its own growing infrastructure, human and social development, technological and institutions needs; here it is no different from other middle-income developing countries. On the other hand, China uses IFIs to expand its economic reach, and access markets and investment opportunities in other developing countries through IFI projects and programmes; and here it is no different from developed countries. In both cases, China is using IFIs to shore up its economic, financial, political and strategic advantages and potential.[20]

Indeed, this raises a significant issue of whether China's interests and position in the IFIs calibrate with those of Africa and if Beijing will reform the status quo of the global economic order or be comfortable with its current setting based on its own interests.

Finally, the need for the development discourse to examine the issue of the correlation between economic development and democratic governance has been mentioned above. In addition, for a more balanced understanding of the unfolding relations between Africa and China, we need to have a clear understanding of the issues discussed in this volume from the perspective of the Chinese government. Future researchers will hopefully address this issue in more detail. The discourse also needs to address the differences in the operations and approaches towards Africa between China's central administration, on the one hand, and its provincial governments, on the other hand, since these entities are not necessarily unified in their dealings with African states, even though their operations are essentially supported by public initiatives for trade and investment.

African governments also need to have well-trained experts and diplomats with a functional knowledge of Mandarin and a robust understanding of Chinese culture and history, not to mention Chinese politics and political processes. This is necessary because China is increasingly becoming well integrated into African economies and the indications are that this will be a long-term effort. Thus, the fact that Beijing has well-trained and well-informed Africanists gives it a tremendous advantage.

But perhaps the greatest challenge facing African governments as they engage the world's next superpower is to see how they can ensure that Smith's theory of 'enlightened selfishness' brings about maximum good for Africa's people. This should be the bedrock of the evolving partnership between China and Africa, and not what seems to be the current state of play of minimum benefits for the few 'enlightened political and economic elites'.

This book, written by sixteen pan-African authors, has provided an historical and geo-political context for understanding the evolving partnership between Africa and China. Nine empirical, detailed case studies spanning four of Africa's sub-regions have provided a sound basis for both comparison and drawing broader lessons from this relationship. The final section on the role of Western and Asian great powers in Africa has provided the comparative frame to assess China's Africa policy and interests in relation to those of other powers. We hope that this volume will broaden the debate on this important topic, and ensure that African voices enrich a discourse that could well determine the future of the continent.

NOTES

1. A. Smith, *The Wealth of Nations* (Cannon edition, Tokyo: Charles E. Tuttle Company, 1979), p. 95.
2. Smith, *The Wealth of Nations*, p. 95.
3. Max Lerner, 'Introduction', in Smith, *The Wealth of Nations*, p. ix.
4. Lerner, 'Introduction', p. viii.
5. Lerner, 'Introduction', p. ix.
6. See E.S. Downs, 'The Fact or Fiction of Sino-African Energy Relations', *China Security* 3(3), 2007: 50.
7. M. Leonard, *What Does China Think?* (London: Fourth Estate, 2007), p. 120.
8. Leonard, *What Does China Think?*
9. Leonard, *What Does China Think?*, p. 119.
10. Leonard, *What Does China Think?*, p. 117.
11. Leonard, *What Does China Think?*, p. 120.
12. H. Broadman, 'China and India Go to Africa: New Deals in the Developing World', *Foreign Affairs*, March/April 2008: 96.

13. Broadman, 'China and India Go to Africa'.
14. Broadman, 'China and India Go to Africa', 97.
15. Broadman, 'China and India Go to Africa', 96.
16. M.C. Lee, 'The 21st Century Scramble for Africa', *Journal of Contemporary African Studies* 24(3), September 2006: 303–30.
17. See H. Melber, 'China in Africa', *Current Affairs Issues* 33 (Uppsala: Nordic Africa Institute, 2007).
18. Melber, 'China in Africa'.
19. Melber, 'China in Africa', p. 8.
20. S. Guttal, 'Client and Competitor: China and International Financial Institutions', in D. Guerrero and F. Manji (eds.), *China's New Role in Africa and the South: A Search for a New Perspective* (Cape Town, Nairobi and Oxford: FAHAMU, 2008), p. 35.

Contributors

Amitav Acharya is Professor of Global Governance and Director of the Governance Research Centre at the University of Bristol, in the United Kingdom. He is the author of *Constructing a Security Community in Southeast Asia*; and co-editor of *Reassessing Security Cooperation in the Asia Pacific* and *Crafting Cooperation: Regional International Institutions in Comparative Perspective.*

Adekeye Adebajo is Executive Director of the Centre for Conflict Resolution, Cape Town, South Africa. He served as Director of the Africa Programme of the New York-based International Peace Academy between 2001–03. During the same period, Dr Adebajo was an Adjunct Professor at Columbia University's School of International and Public Affairs. He previously served on UN missions in South Africa, Western Sahara and Iraq. He is the author of *Building Peace in West Africa: Liberia, Sierra Leone and Guinea-Bissau* and *Liberia's Civil War: Nigeria, ECOMOG, and Regional Security in West Africa*; and co-editor of *Managing Armed Conflicts in the Twenty-First Century, West Africa's Security Challenges: Building Peace in a Troubled Region, A Dialogue of the Deaf: Essays on Africa and the United Nations* and *South Africa in Africa: The Post-Apartheid Era*. He obtained his doctorate from Oxford University, in the United Kingdom, where he studied as a Rhodes Scholar.

Kweku Ampiah is an Academic Fellow and member in the Department of East Asian Studies at the University of Leeds, in the United Kingdom. His research and teaching interests include Japanese foreign policy and international politics. He is the author of *The Dynamics of Japan's Relations with Africa* and *The Political and Moral Imperatives of the Bandung Conference of 1955*. He obtained his doctorate from Oxford University.

Daniel Bach is a Researcher at the *Centre National de Recherches Scientifiques* (CNRS). He is Director of Research and Lecturer at the *Centre d'Éude d'Afrique Noire* of the *Institut d'Études Politiques* at the University of Bordeaux, France, and has previously held teaching appointments in Nigeria and Canada. He is currently coordinating a research network on regional integration in Africa. Professor Bach obtained his doctorate from Oxford University and has published widely on African and African-European international relations.

Mwesiga Baregu is Professor of Political Science and International Relations at the University of Dar es Salaam, Tanzania. Until early 2003, he headed the Peace and Security Research Programme at SAPES Trust in Harare, Zimbabwe. He is a member of the Executive Council of the International Peace Research Association (IPRA) and the Africa Peace Research and Education Association (AFPREA). Professor Baregu is the editor of *Preventive Diplomacy and Peacebuilding in Southern Africa* and *The Conflict Matrix and Research Agenda;* and co-editor of *From Cape to Congo: Southern Africa's Evolving Security Challenges.*

Lucy Corkin was Projects Director at the Centre for Chinese Studies based at Stellenbosch University, South Africa, until 2008. Prior to joining the Centre in 2005, she worked in public relations and issue management for several prominent South African mining houses and corporate firms. She also worked in the Department of Political Science at Stellenbosch University. Ms Corkin holds a Master's degree in International Politics from Stellenbosch University and has published widely on China's relations with Africa in various academic and popular journals.

Devon Curtis is a Lecturer in Politics at the University of Cambridge, in the United Kingdom. Her main research interests and various publications deal with power-sharing and governance arrangements, the transformation of rebel movements to political parties, and security and development. Her field research has concentrated on Africa's Great Lakes' region. Dr Curtis was a Post-Doctoral Research Fellow at the Saltzman Institute of War and Peace Studies at Columbia University, and a Pre-Doctoral Fellow at Stanford University's Centre for International Security and Cooperation (CISAC), in the United States. She has also worked for the Canadian government, the United Nations Staff College and the Overseas Development Institute. Dr Curtis received her doctorate from the London School of Economics and Political Science.

Adam Habib is Deputy Vice-Chancellor, Research Innovation and Advancement, at the University of Johannesburg, South Africa. He was previously Executive Director of Democracy and Governance at the Human Sciences Research Council (HSRC), South Africa, and founding Director of the Centre for Civil Society (CCS) and a Research Professor in the School of Development Studies (SODS), both at the University of Natal, South Africa. He has published extensively in the areas of democratic transitions, political economy, institutional transformation, higher education reform and state-civil-society relations. Professor Habib was formerly editor of the journals *Transformation* and *Politico*.

Garth le Pere has been Executive Director of the Institute for Global Dialogue (IGD) in Johannesburg, South Africa, since 1995. He is the co-author of *China, Africa and South Africa: South-South Co-operation in a Global Era;* and editor of *China through the Third Eye* and *China in Africa: Mercantilist Predator, or Partner in Development?* He previously held academic and research positions at various institutions across the United States, and also held appointments as a researcher in local government (Urban Foundation), senior industrial relations officer (Anglo American Corporation), executive director (United States-South Africa Leadership Exchange Programme) and public administration consultant (New York City Administration). He has published widely on state-society relations, foreign policy, multilateral trade, African politics and public policy. Dr Le Pere obtained his doctorate from Yale University, in the United States.

Sanusha Naidu is a Research Fellow at the Centre for Chinese Studies at Stellenbosch University, South Africa. Prior to joining the Centre, she was a Research Specialist at the Human Sciences Research Council, South Africa, and a Senior Africa Researcher at the South African Institute of International Affairs (SAIIA) in Johannesburg. Ms Naidu obtained her Master's degree in International Relations from Staffordshire University, in the United Kingdom. Her research interests include the implications of China's political and economic engagements in Africa, India's growing Africa strategy and Africa's political economy, subjects on which she has published widely.

Muna Ndulo has been a Professor of Law at Cornell University, in the United States, since 1996. He lectures on international organisations and human rights' institutions, the legal aspects of foreign investment in developing countries and the common law and African legal systems. He is also Director of the University's Institute for African

Development. Dr Ndulo obtained his doctorate from Oxford University. Prior to joining Cornell University, he was Public Prosecutor for the Zambian Ministry of Legal Affairs, Dean of the University of Zambia's School of Law and served on the United Nations Commission for International Trade Law. Dr Ndulo was Political Adviser to the UN Mission in South Africa and advised UN Missions in East Timor and Kosovo.

Alaba Ogunsanwo teaches at Lead City University, Ibadan, Nigeria. He obtained his doctorate from the London School of Economics and Political Science. He has published extensively on the external relations of Nigeria, Algeria, Egypt and China, his major publication being *China's Policy in Africa 1958–1971*, which was published in 1974 by Cambridge University Press. Professor Ogunsanwo served as Nigeria's Ambassador to the European Union, Belgium and Luxembourg, as well as Nigeria's High Commissioner to Botswana and Lesotho. He was a Fulbright Professor at Rutgers University and visiting Associate Professor and Fulbright Fellow at Princeton University, both in the United States, as well as a Japan Foundation Fellow at Mitaka.

Lloyd Sachikonye is a Senior Researcher based at the Institute of Development Studies, University of Zimbabwe, Harare. He holds a doctorate from the University of Leeds, in the United Kingdom. He has edited five books on several themes, including civil society in southern Africa, state-society relations in Africa and labour migration. In 2007–08, he was appointed as a Consultant at the African Union Commission in Addis Ababa. He is also a contributing editor to several journals, including *Africa Development* and *Review of African Political Economy*.

Sharath Srinivasan is a Doctoral Researcher at the Department of International Development, Oxford University, where he holds the Oxford humanities research studentship and is a Clarendon and Chevening scholar. His doctoral thesis examines the impact of peacemaking on conflict politics, and the role of third-party intervention, focusing on the regional peace negotiations in Sudan. He has published on the political situation in Sudan and on China's role in Africa. His research interests also include international normative theory and human development.

Douglas Yates teaches political science at the American Graduate School of International Relations and Diplomacy in Paris, international relations at the American University of Paris, as well as Anglo-American jurisprudence at the French state law school of the

University of Cergy-Pontoise. He holds a doctorate from Boston University, in the United States, and is the author of *The Rentier State in Africa: Oil-Rent Dependency and Neo-Colonialism in the Republic of Gabon*. In addition to edited chapters and journal articles, Dr Yates has co-authored *Oil Policy in the Gulf of Guinea* and *Historical Dictionary of Gabon*.

Suisheng Zhao is Professor and Executive Director of the Center for China-US Cooperation at the Graduate School of International Studies, University of Denver, in the United States. He is the founder and editor of the *Journal of Contemporary China*, a member of the Board of Directors of the US Committee of the Council for Security Cooperation in the Asia Pacific (USCSCAP), a member of the National Committee on US-China Relations and a Research Associate at the Fairbank Center for East Asian Research at Harvard University. He holds a doctorate from the University of California-San Diego, and is the author and/or editor of eight books, including *Debating Political Reform in China*, *A Nation-State by Construction: Dynamics of Modern Chinese Nationalism*, *Chinese Foreign Policy: Pragmatism and Strategic Behavior*, *China and Democracy*, and *Across the Taiwan Strait: Mainland China, Taiwan, and the Crisis of 1995–96*.

Index